# GHANA AND THE IVORY COAST

Edited by
Philip Foster and Aristide R. Zolberg

# GHANA AND THE IVORY COAST

## PERSPECTIVES ON MODERNIZATION

The University of Chicago Press
Chicago and London

*International Standard Book Number: 0–226–25752–5*
*Library of Congress Catalog Card Number: 70–159784*
The University of Chicago Press, Chicago 60637
The University of Chicago Press, Ltd., London
© 1971 by The University of Chicago
Published 1971
Printed in the United States of America

# CONTENTS

# PREFACE

For many years, social scientists concerned with the transformation of West Africa have talked about the potential usefulness of a paired comparison between the Ivory Coast and Ghana, two neighboring countries, which present an intriguing mix of similarities and differences. The present volume is the result of a preliminary effort to transform this aspiration into a reality.

All but two of the papers included were initially presented at a workshop conference held at the Center for Continuing Education of the University of Chicago on 7 and 8 March 1969 under the joint chairmanship of the coeditors. Dorothy Dee Vellenga and Reginald Green were later invited to submit papers they had presented at a panel on the same subject organized within the framework of the 1967 meetings of the African Studies Association by Immanuel Wallerstein and Aristide R. Zolberg.

The 1969 conference was sponsored by the Committee on African Studies of the University of Chicago, which contributed the necessary funds from its share of the Ford Foundation grant to the Center for International Studies of the University of Chicago. In addition to those who contributed papers included in the present volume, the conference was attended by other distinguished students of modernization in Ghana and the Ivory Coast, who acted as discussants. They included David Apter, St. Clair Drake, and Robert Lystad. Michael Cohen and Deborah LeVeen, graduate students in political science at the University of Chicago, acted as recording secretaries during the two days of lively debate which ensued.

In planning the initial conferences and eventually the present book, an attempt was made to obtain parallel analyses of major spheres of activity in each of the two countries. Although the papers by Kraus and Zolberg on national politics and by Kilson and Stryker on local politics do not formally adhere to a single framework, the authors share a common outlook and revised their initial drafts in the light of the other's contributions.

Foster and Clignet, who had collaborated earlier, have done so again in their essay on education. Elliot Berg deals single-handedly with the economics of both countries. His approach is balanced by Green's paper which evaluates economic patterns from a different point of view. Comparative analysis was more difficult to achieve in the sphere of legal modernization. Levasseur covers changes in the sphere of family law in the Ivory Coast from a lawyer's point of view while Vellenga focuses on Ghana from the point of view of a sociologist. Pooley's important contribution to the analysis of legal changes in Ghana which relate to that country's economic life could not, unfortunately, be paralleled for the Ivory Coast.

The editors are most grateful to all concerned for their contributions to the 1967 panel, to the 1969 conference, and, finally, to the present volume. They hope that this book will contribute toward the shared goal of all participants to further the study of the African experience within the context of the contemporary social sciences and on the basis of a genuine interchange between the disciplines.

P.F. AND A.R.Z.

# GHANA AND THE IVORY COAST

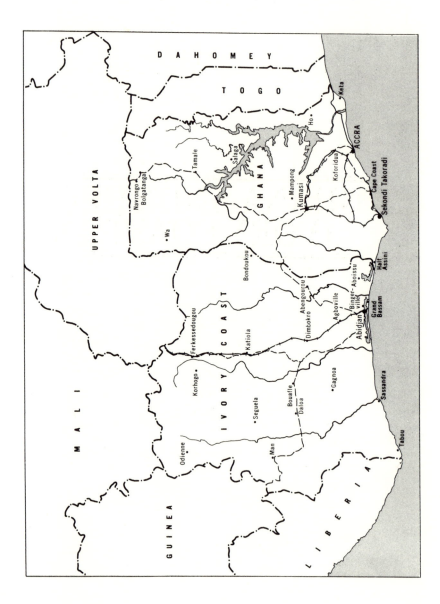

# 1

# INTRODUCTION

## Immanuel Wallerstein

The inspiration for the comparison of Ghana and the Ivory Coast, attempted collectively in this book, has been twofold. First, this particular set of countries has long attracted Africanists as a "natural" opportunity for comparison since so many variables are constant between the two, yet some few variables are both different and significant.[1] A second inspiration was the famous challenge of Kwame Nkrumah to Félix Houphouet-Boigny, made in April 1957, in which Nkrumah acknowledged both the similarities of situation and differences of governmental policy of the two countries and suggested that the success of the competing approaches be assessed after ten years.

An assessment in terms of this challenge would imply acceptance of some generalized theory of social change. The one which seemed to underlie the challenge itself is obscure, weakly validated, and largely disputed. Furthermore, as Berg indicates in his chapter in this volume, the ideological stakes are high. It seems to me, therefore, to be an error of scholarly judgment to attempt the comparisons from this vantage point.

To be sure, politicians may feel inclined or even forced to draw policy conclusions from this comparison even while the evidence is thin and fragmentary and the theory unclear, insubstantial, or debatable. The difference between politicians and scholars is not that the former draw policy conclusions and the latter do not—it is that the former have no choice. Scholars may be permitted to take a more prudent stance, arguing that, since the evidence is not yet in and since the requisite verificational studies have not yet been done to any important degree, it is premature to prognosticate or to prescribe.

1. See my book, *The Road to Independence: Ghana and the Ivory Coast* (Mouton, 1964), based on this comparison; Aristide R. Zolberg, Remi Clignet, Philip Foster, and Robert Lystad have also done work along these lines; and Zolberg and I jointly chaired a collective attempt at the 1967 meetings of the African Studies Association.

3

This does not mean, however, that the present comparison is of no use. It is of use precisely insofar as its intent is exploratory, the establishment of hypotheses which are given prima facie plausibility by the analysis. The essays that follow each suggest in their separate and relatively un-coordinated ways various hypotheses. The reader is at liberty to build from there, to create his own model, reformulate an interrelated set of hypotheses, do further exploratory study, and then perhaps move towards the formulation of an appropriate research design.

I shall not here attempt to design such a research project. Rather I should like to discuss the questions that would have to be answered so that one could decide on the elements to include in it, assuming that the ultimate objective was to explain the paths of national development of an African, or a largely agricultural and dependent, nation-state in the contemporary world.

A first question to clarify, and one upon which our authors differ, is exactly how divergent the paths traversed thus far by Ghana and the Ivory Coast have been. This is basically a question of conceptualization. The typical problem is of the following order: if a difference on some variable can be measured with reasonable accuracy to be of the order of, say, five percent, is it enormous, important, minor, or insignificant? This is not a question of statistical probability but, in fact, of comparing both units involved to the universe of units potentially comparable and of assessing where this particular order of difference (our hypothetical five percent) fits in the curve of paired comparisons. Because we seldom deal with variables that can be measured continuously with any accuracy, we make nominal rank-order distinctions that implicitly summarize undone statistical exercises—that is to say, we "conceptualize."

Let us start with issues related to the internal political system of Ghana and the Ivory Coast. One might argue that the Ivory Coast under Houphouet-Boigny and Ghana under Nkrumah were basically the same because they were both based on one-party systems led by charismatic leaders who emerged out of a nationalist movement that had led the fight for, and made the transition to, independence. Furthermore, both gave short shrift to the opposition, handled coups or putative coups in a similar repressive fashion and held tight rein on nonparty intermediary structures such as trade unions, youth groups, and so on. By this count, the present Ghana regime under Busia is of a different order, since it is a multiparty system, without a heroic leader, which allows a certain liberty of action to voluntary associations.

Or one might argue that the appropriate comparison is to see

Houphouet-Boigny's regime and Busia's as the similar ones and Nkrumah's as the different one. Here one would emphasize that left-wing ideologues were not permitted a significant role in the first two, but were part of the Nkrumah system. In the first two, the key levers of power were held by a growing bourgeoisie who used their administrative positions to enhance their commercial potentialities, whereas in Nkrumah's Ghana this group, while in existence, was constantly harassed by the government or by the party press.

Or one might argue that Ghana, whether under Nkrumah, the *National Liberation Council* (NLC), or Busia, was different from the Ivory Coast because of a tradition of open political debate which survived all attempts at suppressing it, whereas the Ivory Coast at all times had a more secretive, nonpublic, and personally dangerous quality to its public life; that in Ghana the civil service never was without significant political power, whereas in the Ivory Coast it never had it.

Finally, one might argue that there were no significant differences whatsoever between Ghana and the Ivory Coast. Basically both regimes were weakly authoritarian, corrupt, based on shifting consensuses, manipulated by outside forces which had undue internal authority, without a truly disinterested civil service or a critical press.

Which of these pictures is the true one? Of course, all communicate some aspect of reality, as do probably several others. To choose among them is to opt for a theory of social change. But obtaining hypotheses *towards* such a theory is precisely the *objective* of an exploratory study.

Let us now look at the economy. The picture is similar. In this case, some of our authors have divided Ghana into three phases: for example, Green speaks of 1957–60 as (*I*) the "Lewis" phase, 1961–65 as (*II*) the "Mensah-Omaboe" phase, and 1966 to the present as (*III*) the "IMF" phase. Green contrasts Ghana, phases *I* and *III*, plus the Ivory Coast with Ghana, phase *II*. Berg, however, seems to group matters differently. If we use Green's phases, Berg is contrasting Ghana, phases *I* and *II*, with the Ivory Coast. Fitch and Oppenheimer, to whom both refer, would lump all three phases of Ghana plus the Ivory Coast together as variants on a theme.

We could pursue similar conceptual problems in relation to other themes dealt with in this book: the relation of central authority and local communities; the evolution of the legal system; the growth of the educational structures. We could also do it with respect to foreign policy or pan-Africanism, themes not elaborated to any great extent herein.

We could also raise questions about the time and space parameters involved. Which time period is more appropriate: 1957–66, 1957–70, or the experience of both countries from the precolonial period to the present? Some of our authors strain at that bit, and it is also clear that different conclusions can be reached from the comparison of different time segments. Can some of the questions be resolved in a comparison only of the two countries? A number of the authors feel compelled to include some third country or countries to elucidate specific points. This is, of course, essential insofar as one posits a *similarity* of Ghana and the Ivory Coast. In what way we can appropriately "periodize" the history of a country and compare one period against another as though they were two entities is an issue, not only of conceptual judgment (what are meaningful periods?) but also of the degree to which synchronic analyses of diachronic processes are intellectually acceptable. Finally, some would argue that unless the analysis of Ghana and the Ivory Coast were considered in the context of the various international networks of which they are part, it would be void of interest because the analyst might not be able to spot some variables, which, prima facie, some theories take to be determining.

The moral to draw from this discussion is that if we are collectively to build in a fruitful manner on the work done in this book and similar work, we must now turn careful attention to the research design of further systematic work so that we have an explicit and defensible set of premises from which we can infer valid hypotheses and assess the reliability of the empirical research. With this in mind, I shall conclude with a brief discussion of possible strategies of comparative analysis.

Comparison is of course the essence of the scientific method, but there are several varieties of comparison, each appropriate in specific circumstances. One way to categorize social science is by intent. This is not the way it is usually done in expository texts, but it is the de facto mode of classification most social scientists use. In terms of intent, there are two dimensions. Does the study seek to establish generalizations about social action or does it seek to explain specific social actions in the light of general theory? That is, is it theoretical or applied, nomothetic or idiographic, analytic or historical? Is it concerned with the state of knowledge or the state of the world? A second dimension is whether or not clear hypotheses exist prior to the study and the object of the study is to confirm or use them, or whether the development of such hypotheses is in fact the point of the study?

If we combine the two dimensions, we obtain four kinds of studies to which we can somewhat arbitrarily give the names verificational, exploratory, explanatory, and interpretative (table 1).[2]

TABLE 1

| | CLEAR HYPOTHESIS | |
| --- | --- | --- |
| | Exists | Does Not Exist |
| Analytic | verificational | exploratory |
| Historical | explanatory | interpretative |

Without entering now into a complete exposition of the methodological implications of such a morphology, we should underline that one of the most abiding confusions of contemporary comparisons of national societies is between exploratory and explanatory studies. Their intent is totally opposite; and, therefore, they require different methods. Criteria of judging their adequacy are not the same. Yet their superficial similarity of style lends itself to a blurring of the distinction and leads consequently to errors in methods and evaluation.

Both kinds of studies frequently employ only very few cases; the researcher is often immersed in the empirical details of the cases used. However, in an exploratory study, since the object is to establish analytic hypotheses, the crucial exercise is proper conceptualization of the data. To do this requires casting a net for data that is sufficiently wide such that the analyst may have the opportunity to formulate less obvious concepts, without at the same time casting so wide a net that the data become too vague for even minimal measurement. It requires, in short, good judgment about investment of scholarly effort (a sort of cost-benefit analysis) combined with theoretical imagination.

An explanatory study is in many ways far easier to do. It attempts to explain why a particular set of events occurred in the way they did. The comparison is brought in as the control case, replicating many of the same conditions, thereby seeking to demonstrate that the variation in the remaining conditions or happenings explains the differential consequences of the two cases. While straightforward in research design, it requires one prerequisite seldom met in the comparative study of national societies, the existence of fairly well-validated generalizations (theory) on the basis of which inferences may be drawn as to causation in the particular in-

2. This is a very abbreviated version of views developed by Terence K. Hopkins and me in a joint course on the methodology of the comparative study of national societies; they will be presented by us in full in a forthcoming publication.

stance. Even if the hurdle of preexistent validated theory is overcome, an explanatory study requires great psychological self-restraint on the part of the analyst, since the temptation to reinforce one's policy prejudices in the presentation of data is very real.

The present collection, viewed within the context of the suggested classification of comparative studies, is clearly exploratory. Its strengths as well as weaknesses are derived from the very fact that it is an ex post facto exploration by a group of scholars who brought to the task a variety of theoretical, methodological, and substantive concerns. Together, they have cast a wide net. Hopefully, their catch will provide a point of departure for more systematic comparative work on the transformation of African societies.

# 2

# POLITICAL DEVELOPMENT IN THE IVORY COAST SINCE INDEPENDENCE

## Aristide R. Zolberg

The concept "political development" will be used here to refer specifically to the institutionalization in a society of a set of norms, structures, and roles associated with modern political values. These values include, primarily, the transformation of the society into a nation—that is, legitimacy based on popular sovereignty—and the creation of a new political center with authority extending potentially over the entire society. In practice the study of political development draws attention to an examination of three salient problem areas: the extension of political participation and the creation of appropriate mechanisms related to this process; the creation of appropriate instruments to administer modernizing policies; and the diffusion of a political culture congruent with modernizing objectives. My own preference is to examine these problems as much as possible from the point of view of important actors in the system. Hence, I begin with the societal givens which constitute, at any one time, the base line in relation to which change must be defined; I then examine the specific political formula devised by segments of the population who are in a position to initiate political transformation. The analysis proceeds with an examination of the strategy and tactics they use in pursuing their program; of autonomous trends which interact with the political modernizers' pursuits; and of the degree to which at any particular point in time institutionalization has been achieved. Crises provide especially good moments for the examination of the tensions, conflicts, and contradictions generated by modernization.

## THE SOCIETAL GIVENS

Around 1960 the Ivory Coast could hardly be described as a society in the normally accepted sense of the word. The territory carved out by French colonizers in West Africa approximately seventy years earlier

9

contained widely disparate societies interacting with one another to varying degrees and in different ways. Until the 1920s common administration
was but a thin veneer; social and economic change had affected merely
a small proportion of the total population located primarily in the southeastern corner of the country. Although change was accelerated during
the thirty years that followed, and especially after 1945, the vast bulk of
individuals in the country retained a primary identification with the
preexisting societies in the area. By the time of independence, however,
there had emerged a very small stratum that had internalized a commitment to the new territorial unit as a primary referent and a larger stratum
with partial commitment to the same unit.

This situation was reflected in the growth of new patterns of social
relationships based on a modification of primordial ties to ethnic groups
and lineages. The most salient manifestation of this process was the
emergence and the later proliferation of collectivities organized as voluntary associations, but which retained an important element of primordial-
ism. Thus, the "tribes," which usually started out as spatially contiguous
groups, were not necessarily destroyed by the population movements and
the changing orientations that followed modernization; they tended to
become transformed into ethnic groups with rural and urban components
following a process which may be termed "supertribalism."[1] It was estimated, in the early 1960s, that twenty-five percent of the population lived
outside the home areas of the various groups. Two groups in particular
stood out in this respect: forty percent of the Malinké and twenty percent
of the Baoulé lived in rural and urban areas outside those associated with
their traditional location.[2] In the process, however, the definition of the
tribes often underwent some modification as well, usually in the direction
of amalgamation of several distinct, but culturally closely related, smaller
units into somewhat larger ones. The existence of these collectivities was a
determinative factor in shaping patterns of political participation after
World War II.

Although this phenomenon is by no means unique to the Ivory Coast
and is indeed present to a certain extent in all African countries, it is
particularly salient in the Ivory Coast where it constitutes a dominant
pattern of social organization. This can be attributed to a variety of factors.

1. For a fuller discussion of this process and appropriate references see my "Patterns of National Integration," *The Journal of Modern African Studies* 5, no. 4
(1967) : 449–67.
2. *La Côte d'Ivoire 1965: Population—Synthèse—Études Régionales 1962–1965*
(Abidjan: Ministère des finances, des affaires économiques, et du plan, July 1967),
p. 25.

The most important one is the accident of the country's location at the confluence of important African culture areas. Thus, its range of cultural variation among traditional societies is probably greater than in Ghana, for example. Furthermore, there is no core Ivory Coast traditional culture which encompasses a large proportion of the population. Akan-related groups, for example, account for only about one-fourth of the total population; the largest Akan group, the Baoulé, together with the next two largest groups (Malinké, sixteen percent; Sénoufo, twelve percent), constitute slightly under half of the total population, with the remainder scattered among many distinct groups.[3] Historically there were no large-scale political entities in the Ivory Coast at the time of colonial contact comparable with Ashanti in Ghana, Mossi in Upper Volta, or with the resurgent Muslim states of Mali and Senegal.

Other explanatory factors worth exploring are the especially uneven pattern of economic change during the colonial period and the relative lateness of cultural change. Christianity, for example, is much less widespread than in Ghana and never provided a unifying cultural overlay. In comparison with Ghana, the Ivory Coast experienced a much more sudden spurt of modernization following World War II after it had been a colonial backwater for several decades. Suddenly accelerated internal migrations (including migrations to other rural areas, as well as urbanization) may have evoked supertribalism as a natural response, much as appears to have been the case in the Congo-Kinshasa or in Kenya. Supertribalism in the Ivory Coast may be contrasted with the relative salience of regionalism in Ghana, Mali, or Senegal, although regionalism is not totally absent from the Ivory Coast itself.

A new pattern of social stratification emerged during this period as well. In this respect, the Ivory Coast and Ghana are more similar, although they probably vary in the degree to which incipient classes have appeared. The new strata are based on differentiations associated with educational achievement and wealth. Although these two are of course related, they do not by any means coincide. Wealth stems to a considerable extent, as in Ghana, from economic entrepreneurship in the form of independent farming (with coffee added to cocoa in the case of the Ivory Coast), accompanied by small-scale capitalist activity in the form of trucking, brokerage, and related pursuits. Significant variations in access to education and wealth are closely related to ethnic and regional differences; but it is impossible to ascertain on the basis of existing data in what manner

3. Ibid.

access is related to traditional status *within* groups. Around the time of independence there were growing indications that access to education and to wealth were becoming mutually reinforcing avenues of social mobility across generations.[4] In that sense, an incipient bourgeoisie could be identified, following a pattern which began perhaps as much as a quarter of a century earlier in Ghana. The absence of such a bourgeoisie before and immediately after World War II in the Ivory Coast helps explain important differences in the development of the nationalist movement there as against Senegal and Ghana. In the Ivory Coast, there was no Danquah-Busia, or Lamine Gueye, political generation.

A final feature of Ivory Coast society provides a significant contrast with Ghana: the presence of a large non-Ivorian population, both African and European. During the 1920s and 1930s, the Ivory Coast had been viewed as a potential area for European settlement; more land had been conceded to Europeans than in any other West African country. This helps account for the initially radical character of Ivory Coast nationalism. Although the land situation changed after World War II, the European population of nonofficials increased significantly, thus creating a much greater potential for racial antagonism than in Ghana, but also providing the potential for a greater Europeanization of the style of life of the emerging upper strata of the African population, a persistent, striking feature of the Ivory Coast landscape. The European population continued to grow after independence. African immigration into the Ivory Coast also increased significantly with the economic boom of the 1950s. In the 1960s, African immigration continued to grow at the rate of about one percent of the total population annually; in Abidjan, about one-half of the gainfully employed male African population was foreign-born.[5] This factor added to the complexity of the ethnic pattern and was a recurrent source of tension.

## POLITICAL FORMULA

In most of the initial attempts to provide typologies of African political systems, the Ivory Coast was singled out as an example of the "pragmatic," or "nonideological," one-party state. This categorization reflects

4. See R. Clignet and P. Foster, *The Fortunate Few* (Evanston, Ill.: Northwestern University Press, 1967).
5. *La Côte d'Ivoire 1965: Population—Synthèse—Études Régionales 1962–1965* (Abidjan: Ministère des finances, des affaires économiques, et du plan, July 1967), pp. 147, 158.

the fact that no Ivory Coast political leader has yet written a book setting forth his political beliefs, that the policies pursued before and since independence specifically avoid "-isms," and that they tend to be justified on the grounds of a realistic assessment of available choices rather than on the grounds of general principles. But this should not be taken to indicate the absence of a generalized model of political action. To avoid debate on the word "ideology," I shall refer to this model as "the political formula" of the rulers.

This formula appeared around 1950, after the initial spurt of political participation and organization had resulted in severe repression by the French colonial authorities and in an exacerbation of ethnic conflict. The formula was defined by President Houphouet-Boigny who emerged at that time as the sole party leader in a position to influence the course of political events. Its main tenet was that a commitment to rapid political change formulated in the language of the Left threatened to bring about political conflict and hence to undermine both the nationalist organization's support throughout the country and to weaken its bargaining position vis-à-vis the French. The concomitant strategy was the building up of a heterogeneous coalition in which components would retain their distinctive identity. This coalition could be maintained only by enhancing the legitimacy of its leader, Houphouet-Boigny, and by distributing tangible benefits to key components, including the emerging bourgeoisie and the ethnic groups. In order to achieve the latter, economic expansion was critical. Given the Ivory Coast's dependent situation with reference to the market for international commodities and to the absence of internal sources of capital accumulation, good relations had to be maintained with the main sources of economic expansion, metropolitan France and the European population. Mobilization around chiliastic goals and around a totalistic party was therefore deemphasized. Instead, the leadership stressed development of loyal and efficient administrative structures and of a government party capable of managing elections.

In a number of significant respects, this political formula and its economic counterpart is similar to that which arose in France under the Bonapartist Empire of 1852–70. It is sufficiently flexible to accommodate the use of coercion during the periods of crisis and movement in a more liberal direction when the regime has regained confidence. The regime is based on popular sovereignty, but this principle of legitimacy is embodied in one man; political participation is formally broad, but very limited in practice; and the governmental administrative apparatus performs most of the functions associated with a political party.

This political formula is in no sense "conservative." It is genuinely oriented toward modernization, but it is a modernization which is very much guided at the top by Saint-Simonian businessmen and technocrats. From this vantage point, there is no need for a direct confrontation between modernity and traditionalism. Since the capacity of the modernizers is limited, such confrontations would likely be costly. Instead, modernization simply proceeds in the sectors where it is most likely to be successful; it is expected that spillover effects will occur. Meanwhile, traditional features of the society are left to wither slowly; since there is no direct confrontation, traditions can be appealed to when it is useful to do so, much as the Bonapartists could appeal to religion on behalf of the maintenance of order.

The founding of a regime under the guidance of this political formula has been discussed in detail elsewhere. When the Ivory Coast became independent in 1960, the ruling party had achieved an effective monopoly over access to political office at all levels. Its coalition character was manifested in the background of elected office-holders, who included representatives of the most significant ethnic groups (with some over-representation of the president's own) as well as of foreign Africans; of various factions within the dominant party and of former opposition groups which had been co-opted over the years; of important economic interest groups such as coffee farmers, truckers, brokers, and key trade unions (teachers, railroad workers, etc.); and even of ideological dissenters such as leftist ex–student leaders and liberal-minded Catholic activists. Irreconcilable opponents were for the most part in more or less voluntary exile in France or in neighboring African countries; a few had been arrested or had withdrawn into private life.

Although the party was formally prominent and had been reorganized in 1959 in anticipation of renewed activity, in practice it had undergone a severe decline. This was due to internal factionalism based on both personal rivalry and disagreement over issues related to independence, which made any sort of concerted party activity a dangerous occasion for conflict, and to lack of personnel. The first generation of somewhat educated men, who had manned the party in its early years, had moved into governmental posts and were absorbed by their day-to-day tasks; the party's ability to recruit new militants and organizers from the more educated new generations was limited by sharp differences in political outlook stemming from differences in political socialization. Relatively speaking, the governmental apparatus had become the more important instrument of regime-maintenance and of political development. In contrast with Ghana, however, Africanization of the middle and upper levels of both the field administration and the specialized administrative services came late (ca. 1956). In keeping with its general orientation, the regime was reluctant to speed up Africanization of the specialized services, a policy justified in the name of efficiency. But the more political field administration was reorganized shortly after independence and a high priority was assigned to the recruitment and training of politically reliable and administratively effective prefects and subprefects.

## THE CRISIS YEARS

Already in 1958–60, dissent at the highest levels of the party and of the government had come to light. Shortly after the *Parti Démocratique de Côte d'Ivoire* (PDCI) held its long-awaited congress (March 1959), the party's newly elected secretary-general, J.-B. Mockey, "resigned" as minister of interior and was eventually stripped of all the offices he held. The activities of the JRDACI, a youth wing reluctantly created in 1959 in response to vociferous demands voiced by the second generation, were severely curtailed. The regime was unable to control conflicts between native Ivorian and immigrant African workers in Abidjan and in other parts of the country; it resorted to coercion in dealing with students, civil servants, and other labor unions, as well as with ethnic groups which had formerly provided the basis for political oppositions. Hence, the revelation of a serious crisis in early 1963 did not come as a total surprise to knowledgeable observers.[6]

Perhaps as many as 200 persons were arrested, including several cabinet ministers, members of the National Assembly, and recently appointed prefects and subprefects. In the spring of 1963, 126 individuals were formally investigated; 86 were brought to trial in April before a special political tribunal sitting behind closed doors in the president's home in Yamoussoukro and headed by Mockey, who had since returned to the Ivory Coast

6. A somewhat different version of this section has appeared as the appendix to the paperback, revised edition of my *One-Party Government in the Ivory Coast* (Princeton, N.J.: Princeton University Press, 1969). Unless otherwise specified, the materials in this appendix are based on interviews and direct observation during two brief visits in the Ivory Coast in 1963 and in 1964 and on regular reading of the weekly newspaper *Fraternité-Hebdomadaire*. Some of the data and analyses were used in my comparative study *Creating Political Order: The Party-States of West Africa* (Chicago: Rand McNally, 1966).

An analysis of recent transformations with emphasis on the urban setting is being completed by Michael Cohen as a Ph.D. dissertation in political science at the University of Chicago.

and become minister of agriculture after a stint as ambassador to Israel. Of these, 64 were found guilty and received sentences ranging from the death penalty (for 13) to five years of hard labor.

Official accounts eventually specified that the government had learned in mid-1962 that a conspiracy was under way to seize power toward the end of the year, probably by surrounding Yamoussoukro while President Houphouet-Boigny and other officials were gathered there in a council. This information enabled the government itself to set a trap in Yamoussoukro in January. Official comments further referred to the Communist-inspired activities of Young Turks who had retained their leftist orientation since their student days in Paris; using the JRDACI as a cover, they had recruited conspirators at all levels of the society, exploiting latent divisions along tribal or regional lines. Indeed, the examination of the sixty-four individuals condemned in April shows that they included six of the nineteen members of the executive committee of the JRDACI, as well as others known to be local JRDACI officials and former student leaders. Furthermore, many of those tried bore names recognizably associated with ethnic groups which had opposed Baoulé dominance in national political life since shortly after World War II, such as Dioula and Sénoufo in the North, Bété in the West, and Agni of Sanwi in the Southeast.

Before and after the trial the regime took a series of decisions designed to bolster its authority. They included: the passage of a "law for the utilization of persons," enabling the government to mobilize idle men into a labor corps; the reassignment of numerous civil servants; the creation of party committees inside each ministry and at the level of every major administrative district; the negotiation of agreements with generally like-minded African countries to help fight domestic subversion; the retention of a larger number of university-level students at home by reducing the number of scholarship awards; and the requirement of demonstrations of political loyalty as a prerequisite for these awards. In June a spokesman for the president admitted publicly that the senior party leaders who opposed the creation of the JRDACI on the grounds that it would become a party within a party had been correct; hence, the organization was formally dissolved, and its local committees were brought under the direct authority of local party officials. The long-awaited party congress, at which plans for a thorough reorganization of its structures would be discussed, was postponed to the end of the year.

A second act opened when the president, who had left the country shortly after the trial, returned to the Ivory Coast in late August. The popular celebrations usually held upon his return were canceled; instead, he sped to his palace under full armed guard and began a new series of consultations. It was announced in rapid succession that the government intended to create a party militia composed of able-bodied young men and army veterans, that the party congress was postponed once again in order to permit the thorough renewal of party branches, and that government employees, whose salaries had been frozen for several years, would receive a substantial raise. Once again, arrests were not publicized at the time, but it can be estimated retrospectively that they had numbered over one hundred. From information made public later it became evident that the individuals implicated were of even higher political stature than those allegedly involved in the earlier plot and that opposition to the regime had reached to the highest levels of the party and of the government. The most prominent names included five party founders who were members of the Bureau politique and of the Security Court created at the beginning of the year including its president; the three most outstanding leaders of regional movements who had been co-opted into the Houphouet-Boigny coalition during the previous decade; and additional representatives of the university-trained second generation. Six of these men were also cabinet members, including the minister of the interior and the minister of defense; four were members of the National Assembly; and one had recently been president of the Supreme Court. Several long-time French residents of the Ivory Coast were expelled from the country as well.

At his press conference on 9 September the president hinted that this new plot had been "ideological" in character and asserted that while socialism was appropriate for other countries, there was no reason to establish it in the Ivory Coast. A few weeks later Yacé offered a more elaborate interpretation. Tracing the sources of the crisis to 1950–51, when the *Rassemblement Démocratique Africain* (RDA) severed its links with the French Communist party, he asserted that some senior party leaders had stayed in touch with the Communists and had slowly organized a subversive network linking them with ex–opposition politicians, some Frenchmen, and politicians of neighboring African countries. Together, and with the anticipated support of the army, they plotted to establish a tribal federation within the Ivory Coast, which would itself be linked to a socialist-minded multinational union of West African states. The reference here was clear to the then existing union of Ghana, Guinea, and Mali. However, no explanation was given then or later of how known antagonists within the Bureau politique had suddenly become reconciled, how PDCI stalwarts had become the allies of the party's oldest enemies, how party leaders who had opposed the formation of the JRDACI had come to plot with youth leaders, or how any of these alleged leftists had become involved with a conservative Frenchman who had defended to the very end the maintenance of a two-college system in the old Conseil général, except that they were all Freemasons, using their lodge activities as a cover for subversion.

Preparations began immediately for a monstrous rally in support of President Houphouet-Boigny to be held in Abidjan on 28 September, the fifth anniversary of the referendum. The army was disarmed, while order was maintained throughout the city by the armed party militia, described by some observers as "Baoulé warriors" brought in from the president's home region. All activity stopped throughout the country as huge crowds, reported by the government to number about a million, poured into the capital city for an immense political festival.

In their major speeches before the huge crowd gathered in and around the Abidjan stadium, President Houphouet-Boigny and Secretary-General Yacé repeated many of the announcements of the previous weeks. In addition, the president stressed his desire to satisfy the people's legitimate needs: since farmers suffered from the consequences of depressed world-market prices, he was taking over agriculture personally to seek adequate solutions; the government would launch compensatory regional development programs in order to reduce disparities; civil servants would get better salaries; there would be greater freedom for trade unions, so long as they did not engage in political strikes; distribution circuits would be improved to the benefit of African traders; foreign Africans living and working in the Ivory Coast would be granted double nationality; greater control would be exerted over students. But he also warned that corruption and favoritism must be eliminated from all sectors of Ivory Coast life.

A number of these measures and related actions were implemented in the months that followed. The Security Court was reorganized in preparation for the new trial; in addition to the party militia, the government announced the creation of a presidential guard distinct from the regular army; and all students were ordered to join the government-sponsored student union (UNECI) lest their scholarships be withdrawn. The party congress was again postponed, while ad hoc measures for internal reorganization were taken, including the stabilization of ethnic group representation in the Abidjan branches, the renewal of a number of other sections and the creation of additional ones to bring the party in line with territorial administration, and the creation of a "political committee" distinct from the Bureau politique whose ranks had been depleted as the result of the crisis.

In the early months of 1964 the atmosphere appeared to have relaxed somewhat as the regime regained confidence. But the mood changed suddenly on 6 April when it was announced that Ernest Boka, a student leader who had served as minister of education, minister of public service, and president of the Supreme Court, had committed suicide while detained in the president's compound in Yamoussoukro. Rumors that he had been assassinated or died of ill-treatment immediately spread both in the Ivory Coast and abroad. After a number of hasty emergency party meetings, President Houphouet-Boigny convoked an ad hoc national council, to which foreign diplomats, religious authorities, and businessmen were invited as well. Asserting that Boka had been neither beaten nor tortured, he devoted the major part of his address to the reading of a confession allegedly written by Boka before his death, and to his own commentaries upon it.[7]

In this document, Boka admits that he had repeatedly engaged in financial manipulations while holding public office; that he had remained sympathetic to the French Communist party since he joined its ranks while a university student at Grenoble in 1951–52 and had used his influence to place Communists in key administrative posts; and that he had plotted throughout to eliminate those who stood in the way of his self-appointed status as the president's political heir. But the document also contains strange statements concerning Boka's constant reliance on diviners and wielders of occult power to realize his political ambitions. In a final peroration, he repeats his confession of guilt, asks forgiveness for his family, and demands to be immediately executed as an unworthy monster, hinting that he had been in contact with someone who was in a position to poison the president, while also employing an individual "to work on the president's photograph." And he concludes, "It is as if I had assassinated him. May God forgive me!"

After this reading, President Houphouet-Boigny severely condemned "fetishist practices." He asserted that, having been initiated to their use, he knew that fetishes themselves can do no evil, but that evil stems only from the use that can be made of them; fetishes do not kill, only the poison that is behind them. He also explained that the Ivory Coast was suffering from the consequences of the abandonment of traditional religious controls over the use of fetishes, while individuals retained their belief in the

7. The transcripts were published in *Abidjan-Matin* (16 April 1964); and in *Fraternité*, "Supplement" (7 April 1964).

power of the fetishes themselves. "Atheism," especially among the educated young, is therefore a great threat which can be overcome only by the serious practice of Christianity and Islam. Finally, the president displayed as evidence two suitcases allegedly seized from members of Boka's family and others containing magic philters, a variety of fetishes, and small coffins holding his own corpse in effigy.

Additional information concerning the crisis was published about a year later, following a new trial by the Security Court. This time, its verdicts included six death sentences, two life sentences, nineteen jail terms, nineteen acquittals, and eighteen "absolutions" granted to a number of old party militants who had been found guilty but whose previous services warranted forgiveness. These absolutions were conditional upon public confessions before assemblies in Abidjan and throughout the country, in the course of which it was revealed that there had been a second plot to arrest President Houphouet-Boigny when he disembarked in August; the capital would then have been invaded by tribesmen from the North, the West, and the Southeast, who would help bring to power an ethnic federation. Its head was to have been Jean-Baptiste Mockey. At about the same time the Ivory Coast charged that the Ghanaian ambassador had participated in the conspiracy on behalf of his government.

Many aspects of the Ivory Coast crisis of 1962–64 remain obscure. We cannot ascertain whether the various elements involved in one or more attempts to overthrow the existing regime relied on internal resources alone, or whether they benefited from external support, as the Ivory Coast government claimed they did, any more than we can verify the proposition that at least one of these attempts would have succeeded if the regime had not itself benefited from French military support. Even the incomplete account available is useful, however, because it confirms that the origins of the crisis lay in the persistence of old patterns of conflict characteristic not only of the Ivory Coast, but of other new African nations as well. One major source of strain stems from the cleavages between ethnic groups discussed above. It confirms the hypothesis that in the short run, at least, processes of social, economic, and political modernization increase rather than reduce the likelihood of severe conflict. The other major source of strain stems from the deep cleavage between the founding generation of nationalist leaders and the generation of potential successors, who view themselves as better qualified to rule on the basis of their higher education. In the case of the Ivory Coast, President Houphouet-Boigny's persistent avoidance of militancy in the fields of foreign affairs and economic development insures that these oppositions speak in the name of the Left; but the experience of similar sources of opposition in other African regimes who themselves identify with the Left suggests that ideology as such is not a determining factor. The allusions to magic and witchcraft which emerged in the course of the crisis were, so far as I know, the first public references by the Ivory Coast regime to processes that are often hinted at by Ivorians discussing politics privately. Are these references to be dismissed as trumped-up accusations, in this particular case, and as irrelevant lurid gossip, more generally? What matters is not whether or not a specific individual resorted to such means but rather whether actors involved in important social and political processes *believe* that such means are used and that they can be effective, as is indeed the case in the Ivory Coast. At the most manifest level, these beliefs contribute to the generation of a climate of great suspicion, especially among individuals who are closely associated with one another; and this climate itself contributes to the fulfillment of the prophecy. But at a less manifest level, these beliefs are associated with a sense that the equilibrium which prevailed in traditional society between the use of occult powers and controls over the circumstances and consequences of this use has been lost. How can it be restored? Only by creating a new reliable order of society. Initially, for many Africans, this order was sought in the political realm. But as recurrent disturbances demonstrated the failure of this strategy, or as the costs of political fervor came to be viewed as overly high, one could expect the emergence of alternatives. Viewed in this light, President Houphouet-Boigny's appeal for participation in Christian and Muslim religious activities and the subsequent implementation of this appeal by means of specific efforts, must be taken as an important key to the understanding of the institutionalization of patterns of integration in the Ivory Coast.

## INSTITUTIONAL RENOVATION

The experience of the crisis years had revealed that existing party structures were faction-ridden, that they were inadequate instruments of control over the administration and over the population, and that they did not provide an effective network of political communication. Although party reconstruction began immediately, the record of the last five years confirms that the Ivory Coast regime has come to rely much more heavily on the development of an effective territorial state bureaucracy for the performance of critical tasks. Furthermore, although the party, the National Assembly, and regular elections remain the formal nexus for popular participation in political life, in effect this nexus seems to have become merely one component of an incipient institution which can be called the "estates-general" of the Ivory Coast.[8]

At the time of independence, the Ivory Coast was still divided territorially into *cercles* and *subdivisions* manned primarily by French colonial officials with some African aides; below this, in the rural areas, the *canton* was still functioning as a unit headed by an appointed African chief. It is in this sphere that the most significant institutional innovations have taken place following a strategy discussed in Stryker's contribution to the present volume. By the end of 1965 the *cercles* and *cantons* had been eliminated, and the country had been reorganized into six *départements*, each headed by a *préfet*, and further into approximately one hundred *sous-préfectures*, each headed by a *sous-préfet*. More recently this administrative network has been further extended by the creation of several *centres d'état-civil* below the *sous-préfecture* level. The organizational model is clearly that of contemporary France; but the spirit in which the organization operates appears to be closer to that of the French Second Empire. The prefects are the president's personal representatives at the regional level, endowed with broad authority to implement his directives; several of them are members of the Bureau politique as well. The subprefects are usually products of the National School of Administration, but political criteria enter into their recruitment and assignment to specific posts.

The role of the subprefect in the Ivory Coast and of equivalent officials elsewhere is critical in the overall process whereby a modernizing center attempts to reach into those spheres of society least affected by social change. This is clear from the extent of the tasks that have been entrusted to them: they are in charge of the newly created civil registry services whereby the most intimate aspects of social life become publicly regulated acts; they "animate" development policies and coordinate the activities of technical officials in their district; they report on political life in the area by keeping track of the activities of individuals and groups.[9] There are no assemblies with decision-making authority at this level in the Ivory

---

8. A most useful source of detailed information on recent Ivory Coast institutions is Conférence Olivaint de Belgique, "La Côte d'Ivoire, Chances et risques" (mimeographed report, 1966; 71, avenue de Cortenberg, Brussels 4).

9. See Robert Guidon Lavallée, *Le manuel du sous-préfet* (Abidjan: Editions Africaines, n.d.). Party bureaucratization and the political role of the state apparatus are well discussed in Martin Staniland, "Single-Party Regimes and Political Change: The P.D.C.I. and Ivory Coast Politics," in Colin Leys, ed., *Politics and Change in Developing Countries* (Cambridge: Cambridge University Press, 1969), pp. 135–75.

Coast but merely a Conseil des notables of from eight to sixteen members who must be consulted by the subprefect at least once a year. The status of chiefs is very ambiguous. Although the 1934 law concerning their recruitment and functions has never been abolished, the administrative chiefs have been stripped of their authority in the fields of tax collection, judicial arbitration, and the police. During their lifetime they are consulted by the subprefect; but the government has not been recruiting successors when the incumbents die.

From mid-1964 on, the PDCI's territorial organization was modified to parallel the territorial state bureaucracy; approximately forty new sections corresponding to the new subprefectures were created. As in the past, these sections are divided into village committees in the rural areas, and into ward or ethnic subcommittees in the towns. In keeping with a long-standing suspicion of regional centers of power, there is no party organization corresponding to the departmental level. In preparation for the party congress of September 1965, national teams supervised the election of secretary-generals in the new sections and in old ones where officials had been dismissed during the crisis; unusual publicity was given in the party press to the democratic character of the electoral process by citing actual results.

The congress's main task was to replenish the membership of the party's governing bodies, one-third of whom had been involved in oppositional activities. The congress maintained all ten remaining members of the Bureau politique and selected fifteen new members, for an enlarged total of twenty-five. About two-thirds of the additions appeared to be old "companions," individuals who had been active at the local level in the late 1940s; the remainder were technocrats who had remained faithful to the president throughout the crisis, including some outstanding members of the university-trained second generation. Significantly, these men were selected as individuals rather than as representatives of organizational components of the party. The Comité directeur was enlarged to eighty-five (including the twenty-five members of the Bureau politique). Its membership consisted mainly of old and new secretary-generals and the only visible innovation was the inclusion of ten women.

The congress was also concerned with finances and communications. In recent years the payment of party dues has become such a universal phenomenon that it may be assimilated to the payment of a head tax. Indeed, the secretary-general has become a tax farmer, since he retains approximately one-third of the proceeds gathered in his section, much as the *chef de canton* did in respect to the head tax before it was abolished.

Furthermore, although the basic rate has been set at 200 C.F.A. francs a year (approximately 80 cents), a lower rate has been set for poorer areas. Besides the secretary-general's share, half of the proceeds are allocated to the national headquarters, leaving only approximately fifteen percent for the activities of the section and the local committees, including their building program. The party has increased the production of its weekly, *Fraternité-Hebdomadaire*, to nearly 20,000 copies, but it can be guessed from recurrent complaints and appeals for subscriptions that actual readership is very much lower. Little imagination is used in party propaganda.

Finally, the congress of September 1965 formally nominated candidates to the National Assembly whose mandate expired in November. Its membership, which had been reduced from 100 to 70 in 1960, was increased to 85. Of the 70 members elected in 1960, only 48 were renominated. Of the remainder, approximately one-third had been appointed to other positions (ambassadors, heads of administrative agencies, etc.); about one-third had been arrested; and the others included some deaths and retirements. Official statements concerning the 37 new candidates stressed only that for the first time they included 3 women. The others appear to have been selected, as in the past, for their representative character according to ethnic criteria (including 3 foreign Africans), or to functional criteria (through their role in important associations); many of them were "old companions" as well. The elections for the National Assembly, the presidency, and the general councils at the departmental level —those elected in 1960 had never met—were held simultaneously in November 1965, following the pattern of 1959 and 1960. The new government which was formed in early 1966 signaled a deconcentration of the offices gathered under the presidency during the crisis and the elimination of the last non-African from the cabinet. With 2 additions in later months, its total membership was brought to 18, excluding the president. Eight of the cabinet ministers are also members of the Bureau politique; but this included several individuals who were co-opted to the party's governing body because of their effective performance in government service. Several younger men with high professional qualifications were included as junior ministers and later promoted to full cabinet rank.

In other institutional spheres the regime remained consistent with its earlier approach, stressing the unification of major functional associations such as labor unions, businessmen's groups, women's organizations, and youth under government and party sponsorship. It continued to experience difficulties in dealing with labor and, particularly, with university students.[10] The JRDACI was completely dismantled to avoid the formation of a party within the party; youth who want to participate in politics must do so as individual members of party sections and committees.

In spite of these occasional difficulties there was a general relaxation of the political atmosphere after 1965 and particularly after the fall of Kwame Nkrumah in early 1966 removed what the regime believed to be the main source of external support for internal opposition. In recent years, there has been less reliance on coercive measures. A number of political prisoners were released to celebrate the 1965 elections while others had their sentences reduced; the last seven, all of whom had initially received death sentences, were freed on the occasion of the state funeral for President Houphouet-Boigny's maternal aunt in May 1967. Sanwi exiles in Ghana were returned by the new Ghanaian government and forgiven after a public confession of their subversive activities. In 1966–67 the presence of President Nkrumah in Guinea was a new source of international tension, but there is no evidence that it affected internal political processes.

The general patterns of political control and of participation with the Ivory Coast version of the West African party-state appear to be fairly well institutionalized for the time being. Their major locus is not the party, nor the government, nor formal representative assemblies, but rather a national council convened by the president whenever important issues arise for a face-to-face encounter. The composition of this body varies, but most of the time it includes the Bureau politique, the Comité directeur, the remaining secretary-generals of hinterland sections, the secretary-generals of ethnic committees and of foreign African committees in Abidjan; the cabinet, heads of government services and agencies, prefects and subprefects; the National Assembly, members of the Economic and Social Council, and of the departmental general councils; labor leaders, representatives of veterans and of women as well as student spokesmen; and, finally, "notables" not included in the above categories, such as traditional chiefs who retain some influence and leaders of the Catholic, Protestant, Harrist, and Muslim religious communities. Since there is a lot of overlap among individuals in these various categories, the total probably ranges from four

10. Victory D. DuBois, "The Student-Government Conflict in the Ivory Coast," *American Universities Field Staff Reports Service*, West Africa Series, vol. 8, no. 1 (Ivory Coast), 1965. On youth, more generally, see Lyman Drake, "The Anxious Generation" (Ph.D. dissertation, M.I.T., 1968).

to eight hundred people. These estates-general function as a parliament with a limited but genuine role in decision-making, informing the president of the state of affairs in the country and disseminating his directives downward into every sphere of Ivory Coast society. They do not have the power to initiate decisions or to oppose presidential initiatives, but rather to influence the extent of their implementation and to help establish priorities. Their negative response to the announcement of a new policy may even lead to the withdrawal of presidential initiative, as seems to have been the case with the proposal to extend Ivory Coast citizenship to the foreign Africans who constituted about one-fourth of the country's total population in 1966–67.

At the top all of these institutional segments coalesce but beneath they remain distinct. The two key roles are probably those of the party secretary-general and of the subprefect, who constitute the locus of interaction between local and national concerns. As we would expect, the relationships between the individuals who occupy these roles are tense. It is probably through an investigation of these relationships, however, that we can make further progress in understanding the process of political modernization in the Ivory Coast.[11]

## MODERNIZATION POLICIES

The study of political modernization, however, requires not merely an understanding of political institutions and processes, but also an understanding of the eventual political consequences of changes in the nonpolitical sectors of the society. These changes occur in part autonomously, from the point of view of the political system, but to a varying extent they are themselves the result of political decisions to pursue specific policies in such obviously important fields as education and economic development, as well as in less obvious ones which impinge on the character of social relationships, such as family law. Since several of these aspects will be discussed in other chapters, I shall merely indicate their relationship to politics.

From 1950–51 on, the achievement of maximum economic growth was given precedence over most other goals. While most other underdeveloped countries also assign a high priority to this goal, the Ivory Coast regime is distinguished by its great consistency in this respect and by its willingness

11. See Staniland, "Single-Party Regimes," pp. 168–75.

to sacrifice to it possible political satisfactions derived from militant nationalism. As elsewhere, economic policies are intimately connected with political policies properly speaking; but while in some cases, such as Mali or Ghana during the late Nkrumah period, economic decisions reflect a desire to achieve immediate regime needs, such as the creation of economic structures dominated by nationals and which provide the party-state with physical evidence of its reality, in the Ivory Coast these decisions reflect a belief that economic growth achieved by the most effective means, including dominance by foreign personnel and capital, will maximize the regime's capability for distributing material benefits to its population and hence foster support.[12]

The results of this orientation, whose details are examined by Berg in his contribution to the present volume, have been that the Ivory Coast has experienced the most spectacular rate of economic growth in tropical Africa during the last decade. Whether it is accurate to characterize the Ivory Coast pattern as "growth without development," as some have done, in the sense that its economic structures are unlikely to lead to take-off but rather to increased external dependence and internal blockages, is more properly an economic question.[13] From a political point of view, there is little doubt that on balance economic policy choices have achieved the results desired by the regime at least in the short run. Demands continue to be voiced by workers, employees, and farmers for a greater share of material benefits, but it has been relatively easier to satisfy these demands than it would have been under conditions of economic stagnation. The political costs of avoiding socialism have been most obvious in the tense relationships between the political generations; but it is possible that these tensions are independent of ideology, and in any case they are somewhat balanced by the regime's ability to eventually co-opt members of this generation by recruiting them to rewarding positions whose establishment is made possible by economic expansion itself. In the longer run, the regime is betting on the contributions that economic growth will make to the transformation of social relationships by fostering national transaction flows. That is a more problematic question, however, since political crises of great depth often occur precisely during periods of rapid economic

12. For the contrast with Mali see my chapter "The Political Use of Economic Planning in Mali," in Harry Johnson, ed., *Economic Nationalism in Old and New States* (Chicago: The University of Chicago Press, 1967), pp. 98–123.

13. The most detailed study is Samir Amin, *Le développement du capitalisme en Côte d'Ivoire* (Paris: Les Editions de Minuit, 1967). See also Berg's discussion in the present volume.

growth as a result of the structural upheavals this growth generates in the society as a whole.[14]

The modernization of social relationships remains a subject of great concern not only for its own sake but also because it is believed that it is a prerequisite to further economic development and that enemies of the regime can manipulate traditional relationships and beliefs to achieve their own political purposes, as revealed by the crisis of 1962–64. The president's attack on fetishism and atheism during the Boka affair can be seen as the source of a campaign to raise funds for the building of Catholic, Protestant, Harrist, and Muslim religious edifices in Abidjan launched at the beginning of 1965. This was an extra-governmental policy entrusted to the party and to specially created associations; but there is no doubt that it ranked in importance with major governmental decisions. Initially, the president of the republic, the president of the National Assembly, and the president of the Supreme Court, each contributed approximately $1,000 to the fund; mandatory contributions were imposed on lower officials as well. A special assessment, to be collected by the party from each family in the country, with a lower rate in poorer areas of the North, was announced; the collection of this assessment constituted a major party activity during the rest of the year.

The major strategy for modernizing social relationships has been the creation of a new national civil code pertaining especially to family law. The code was radically innovative in that it deliberately avoided the codification of existing customary law and formally abolished three major social institutions: bride price, that is, dowry paid by men, in the West; matriarchy, that is, matrilineal inheritance from uncle to nephew, in the Akan culture area; and polygamy, in the North as well as throughout the country, more generally. It was made clear from the outset, however, that the government had no intention of enforcing all the provisions of the code everywhere and immediately. Presently, it stands as a major symbol of the orientation of the Ivory Coast toward modernity; it also provides a new legal framework toward which individuals already imbued with modern values can orient their behavior; and it serves as a model against which existing practices can be evaluated. The slow task of diffusing the norms the code embodies is shared by the major political institutions: while the government has been investing resources in the creation of appropriate

14. Similar questions can be raised about the impact of educational development. See particularly Clignet and Foster, *The Fortunate Few*. Rising tensions between the government and key labor unions in 1969 are analyzed by Michael Cohen in a forthcoming Ph.D. dissertation, University of Chicago.

civil registry services at the local level, party officials and the party press function as educators. But the results of all these activities remain extremely limited, as indicated in the discussions of Ivory Coast law elsewhere in the present volume.

## CONCLUSIONS

Toward the end of its first decade of independence, the Ivory Coast stands out as one of the few African countries which has not experienced a discontinuous change of regime. Although this should not be taken as the sole indicator of success in achieving a measure of political development, there is little doubt that it is a significant indicator of the regime's capacity to handle some of the crises African nations normally experience. I have tried to indicate in this chapter that this capacity is related to the regime's ability to devise a flexible political formula which has in turn enhanced its ability to learn from the crises it has experienced. It may be that even this limited success in weathering early crises has significantly reinforced the institutionalization of a set of political structures by enhancing their legitimacy. The longer these structures last, the more likely they are to constitute a permanent layer of societal sediment which will not be easily eroded even if a tidal wave were to occur as a result of future crises.

As in other new nations, the establishment of legitimacy remains a key to political development. We still know very little, however, about how power is transformed into authority. One important aspect of this process is probably the achievement of a certain degree of success in solving crucial political problems such as the maintenance of civil peace. Although this is perhaps a universal phenomenon, it appears to be particularly salient in Africa where it may be related to deep seated beliefs in the relationship between man and nature. The repeated demonstration by a man, or group of men, of their ability to surmount challenges through the use of specific techniques of control, may earn them the sort of respect that a willingness to obey entails. Although this process is independent of the regime's ability to satisfy demands, it is, of course, affected by the latter.

The Ivory Coast appears to have been relatively successful in these respects in comparison with most other African countries. But this success is due to a considerable extent to the lasting power of a single individual, President Houphouet-Boigny. That he remains, for the time being, the major source of legitimacy, is evident. For example, when he led the country in the celebration of a national funeral for his deceased maternal aunt at Yamoussoukro in 1967, the president used the occasion for a sermon on the Ivory Coast's approach to modernization. Why, he was asked, did he celebrate a "pagan" funeral at great expense, when he had himself often urged the abolition of such practices? He explained that his aunt, who was in effect his mother since the death of the latter many years ago, had agreed to the abolition of "matriarchy," and specifically that she had foregone her son's right to inherit from the president, in exchange for the promise of a dignified funeral. Already, the president went on, he had knowingly violated his family traditions in order to modernize them: there were no human sacrifices at the funeral; the ceremonies were celebrated in broad daylight and in the presence of strangers; the burial was not carried out by family members but by a public undertaker. He deplored having to abide by the "anachronistic, noneconomic" practice of displaying wealth which would then be withdrawn from commercial circuits, rather than invested, but concluded that deeply rooted traditions can be eliminated only gradually.

On this occasion the party newspaper commented that the Ivory Coast "was united as a single tribe and a single family." Although traditions remain important, the meeting at Yamoussoukro "proves that our country has not awaited the disappearance of tribal customs to achieve its unity." A nation is to be created not by revolution but by the growth of a common sentiment of belonging together. At Yamoussoukro, "all the races of the Ivory Coast" renewed their pledge of allegiance to Houphouet-Boigny, the "cement that binds the nation."

The president of the Ivory Coast provides an interesting test of the heuristic value of the concept "charismatic leader" when used in a serious analytic sense to understand authority relationships in new nations. According to David Apter's recent restatement, "The true charismatic leader accepts his own mystique, his consciousness of his role in history, so that the public or a significant subgroup allows him to relate his personal political goals with a wider moral vision and thereby affect public action."[15] In the light of Houphouet-Biogny's effective role, as revealed by his repeated citation of personal beliefs and experiences to justify policies, as well as by the responses to these attempts on the part of much of the Ivory Coast public over a quarter of a century, I conclude that the concept does have some explanatory value in this case. But many others, including Apter, disagree.[16] Why? I think it is because in spite of efforts to dissociate the analytic use of charisma from its more popular usage, observers

15. David E. Apter, "Nkrumah, Charisma and the Coup," *Daedalus* 97, no. 3 (summer 1968) : 760.
16. Ibid., p. 789, n. 8.

commonly seek evidence on the basis of their own subjective responses to a leader's presence. It is fairly obvious that an African leader who almost always dresses in elegant continental suits, who usually expresses himself, when speaking for foreign ears, in the vocabulary of the French Center-Left, and who has pursued "moderate" policies for nearly two decades, hardly evokes feelings of moral fervor among Western social scientists. But our own feelings are a poor test of charisma in a new nation. For many Ivorians, the personal world of Houphouet-Boigny does provide a moral, future-oriented vision, on the basis of which they are willing to obey. Paradoxically, what makes it most difficult to perceive the charismatic aspects of Houphouet-Boigny's leadership is that the landscape has been filled out by an elaborate political machine. But does that not suggest that we may have before us a rare case of relatively successful routinization of charisma?

There is but one possible test of the hypothesis and this must await the passing of time. But if routinization is indeed occurring, it is noteworthy that what is being institutionalized in the Ivory Coast is not a regime based on an all-encompassing, integrative party, but rather a regime centering on a political bureaucracy. Earlier in this chapter reference was made to some similarities between the Ivory Coast and Bonapartist France of the mid-nineteenth century. It may well be that the resemblances are not fortuitous, not because of continued French influence on the Ivory Coast but because the "political bureaucracy" model provides a pre-Leninist strategy well suited for use by political elites with a limited mobilizational capability, operating under conditions of formal popular sovereignty which includes irreversibly universal suffrage.

Although the undoubted success of the regime noted at the beginning of this concluding section may well have contributed to the reinforcement of its legitimacy, we must remember that this is being evaluated in relation to other comparable African experiences. On any universal scale the degree of institutionalization achieved by the Ivory Coast regime remains very low. Ethnic tensions remain high; intergenerational conflict is endemic; incipient classes may well crystallize. Hence, the safest prediction is that sooner or later, in the medium run, discontinuous change of political incumbents will occur in the Ivory Coast as it has elsewhere. But it is equally safe to predict that the characteristic political processes sketched out in this chapter will outlast short-term political upheavals.

# 3

# POLITICAL CHANGE, CONFLICT, AND DEVELOPMENT IN GHANA

## Jon Kraus

Many of the recent ventures that attempt to specify the elements of political development stress functional differentiation of governmental and nongovernmental political structures; growing subsystem autonomy; increasing capability of the political system in a number of areas; expansion of political participation; secularization of the political culture; and shifting orientations of members from parochials to subjects and then to participants in the national political system.[1] Yet, one must be concerned with the applicability of approaches derived from the experience of Western democracies to the situation in contemporary new states. Biased toward a view that democratic regimes are inherently more capable of performing political functions, these approaches neglect the problem of the variable requirements of political systems at different levels of development. In particular, they have not focused on the types of structures, processes, and capabilities required to *establish* political systems in the first instance, particularly in countries confronting simultaneously, rather than consecutively, the various crises of political development. Furthermore, these approaches fail to deal with the relationship between social structures and dominant strata and neglect the possibility that structural conflicts may be inherent to different stages of political development.

The contrast between the problems of political development which confront contemporary Africa and the Western experience is most vivid.

Much of the material in this chapter is drawn from the author's unpublished Ph.D. dissertation on the emergence of the single-party state in Ghana.

1. See Gabriel Almond and G. Bingham Powell, Jr., *Comparative Politics: A Developmental Approach* (Boston: Little, Brown, 1966); Gabriel Almond and Sidney Verba, *The Civic Culture* (Boston: Little, Brown, 1965); the series of volumes on political development published by Princeton on the relationship of communications, bureaucracy, political culture, education, and political parties to political development; and Robert Holt and John Turner, *The Political Basis of Economic Development* (Princeton: Van Nostrand, 1966).

Almost without exception, the new African states are artificial political
entities, embracing heterogeneous traditional societies which often retained their coherence and distinctiveness during the fifty or sixty years of
colonial rule. Given low levels of socioeconomic development, there were
few stimuli toward national integration in the sense of linking these persisting societies to the new national center. The degree of institutionalization of modern political structures at the end of the colonial period was
also low. At the time of independence, most countries were faced simultaneously with all the major problems of political development: the establishment and legitimation of a national political system and of new authority
roles; the creation of mass-elite and local-national linkages through political and administrative organizations; and the development of a national
economy.

Given these unfavorable conditions and these heavy tasks, as well as
the narrow limits of choice which the social environment and the economy
impose upon them, the rulers of new African states have adopted political
strategies which are often characterized as authoritarian. Yet, one observer
has suggested that envisaging these states as "*pre*democratic rather than
*anti*democratic . . . allows us to view certain institutions of coercion as
perhaps necessary to the organization and integration of a modernizing
community."[2] Such a view minimizes, at some stages, the importance of
some of the criteria of political development referred to earlier, and allows
us to direct attention to the conflict between certain aspects of change and
development. Social mobilization, often induced by political instruments,
may result in a broader economic base, increased secularity, and structural
differentiation; but it is also likely to be initially disruptive of institutionalization. Similarly, the development of new national state structures,
partly through the centralization of power, may maintain and legitimize
national political roles and structures; but it may also erode or ritualize
political participation and reduce subsystem autonomy (e.g., of traditional
states and authorities, of particularistic political movements, and of associational groups).

The present analysis of political change and development in Ghana
focuses on a set of interrelated political dimensions which are regarded
as fundamental. First, it deals with political participation: its expansion,
the context provided by political culture, its socioeconomic basis, the differentiation of political roles and structures which accompany it, the
growth of political linkages it entails, and the structure of political conflict

2. David E. Apter, *The Politics of Modernization* (Chicago: University of Chicago
Press, 1965), pp. 2–3.

which emerges. Second, it deals with the development of state structures: territorial and institutional integration, legitimation of national authority, penetration by the center into hitherto unintegrated subsystems, and the accompanying growth of specialized and differentiated structures to implement government policies. And third, it assesses the capability of the political system to accommodate and manage political change and conflict, as well as to implement strategies of economic development. The analysis is prefaced by a brief survey of relevant aspects of Ghanaian society and concludes with an examination of trends since the coup d'etat which ended the Nkrumah regime in early 1966.

## THE GENERAL BACKGROUND

Ghana contains a large number of persisting subsocieties which were formerly separate traditional states. While there are a relatively small number of ethnocultural groups—the Akan (forty-five percent of the population in 1960), Ga-Adangbe, Ewe, Guan, Gurma, and Mole-Dagbani— this relative homogeneity did not provide a basis for national political solidarity. On the contrary, there were intense, historically-rooted antagonisms and conflicts; ethnoculturally similar, but politically distinct states, often regarded each other as aliens, "strangers." There were some sixty-two distinct traditional states in the southern colony area.[3] In Ashanti, there were sixteen distinct Ashanti "divisions" or states and ten Brong states, whose precolonial subordination to the powerful Ashanti Confederacy bred enmities, which continue to manifest themselves in the contemporary political arena. In the Northern Territories some two dozen distinct political units were recognized by the colonial government; but this figure ignores, as in Ashanti, the virtual autonomy of many of the substates.[4] Colonial administrative practice preserved regional demarcations. More significantly, although the British practice of indirect rule sustained the identity of traditional states and communities, it ultimately eroded traditional authority. In the Akan chieftaincies of southern and central Ghana indirect rule exacerbated conflicts between commoners and chiefs by making the chiefs local agents of the colonial administration, by assigning them nontraditional political roles unchecked by community norms, and by attempting to maintain them in power in the face of frequent popular attempts to unseat them. The commoners correctly perceived the

3. Gold Coast, *1931 Census: Appendices*, table 20, p. 21.
4. J. D. Fage, *Ghana, A Historical Interpretation* (Madison: University of Wisconsin Press, 1959), p. 26.

colonial-traditional structure of authority as an impediment to their access to new social, economic, and political roles to whose possibilities socioeconomic change and education had introduced them.

Socioeconomic change in preindependence Ghana was sharply skewed both ethnically and regionally. In terms of urbanization, wage labor, participation in the market economy, education, and exposure to modern ideas through various media, the colony area was the most developed; Ashanti followed; the British Togoland Protectorate (especially its southern portion) was next; and the vast underdeveloped Northern Territories was last in all respects.

By the end of World War II socioeconomic change had resulted in the emergence of modern and quasi-modernized strata, which viewed in terms of action on behalf of economic interests and values could be seen as incipient classes. A very small merchant-professional bourgeoisie, which also included the top educators and bureaucrats, was politically dominated by lawyers and had a relatively high level of class consciousness; this stratum was located exclusively in the colony. There was a much larger middle and lower-middle class composed primarily of teachers, the multitude of clerks spawned by a colonial bureaucracy and expatriate businesses, traders, cocoa brokers, small contractors, pharmacists, and journalists. A small but significant number of the 500,000 or so cocoa farmers (1960) had incomes and values which placed them in the middle class.[5] Straddling the line economically between the working class, lower-middle class, and cash crop farmers were the thousands of primary and middle school leavers who were commoners in the traditional Akan stratification system. They had great difficulty finding positions commensurate with their ambitions (and thus experimented with many), participated in commoner-chieftaincy conflicts, and found in nationalism the promise of both freedom and opportunity. There was a lower class, composed largely of the rapidly increasing number of wage laborers (183,000 in 1956), a large portion of whom were non-Ghanaian migrants who remained outside the mainstream of political life. Peripheral to the emergent class strata were all those who derived their values, role identities, and behavior in large measure from primary affiliations of kinship and com-

5. The contrast in income levels between cocoa farmers and the wage earners and salariat can be found in Ghana, Office of Government Statistican, *Survey of Population and Budgets of Cocoa Producing Families in the Oda-Swedru-Asamankese Area, 1955–1956* (Accra, 1958), pp. 72–77, and *Survey of Cocoa Producing Families in Ashanti, 1956–57* (Accra, 1960), pp. 58–65; Ghana, Ministry of Trade and Labour, *Annual Report on the Labour Division, 1956–57* (Accra, 1959), pp. 66–67.

munity, whether or not they were involved in the market economy. In contrast to the experience of the Ivory Coast, whose belated economic and educational development precluded the emergence of competitive class strata during the initial nationalist period, the relatively early emergence of these strata in Ghana provided lines of cleavage as important for the structure of political conflict as the politicization of traditional ties.

## POLITICAL PARTICIPATION

Political participation expanded greatly in Ghana (then, the Gold Coast) after World War II, stimulated by different elements on behalf of diverse values. Initial demands were animated by the drive for social, economic, and political mobility and by a diffuse anticolonial nationalism among the strata who felt constrained by the colonial and traditional authority structures. With a long tradition of respectable, anticolonial reformism, the merchant-professional bourgeoisie, in competition with the indirect rule chiefs, laid claim to power and established the United Gold Coast Convention (UGCC) in 1947 to broaden its base of support. A faction led by Kwame Nkrumah broke from the UGCC to form the Convention People's Party (CPP) in 1949. The CPP launched a program of militant nationalism that was populist in appeal and antagonistic to traditional authority. It derived its strength from its strident anticolonialism, Nkrumah's charismatic authority, and the mobility aspirations of educated commoners in small towns and rural areas, organized in numerous youth associations in the Colony and Ashanti. Nkrumah's and the CPPs challenge to authority in the name of the people, nationalism, and modernization was not directed against British colonialism alone. It threatened the traditional authority of the chiefs, rooted in social structures and values sanctioned by the past, as well as the claims of the professional bourgeoisie as the rightful heirs to the British on the basis of their education, values, and property.

Political change and development were decisively shaped by the nature of the political groups which arose to channel participation and to shape diffuse demands for self-government, a better life, more education, and jobs. Almost all the major political groups were party movements, of either a patron or mass type, animated ultimately by semisacred ends which were not up for bargaining; they tended to accept compromise only in the last resort, if they could not shape the new political system.

The CPP, which was a mass party movement, came to power in the largely indirect 1951 election within the framework of limited internal self-government. With the shift in authority to secular, African-controlled political structures at the parliamentary and local levels, and the expansion of political participation through further extension of the franchise, there was a vast inflation of political demands from different communities, traditional states, ethnic groups, regions, and modern groups for a just share in the power, status, and material rewards of self-rule. The sharp shift in the location of power from the chiefs in traditional councils to the commoners in local councils produced a continuing and bitter authority struggle. Modern groups such as trade unions, associations of farmers, exservicemen, contractors, merchants, and teachers, as well as various communities made extensive economic demands upon the CPP government, whose ability to respond was limited; it did not control the budget until 1954, after which expenditures rose dramatically. The leaders of most of these modern associational groups were drawn from the same middle and lower-middle class strata as were CPP leaders; many both identified and competed with the CPP for material allocations and power positions. Although the CPP sought with some success to align them with or integrate them within its own structures in order to control the level of demands and maintain support, this caused resentments and periodic conflict.

In addition, the territorially skewed pattern of socioeconomic change meant that variable levels of modernity and consequent claims for advantage reinforced rather than crosscut traditional cleavages. More generally, when political groups arose to compete with the CPP, they politicized primordial, local solidarity ties on behalf of both traditional and secular demands. Many chiefs and others remained fundamentally dissatisfied with the new, modern attitudes and norms which regulated participation, defined legitimate authority, and subordinated local identities and subsystems to a national political system. They were quick to ally themselves with particularistic (local, regional) secular demands for power, status, and resources often made by the new strata and reinforced these demands by endowing them with sacred sentiment. Both the great *quantity* of demands and their particularistic, often sacred, *quality* fundamentally undermined support for the CPP. Their appeal to tradition was in conflict with the secular values on which the CPP was founded and which it advocated as a goal for the nation-state. Apter indicates that in the early 1950s "the reality of the battle between parties and . . . over constitutional forms (i.e., federalism and unitarism) was less in the spirit of constitutionalism than in a conflict of charismatic authority with traditional authority . . . the confrontation between tradition and charisma was inevitable."[6] This is one side of a complex reality. Conflicts over legitimate authority, power, and distribution of advantages, were fused, as indicated by the following examination of some examples of anti-CPP activity.

The Togoland Congress, an intermittent coalition of patron groups organized in 1951 among the Ewe of British Togoland, appealed to their sense of being economically ignored and sought to preserve a distinctive Ewe identity through a part ethnically and part historically-based irredentism that advocated territorial separation and joining French Togoland. The patron Muslim Association Party (MAP; 1953) militantly articulated the distinctive social and economic neglect of Gold Coast Muslims and appealed for solidarity on the basis of religious ties. The Northern People's Party (NPP; 1954), ethnically diverse but regionally exclusive, was a protoparty, a conglomeration of chief-led groups represented nationally by educated chiefs and their clients; it articulated the development demands of the backward North and northern fears that anti-chief southern politicians would disrupt the still powerful traditional chiefs and authority systems and dominate the society. The National Liberation Movement (NLM), a patron movement launched in Ashanti in 1954, was animated by grievances which stemmed from a prevailing low cocoa price, insufficient development projects, and inadequate representation and power. It fought vehemently to preserve the power, prerogatives, and dignity of Ashanti and of its chiefs against the southern people they had conquered in the past. The merchant-professional bourgeoisie, regrouped in the Ghana Congress Party (GCP), scorned the CPP leaders as "verandah boys" of meagre means and attainment whose claims to authority were unjustified; the party found support primarily by developing links with traditional authorities through the family ties of its leaders in such states as Wenchi and Akim Abuakwa.

That the CPP could be undermined as readily as it was in Ashanti by the NLM, among the urban Muslim community by the MAP, and in the southern half of British Togoland by the Togoland Congress is indicative of the unintegrated nature of the society and of the CPP itself. In its inception the CPP was a loosely structured movement, composed of individual members as well as of a wide range of local and associational organizations. As a party in 1951 and after, its support was structured around parliamentary constituencies, local councils, and various associational

6. David Apter, *Ghana in Transition* (New York: Atheneum, 1963), pp. 329–30. This thought appears to be slightly qualified by Apter in "Nkrumah, Charisma, and the Coup," *Daedalus* 97, no. 3 (summer 1968) : 765–73.

groups (e.g., the United Ghana Farmers' Council and its local affiliates) on the one hand, and around Nkrumah's personal popularity and the organizational efforts of his small band of lieutenants, on the other. The top leadership's orientations were national; the allocation of resources and jobs through government power drew attention to the need to articulate demands effectively at the center and to anticipate government policy. Nkrumah's charisma and the CPPs nationalism performed as socializing agencies.

Two interrelated factors posed a threat to CPP coherence: the weakness of its local roots and the competition for office and status among its lower echelon leadership. First, although the CPP recruited its national and local leadership from the emergent middle and lower-middle classes, party membership at the local level was solicited through the youth associations and through local kin, clan, and ethnic affiliations. While the CPP had derived much of its local impetus and energy from the affiliation of commoner youth associations in revolt against traditional authority, the conflict was with traditional *authority*, not with all traditional relationships. With local roots in distinct subsocieties, the CPP and its local leaders were susceptible to local sentiments, interests, and conflicts. As the crisis period of the anticolonial struggle passed, and CPP militants became well-paid legislators and ministers, the nationalistic orientation which Nkrumah and the CPP had lent to particularistic demands gave way to a reassertion of specific interests and of local and ethnic orientations concerning participation in the power and material dividends of self-government.

Second, the national leadership of the CPP was composed largely of former teachers, traders, and clerks who were only the more fortunate of the primary and middle school leavers in the incipient middle and lower-middle classes. There was a high level of competition for political office and the power, wealth, and status that accompanied it as well as for remunerative and prestige positions in public corporations. The inflation of demands within the CPP for office manifested itself in 1954 when over 1,000 candidates sought nomination for 104 seats; over 100 ran as CPP rebels when they were refused nomination. In Ashanti, for example, there were at least 27 CPP rebels who received 25 percent of the total Ashanti vote. They articulated Ashanti antagonism toward the national government and provided much of the leadership in stimulating the rise and organization of the NLM which sought to replace centralized government with a loose federation. Although the NLM set up branches, acquired the support of the Ashanti-based associational groups, and had an executive committee composed primarily of modern leaders, it was fundamentally organized around and through the chiefs and councils, with the use of traditional norms and authority as appeal and sanction. The CPP was torn asunder in Ashanti; its electoral strength dropped from 59 percent in 1954 to 43 percent in 1956.

In the political conflict which raged between 1954 and 1957, there was a fairly high level of intimidation and violence in CPP encounters with the NLM and MAP.[7] There were no commonly accepted norms which regulated behavior in these conflicts in the emergent political system between political groups with diverse and highly valued goals. Nkrumah and other leaders regarded the CPP not only as a basis of power but as the incarnation of the incipient nation, to be generalized throughout the society, a view which made them quite inhospitable to the demands of new groups, whose claims were legitimized on the basis of parochial appeals and values. In return, the 1954–56 national assembly was regarded by newly arisen opponents as illegitimate, dominated and manipulated by an essentially dictatorial CPP. Parliamentary authority, like Nkrumah's charismatic authority, was a casualty of the 1954–57 conflict, and in the absence of legitimate authority there was social and political conflict. Even after the CPP victory in the 1956 election in which it won 72 out of 104 assembly seats and 57 percent of the vote, the opposition parties, except for the NPP, continued to contest the legitimacy of CPP government authority. They periodically boycotted the assembly and refused to negotiate the independence constitution until the British colonial secretary acted as mediator.

The high level of distrust between CPP and opposition as well as the forced compromise nature of the 1957 constitution meant that the parliamentary structure and its CPP occupants were, in fact, regarded with relatively little legitimacy, despite the aura which surrounded the celebrations of the first black African colony to receive its independence. The outbreak of both structured and anomic disorder indicated to Nkrumah and the CPP leadership that there would be little respite from the inflation of political demands, and that these would be exploited by the opposition in an effort to discredit and bring down the CPP government. Within a short time, the CPP had to face a small-scale Togoland Congress rebellion and more widespread Ewe disorders; the militant, angry rise of the *Ga Shifimo Kpee* in Accra itself; many important labor strikes and threats of strikes by government unions; demands of the CPP-led Ex-Service-

7. See Geoffrey Bing, *Reap the Whirlwind* (London: MacGibbon and Kee, 1968), pp. 179–94.

men's Union whose members threatened to march on Nkrumah's residence, as they had in 1948 on the British governor's; a revolt by CPP backbench National Assembly members, with some members aligning themselves with CPP dissidents in the unions and the Ex-Servicemen's Union. Many others threatened to "cross the carpet" to the opposition.

The attitude of Nkrumah and the CPP towards political participation thereafter spoke of a growing conflict between the desire for order and the desire for change, increasingly resolved in favor of order. Basic to the nationalist ideology of Nkrumah and CPP leaders was the belief in the virtue if not sanctity of political solidarity and the fundamentally malign intent of those who perpetrated social and political conflict on behalf of their specific interests.

The CPP government was in part unable and in part unwilling to satisfy the high levels of demands by participants upon the material resources, power and status available to the political system. On the one hand, they sought to maintain support through the distribution of resources and patronage, by increasing organization and integration of all social elements around the party, and by providing psychic participation through symbol manipulation such as the Nkrumah personality cult imbued with a diffuse ideology of nationalism, Pan-Africanism, and socialism. On the other hand, in an effort to diminish the level of demands, they started to employ increasingly negative sanctions against political participants and structures, including those within the CPP.

The consequences of this restriction of participation varied with the roles and structures involved, their degree of institutionalization, and general economic conditions. Until 1960 large annual increments of government and private consumption expenditure occurred while prices remained stable. After 1960–61, the precipitous decline in the world cocoa price, the great increase in crop tonnage and thus domestic receipts, the establishment of import controls, and vastly increased government expenditures which regularly outstripped revenues caused considerable inflation, severe shortages of consumer and other goods, unemployment, and a decrease in the living standard. Economically inspired dissidence and political conflict over ways to promote economic growth increased after 1960–61, making the regime less secure and increasing the use of repressive sanctions.

Sanctions employed against chieftaincy and chiefs such as the denial of resources, removal of certain prerogatives, and destoolments in favor of pro-CPP candidates appear in many instances to have resulted in local reconciliation with the party in formerly hostile areas; this in turn tended to diffuse the local CPP. In addition, chiefs sought, and some government agencies allocated to them, certain important modern functions. One consequence of this as Benjamin notes in the case of the Upper Region, was "the failure to develop fully the alternative lines of communication between the Government and the people."[8] There was less need to differentiate, specialize, and institutionalize the roles of the local CPP elite where this had not already occurred. Chiefs did not disturb the CPP regime much; chieftaincy and traditionality did.

The familiar catalogue of government inducements and sanctions was visited upon the opposition. Except for some MPs who steadfastly refused to cross the carpet to the CPP, opposition had effectively vanished by 1961, although, in practice, it was inoperative long before this date. To the extent that it was structured around chiefly support, it had lost its base, and with the exception of the NLM none of the opposition groups had much of an organization. To the extent that it was structured around ethnic and local relationships and interests, opposition remained; but it was rendered inarticulate or was now channeled through CPP structures. Disaffection from the CPP party-state persisted, of course. Under adverse conditions, leaders and many followers simply withdrew from political life.

An important result of the oppositions' decline was that CPP branch and constituency organizations were without political opponents and lost their raison d'être and energy. Further, the branch base became more diffuse as the party sought to recruit everyone into its ranks, including the opposition, in order to bind community wounds and to stimulate local solidarity on behalf of local projects. The CPP unit became primarily interested in furthering local interests, whether in terms of acquiring amenities or pursuing conflicts with neighboring communities or chiefdoms. Local issues became more substantive, national issues more a matter of ritual. This meant that there was notably less integration in terms of building value consensus on substantive issues but also that national government was not jeopardized by endemic local conflicts. The expansion of local government activities and projects provided for some specialization of roles, as did the recruitment of leading activists into the network of organs comprising the party-state: the district commissioners, Workers Brigade, Young Pioneers, and United Ghana Farmers Council (UGFC). Local

8. Ernst Benjamin, "The Persistence of Tradition in Ghanaian Politics," paper delivered at the 1965 meeting of the African Studies Association, p. 18. See also St. Clair Drake, "Traditional Authority and Social Action in Former British Africa," reprinted in William J. Hanna, ed., *Independent Black Africa* (Chicago: Rand McNally, 1964) and David W. Brokensha, *Social Change at Larteh, Ghana* (Oxford: Clarendon Press, 1966).

roles in these organizations linked these activists and, in part, the community to national structures.

While particularistic demands were considered illegitimate, the regime still had to contend with the secular claims made by various occupational and interest groups, many of which were affiliated with the CPP. These included: (1) wage and salary earners, organized in trade unions, as well as teachers and civil servants organized into associations later transformed into trade unions; (2) cocoa farmers, who were organized under the United Ghana Farmers' Council to whom they mandatorily sold their cocoa; (3) self-employed traders and merchants (54,300 men and 258,000 women in 1960),[9] with the market women well organized in the large urban markets and the larger merchants organized in a chamber of commerce, headed by important CPP leaders; (4) timber and building contractors, organized in respective associations and vying with expatriate concerns; and (5) quasi-professional skill groups like accountants and nurses, some salaried and others self-employed. The CPP government sought to control the level of demands from most of these groups, especially claims for wage and salary increases and for higher cocoa prices, but in 1960 the market women, merchants, and contractors had influential representatives in high party and government offices. Indeed, not a few of the party leaders, including many MPs and ministers, for whom the CPP had been a vehicle of mobility, had acquired significant economic interests as merchants and contractors. Competition for power and office also continued. Regional and national level CPP leaders and those in affiliated organizations such as the Trades Union Congress (TUC), UGFC, Ex-Servicemen's Union, and party press who had not received well-remunerated parliamentary seats, ministerial roles, or positions in state corporations, energetically sought offices which would afford them power, prestige, and higher incomes.

Conflict and competition over the arrangement of power within the Nkrumah regime from 1960 on revolved largely around the determination of economic policy and political strategies for establishing a nation, which came to mean creating an integrating political consensus which would sustain the power and authority of Nkrumah and the CPP. On the political side, CPP leaders were disturbed by the inadequate enthusiasm and support shown for the party in the first day of voting, in Accra in the mid-1960 republican and presidential plebiscite. Only forty-five percent of those registered voted, and Nkrumah's candidacy was opposed by thirty-

9. Ghana, Census Office, *1960 Population Census of Ghana, Advance Report on Volumes III and IV* (Accra, 1962), p. 51.

five percent of the voters. This stirred the CPP to greater and probably some fraudulent efforts in the following two voting days, so that the eventual CPP margin of victory was a suspicious ninety percent, though the poll was only fifty-four percent of those registered. Obvious remedies included party reform and government spending. In addition, a number of factors induced Nkrumah and part of the CPP leadership to opt for a large state role in economic development. The political factors that led to this emphasis included the colonial legacy of a bureaucratic orientation, strong nationalism, a suspicion of foreign economic interests, a partly antieconomic ideological preference for socialist ideals, and a crystallization of the class interests of much of the middle and lower-middle class around an affirmative use of state power. Economic factors included a conception of economic development as industrialization, the small inflow of foreign private capital, the inability of indigenous entrepreneurs to provide adequate capital, the need to initiate import controls in 1961 due to the vast increase in import demand, the determination to develop an internal market, and the need for rapid development in order to provide jobs for a burgeoning population of school leavers. Thus, a socialist pattern of development responded to both political and economic pressures, and most sanctioned political participation took the form of mobilization for socialist development. In this process conflict occurred between the structures developed to carry out these tasks and those who resisted the attack upon their power and status that the strategy implied. Furthermore, the mobilization apparatus was not capable of or, in some cases, permitted to induct "mobilized persons into some relatively stable new patterns of group membership, organization, and commitment."[10]

The campaign to renew the party started in 1960 and had several important elements. There was a much heralded national party reorganization, a new general secretary, Tawia Adamafio (not a member of the old guard, having joined the CPP in 1953), and an assertion of party supremacy over government in order to upgrade the CPPs status. In line with this was a new effort to integrate the TUC and UGFC more closely with the party and to give them new economic and political roles. There was a sustained attack upon the corruption and incompetence of the party old guard, members of Parliament, ministers, and some party leaders. There was also an attempt to raise the level of ideological competence within the party to prepare it to perform new tasks. This meant a change in the character of the party from a mass nationalist party that sought to

10. Karl Deutsch, "Social Mobilization and Political Development," *American Political Science Review*, 55, no. 3 (September 1961): 494.

incorporate everyone, to a cadre party that was more selective in the recruitment of leaders and members. The National Association of Socialist Student Organizations (NASSO), a heretofore small group of ideologically interested activists which had been kept in the background, set up new branches in the urban areas. It recruited into its study groups a relatively large group of critically-minded or opportunistic persons both party and nonparty, who were interested in effecting political change. In late 1960 and early 1961 there were numerous mass meetings of NASSO and smaller study group sessions at which resolutions were passed to purge corrupt, antiparty, and antisocialist elements. There was an intense, public conflict between members of Parliament and the new socialist militants in NASSO, TUC, and the party press which culminated in Nkrumah's famous Dawn Broadcast in April 1961 in which he criticized both sides in the conflict but came down hardest against corruption and "self-seeking careerists" in the National Assembly. In early May Gbedemah and Botsio, Nkrumah's top lieutenants and ministers, were downgraded in a cabinet change; in late September they were dropped entirely, along with several other opponents of the new socialist militants. Adamafio became Nkrumah's chief lieutenant, as minister of presidential affairs with wide powers.

But the socialist militants were by no means completely successful. The new specialization of offices called for in the CPP secretariat remained uncompleted. New, younger CPP regional secretaries and assistant secretaries were selected and their salaries raised, but their functions were no more extensive than before. The ideological secretaries were not ideologues, except the national secretary; sometimes they worked with the regional party in conveying government policies, as in the Eastern region; elsewhere they fought with it, as in Ashanti; sometimes they were appointed because of close ties to a ruling paramount chief, as in Brong-Ahafo. The local party with its entrenched old guard was difficult to reform.

Personal abuse and recrimination, charges of disloyalty, rumor-mongering, public attacks upon party leaders, factionalism, and the use by party leaders of *juju* (magic) for self-protection and for inflicting harm on enemies profoundly divided the party, raised fear to a high level, and demoralized many of its leaders. The violent rejection of CPP leadership manifested in the wide-scale support of the Sekondi-Takoradi strike in September 1961 made it clear that the workers did not share the militants' enthusiasm for the July 1961 "socialist" budget and its austerity provisions. Suspicious of the ambitions of Adamafio and Tettegah and

monopoly to undertake systematically every form of thievery and corruption.[13] Moreover, by the early 1960s it had become wholly dominated by the Ashanti.

In the last four years of the Nkrumah regime, the National Assembly remained the most important structure for political participation. Without a doubt it was manipulated, often adulatory, uncritical, uninformed, and unprepared, in part due to the government propensity to attach certificates of urgency to bills. During several periods it suffered a severe decline in status due to sustained attacks by the socialist militants. However, if it was, as an opposition member of Parliament noted in 1958, an "apparatus . . . to give legal effect to what has been decided elsewhere" and "a ritual dance," there was some response to the plea that "the Government will be good enough, at least when our turn comes for the dance, to listen patiently." Not a few members of Parliament felt, like S. I. Iddrissu, the most critical CPP member, that the assembly "is in the only place in the country where irregularities can be checked."[14] With regard to the post-1960 period, CPP members of Parliament served an important critical function in informing the government of public grievances and discontent within the party. It is clear that many ministers listened more closely than did Nkrumah, who tended to buy off dissent. Between 1957 and mid-1963 eighteen bills were withdrawn by the government in the face of strong assembly protests. When exposed to attack in 1961, CPP members overwhelmingly refused to accept the progress report of Minister of Information Kwaku Boateng, the chief ministerial ally of the socialist militants, who was then temporarily removed from the cabinet.[15] There are innumerable lesser instances which provide clear evidence that many members of the government were responsive to the criticisms of CPP MPs. If measures of adulation of Nkrumah were deemed appropriate, or even compulsory by many, the gap between principle and practice in the regime was regarded as a legitimate basis for criticism. But it could not be aimed at Nkrumah directly but only by implication. The right and the usefulness of parliamentary criticism by MPs was frequently protected, reaffirmed, and even encouraged, though there were times when it was constrained. The right to publicly criticize many aspects of government was institu-

13. See Ghana, *Report of the Committee of Enquiry on the Local Purchasing of Cocoa* (Accra, 1967), pp. 14–21.

14. *Parliamentary Debates: Official Record*, 11 (9 July 1958) : 313; 30 (5 Dec. 1962) : 61.

15. Boateng was undoubtedly the most disliked CPP member; Nkrumah refused to heed CPP opinion and soon after made him minister of interior, where his use of preventive detention made him all the more hated.

tionalized. In the last year and a half of the regime there was a chorus of criticism of the wretched economic performance of various state enterprises such as the state farms, the UGFC, and the Ghana National Trading Corporation (GNTC),[16] and it was the assembly's attacks which produced a commission of enquiry into the GNTC's operations.[17] Many ministers responded to these criticisms, but Nkrumah was incapable of acting decisively in the face of economic deterioration. Not a few MPs were in reasonably close and regular touch with their constituencies. They represented their interests in attempting to secure development allocations on everything from schools to state farms and became skillful at extracting funds and projects from ministries.

Leadership insecurity in the context of a modernizing, poorly integrated society nurtured notions concerning the necessity for unity and the evils of competition. Party-government sanctions were thus utilized to repress participant groups, political or not, in a parochial society which sought to become modern. Nkrumah's insecurity was furthered by several attacks on his life, fears of plots, and the political ambitions of others. The felt need for order drove Nkrumah to attempt to control or keep in close bounds all political participation and to regard the society as a corporate whole whose parts could be represented within the CPP.[18] The felt need for change, dramatic revolutionary change, inspired vanguardist conceptions of political roles, which were not given substantive functions after 1960–62 because of a fear of their disruptive effects upon the party and social whole. The political participation that did occur was largely ritualistic: rallies, speeches, a rigged referendum in 1964, and an important parliamentary renewal in 1965, in which there was participation by party branches in nominations, no opponents, and no election. The socialist militants were primarily confined to propaganda and ideology, but they had the capability to censure efforts in other areas. What was lacking in Ghana for a disciplined organizational effort, besides sufficient interest on Nkrumah's part, was a well-educated group of organizers who would be assigned specialized functions. The manpower was unavailable to the

16. See *Parliamentary Debates*, vol. 37 (1 October 1964), on state farms and UGFC; vol. 38 (23–24 March 1965), on GNTC; vol. 38 (28–29 January 1965), on Ministry of Food and Agriculture, state farms, and UGFC; vol. 39 (20–21 May 1965), on price controls and GNTC; and vol. 40 (7 September 1965), on implementing the Dawn Broadcast.

17. See Ghana, *Report of the Commission of Enquiry into Trade Malpractices in Ghana* (Accra, 1965).

18. See Jon Kraus, "Ghana's New 'Corporate' Parliament," *Africa Report*, 10, no. 8 (August 1965) : 6–11; Aristide Zolberg, *Creating Political Order* (Chicago: Rand McNally, 1966), chapter, "The One-Party Ideology," pp. 37–65.

CPP, and certainly the Kwame Nkrumah Ideological Institute was not going to produce this cadre. It was so heartily and vocally disliked, and feared, within the party that its graduates could often not even return to their former positions in their original organizations. In the absence of such a cadre, mobilization was, in fact, elicited by civil servants working in the field.

During this period, there was little development of political skills, little learning of the habit of bargaining over legitimate interests. All public decision-making was not reserved to Nkrumah. He was liable to suggestion and vacillated considerably. Since his inattention to national affairs was obvious, a number of individuals, groups, and institutions, such as the leaders of the TUC and UGFC, ministers, and heads of state corporations behaved much as they pleased. The opposition parties had represented the interests of subsocieties and as political structures were minimally differentiated from those societies. The autonomy of not only these but of more differentiated, specialized structures such as associational groups and party units was conceived as a danger to the system. Thus, except when articulated and aggregated through the National Assembly and the efforts of MPs, political demands were pursued on the subterranean level: through personal, kinship, ethnic, and institutional ties. Due to difficulties of access, interest articulation and aggregation tended to be intermittent, not infrequently anomic, the most important instance being the 1966 coup by elements of the army and police.

## THE DEVELOPMENT OF STATE STRUCTURES

### TERRITORIAL INTEGRATION

Territorial integration is obviously basic to the existence of the state. The opposition movements in Ashanti and British Togoland, the NLM and the Togoland Congress (TC), were regarded as genuinely separatist movements. Although it was the central aim of both to maintain the distinctiveness and autonomy of their regions, the NLM sought federation with significant and reserved powers for the regions, while the TC advocated the complete separation of British Togoland from the Gold Coast. Once Ghana was independent, the CPP government had the means to ensure Ashanti's integration and was willing to use them in response to political violence, the repeated unwillingness of NLM-controlled structures (the local councils and the Ashanti Confederacy Council) to deal routinely with the central government, and the virtual inability of CPP government

members to appear there from 1954 to 1957. Southern British Togoland
was a different matter. It had better communications with the state it
wished to join than it had with Ghana; TC leaders had a close and continuing association with political leaders in French Togo; there were close
ties between the related Ewe on both sides of the frontier; refusal by TC
leaders to accept the results of the U.N.-administered 1956 plebiscite (in
which the majority vote in southern British Togoland against integration
with Ghana was more than offset by the vote in the northern section for
integration) was accompanied by threats. The TC also inspired an uprising
and disorders at independence. Strong security precautions were taken,
and Krobo Edusei was appointed minister for Trans-Volta Togoland as
well as minister for interior. The involvement of M. K. Apaloo, a TC
leader, and his kin in French Togo in a plot against the government
(the Awhaitey affair), Togo's demand for the "return" of British Togoland, and rumors of French military intentions in Togo illustrate the basis
for Ghana's concern. In fact Ghana's notoriously poor relations with Togo
were not simply a matter of Ghana's undoubted ambition to have Togo
unite with it.[19] Some of Ghana's road development was deliberately
planned to integrate the Volta region physically, and internal security in
the area was a continuing concern to Nkrumah. Ghana and Togo accepted
each other's refugees and periodically undertook subversive efforts against
one another. Since the 1966 coup, the former TC leaders have not called
for separation again.

## LEGITIMATION OF AUTHORITY

A new state's central need is a common value structure. Nationalism
was the central value diffused through Nkrumah's charisma, and it soon
confronted the counter-values and norms of ethnicity, localism, and traditional authority. The legal-rational values inherited from the British
and suffused through the parliamentary and bureaucratic structures were
useful and used. They were, however, inadequate and considered so as a
basis for inspiring loyalty to the new state and its central authority structures, including Nkrumah's role as leader.

The attempt to reinforce Nkrumah's declining charismatic authority
through the development of a cult started in the early 1950s, but this
effort was greatly multiplied after independence. Nkrumah strongly be-

19. See Claude Welch's study of the Ewe movement and Ghana-Togo relations in
*Dream of Unity: Pan-Africanism and Political Unification in West Africa* (Ithaca:
Cornell University Press, 1966), pp. 37–147.

lieved in his personal mission, which was reinforced by the calculation that Africa no less than Ghana required a hero. There is no indication that he did anything but encourage the development of his cult; even if, in 1964, he allowed a brief critical discussion of it, he soon turned that to his own advantage.

The function of the cult was not only to create a national symbol with which Fanti, Ewe, Ashanti, Brongs, and Dagomba could identify but also to elevate his person and power beyond reproach or challenge. Since other CPP leaders had a stake in the Nkrumah cult, for it protected their power and status as well as Nkrumah's, it was purposely manipulated to that end. As Adamafio, the most sycophantic of followers, suggested: "We must look upon the Osagyefo as our Savior and Messiah. Let us exploit him for the benefit of the nation. Let us make an institution out of him."[20] It was necessary for the cult to have multiple connotations—traditional, radical, Pan-African—for it was addressed to diverse audiences. This also explains in part why to many the development of ideologies, by whatever name, associated with Nkrumah seemed to lack coherence.[21] The salient religious elements of the cult, which played upon Christian as well as traditional beliefs, were designed to inculcate in a population, to whom the life and efficacy of spirits are very real, Nkrumah's extraordinary character and the existence of divine intercessions on his behalf. The legitimacy or moral acceptability of authority is dependent upon the worth attributed to both the authority role or role holder, and to the satisfaction with the manner in which authority is dispensed. When the party undertook political or other innovations or when deteriorating economic conditions created grave public dissatisfactions, the cult was intensified. While it is clear that there was widespread public disaffection and alienation from the regime, it is still difficult to evaluate the effectiveness of the cult. The assumed effectiveness of the cult protected Nkrumah from challenge and placed him and his role above overt criticism by other CPP leaders. But toward the end their awareness of manipulation, their subjection, and their frustration with trying to work within the cult to improve

20. *Ghanaian Times*, 10 April 1961, p. 6. See also Tawia Adamafio, *A Portrait of the Osagyefo Dr. Kwame Nkrumah* (Accra: Government Printer, 1960).

21. See Kwame Nkrumah, *Towards Colonial Freedom* (London: Heinemann, 1962), *Consciencism* (London: Heinemann, 1964), and *Some Essential Features of Nkrumaism* (New York: International Publishers, 1965); Central Regional Secretariate, CPP, *Seminar Report on "Nkrumaism"* (Cape Coast: CPP, 1962); and the changing interpretation given by Kofi Baako, Nkrumah's lieutenant, *Ghanaian Times* (25 March to 4 April 1961 and 4, 25, 26, 28, 29 January 1961).

conditions created cynicism, demoralization, and apathy. When the regime ended it was with a whimper rather than a bang, with few bewailing its passing and many expressing relief.

The Nkrumah regime also attempted to build and sustain its legitimacy by bringing about economic change in a tangible form. It conceived of economic development in terms of the provision of jobs, which it found increasingly difficult and expensive to create, and in terms of larger expenditures, which provided a variety of amenities for the rural and urban areas. By the 1960s budget deficits were continuous as increases in expenditures outpaced revenues. Deficits ran from one-sixth in 1963–64 to one-third of the revenue in 1961–62 and 1962–63. But these deficits were financed by the creation of money which fed inflation. To counteract it, the government froze wages and reduced expenditures on certain popular amenities at a time when Ghanaians witnessed expenditures on prestige projects, heard about the state enterprises operating at a deficit, and freely exchanged tales about corruption. Prices of local foods as well as imports soared in 1965; for several years there were shortages of many essential goods, some of which could only be bought at black market prices. Meanwhile, unemployment was growing.

## PENETRATION OF STATE STRUCTURES

Constitutional and legal centralization of power commenced soon after independence. The result was to reduce the power of traditional rulers, to centralize formal rule-making first in the National Assembly and then, under the 1960 constitution, in the president and assembly, and to make the instruments of law readily available to the party-state. Although the severity of legal sanctions increased during the tenure of the regime in a reasonably direct proportion to the decline in its authority, the use of sanctions was more arbitrary than systematic, and cyclical rather than constantly increasing. Times of crisis and detentions were interspersed with peace and gestures of magnanimity such as the release of detainees.

The territorial administrative structure of the Nkrumah regime was an extended, less hierarchical, and more direct and politicized version of the colonial structure. It involved a meshing of party and state roles and structures at all levels. Eight MPs were appointed in 1957 as regional commissioners to replace British regional officers; they were also ex-officio ministers and were the regional heads of the CPP until 1960. They were aided by an increasingly extensive regional organization, which included the appointment of party activists to replace the civil service district commissioners. The new district commissioners lost some of the administrative and judicial functions which the civil servants had held, and these functions were assigned to specialized government agencies which established regional and district offices (e.g., in health and the judiciary).

The appointment of political district commissioners (DCs) started experimentally in the Volta region in 1958 (because of the TCs irredentist threat) and then was extended to all regions in mid-1959. Armed with government power and largesse, the regional commissioners (RCs) and the forty-three DCs, worked in close cooperation with the local party to cajole, threaten, and induce opposition forces and local chiefs to show proper deference to CPP government authority. They were helped in this by members of the new Builders' Brigade (established to take up unemployment among school leavers) and exservicemen, and branches of the UGFC, invigorated with a government grant.

Coincident with the attempt to reinvigorate the party between 1960 and 1962, the number of DCs and districts was increased from 43 to 155 (see table 1). This penetration of the local society by DCs, toward whom def-

TABLE 1

NUMBER OF DISTRICT COMMISSIONERS BY REGION AND PERIOD

| Dates Appointed | North- ern | Upper | Volta | Brong- Ahafo | Ashanti | Cen- tral | West- ern | East- ern | Accra |
|---|---|---|---|---|---|---|---|---|---|
| 7/59 | —12— | | 5 | 4 | 7 | —9— | | 6 | 0 |
| 7/60 | 8 | 7 | 7 | 4 | 8 | 5 | 8 | 7 | 0 |
| 10/60 | 10 | 11 | 10 | 7 | 9 | 11 | 11 | 13 | 0 |
| 3/62 | 15 | 18 | 14 | 8 | 14 | 14 | 11 | 18 | 5 |
| 12/62 | 19 | 23 | 16 | 12 | 22 | 21 | 17 | 18 | 7 |

SOURCE: Information from issues of *Ghana Gazette*.

erence had been deeply inculcated in the rural areas during colonial rule, was intended to significantly increase the government's regulative capability. The DC was an active party-state official; he was usually drawn from the ranks of party activists, many of whom had relatively low levels of education—middle school, sometimes teacher training—and had received little administrative instruction. He was responsible for and head of the district CPP organization, which became the main local unit in 1962. He diffused information on government policies, superintended local councils, worked with Village Development Committees and with labor committees to find jobs for school leavers, and frequently arbitrated the numerous disputes of local society. He was an administrator, coordinator, and exhorter. The district party executive worked out of his office, and he was on intimate terms with regional party personnel. Although the DC was a mobilizer, his role was limited by the fact that the CPP itself was often closely integrated into local life and institutions and reflected local beliefs and preoccupations.[22] Assigned to his own home area, the DC himself was susceptible to pressures of kinship and local loyalties. It was only in late 1964 that a systematic effort was made to place DCs in other than their own areas. Many were plainly incompetent. Furthermore, Ghanaian newspaper reports indicated that the DCs frequently abused their office. Some extorted money from individuals, misappropriated funds from local council treasuries, seduced young school girls, and occasionally detained local enemies or "saboteurs." As new local elites many engaged in continual conflicts with the MPs from the area, with whom they often refused to cooperate.[23]

After 1962, the government attempted, with little success, to coordinate party-state structures by establishing the district as the basic local unit for local administration, the party, and national representation. The UGFC was also established at the district level in many regions.

The RCs were directly responsible to Nkrumah, and the DCs to the RC, Nkrumah, and the minister of local government (on local council affairs). RCs usually went to cabinet meetings once a month, and channels of communication between Accra and the regional offices were available, by police radio if by no other means. Particularly after 1960, the party matters with which RCs were concerned were essentially trivial. Their substantive role was head of a regional state bureaucracy, which varied in size by region. This involved them in administration, budgets, projects, and liaison with ministers. And, as governors of near or distant provinces, they went on tours into the bush. The RCs rather than the CPP regional secretaries were the main source of power in the region.

Though it has been asserted that each RC and DC was literally rather than formally Nkrumah's personal agent,[24] there was in reality relatively little direct control exercised by Accra over the RCs and less still over the DCs.[25] Certainly Nkrumah received information from the police on ac-

22. See Brokensha, *Social Change at Larteh, Ghana*, pp. xix, 103–28.

23. See, for example, discussions on precedence between these officials in *Towards Socialism* (Accra: Government Printer, 1963), pp. 12, 26–27.

24. Henry Bretton, *The Rise and Fall of Kwame Nkrumah* (New York: Praeger, 1966).

25. This judgement is informed by research and interviews at the regional level in the Central, Western, Eastern, Ashanti, and Brong-Ahafo regions in 1964, as well as access to files.

tivities at the regional and district levels, and party leaders were forever appealing to Accra to settle local squabbles and conflicts. But the regional headquarters, especially the more distant ones, were in some senses provincial satrapies, which included in their realm the regional and district outposts of central government institutions such as the police and information services. Most of the RCs appointed in 1957 lasted until the end of the regime. Nkrumah seldom traveled outside Accra after 1962. The regions, too, had certain interests and prerogatives to maintain and grew fractious if there was intervention from the center (which one side to a dispute often sought).

The administrative structure was assisted by the regional offices of an increasingly extensive, professional, and specialized bureaucracy. This made available technical skills to support national development projects in the region and local development projects financed from the regional development grant which each region received annually to help finance local council and village projects. These latter were aided by a well-established Community Development department. Other ministries which had offices in many regions were Works and Communications (with the Ghana National Construction Company, good for party employment), Education, and, particularly, Agriculture, which also had some district offices. In terms of penetration of the society, the two most effective state structures were Agriculture, with an excellent extension service, and Education. By 1966 there were 1,480,000 primary and middle school students.[26] These were instructed in a standard curriculum and introduced to the symbols of nationhood. An enormous expansion of certain state corporations also took place, including the Ghana Commercial Bank, State Farms, and the Ghana National Trading Corporation, though the latter two were enormously inefficient. The local establishment of both State Farms and Workers' Brigade camps were eagerly sought after for they provided rural wage employment.

As the central government bureaucracy grew rapidly in the 1960s in response to a large number of specialized new functions to which it was assigned, a number of ministries were so overburdened with sensitive tasks that they became both inefficient and corrupt.[27] A pattern of increas-

26. Ghana, *Statistical Yearbook, 1964*, p. 182; *Parliamentary Debates: Official Record* (1 February 1966), pp. 11–12. It was reported that the number of Young Pioneers had increased from 240,067 in 1962 to 372,229 in 1963 and to 479,059 in 1964 (*Statistical Yearbook*, 1964, p. 253) ; I do not believe it.

27. Cf. Ghana, *Report of Commission of Enquiry into Alleged Irregularities and Malpractices in Connection with the Issue of Import Licenses* (Accra, 1964), Akainyan report; Ghana, *Report of the Commission of Enquiry into Trade Mal-*

ing differentiation and specialization did develop, however, as a substantial group of civil servants of the administrative class received specialized training, in Ghana and abroad, to enable them to cope with new government roles. A number of specialized secretariats emerged, including the Planning Commission, State Control Commission, Productivity Center, Water Resources and Power Secretariat, and Volta River Authority, among others.

This bureaucracy was subjected to institutional, ideological, and personal controls. Many CPP leaders, including Nkrumah, had long harbored suspicions concerning the attitude of the civil service towards the CPP, the Nkrumah government, and development problems. They also suspected it of a class bias which made it favor the opposition. It was undoubtedly necessary for the Nkrumah government to apply some direct pressures to the civil service in order to undermine, somewhat, its great devotion to essentially colonial bureaucratic norms, regulations, and attitudes. The government also wished to infuse it with a sense of urgency and a developmental orientation and prevent it from pursuing its own autonomous goals, which were not necessarily those of the regime.

During 1960–62, under the banner of the "Party is Supreme," the CPP intervened more directly in the bureaucracy, through political interference with bureaucratic functions by CPP associational wings, or through outright takeover of these functions. For example, the TUC had long wanted to control the Labour Department, and Tettegah entertained the thought of being appointed permanent secretary while remaining TUC secretary general. Instead, responsibility for labor was transformed briefly to Flagstaff House so as to provide ready access, and the TUC came to exercise a veto over certain Labour Department functions. Adamafio, as minister for presidential affairs, took a major interest in the bureaucracy, particularly in the Establishment Secretariat, where he worked some changes and brought some highly trained party leaders into the civil service as permanent secretaries. He is remembered there as being a competent innovator. When the UGFC received the cocoa buying monopoly, it saw to the total elimination of the Department of Cooperation, and then in 1963 took over the extension services of the Ministry of Agriculture. Despite UGFCs attempts at takeover, however, the officers in the extension service remained civil servants and thus retained some independence.

---

practices in Ghana (Accra, 1965), Abraham Report; and the postcoup, Ghana, *Summary of the Report of the Commission of Enquiry into Irregularities and Malpractices in the Grant of Import Licenses* (Accra, 1967), Ollennu report.

A large number of government departments were placed under the direct control of the president's office. This facilitated personal intervention as in the case of removal of the Budget Department from the Finance Ministry during 1961–62 in order to institute a discretionary contingency fund of two million pounds. It also led to mixed forms of institutional and personal control, as when Nkrumah's strong interest in Pan-African politics led him to establish an African Affairs Secretariat, divorced from the Foreign Ministry but staffed by civil servants, which handled relations with African states. In a number of instances government departments were placed directly under Nkrumah in order to protect them from party intervention and in others to give direct presidential sanction to decisions.

There were also forms of ideological intervention, particularly during 1960–62. Civil servants were pressured into becoming members of the CPP and of the TUC. Party study groups were started in a number of ministries and secretariats. These were often headed by a clerk of inferior rank who informed senior civil servants about the necessity for socialist development. Although these groups were short-lived, ideological intervention was highly demoralizing while it lasted.

Since the party was unreliable, the Nkrumah regime came to rely increasingly on the bureaucracy; as this occurred Nkrumah sought further means to control it. Nkrumah also undertook to protect civil servants from personal and ideological pressures, and they were grateful for this "magnanimous intervention," which helped to strengthen direct loyalty to Nkrumah who, it was believed, would allow them to do their work undisturbed. In 1965 the Civil Service Commission was abolished, and its functions of assigning and promoting civil servants lodged in the Establishment Secretariat in the president's office.[28]

As the Nkrumah regime lost popular support and legitimacy, it turned to institutional instruments of coercion in order to retain its power. As the power flowing from authority declined, power increasingly derived from direct force or the threat of force.

The military and police were instruments of coercion which had basic roles in internal security.[29] Both underwent rapid expansion after 1960, the army in large measure due to Nkrumah's interest in creating a Pan-African military force. Senior army and police officers in each region sat

28. On the evolution and crises in the judiciary, see William Harvey, *Law and Social Change in Ghana* (Princeton: Princeton University Press, 1966).

29. On the role of the army and police under Nkrumah and in the coup, see Jon Kraus, "Arms and Politics in Ghana," in Claude Welch, ed., *Soldier and State in Africa* (Evanston: Northwestern University Press, 1970) and A. K. Ocran, *A Myth is Broken* (Accra: Longmans, Green, 1968).

on a security committee with the RC. And after the Kulungugu assassination attempt in August 1962 and the bombing which followed in Accra, the army was given wide powers in the North and in Accra. But neither the police nor army, with their strong pro-British orientation and sense of professionalism, satisfied Nkrumah's security needs, and after Kulungugu he no longer trusted the police.

In 1963 he started to develop a National Security Service (NSS) which was a complex civilian-military security force directly responsible to him.[30] Included within the NSS was a military intelligence section, set up after the Africanization of the officer corps in late 1961 as a means of obtaining information on officers. Its head, Lieutenant Colonel Hassan, was profoundly disliked in the army, and his informers inspired great caution among officers. There was also a special intelligence unit, headed by Ambrose Yankey, like Hassan and Nkrumah, an Nzima, and some officers of the police Special Branch were assigned to it. This angered the police. Police-military competition was encouraged. Within the army Nkrumah fostered distrust by having certain officers whom he trusted, General Barwah in particular, report to him over the heads of the army commander and chief of defense staff. After 1961 the National Defense Council, which was the civilian-military council and regulator of terms of service, was not reconvened, and military fringe benefits were eliminated without consultation. On a number of occasions after 1962 Nkrumah sought to introduce the party into military life and to persuade the army to accept Russian weapons and cadet training, both of which they resisted and resented. Periodic affirmations of fealty to Nkrumah as head of state *and* of the CPP were required. After the January 1964 assassination attempt on Nkrumah by a policeman, Nkrumah dismissed and jailed eight senior police officers whom he accused of the plot, disarmed the police, and transferred the whole of the Special Branch to Flagstaff House. In mid-1965 he "retired" the heads of the army and defense staff.

The primary instrument of security which Nkrumah developed was the President's Own Guard Regiment (POGR), originally an honor guard. Its officers and men were recruited from the Army, but it formed a part of the NSS, a counterweight to military and police power. Starting in 1962, Nkrumah expanded the POGR to battalion size (50 officers, 1,142 men, by the coup) and started to form a second battalion; he armed, paid, and supplied the regiment much better than the regular military and covertly severed it from army command in order to make it directly responsible to

---

30. See Ghana, *Nkrumah's Subversion in Africa* (Accra, 1966), pp. vi-ix, 1–3, 28–36.

himself. Learning of this slowly, the army leaders were both humiliated and outraged. The POGR was counterproductive in its effect and may well have been the most important element among many that incited the coup leaders in February 1966.

## POLITICAL CAPABILITIES

The regime's responsive capability was basically undermined by the decline in information which reached Nkrumah and to which he paid attention. The rise in the use of coercion, the insecure base of politicians vis-à-vis Nkrumah, and the level of disquiet among both politicians and civil servants made most of them increasingly reluctant to press critical information upon him.[31] Nkrumah's reciprocal demands that the regime overcome endemic corruption, in which few thought him personally involved, were limited to rhetoric and tactical sacrifices, for, in practice, money and other gifts were the lubricant of personal loyalty.[32] New norms would have required party manpower drawn from another stratum and, possibly, another society, for office was the avenue to monetary reward; ostentation, not modesty, brought status. There were considerable pressures in 1964–65 for reorganizing the UGFC into a true cooperative which would be responsive to the needs of farmers and be less corrupt. But the fact that the UGFC was financially successful, controlled the farmers, and that it was necessary in 1965 to reduce the cocoa price once more meant that the regime left it unchanged.[33] Instead of constructing a stable party hierarchy, Nkrumah manipulated the Central Committee, a body that was a mystery even to the party leadership; it was unaccountable because its membership was unknown, with individuals called on to attend one time and not the next, unsure whether or not they were, in fact, *members.* To socialist demands for radical representation, Nkrumah responded with a 1965 National Assembly that represented all tendencies, militants and old guard, but with no radicals in the cabinet.

31. See Douglas Rimmer, "The Crisis in the Ghanaian Economy," *The Journal of Modern African Studies* 4, no. 1 (May 1966) : 17–32; Tony Killick, "The Possibilities of Economic Control," in W. Birmingham, I. Neustadt, and E. N. Omaboe, eds., *A Study of Contemporary Ghana: I. The Economy of Ghana* (Evanston: Northwestern University Press, 1966), pp. 411–38.

32. For an account of Nkrumah's acquisition and use of wealth, see Ghana, *Report of the Commission to enquire into the Kwame Nkrumah Properties* (Accra, 1966), Apaloo commission.

33. "Report of the Cabinet Committee on the Re-Organization of the Cooperative Movement in Ghana" (mimeograph, limited circulation, 1964) ; *Report of the Committee of Enquiry on the Local Purchasing of Cocoa*, pp. 7–8.

But the most striking flaw in the regime's responsiveness was Nkrumah's inability and unwillingness to demand accountability from those with responsibility or to exact some measure of discipline. The latter was the most elusive element in Nkrumah's rule and personal political behavior. This undoubtedly derived from the society's cultural norms and relaxed pace of life. In some cases, the failure to demand accountability, as from heads of state corporations who failed to turn in annual reports for several years, stemmed from Nkrumah's basic lack of interest in economics, despite his socialist language. Nkrumah was himself not ruthless, though he used and allowed others to use intimidation. Power was limited and was most effectively exercised to inflict negative sanctions, to limit and repress; it was used less, and was more ineffective in inducing compliance with affirmative goals. Ultimately, there was relatively little emphasis upon accountability or discipline because the regime became a holding operation, where the felt need for change was hedged by the necessity for safety. And when fealty is more important than performance, ritual develops a reality of its own.

Ritual and reality were involved in Ghana's planning exercises, as were role conflicts and indulgences by Nkrumah which suggest a refusal to routinize his role in the system.[34]

The several economic development plans which Ghana had devised before 1961 were essentially "laundry lists": projects were totaled up by each ministry, then examined by a committee which limited its function to the paring of the least essential items on the list. After Nkrumah's two-month tour of Communist countries in summer 1961 he became persuaded that the Ghanaian Second Five-Year Plan was not a plan at all. It was scrapped on his return and he instructed officials to prepare a new, Seven-Year socialist plan. Although he even brought a Hungarian economist to write it, the plan was developed in the end by a Ghanaian economist, J. H. Mensah. In order to coordinate economic activity within the framework of the plan, a small planning body, the State Control Commission, was established in 1961. It functioned through 1962, until the August assassination attempt; afterwards, it met only once more. In early 1964 Nkrumah announced the formation of two new planning bodies. A National Planning Commission, which comprised political representatives, was estab-

34. The following case is derived from this writer's study of the work of the Planning Commission in Ghana, access to files, and interviews with planning officials in 1964 and 1966. See also, E. N. Omaboe, "The Process of Planning," in Birmingham, Neustadt, and Omaboe, pp. 439–63.

lished; but it also met once only. The other body was the State Planning Committee, to which proposals drafted in the various ministries were to be submitted in order to determine whether they fitted within the Seven-Year Plan. Three leading CPP politicians were initially included, but later dropped, leaving the committee membership as follows: Nkrumah; Foreign Minister Botsio; Finance Minister Amaoko-Atta; the president's financial adviser and bag man, Ayeh-Kumi; the governor of the Bank of Ghana, Halm; and four senior civil servants, including J. H. Mensah, head of the National Planning Commission. These latter were to service the committee.

The State Planning Committee's operations reveal the contradictions which stemmed from the disparate commitments of administrator/technocrats (both in the Planning Commission and in the ministries); politician/ministers; Nkrumah; and the socialist militants. The administrator/technocrats in the planning commission believed that the ministries would readily submit their development budgets. Only two were represented on the committee, however; the administrator/technocrats and politician/ministers in other ministries had long been accustomed to making up their own shopping list of projects, getting cabinet approval, and going ahead with them, without relevance to plans. They remained extremely resistant to the notion that their projects should be critically examined elsewhere. J. H. Mensah eventually came to believe that the planning process would be more effective if other ministers had a direct stake in the planning process; but by the time he suggested this to the president, it was too late to effect.

The ministries thus continued to operate more or less autonomously. For example, the deputy minister of Works and Communications thought it an excellent idea for his own region (the East) to draw up a regional seven-year development plan and attempt to have its projects inserted in the development plans of the relevant ministries. In mid-1962 the CPP Regional Steering Committee accepted the idea and had all DCs prepare lists of projects for their areas. They were examined and pared in a series of conferences over a fortnight and printed as a "plan." The deputy minister then persuaded each of the relevant ministries to include these projects in their own segment of the Seven-Year Plan. At no time did he contact the State Control Commission. Naturally, not all his projects fitted in with the Seven-Year Plan then being prepared. Within a short time, the flow from the cabinet of development projects requiring State Planning Committee investigation and approval began to slow down.

Nkrumah was a leading advocate of central planning; but he also retained presidential discretion, negotiated prestige projects without reference to the plan, accepted kickbacks, and remained indulgent towards his ministers. The socialist militants acted as Nkrumah's conscience and sought to preserve the socialist orientation of the plan. Before J. H. Mensah left for an overseas financial meeting in August 1964 he gave an unpublicized talk on development to the Economic Society of Ghana. He noted, among other things, that private capital, including foreign private capital, could be useful in development and that the Eastern European countries might well not be models for Ghana. After he had left, a long, learned, pseudonymous article was published in *The Spark* denouncing this capitalist conception of development and pointing out all Mensah's fallacies, without drawing attention to his office. Mensah had previously had excellent relations with Nkrumah. As a trained economist he spoke to Nkrumah with assurance, and Nkrumah had listened. After the article was published, meetings of the State Planning Committee were not resumed. That Mensah was deemed a "capitalist" by ideologues was obviously important to Nkrumah; some time later his resignation was accepted.

However, at Mensah's suggestion, the State Planning Committee was reborn in June 1965 under a new executive director, B. K. Mensah. Nkrumah was largely preoccupied with the upcoming OAU conference in Accra (the conference hall was not in the plan), and he made Kojo Botsio minister of planning. The new committee was strong, tough on those who came before them to explain their projects, and political: in addition to Botsio, who was not only competent but in daily contact with Nkrumah, and the critically minded socialist finance minister, Amoako-Atta, Kwesi Armah, minister of foreign trade, and F. A. Jantuah, minister of agriculture, had joined the committee. Both were new to the cabinet and were undaunted. The minister of industries, a member of the old guard, and three high civil servants were also members.

Ghana was in somewhat desperate financial straits, and a visiting International Monetary Fund mission strongly suggested a top limit to the budget which would have left a more manageable deficit. Planning committee members, especially the principal politician/ministers, took this warning seriously and severely cut the budgets of the other ministers who appeared before them. The committee had full decision-making powers, for the cabinet no longer discussed development projects; it required only Nkrumah's approval. In February 1966 committee members anticipated that, given the cuts they had made, ministers would go to Nkrumah seeking supplementary budgets. They decided to forestall this possibility by reiterating the importance of the budget limit, which Nkrumah had already publicly asserted.[35] A subcommittee, the Central Treasury Committee, approached Nkrumah, who in the next two days undid their disciplined efforts and wantonly restored all the cuts that had been made (including that in the military's budget), perhaps, in part, to bolster regime legitimacy through sustained public spending. In this response to Ghana's economic crisis, Nkrumah's prerogatives were asserted, budgetary discipline was again shattered, and ministers were once more assured, in effect, that they would not be held accountable.

## POSTCOUP POLITICS

The coup d'état was greeted with tumultuous jubilation by Ghanaians, the only resistance coming in the first day from the POGR in Flagstaff House, from which Nkrumah was absent, on a trip to Hanoi.[36] An eight-man, army and police National Liberation Council (NLC), headed by the previously "retired" General Ankrah, was established on 24 February 1966 and ruled until 30 September 1969 when civilian government was restored. The NLC gained widespread support for turning out Nkrumah and promised the restoration of democratic rule; it effectively reinforced its reputation by setting up numerous commissions of enquiry which held public hearings and exposed the depth of the Nkrumah regime's abuse of power, its corruption and mismanagement. The basic structure of NLC rule was a military-police and bureaucratic administration, supported by advisory bodies. An Executive Council of well-known senior civil servants was established in July 1967 to head the ministries, with the exception of defense, external affairs, interior, and finance, which were held by General Ankrah, Police Superintendent Harlley, and Brigadier Afrifa.

In the NLCs three-and-a-half years of rule, during which it sought to restore economic health and restructure political institutions, it demonstrated considerable agility in coping with political demands and potential conflict. While the interim nature of its rule prevented a high level of opposition, it had to manage demands for material goods and participation under extremely adverse economic conditions. Compelled to retrench economically, stop inflation, renegotiate a staggering burden of external debts, and reduce Ghana's large balance of payments deficit, the NLC drastically reduced government spending. This meant prolonging the recession of the last years of Nkrumah's rule. With a 3.5 percent annual rate

35. Cf. *Parliamentary Debates* 43 (1 February 1966) : 8.
36. Ocran, *A Myth is Broken*; A. A. Afrifa, *The Ghana Coup* (London: Frank Cass, 1966) ; Kraus, "Arms and Politics in Ghana," in Welch.

of population increase, Ghana's low real rate of growth in GNP (0.6 percent in 1966, 2.4 percent in 1967, and 0.8 percent in 1968) meant a continuing decline in per capita income and a high level of unemployment. In 1968 about 25 percent of the previously employed wage-labor force of 600,000 was unemployed; there was an additional decline in nonwage employment and an estimated 300,000 people seeking to enter the wage-labor market.[37] The situation was so desperate that soon after it came to power in late 1969 the civilian Busia government ordered mass deportations of parts of the large foreign population in order to open up employment opportunities for Ghanaians. This bleak economic picture was somewhat offset by a rise in world cocoa prices from 1966 on. Though the NLC immediately banned not only the CPP but all political groups, its intent to restore democratic life, its need for support, and its desire to rule in as nonauthoritarian a fashion as possible rendered it sensitive to public demands. And while it could not and did not comply with many of the demands made upon it, it gave strategic groups a representative, unfettered voice in public institutions and advisory bodies.

The most vocal demands for resources and participation came from the merchant-professional class, now supported by a much larger middle class of farmers, workers, and chiefs. The merchant-professional and middle classes, especially the most important former opposition leaders, immediately sought a role in NLC rule. The NLC quickly recognized them as legitimate national political leaders with whom it should consult toward the creation of new political institutions. Though the merchant-professional and middle classes include the salaried as well as the self-employed, they are fundamentally different in character from the lower-middle and middle class supporters of the CPP in that they are less economically dependent on state action. Heavily represented in the constituent assembly, representatives of these classes voted against salaries for MPs to keep out those who sought office for wealth. The former UP leaders, who saw some senior civil servants as accomplices in Nkrumah's regime, also objected to NLC dependence on the civil service.

These strata dominated the twenty-three-member Political Committee, established by the NLC in June 1966 to advise it on past and future decisions, as well as the National Advisory Committee that replaced it in July 1967. The latter was headed by the former Supreme Court justice, Akufo Addo; its vice-chairman was Professor Kofi Busia, former leader of the UP. No less than fourteen of the twenty-seven members were former

37. *West Africa* (1 November 1969), p. 1318.

opponents of the CPP, ten of them former UP leaders. This heavy influx of former opposition politicians drew criticism, and the committee was later broadened. The Constitutional Commission appointed to draw up a draft constitution was also headed by Chief Justice Akufo Addo and its members recruited almost wholly from the merchant-professional and middle classes. Lawyers again dominated the political scene. The NLC also responded to the economic demands of the merchants and entrepreneurs, not least because it required private investment to compensate for the decline in government spending. It arranged for credit facilities, encouraged and coordinated links with foreign private capital, and in January 1969 restricted certain areas of commerce to Ghanaians only.[38] There has been a marked de-emphasis of the now severely controlled state enterprises, several of which have been sold to Ghanaian businessmen.

The NLC quickly sought the support of the chiefs, who, in turn, demanded the voiding of destoolments carried out during the Nkrumah regime and requested participation in local and national government. The NLC restored many former chiefs to their stools, and destooled or demoted many who had been raised by Nkrumah. Under the new constitution traditional representatives have been given two-thirds of the seats in local councils and one-third in district councils. Although this is a deliberate attempt to combine modern and traditional councils in one institution in order to render local government both meaningful and legitimate, it may well revive the commoner-chieftaincy conflicts of old. Through their Regional Houses the chiefs nominate eleven percent of the electors to the college which selects the powerful, nonexecutive president. Chiefs are also members of the president's advisory Council of State and have appellate jurisdiction in chieftaincy cases in a National Assembly of Chiefs.

The TUC received less satisfaction from the NLC, due to the increasing rate of unemployment and NLC dismay at the large number of strikes that occurred, including one in 1968 in which the police killed several miners. The TUC, headed by Bentum, worked with the NLC in trying to relieve unemployment, and representatives of the TUC were appointed to far more public bodies than in the Nkrumah regime, including nine to the Constituent Assembly. But the TUC saw a growing disparity of incomes and was increasingly at odds with the NLC over treatment of strikers. In the 1969 elections it decided that it would not officially support any party.

38. Taxi operations; small scale businesses with under 30 employees; retail trade with a sales volume of less than about $500,000; wholesale trade with sales of less than $1 million; and representation of overseas manufacturers (*West Africa*, 13 July 1968, p. 819).

The cocoa farmers, and the NLC governments as a whole, benefitted from the rapid rise in world cocoa prices which started in 1966. Cocoa prices paid to producers were raised several times during 1966–69. The cocoa farmers are not yet organized into a national farmers organization, but there are a number of regional bodies; the one in Ashanti supported Busia's party in the 1969 election. Representatives of the cocoa farmers have also been appointed to the Cocoa Marketing Board.

There were problems and hesitations, and public criticisms of the NLC, concerning the dates for lifting the ban on parties, holding the elections, and returning to civilian rule. But the major internal issue was whether or not to ban former CPP leaders from public office for a period. The NLC passed a number of different decrees excluding former CPP leaders, starting with one in January 1968 under which some 5,000 former members were banned to a final one on 30 April 1969, which specified that anyone who at the time of the coup was a CPP leader in a range of national and regional offices, including those of DC and RC, but excepting MPs, could not be a party official or MP. The NLC also forbade the creation of tribal, ethnic, and regional parties.

The new constitution was approved in mid-1969 by a constituent assembly whose members were nominated by representative groups. The constitution established a political system with separation of powers and many checks and balances to guard against further abuses. The constitution, rather than the unicameral National Assembly of 140 members, is supreme. There is a dual executive, in which the president, elected by an electoral college of the MPs, chiefs, and district council representatives, for a single eight-year term, selects the most important state officers with the advice of a Council of State. He can veto assembly bills, and a two-thirds majority is required to override him. The Supreme Court has jurisdiction in a large number of areas and can entertain a challenge to the constitutionality of any law or bill by anyone. The constitution was not ratified but simply promulgated. In addition, the NLC launched a move toward administrative decentralization to the regional level.

The major parties formed in mid-1969 were: the Progress Party (PP), headed by Kofi Busia, the most prominent civilian figure, which attracted a large number of well-known former UP leaders; the National Alliance of Liberals (NAL), led by Komla Gbedemah, Nkrumah's former lieutenant and finance minister, who had fled the country in 1961; the United Nationalist Party (UNP), led by Joe Appiah, a lawyer and former NLM and UP leader, who allied himself with Ga lawyers in Accra and made a bid for support in the North and among cocoa farmers; the All People's Republican Party (APRP), led by P. K. K. Quaidoo, a businessman and former CPP minister, who was detained briefly in 1961; and the All-People's Congress, which billed itself as a "third force," but vanished before the election.

Busia's PP won the August 1969 election by an overwhelming margin, taking 105 of the 140 seats with 59 percent of the votes. Gbedemah's NAL came in second, with 29 seats and 30 percent of the vote; the other parties fared disastrously.[39]

The obvious fact that the PP won overwhelmingly in the Akan areas and the NAL in the predominantly Ewe area has raised the possibility that Ghana will again have parties organized along ethnocultural and regional lines. However, the PP election victory can most readily be explained by three factors. First, the PP won because its leaders were recognized as national leaders by the NLC and were thus most well known. They looked like winners and thus attracted candidates who wished to gain from the material and status benefits of victory and electors who readily identified with the stronger force. The large PP vote in Ashanti (77 percent), Brong-Ahafo (85 percent), the Central region (71 percent), and the Eastern region (59 percent) makes it clear that it was the party rather than individual candidates that was decisive. Second, the PP was regarded as anti-CPP, while Gbedemah and the NAL were identified with the CPP. The PP thus benefited from continuing revulsion against the recent past. The ethnocultural cleavage visible in the voting results in southern and Central Ghana demonstrates diffuse fears of Ewe domination which were freely voiced during the NLC rule and the election campaign. Three of the main coup leaders were Ewe; it was alleged that Ewes were replacing others in government jobs. These fears undoubtedly compounded the anti-NAL sentiment, and, in turn, created a defensive solidarity among the Ewe in support of the NAL. The voting in the Northern and Upper Regions was more evenly divided between the PP and NAL.

Though there were some initial complaints by the defeated parties, all accepted the election results, and Busia took office as prime minister on 1 October 1969. Busia's cabinet included eight former UP leaders, three former senior civil servants plus several other lawyers, a doctor, and a professor. It looked initially as if the NAL, with appreciable strength in four regions (including greater Accra) outside the Volta region, would play a strong opposition role and benefit from the fragmentation which

39. Derived from election figures in *The Legon Observer*, 4 (5 September 1969). The UNP won two seats in Accra, the APRP won one seat, and the People's Action Party won two seats in the Nzima areas.

will probably occur in the PP. But it was hampered by the fact that after the election the Supreme Court found Gbedemah's candidacy illegal, and he lost his seat.

Several factors are important in assessing the relationship of the military to the new system. Within the military itself, the coup created some divisions. The precedent prompted an attempted coup by several young officers in April 1967; NLC chairman General Ankrah was removed from office and replaced by Brigadier Afrifa in early 1969 on the grounds that he had received money to promote his presidential candidacy. Ethnic divisions, postcoup purges, and a slowdown of promotions due to the young age of senior officers, all induce tensions.

The military has insured that the new constitutional arrangements will protect its autonomy and professionalism by dividing authority over the military between the prime minister and president; it has also raised its budget to over ten percent of the total in order to resupply itself. At the last moment, it asked the constituent assembly to substitute for the presidency a presidential commission composed of the three leading NLC members, Afrifa, Harlley, and Ocran. This was approved for a period of three years. The commission may be a useful transition mechanism, which is all that PP leaders will allow it to be. The problem of a civilian government giving directions to its former rulers has been eliminated by the decision of Afrifa, Harlley, and another NLC policeman to resign their posts.

## CONCLUSION

One knows too little, and the available measures are too gross, to permit other than a rough estimate of the extent of Ghana's political development during the last two decades.

Ghana is doubtless a better integrated country than it was twenty years ago. There is less resistance now to a strong government than before independence, as indicated by the absence of new demands for federation. The experience of being a united country and increased economic integration have probably been important contributors to this state of affairs. However, the determinative factor may have been the CPP which, with broad local roots established in the pre-independence period, helped to legitimize notions of a national society in which diverse peoples in Ghana played a role, to attach subelites to a national regime and give them national and participant orientations. Ironically, it is possible that the CPP facilitated the development of those orientations by becoming more particularistic over time; too rigorous an assertion of a distinct national identity might have made it too difficult for subelites to develop these orientations. It is also possible that an independence regime dominated by merchant-professional-class leaders would have been less successful in these respects because of their limited penetrative capacity and their dependence upon alliances of convenience with traditional leaders. Had they been in power, they would have cohered as a distinct subsociety more oriented to British than to Ghanaian norms and values.

The Nkrumah regime's reliance upon the allocation of government resources as a major source of support, even if inefficient and economically costly, had the effect of orienting people to government output and to the need to affect government decision-making. Furthermore, the populist orientation of the CPP drove it to broaden the educational system, a decision which the merchant-professional class opposed because it would lead to a decline of educational standards. The result is that hundreds of thousands of Ghanaians have now passed through primary and middle school. These national, secular institutions have equipped them to become potential political participants rather than parochials or simply subjects, endowed with a belief in the possibility of change in their life chances. In these respects, it is possible that the Nkrumah regime's use of its regulative capabilities, which were most effective for taxation and repressive purposes, gave Ghana the time to create Ghanaians.

Furthermore, social and economic change came to be valued more highly than the institutionalization of political and administrative procedures; equality became an important feature of the political culture. Identities can be forged through ritualistic and psychic participation, as with the development of pride in Ghana as being a leading Pan-African force (though there was much criticism here too). Initially the regime channeled broad political participation into a *national* political structure, and later it facilitated a fairly high level of social participation through expanding education and employment that undoubtedly mobilized many from parochial identities. In these ways, the regime certainly dramatically broadened access to the national system.

However, to the extent that authority rests on consent and not simply on force, one may question just how far the Nkrumah regime contributed to the building of national political authority and to the centralization of a poorly integrated society, since it permitted increasingly less substantive political participation.

The regime's monopolization of political choice, arbitrary use of power with intimidating effect, and inability to co-opt opposition leaders into significant roles, all reduced its ability to elicit a sense of shared purpose and participation. It was too strident and abusive, provoking anger at the "socialist boys." The regime's increasingly poor economic performance compounded this inability. This and the prevalence of corruption disaffected many and created negative sentiments about national government and authority.

Struggles over legitimate authority will doubtless recur in Ghana and may well politicize parochial social cleavages. But one legacy of the Nkrumah regime is that it seems unlikely that traditional authority will again challenge secular authority at the national level. This holds true for many local areas as well. Henceforth, conflict over legitimate authority is likely to occur between modern contenders for power. Whether the new Busia government will be able to legitimize the new regime (including the constitution) will depend on a variety of factors. Among them will be success in improving economic conditions; the extent to which the regime affords some access to decision-making processes to a variety of important parochial, associational, and institutional groups and thereby gives them a stake in the regime and its norms; and the extent to which the government and currently dominant social stratum is confident enough in its power to regard political conflicts as manageable rather than destructive of the party regime.

# 4

# POLITICAL AND ADMINISTRATIVE
# LINKAGE IN THE IVORY COAST

## Richard E. Stryker

This chapter is concerned with structural relationships (linkages) between central and local (or national and subnational) public life in the context of a new state, the Ivory Coast.[1] The development of such linkages, at several levels, during precolonial and colonial phases in the history of the area encompassed by the contemporary Ivory Coast is an indispensable secondary aspect of this concern. It should be noted that the empirical focus of my research has been the northwestern part of this country, more specifically the Malinké areas plus the proximate town of Man, though I have drawn on materials for other parts of the Ivory Coast, where appropriate and available.

In using the phrase "public life," especially with respect to *local* public life, I do not intend to stake out a range of phenomena distinct from that usually conveyed by local government and politics. The influence of M. G. Smith has, however, induced me to conceive government (the regulation of public affairs) as an inclusive rubric, subsuming politics (competition in power to influence decision-making) and administration (authorized procedures for implementing decisions).[2] Yet the normal connotations of government are weighted on the output side, which may be empirically appropriate in the case of contemporary Ivory Coast but which, nevertheless, is not my sole concern. Public life provides an alternative inclusive term, perhaps more common, and which I particularly like because of its "vital" reference. For reasons of space and relative lack of data, many aspects of local public life, such as cooperatives and other social and eco-

1. This chapter is part of my "Center and Locality: Linkage and Political Change in the Ivory Coast" (Ph.D. Dissertation, U.C.L.A., 1970). I am grateful to the Foreign Areas Fellowship Program for its support of my field research during 1965–67.
2. See, for example, M. G. Smith, *Government in Zazzau* (London: Oxford, 1960), pp. 15–33.

nomic associations, will not be treated here; the focus will be limited to the major, explicit political and administrative organizations.[3]

That the study of central-local relationships in contemporary Africa has been slighted is a well-worn theme. Anthropologists have been criticized for narrow concentration on communities as self-contained systems, and political scientists have been charged with unwarranted specialization on personalities and institutions at the new centers.[4] This situation, with respect to contemporary public life, has been improved in recent years,[5] but the analysis of central-local relationships in precolonial and colonial Africa remains a seriously neglected subject.[6]

A brief note on the concept of linkage should be included before proceeding. The term refers here to structural relationships between a given center (political-administrative leadership, the "capital" of a polity or "headquarters" of a sub- or supra-polity unit) and its constituent members. These members may act and/or be treated as citizens, subjects, groups, localities, or some other unit; but our concern will focus on territorial localities. Structural relationships are institutionalized roles and organizations through which demands and supports can be transmitted between a center and its members. An extreme formulation of, what we may call, the "linkage problem" in new states has been offered by Douglas Ashford: "The dilemma of government in the new nation is that it is all-powerful in the decision-making sense, but that it is utterly devoid of structural rela-

3. Since cooperative organization and programs for "animation rurale" are relatively underdeveloped in the Ivory Coast, they have been little studied. See, however, John C. de Wilde, *Experiences with Agricultural Development in Tropical Africa* (Baltimore: Johns Hopkins, 1957), vol. 2, pp. 391–414.

4. See, for example, Aristide Zolberg, *Creating Political Order* (Chicago: Rand McNally, 1966), p. 153. Community studies in general have long suffered from being minimally related to "the larger political systems in which they operate" [Morris Janowitz, *Community Political Systems* (Glencoe, Ill.: Free Press, 1961), p. 13].

5. Among the recent studies of contemporary African politics which seriously analyze the relationships between local and central institutions are Douglas Ashford, *National Development and Local Reform* (Princeton University Press, 1967); Martin Kilson, *Political Change in a West African State* (Harvard University Press, 1966); Henry Bienen, *Tanzania: Party Transformation and Economic Development* (Princeton University Press, 1967); and Clement Moore, *Tunisia since Independence* (University of California Press, 1965). An earlier classic is A. L. Epstein, *Politics in an Urban African Community* (Manchester University Press, 1958).

6. On the neglect of such studies in precolonial Africa, with the major exception of S. F. Nadel's *A Black Byzantium*, see M. G. Smith, "Pluralism in Pre-Colonial African Societies," in Leo Kuper and M. G. Smith, eds., *Pluralism in Africa* (Berkeley, Cal.: University of California Press, 1969), p. 105. For colonial Africa, the exceptions would include Kilson, *Political Change*; Martin Klein, *Islam and Imperialism in Senegal* (Stanford University Press, 1967); and Jean Suret-Canale, *Afrique noire: L'Ere coloniale* (Paris: Editions sociales, 1964).

tionships to the society that make it possible to extend the meaning of development."[7]

Linkage is to be conceived as a dual process: from the center to its members, which is the administrative aspect (penetration); and from the members to the center, which is the political aspect (participation). We may regard a parallel establishment of administrative and political linkage (a two-way flow) between a center and its members as a necessary but not sufficient condition for political integration and political development of any unit, however these latter concepts are defined.

Various types of linkage, whether administrative or political, can be termed "demands" and "supports." These concepts are familiar from the work of David Easton with respect to members' demands on and supports for the center.[8] We can, equally, qualify the center's relationships to its members as demands (in the sense of extractions) and supports (in the sense of services).

Finally, it is necessary to specify spheres of life within which linkage may or does occur. The number of relevant spheres is theoretically as large as the distinctive activities carried on in society. Illustrative and important spheres within which linkage is most frequently sought by centers and/or members are the ritual-symbolic, the economic, the legal-adjudicative, the educative, the protective and punitive (military and police), and that of physical well-being (health, social security, etc.). Many others are possible, of course, and some of those listed (e.g., the economic) could be broken down into a vast number of subdivisions. We will not regard the political and the administrative as spheres of life at the same level. Penetration and participation are instrumental aspects of linkage in any sphere of life, though they are, of course, often valued in themselves.[9]

Implicit in the local component of our subject is a reference to a higher, or central authority: local public life can only exist within the boundaries of a larger scale public. The reference is also most commonly territorial or spatial, the most distinctive image being the hinterland with respect to a capital. Not all polities can be conceived in this perspective, only those where a center exists, possessing some capability and intention of making decisions for its localities.

Prior to the establishment of administrative control by the French, there was no center for the territory which became the Ivory Coast.

7. Ashford, *National Development*, p. 8.
8. Easton, *A Systems Analysis of Political Life* (New York: John Wiley, 1965).
9. These concepts are explicated in greater detail in chapter 1 of my dissertation.

Unlike many other parts of West Africa, this territory contained no states of really significant scale, and only a few polities with administrative centralization over rather limited areas. These included, most importantly, the Malinké kingdoms of Kong (Watara dynasty) and of Kabadugu (Touré dynasty); the Koulango kingdom at Bouna (of Dagomba origin) and the Abron kingdom in the Bondoukou area (of Akan origin); the Agni kingdom of Sanwi (and the lesser ones of Indénié and Moronou) and the Baoulé kingdom of Sakassou. Only Kabadugu and Sanwi survived the nineteenth century essentially intact, to be dealt with by the French administration; Sakassou had early dissolved into a group of small-scale chiefdoms, and the kingdoms of Kong, Bouna, and Bondoukou were subjugated and destroyed by the forces of Samory. The Samorian state itself possessed the most impressive potential center in the precolonial history of the region, in terms of military and administrative capability and of intention to centralize decision-making, territorially and functionally.

Our knowledge of precolonial public life in the Ivory Coast is limited in the extreme; but the general pattern within these various chiefdoms and kingdoms was the persistence of a great degree of local autonomy, subject to higher ritual authority and to intermittent demands from the center in the economic and military spheres. Boundaries were ill-defined, and political relationships (at least in the North) were seldom coterminous with economic or other social relationships. Linkage between center and locality existed only with respect to a limited number of affairs, conditioned by the crucial variable of territorial distance between the center and any given locality. For present purposes, it is sufficient to indicate that, even among the traditional states of this area, there was little impingement by *any* center on the localities of the Ivory Coast until quite recently. This is a legacy in contrast to large areas of contemporary Mali, Upper Volta, Senegal, or Nigeria.[10]

The center for the new administrative organization to which inter alia, the peoples of the Ivory Coast were subjected following the French conquest was ultimately the imperial capital of Paris. From this perspec-

10. The bibliography on precolonial public life in the Ivory Coast is neither extensive nor, with few exceptions, of high quality. The outstanding exception deals with an "acephalous" polity: Claude Meillassoux, *Anthropologie économique des Gouro* (Paris: Mouton, 1964). On Kong, see E. Bernus, "Kong et sa région," *Etudes Eburnéennes* 8 (1960): 239–325. On Bondoukou and the Abron kingdom, see L. Taxier, *Le Noir de Bondoukou* (Paris: Leroux, 1921). On the Agni, see F. J. Amon d'Aby, *Croyances religieuses et coutumes juridiques des Agni de la Côte d'Ivoire* (Paris: Larose, 1960). Information on Kabadugu is derived from personal interviews by the author in the Odienné region.

tive, local government might seem to refer to the level of the constituent territories which made up the empire, or even to the level of the several federal administrative units, such as AOF. A generous interpretation of the minimal French effort to develop representative institutions at *more* localized levels, even after 1946, might be that "the overseas territories were themselves viewed from Paris as the equivalent of French departments. The elected territorial assemblies . . . were considered local councils; indeed until 1952, they were called *conseils généraux,* as in French departments."[11]

In a similar vein, Zolberg has commented that "there is no adequate explanation for this lack of development of local government, except to note that the French are less concerned with 'grass-roots democracy,' perhaps, than are Anglo-Saxon countries."[12] Whether or not British administration was ever truly devoted to grass-roots democracy in Ghana and Nigeria, there can be little doubt that the French undermined indigenous local public life in the Ivory Coast and elsewhere, not through imperial oversight or cultural idiosyncrasy, but intentionally, in order to weaken organized opposition. Influential French critics of their country's colonial administration in West Africa, from as early as the 1920s invariably insisted upon the need for effective representative councils at subterritorial levels.[13] The problem, then, of local public life to be considered here is situated at levels inferior to that of the territory called the Ivory Coast.

Colonial decision-making, at least with respect to economic policy, appears to have been highly centralized in Paris. Suret-Canale has shown the extent to which the great French commercial monopolies, "with their men located in the highest administrative echelons and especially in the offices of the 'rue Oudinot,' " were able to impose their interests on the administration.[14] According to former governor Deschamps, "the influence of the 'Colons' and businessmen, and especially of the large companies, was frequently felt in Paris and made the governors 'jump' when they did not prove themselves 'understanding.' "[15]

11. M. J. Campbell et al., *The Structure of Local Government in West Africa* (The Hague: M. Nijhoff, 1965), pp. 712–72.
12. A. Zolberg, *One-Party Government in the Ivory Coast* (Princeton University Press, 1964), p. 84 n.
13. See, especially, Henri Cosnier, *L'Ouest africain français* (Paris: Larose, 1921), pp. xiii, 141–48, 162–66; and Henri Labouret, "A la recherche d'une politique indigène dans l'ouest africain," *L'Afrique Française* 6 (June 1931) : 403.
14. Suret-Canale, *Afrique noire,* p. 395.
15. H. Deschamps, cited in Suret-Canale, *Afrique noire,* p. 395.

While the grand colonial options were defined and the great economic interests defended in Paris, the degree of de facto administrative decentralization was very great indeed. The evolution of the power struggle between the various segments of the colonial administration (the minister of colonies, the governor-general, the territorial governors, and the local administrators), and between this administration and the various military and technical ministries, is a subject beyond the scope of this chapter, except to indicate that "the administration" was far from a monolithic entity and was itself a political arena.[16] The major beneficiary of these struggles came to be the governor-general (of AOF in the case discussed here), where major administrative, financial, and technical control was concentrated from as early as 1904. Yet, as Crowder has rightly insisted,

. . . in the early days the Governor-General, arrayed as he was with a vast body of powers, had in practice to leave much of his power in the hands of the Lieutenant-Governors [redesignated "Governors" in 1937] on the spot. With responsibility for a sizeable bureaucracy in Dakar, and unable to travel in the colonies frequently because of the poor communications that existed at the time, he had to trust their judgment in all but the most important political decisions. Similarly, the Lieutenant-Governors, bogged down with paper work and restricted in their ability to travel, were very much dependent in the administrator on the spot, and so it is that in the early years of the federation . . . the most important agent of the "mission civilisatrice" was the *Commandant de cercle*.[17]

To a significant extent this de facto decentralization to the local administrator remained in effect throughout twentieth-century colonial rule, so that the *commandant* was not only the referent center for most Africans, but probably the most effective policy maker. In any given *cercle* this policy was likely to be erratic over time due to the "continual coming and going" of officials, each "reorganizing things in his manner," and each "complaining that his successor completely ruined his accomplishments."[18] Former commandants such as Maurice Delafosse reported that they "administered haphazardly [au petit bonheur]," and, for the most part, took "decisions . . . that no text, recent or ancient, could have justified. . . ." Likewise, Robert Delavignette noted that "the *commandant* was not waiting for orders from the governor"; because "there are never

16. This subject has been insufficiently explored. An interesting contribution, however, is Charles Cutter, "The Popular Front in the French Soudan: Colonial Bureaucracy as a Political Arena," unpublished ms.

17. Michael Crowder, *West Africa under Colonial Rule* (Northwestern University Press, 1968), pp. 180–81.

18. Cosnier, *L'Ouest africain français*, pp. 143–44.

ready-made solutions, there is [simply] the locality and its administrator. ...."[19] Thus, French colonial administration was neither centralized direct rule nor was it noninterventionist, or indirect rule; it was the paternalistic *régime du commandant*.[20]

French colonial strategy, contrary to the long-prevailing myth as to its monolithic and doctrinal character, was essentially reactive and lacked any consistent coordination. There was continual vacillation at higher administrative levels on nearly every aspect of relationships with existing African polities.[21] The only consistent principle, which provided little situational guidance, was the necessity to establish French authority (whether as an end in itself or as an adjunct to commercial exploitation became almost inextricable questions). Comparable vacillation was evident at the territorial and local levels of the Ivory Coast colony. One of its consequences was a serious linkage problem for the French administration.

The explorer and first governor of the Ivory Coast, Binger, intent on subjugating the centralized Malinké polities of the northern region, ordered his officials to "protect all the small states against the large ones; divide the large states [into smaller units] . . . ; prevent any chief from increasing his power at the expense of another. . . . But to do this, we must be there, be able to operate efficiently and direct the internal politics of each locality."[22] Only a few years later, Governor Roberdeau criticized "excessive" administrative intervention into local affairs: "The necessity of collecting taxes in the near future requires that the chiefs have more extended and effective authority. . . ."[23] Clozel agreed with this position, even remarking that "our duty is simply to take the institutions as they are and aid in their development and natural progress. . . ."[24] However, when he became governor shortly thereafter, Clozel favored intervention on behalf of the Sénoufo, for example, who had earlier come under

19. M. Delafosse, *Broussard* (Paris: Larose, 1922), p. 137; and R. Delavignette, *La Paix nazaréenne* (Paris, 1943), p. 91, as well as *Service africain* (Paris: Gallimard, 1946), p. 34.

20. These terms are derived from Crowder, *West Africa*, pp. 69–71.

21. On the evolution of French strategy with respect to chiefs, see R. Cornevin, "L'Evolution des chefferies dans l'Afrique noire d'expression française," *Recueil Penant*, no. 686 (April-May 1961) : 235–50, and no. 687 (June-August 1961) : 379–88; and Jacques Lombard, *Autorités traditionnelles et pouvoirs européens en Afrique noire* (Paris: A. Colin, 1967), pp. 91–144.

22. L. G. Binger, cited in Cornevin, *Recueil Penant*, no. 686: 244.

23. Circulaire du Gov. Roberdeau, in *Recueil Penant*, no. 686: 244–45.

24. F. J. Clozel and Roger Villamur, *Les Coutumes indigènes de la Côte d'Ivoire* (Paris: Challamel, 1902), p. 70.

Malinké domination.[25] Intervention reached its culmination, militarily and administratively, under Governor Angoulvant in the years preceding World War I; then the pendulum swung back again, with governors favoring respect for chiefs and the restoration of traditional administrative and conciliar institutions.[26]

The consequences of inconsistent administrative interference, dictated by immediate situational needs rather than by any coherent strategy, varied in time and locality. It alternatively degraded and artificially reinforced traditional institutions, but the dynamics of all types of indigenous polities were fundamentally altered. Recruitment to chieftaincies became the prerogative of discontinuous commandant policy, which might respect, rigidify, or disregard traditional criteria. Conciliar institutions were ignored or rendered ineffective, so that whatever constitutional elements did exist in traditional polities ceased to function, at least above the village level. Village chiefs and councils were only minimally altered (new tax functions, commandant approval of successions) and remained representative; but almost nowhere was the village an isolable political unit, so its character was unavoidably changed with the disruption of traditional polities.

The key to this disruption was the reorientation of the chieftaincy itself, dependent now upon the will of a superordinate center rather than upon its own constituency. This was a fortiori the case in traditional polities previously lacking centralized chieftaincies. Not the least of the resulting alterations was the breakdown of whatever linkages had existed between the traditional centers and their localities. This posed an almost insuperable dilemma for an understaffed, nearly nomadic colonial administration, because its most pressing need was for *interlocuteurs valables*.[27]

Empirical illustrations of this linkage problem can be briefly examined in two types of traditional polity in the Ivory Coast: the kingdom of Kabadugu, and the acephalous polities of the Forest Mandé. In the Odienné area, formerly the center of Kabadugu, the incumbent chief in the ruling Touré line at the time of the French occupation was "exiled for non-

25. See Clozel, *Dix ans à la Côte d'Ivoire* (Paris: Librairie maritime et coloniale, 1906), pp. 114–16.

26. See G. Angoulvant, *La Pacification de la Côte d'Ivoire* (Paris: Larose, 1916). The erratic evolution of colonial policy toward traditional chiefs in the Ivory Coast is summarized, though with insufficient attention to the northern areas, in F. J. Amon d'Aby, *Le Problème des chefferies traditionnelles en Côte d'Ivoire* (C. H. E. A. M., doc. no. 2778, 1957).

27. Many of these points are discussed in detail in Lombard, *Autorités traditionnelles*, and Suret-Canale, *Afrique noire*.

cooperation," as was his successor. The third Kabadugu chief in less than four years, Ibrahima Touré, fell in and out of favor with successive commandants; but Governor Clozel personally intervened to insist that his administrators support the chief, or the French might be faced with massive popular hostility in the area. At about the same time, the administration freed the Sénoufo war captives held in Kabadugu (12,000 in 1907) and began to dismantle the territorial authority structure by granting administrative autonomy to many of the villages and provinces which had come under Touré domination a century earlier.

These actions, in which Ibrahima acquiesced as a condition for remaining in office, albeit now merely as an administrative *chef de canton*, turned the Touré nobles solidly against both the French and Ibrahima. The hostilities provoked by this intervention led commandants in other areas, such as nearby Boundiali, to protest against "too abrupt an emancipation of the Sénoufo which could lead to regrettable reprisals [from the dominant Malinké]." Successive administrators in Odienné, from about 1908 until the late 1920s, interfered less and less with local Touré rule, reporting that "this is a bad time to modify a state of affairs which our lack of personnel does not permit to replace with an organization more in conformity with our own customs." Thus the French continued to support Ibrahima, who remained chief until 1934, despite widespread local opposition to him, complaints from village chiefs about his arrogant and unwarranted meddling in their affairs, and several attempts by the Touré nobles to replace him. A commandant received orders from the governor as late as 1928, "to seize every convenient occasion . . . for reaffirming the authority of Ibrahima. . . . For example, call him obviously first to public meetings and seat him at your right." Four years later, the commandant's reports continued to emphasize "the crisis of authority" in the area and the lack of reliable cadres linking his office to ongoing affairs in the villages.[28] Although the French apparently gained a loyal ally for their administration in Kabadugu, the chieftaincy had been seriously discredited. The commandant could not, by fiat, develop linkages between his headquarters and the villages.

At the other end of the continuum of traditional polities in the Ivory Coast, there were many autonomous, localized villages, usually interlinked over a given, limited area through ties of clanship, marriage, and ritual. They lacked centralized offices, or chiefs, at any level above the village and were often even without village chiefs. This type of polity was widely

28. This section is based on administrative reports in the Archives of the Ministry of Interior, Abidjan, Ivory Coast, "Cercle d'Odienné," 1898–1935.

scattered in the forest area of the western Ivory Coast among many of the Forest Mandé (Dan, Wobé, Gouro) and other peoples. They successfully resisted the intrusion of Samory and earlier Malinké warriors for the most part, and they offered the most sustained military resistance that the French met in their conquest of the Ivory Coast.

Here the colonial regime altered the traditional polities, not by circumscribing, but by creating chieftaincies "from scratch." Villages were forcibly regrouped into artificial cantons, and men utterly without traditional authority were installed as chiefs, backed by French arms and sustained through special privileges and economic advantages. Needless to say, such chiefs found little support among their own people, and the French remained frustrated in their search for the elusive linkage between administrators and village. An unusually frank commandant in the Man area in the mid-1920s complained that "as for the chiefs which we have created from scratch and named, let's be honest, *by force alone*, they exist undoubtedly, but their authority is entirely theoretical."[29]

These administrative chiefs, themselves, benefitted materially and politically from office, benefits which were accumulated over time into significant power resources, and which enabled most chiefs to weather successfully the "time of politics" in the Ivory Coast following World War II.

They received a salary and a part of the taxes collected. They were also empowered to designate the men . . . to be taken for recruitment [military and forced labor]: few direct dependents of the chiefs were hit. Disposing of money and a nearly intact family labor force, sometimes even of recruited laborers, the "chiefs" were in a position to undertake the first plantations, . . . thus to enrich themselves and exercise the patronage functions expected from an eminent man.[30]

They developed into the upper strata of an emergent peasant nobility, based on wealth and prerogatives rather than on traditional status. While they performed critical functions for the colonial administration, they became increasingly assimilated to the status of indigenous *fonctionnaires*, serving far more as obstacles than as channels to broaden support for that administration. There were French efforts, especially in the 1930s, to cope with their lack of linkage to the localities. Means were sought to enhance the representativeness of chiefs, and local conciliar organs were revived periodically; but the policies proved abortive even before the outbreak

29. R. Vendiex, "Rapport politique—Man" (Ministry of Interior Archives, Ivory Coast, 1923).

30. Meillassoux, *Anthropologie économique*, p. 316.

of the war. An irreparable breach existed between the administrative chiefs and their people.[31]

There were other chiefs, however, who maintained much of their traditional integrity, albeit at the cost of exemption from the privileges which accrued to "cooperative" administrative chiefs. Many indigenous chiefs, primarily at the village level, had a "straw chief" presented to the commandant as the local representative. Such a man was usually a client or dependent of the actual chief, whose position thereby remained uncompromised in the eyes of the people. The straw chief frequently operated as a buffer between the administration and the village, limiting colonial penetration and preserving the authority of the actual chief. This was particularly evident in the legal-adjudicative sphere: despite the efforts at judicial aggrandizement by the official courts of the commandant, indigenous chiefs continued to settle most civil and even criminal disputes throughout the colonial era.[32]

The commandant, as the linchpin of the colonial system, clearly occupied a very powerful role. He was able to impose arbitrary sanctions on recalcitrant individuals or entire villages. However, he did not represent a center with a very imposing coordinating capacity, due to the lack of reliable linkages, or even *interlocuteurs valables*, with the subjects of colonial rule. In their absence, the commandant was far too limited in personnel and other resources to enable him to play, very consistently or thoroughly, the role of heroic demiurge that he often fancied for himself. The rapid turnover of local administrators, instituted as a deliberate policy after World War I (the *système de la plaque tournante*) to ensure that administrative units did not become personal fiefdoms of zealous officials, rendered the second generation of administrators unavoidably ignorant of local affairs. It frequently meant that officials were delivered "into the hands of African interpreters [and *gardes de cercle*] who all too often became the powers behind the commandants' desks."[33] The cursory

31. See Lombard, *Autorités traditionnelles*, pp. 105, 126, and passim.

32. "Straw chiefs" have been reported from nearly every area of ex–French West Africa: among the Dan and others in the western Ivory Coast in M. Allusson, *Etude générale de la région de Man* (B. D. P. A., Ivory Coast Planning Ministry, ca. 1965) 4: 11; and more generally in Delavignette, *Service africain*, p. 124. On the legal-adjudicative role of chiefs, see Zolberg, *One-Party Government*, p. 54; Crowder, *West Africa*, p. 192; and R. L. Buell, *The Native Problem in Africa* (London: F. Cass, 1965), 1: 1006–8.

33. Pierre Alexandre, "Social Pluralism in French African Colonies," in Kuper and Smith, eds., *Pluralism in Africa*, p. 204. See also Labouret, *L'Afrique française*, p. 403.

and infrequent character of *tournées* outside the administrative head-quarters further limited the ability of officials to coordinate any but the most urgent affairs within their domain.[34]

Finally, it must be noted that, until after World War II, there were no meaningful participatory linkages at any level within the Ivory Coast, and certainly none that affected the mass of Africans. Neither at the territorial level, in the growing urban centers, nor in the rural *cercles* were there representative councils of any significance to link administrative policy with popular demands and supports. The much-publicized *conseils de notables* at local levels were ineffective, because they were seldom representative and were treated with disdain by the commandants. These councils also lacked substance as linkage institutions because local adminis-trative units had no financial autonomy; so decisions in the all-important spheres of taxation and public works were taken beyond the range of any local participation. The colonial cooperative organization (the *Sociétés Indigènes de Prévoyance*) was equally removed from any control by its members: the societies "belong[ed], in the most absolute sense of the word, to the administrator."[35] Their budgets functioned as a general pur-pose *caisse noire* for the commandant, enhancing his autonomy but stultifying the political linkage which the colonial regime so desperately needed.[36]

The territory of the Ivory Coast was a unit only with respect to a uniform administrative superstructure, and, as noted, this was consider-ably less centralized than the rhetoric of French colonial hierarchy would indicate. There was a virtual absence of political linkage, and the skeletal local administration was linked precariously at best to a vast "residual political space." Residual from the perspective of an aggrandizing center, but because this space was indeed "filled by other structures," one might more accurately term the spheres of life wherein the colonial center lacked linkages as "competitive political space."[37] The colonial Ivory Coast did not possess a politically integrative center, and competition to fill its political space began in earnest with the organization of the *Parti Démo-cratique de Côte d'Ivoire* (PDCI) at the end of the war.

The evolution of public life in the Ivory Coast over the past two and

34. See Suret-Canale, *Afrique noire*, pp. 392–95; and Labouret, *L'Afrique française*, p. 403.

35. Cosnier, *L'Ouest africain français*, p. 241.

36. See Suret-Canale, *Afrique noire*, pp. 299–310.

37. See Zolberg, *Creating Political Order*, p. 133.

one-half decades will be discussed here, first from the perspective of the development of political participation through the dominant party organization, then in terms of administrative penetration by the new Ivorian center since independence, and finally I will return to the question of political linkage via governmental conciliar institutions. The political history of the PDCI during the period in which it organized and consolidated its challenge as a rival center to the colonial regime has been documented and analyzed more fully than perhaps that of any other French-speaking African political organization.[38] Several aspects of the party's evolution from a local perspective should, however, be emphasized.

Neither the PDCI nor its parent organization, the *Syndicat agricole africain* (SAA), ever developed the characteristics of a mass-based organization, even at their apogee. Both, indeed, "grew from the top down,"[39] and both were oriented to a clientele predominantly southern, monetized, and Baoulé or of the Lagunaire group.[40] The need to negotiate directly with northern chiefs for the recruitment of labor led the SAA to expand its organization into the savanna zone; and the need for votes led the PDCI to expand its coalition to include several other critical groups.[41] Yet the SAA remained a rather elite group of larger southern planters, perhaps 20,000 at the outside.[42] The PDCI, in spite of its electoral successes, only represented, in terms of votes cast, six percent of the adult population in the elections of 1946 and 1952 (under conditions of limited suffrage) and still less than fifty percent in the 1957 election, when universal suffrage existed and with no more than token opposition.[43] The nearly unanimous PDCI vote in subsequent, uncontested elections must be regarded as utterly ambiguous in significance.

---

38. Zolberg, *One-Party Government*; Zolberg, "Ivory Coast," in Coleman and Rosberg, eds., *Political Parties and National Integration*, pp. 65–89; Zolberg, "Mass Parties and National Integration: The Case of the Ivory Coast," *Journal of Politics* 25, no. 1 (February 1963): 36–78; Zolberg, *Creating Political Order*, passim; Ruth Morgenthau, *Political Parties in French-Speaking West Africa* (Oxford University Press, 1964), pp. 166–218; Amon d'Aby, *La Côte d'Ivoire dans la cité africaine* (Paris: Larose, 1951) ; I. Wallerstein, *The Road to Independence* (Paris: Mouton, 1964) ; Georges Chaffard, *Les Carnets secrets de la décolonisation* (Paris: Calmann-Levy, 1965), pp. 29–59, 99–132; and French National Assembly, *Annexe No. 11348: Rapport sur les incidents survenus en Côte d'Ivoire*, reprinted by the PDCI (Abidjan, 1965).

39. Zolberg, *One-Party Government*, p. 67.

40. Opposition political parties were also oriented to a predominantly monetized clientele, but with different ethnic bases.

41. See the testimony of J. Anoma, president of the SAA, in French National Assembly, *Annexe No. 11438* 1:396; and Zolberg, *One-Party Government*, pp. 70–71.

42. Testimony of Houphouet-Boigny in *Annexe No. 11348* 1:10.

43. Zolberg, *Creating Political Order*, pp. 15, 25.

It is also worth noting that the original political demands of the Houphouet-Boigny organization in 1945, while radical in comparison to those of his elitist opponent, K. Binzeme, included only the most modest political reforms: citizenship for *évolués*, creation of a territorial assembly (with both Europeans and Africans), and new municipalities.[44] Houphouet-Boigny's very success in identifying himself with the abolition of forced labor and the *indigénat* has obscured the minimal extent to which he sought the creation of a new, participant public life. There were no demands for the election of chiefs, the creation of rural councils, changes in the structure of local administration, or universal suffrage.[45] His pre-occupation with the territorial arena at this stage is certainly understandable; but the emphasis on select socioeconomic issues, at the expense of efforts to restructure local public life so as to develop participant local and national communities, has been an enduring feature of the Houphouet-Boigny regime.

Any analysis of the PDCI organization must consider at least two levels of internal linkage: between the territorial or national arena and the intermediary *sous-sections;* and between the latter and the localized *comités* at the level of village and urban *quartiers* the key role in this structure, at the head of each sous-section, is the secretary-general. Linkage between the central leadership of the party and its members is only possible where the secretaries-general fulfill a dual responsibility in co-ordinating the flow of demands and supports from above and below.

The sous-sections (originally some sixty units at the level of the administrative subdivisions) did not develop from nor were they necessarily responsible to the localized comités. Membership in the rural comités was and remains coterminous with membership in the traditional community, while membership in the urban comités is ethnically specific even where residential areas are mixed. Zolberg's comment on the party organization in Treichville would appear to hold throughout the country: "Except at the uppermost echelons, the [PDCI] . . . provides little or no opportunity for horizontal communication between members of different ethnic groups."[46]

The leadership of the sous-sections was seldom, and in some cases has never been, elected by the constituent comités. Rather, personal representatives of Houphouet-Boigny (e.g., Ouezzin Coulibaly for much of the northern Ivory Coast) selected prominent individuals whom they knew

44. See Zolberg, *One-Party Government*, p. 72.
45. I am grateful to Martin Staniland for bringing this to my attention.
46. Zolberg, "Mass Parties and National Integration," p. 42.

and trusted as the secretaries-general of the sous-sections. These men, in turn, selected the membership of the party bureaus at this level. "Instead of being the apex of a hierarchical organization of committees, the *sous-section* became a sort of caucus of the indirect type,"[47] whose bureaus might or might not be representative of the political forces in the area. The concern of PDCI officials was simply to find, as quickly as possible, local leaders who could be entrusted with the task of organizing support of Houphouet-Boigny's campaigns in the territorial arena.

There have not been any levels of party organization intermediary between the sous-sections and the territorial organs since the suppression of the "undisciplined" *comités régionaux* in 1947. The rare territorial congresses and the, apparently inoperative, *Comité directeur* are creatures of the central Bureau politique, not of the sous-sections. In turn, central party direction emanates less from the Bureau politique than from an informal coterie around President Houphouet-Boigny and Party Secretary Philippe Yacé.[48]

The men who became secretaries-general were political entrepreneurs in their own right, with varying goals and varying perceptions of the relevant public arena. Some had ambitions in the territorial arena and found their local party offices a convenient mode of access to higher positions in the National Assembly and the civil service, especially after independence. For many, however, local party office (as well as higher positions) served to enhance or consolidate localized political and economic ambitions.

At the local level, the PDCI, because its goals and ideology were diffuse and its prospective clientele universalistic, was a highly flexible organizational weapon, suddenly available to particular individuals representing particular groups and interests. The identification of just whom secretaries-general represent has been variable over time and by locality. Yet the general trend had favored elders as against youth; locals or natives as against strangers; men with a combination of traditionally-ascribed and economically-achieved characteristics as against those lacking one or both qualities; and residents of a *chef-lieu* as against residents of the villages. Such a categorization, of course, provides only the roughest kind of guide to the dynamics of local politics in any given sous-section;

47. Zolberg, *One-Party Government*, p. 117.
48. This summary is derived from a variety of sources, including the writings of Zolberg; Francis Wodie, "Le Parti démocratique de Côte d'Ivoire," *Revue juridique et politique* 22, no. 4 (October-December 1968) : 987–1018; and personal interviews by the author with PDCI officials.

but the point is that the PDCI, which, at least for a time, was a party in the territorial arena, is often no more than a clan or faction or ethnic category in the local arena.[49]

This is not to say that all PDCI sous-sections are grossly unrepresentative of their constituents. But there have been few institutionalized restraints on the secretaries-general, and their roles have permitted a great deal of self-definition. Almost all of the party comités, especially in the rural areas, were organized *after* the constitution of the higher-level sous-sections, and the yearly election of secretaries-general, required by party statutes, has never been observed. Thus these local party leaders have enjoyed almost complete immunity to challenges from below.

The key variable in a secretary-general's tenure is support from the territorial leadership, particularly from the president himself. This support is conditioned by several factors: loyalty to the president in times of crisis; political status as an "old-militant" who fought and perhaps suffered during the period of colonial repression against the PDCI; and services to the regime—honesty and efficiency in the delivery of party dues and in the fulfillment of other central demands, whether economic or political. With such support, a secretary-general can avoid local electoral challenges almost indefinitely; have an election managed so as to ensure the defeat of opponents (e.g., in Mankono in 1964); or have the results of an electoral defeat annulled and reversed by Abidjan (e.g., in Séguéla in the late 1950s and in Katiola in 1966). In many of these cases, the PDCI has become essentially the party of the elders in the local arena, as the challenges came from younger, better-educated men, whose disaffection from the party in general seems to be regularly exacerbated.[50]

On the other hand, due to the lack of regular channels of communication between national and local party officials, much less between national officials and private citizens with grievances against the local party, secretaries-general were able to gain extensive de facto autonomy from higher control. As Zolberg observed, they "often took advantage of the situation to extend their authority over many spheres of life unrelated

49. A similar phenomenon was described over a decade ago with respect to the African National Congress in Northern Rhodesia by A. L. Epstein, *Politics in an Urban African Community*. Subsequent studies of local party politics in Africa have frequently noted the lack of structural congruence between local and national party arenas.

50. Information on the Katiola case comes from research by Staniland, who also studied the Bouaflé and Bongouanou sous-sections. My own research centered on Mankono, Séguéla, and Man. On youth attitudes toward the party and the Ivorian regime, see Lyman Drake, *The Anxious Generation* (Ph.D. Dissertation, M.I.T., 1968).

to the party's concern." They frequently "settle family disputes and perform other chiefly functions. Transmission of party office has sometimes taken on dynastic connotations; at the death of the incumbent, his heir according to custom may become the new party secretary."[51]

The absence of regular linkage between the center and the party soussections has often had serious local consequences. I will limit myself to two indicative examples. In reaction to demands from the territorial leadership for reconciliation with former opponents at the local level following the PDCI victories of the mid-1950s, some of the militants in the western town of Man undertook a campaign of intimidation and violence against traitors (neither faction being ethnically homogeneous). Although Abidjan had forbidden such reprisals, legal action against the militants was dropped.[52]

There were other accounts to be settled in Man as well. As in most urban centers of the Ivory Coast, the majority of the town population in Man are *dyula*, "strangers" to the area, but economically and numerically dominant in the town since its creation by the French. The majority of PDCI militants in Man were also dyula, and they indeed "made dramatic sacrifices during the [colonial] repression."[53] The Man sous-section, however, covers an area wider than the town (which is everywhere the case except in Abidjan and Bouaké), and the rural party committees outnumber those in the town. This distribution ensures the continuing tenure of the secretary-general, who is a local (a Yacouba), in spite of dyula control of most town committees.

Following the incidents noted above, the secretary-general and his allies began a purge of dyula militants on the sous-section bureau, replacing them with locals and a few dyula who owed personal loyalty to the secretary-general. The dyula militants protested to Abidjan, but the lack of regular links between the base and the leadership rendered evaluation of demands exceedingly difficult; and the Man case was far from isolated. As was generally the case elsewhere, the secretary-general was upheld, though forced to add a prominent, but nonmilitant, dyula to his bureau. Demands of the dyula militants for a separate sous-section were denied. Since then, much of the local dyula leadership has ceased to participate in party affairs, and a certain disaffection from the party is widespread

51. Zolberg, *One-Party Government*, p. 120, and "Ivory Coast," p. 72. See also Morgenthau, *Political Parties*, p. 211.

52. Some aspects of these incidents are reported in Morgenthau, *Political Parties*, pp. 206–7.

53. Ibid., p. 208.

among the dyula of Man. Participation in party affairs in Man as elsewhere is, in any case, "restricted almost exclusively to the activities of the *bureau* of the *sous-section*," under the "increasingly caucus-like authority" of the secretary-general.[54] The position of the latter was further solidified by his appointment to the national party's Bureau politique in 1965.

Thus, a failure of linkage at one level (between the center and the intermediary sous-section) was the permissive condition for a partial structural breakdown at another level (between the sous-section and local members). In Man, the PDCI has not provided a structure for integrating local diversity. Indeed, the party has been a factor in exacerbating existing ethnic cleavages.[55]

Perhaps a more blatant, but likely more common, example of the autonomy of local party leadership comes from the northern area of Séguéla, where the secretary-general was an old militant and long a local law-unto-himself (he died in late 1968). It concerns the authorization of village markets and schools, supposedly a governmental rather than a party function. A longstanding feud between the villages of Tjemassoba and Gbogolo, only a few kilometers from Séguéla, broke into violence in 1965, requiring the attention of the district administrator. Upon investigation, it was revealed that a market traditionally located in Tjemassoba had been transferred to Gbogolo and that construction of a primary school in Tjemassoba had been halted and was to be transferred to Gbogolo. These actions were taken on personal orders from the secretary-general, although the market and school authorization had come from an earlier district administrator.

It seems that the secretary-general frequently complained to the people of Tjemassoba that they were "bad Muslims" because they did not give him many gifts. Yet the village chief testified that they had given the secretary-general "three sheep, a large goat, a sack of rice, and 20,000 francs," so he would give them back their market and school. Apparently the market and school went to Gbogolo because they were better Muslims, whose gifts to the secretary-general amounted to "130,000 francs, a cow, some rice, and much oil." When the village chief of Tjemassoba complained, he was arrested by the secretary-general for several weeks, unknown to the administration. The incident eventually required the intervention of higher authority than the district administrator, and a compromise was imposed on the two villages. However, there were no apparent, at least no public, sanctions against the secretary-general, whose

54. Zolberg, *One-Party Government*, p. 186.
55. This account is based on interviews with the principals in Man, 1966–67.

line of political support was said to lead directly to the president himself. The district administrator, who intervened in a number of such cases, was transferred from Séguéla in 1966, because of "bad relations" with the secretary-general—a fate shared by his predecessor and not uncommon in similar circumstances elsewhere in the Ivory Coast.

This example of ultra vires action by a secretary-general illustrates not only the diffuse character of the critical linkage role between the party center and its members, but it indicates the manner in which the party remains a "partisan" rather than an integrative organization. Furthermore, poor linkage within the party can operate as an impediment to linkage within the administrative structure.[56]

The PDCI has failed to provide a reliable organization for linking the Ivorian center and its members. Consequently, the Ivorian regime has minimized the developmental role of the party. While the party is proclaimed to have an "explanatory and persuasive role" in promoting local development, this is irregular at best, and the regime has placed little reliance on the PDCI for either educational or organizational tasks. In analyzing the Provisional Plan for 1962–63, a commission of the Economic and Social Council noted that there was no reference therein to, so presumably no role for, the party—an "omission" the council thought should be rectified. The more recent and far more elaborate Ivorian Plans equally omit any mention of the party's role, and there is little indication that the leadership foresees any significant recourse to the PDCI organization in future local development.[57]

Over the past five years, the party has operated less and less as a discrete institution at the territorial level. A new organ, the Conseil national, which Zolberg aptly terms a kind of Estates-General of the Ivory Coast, has become the preeminent forum for formal communications between the regime and diverse notables of the realm.[58] This forum includes the secretaries-general, of course; but the important point is that the party is not treated as a privileged structure for linking the regime and Ivorian citi-

56. This account is based on interviews and documents in the local archives in Séguéla, 1966–67. Transfer of district administrators in cases of conflict with secretaries-general has been documented elsewhere: for example, in Bouaflé by Staniland and in Dimbokro by Leonard Jeffries.

57. *Journal officiel de la République de la Côte d'Ivoire* (1962), no. 28, p. 672. See also M. Diawara, "Le Second plan," *Fraternité* (2 August 1968) ; and *Perspectives décennales de développement, 1960–1970* (Monaco: P. Bory, 1967). This subject is treated at greater length in my "A Local Perspective on Developmental Strategy in the Ivory Coast," in Michael Lofchie, ed., *The State of the Nations: Power Structures in Independent Africa* (forthcoming, 1971).

58. On the *Conseil national*, see Zolberg's chapter in this volume.

zens. It would appear that the status of privileged structure has been appropriated by the territorial governmental apparatus.

The fusion of party and governmental authority at the center in many new states has often been noted. In the Ivory Coast, one even finds the national secretary-general of the PDCI, Philippe Yacé, on a recent tour of the interior, everywhere stressing "the need for union and the *precedence* of the administrative power over local party leaders."[59] Ivorian-style linkage has become focused on the penetration of a highly centralized bureaucratic apparatus into the hinterland. This indicates, of course, an effort by the regime to give priority to the flow of demands and supports from the center over those from constituent members.

Penetration by the center is achieved through the deconcentration of administrative and technical field-agents from the capital into the hinterland. Deconcentration must be distinguished from decentralization; the latter refers to the devolution of certain statutory powers to locally elected organs, which thereby possess a sphere of autonomy. On the other hand, "deconcentration consists in augmenting the powers of the local representatives [field-agents] of the central power. . . ."[60] Deconcentration is the method, par excellence, for achieving administrative linkage by a newly established center: it facilitates the spread of basic public services and permits "a substantial increase in the center's potential for control over the localities."[61] Thus, deconcentration is a technique for increasing *centralization*, or, in the words of an Ivory Coast administrative manual, for "crush[ing] all local public life. . . ."[62]

The organization of Ivorian field administration, until late 1969 was based upon a division of the country into six *départements* (regions), headed by high-level administrative cadres who also possess important political credentials—the prefects. Hierarchically subordinate to the prefects are the subprefects, who administer the 113 district prefectures. These officials, field-agents of the Ministry of Interior, provide considerably more localized administration than did their colonial counterparts; but the differences are more symbolic and potential than actual. Further deconcentration is to be effectuated "as financial means and personnel permit." Plans were announced in 1969 to increase the number of départe-

59. *Réalités Ivoiriennes*, no. 68 (October 1967). My emphasis.
60. A. de Laubadère, cited in Campbell et al., *The Structure of Local Government in West Africa*, p. 12.
61. Zolberg, *Creating Political Order*, p. 115.
62. R. Guidon-Lavallée, *Le Manuel du sous-préfet* (Abidjan, ca. 1965), p. 5.

ments from six to twenty-four, in order to further localize central services and controls, and "so that the prefects can better animate, co-ordinate and control the sub-prefects."[63]

Other ministries have their own field-agents (agriculture, education, justice, etc.), whose geographic responsibilities do not always coincide with those of the Ministry of Interior agents. By statute, the regional prefect represents the entire government and each ministry within his département, with the exception of Justice, whose agents are legally independent from prefectoral control. The role of the prefect and, to a more limited extent, of the subprefect within his domain, is conceived as primarily a coordinating and supervisory task. However, neither official possesses sufficient resources to carry out these responsibilities, and little coordination has been manifested as yet at either administrative level. The technical field-agents operate quite independently of each other and of the administrative representatives; and the latter devote most of their time to strictly "interior functions: the maintenance of order, civil registration, and application of a wide range of economic and social regulations."[64]

The subprefectures represent the most localized official government presence, but their proliferation in recent years has unavoidably entailed the posting of minimally qualified personnel with scant resources. Outside the major towns, a subprefecture often consists of little more than "a single clerk frequently lacking even a typewriter; to send out the mail requires going to the neighboring town."[65] Many of the newer subprefectures, particularly in the northern and western parts of the country, have neither administrators nor staff. There is not only an insufficient number of trained Ivorian administrators, but they are heavily concentrated in the capital. A recent study found that eighty-six percent of top-level administrative cadres (a majority of whom are still French) and over forty percent of the entire civil service resides in Abidjan.[66] By comparison, about two and one-half percent of civil servants in France are located in Paris, ten percent of American federal civil servants are in Washington, and some forty percent of British central administrative per-

63. *Fraternité* (6 June 1969).

64. Staniland, "Local Administration in Ivory Coast," *West Africa* 2649 (9 March 1968). My own observations of prefects and subprefects over an extended period of time in northern areas would tend to confirm these generalizations.

65. Moussa Konet, deputy from Man, *Débats de l'Assemblée nationale*, J.O.R.C.I. (1962), no. 16.

66. Study by the French Company, S.E.M.A., 1965, cited in Samir Amin, *Le Développement du capitalisme en Côte d'Ivoire* (Paris: Editions de Minuit, 1967).

sonnel are in the entire London region.[67] Penetration by the Ivorian center remains significantly limited.

Below the level of the subprefectures are the roughly 8,600 villages of the Ivory Coast, as yet untouched by any administrative presence. The vast majority of these have less than 600 inhabitants; nearly fifty percent have fewer than 200.[68] The Ivorian administration has divided the country, theoretically, into over 1,000 *centres d'état civil secondaire*. Agents are to be posted to these local sites in order to register vital statistics and to aid in enforcing the provisions of the new Civil Code, which imposed a uniform system of law relating to personal status on the country. But enforcement of the code has been sporadic at best due to lack of personnel and to widespread ignorance of or hostility to the new law. This effort at administrative aggrandizement does represent an officially sanctioned model for future development and a legal support for those, primarily youths, who seek to escape traditional modes of regulating personal rights and obligations. However, at present, for most Ivorians, the center's penetration in this sphere is little more than symbolic—some would even label it fantasy.[69]

Under the colonial regime, as discussed above, the chiefs at the canton, village, and urban quartier levels performed important official functions in the taxation and policing domains and also maintained a significant judicial role despite colonial efforts to circumscribe that role. Under Ivorian leadership, chiefs supposedly no longer have "any defined functions," apart from "assisting the subprefect in his diverse administrative tasks." Even their policing function is now limited to "informing" the subprefect of any disorder. Furthermore, "it is forbidden for customary chiefs to assume jurisdiction in disputes between their subjects, much less to take decisions which would have no legal value."[70] The center's aggrandizement in these spheres has almost eliminated the formerly powerful role of the *chefs de canton*, and their office faces progressive extinction. However, the village and urban quartier chiefs are still recruited for the most

67. See Brian G. Smith, *Field Administration* (London: Routledge and Kegan Paul, 1967), p. 4.

68. Ivory Coast Ministry of Finance, Economic Affairs and Planning, *La Côte d'Ivoire, 1965: Population-synthèse-études régionales* (Abidjan, 1967), p. 37.

69. Two recent papers presented to African Studies Association meetings raise interesting questions concerning the "fantasy law" character of the code: Dorothy Vellenga, "Attempts to Change Family Law in Ghana and Ivory Coast" (1967), and Jeswald Salacuse, "Modernization of Law in French-Speaking Africa: Revolution or Fantasy?" (1968). A revised version of the Vellenga paper is included in the present volume.

70. *Le Manuel du sous-préfet*, pp. 26, 112.

part according to traditional rules of succession. On the basis of rather unsystematic observation, it appears that these indigenous chiefs continue to fulfill an important mediating role in local disputes.

The most effective penetration of the village by the colonial regime was in the collection of taxes. Today it is through the yearly campaigns to collect party dues, which closely approximate the character of the old head tax. The subprefects and the chiefs are encouraged to assist in these campaigns, and they frequently do, but the key role belongs to the party secretaries-general and the comité leaders. Not surprisingly, this has occasioned frequent conflicts between village chiefs, jealous of their former prerogatives, and local party leaders, anxious to exert new prerogatives. In many respects, as noted, local PDCI leaders have functionally supplanted the chiefs. Yet, in many areas, the chiefs remain in competition with local party and government officials and the local deputy to the National Assembly. All of these figures remain engaged in an unresolved struggle to fill political space at the local level.

In many respects, Ivorian local administrators face the same problems as did their colonial predecessors. Although African, and therefore more acceptable to the population than were Europeans, the subprefect is always a stranger in his assigned district (by official policy to discourage nepotism), and he is usually as dependent upon interpreters as was the commandant. Administrative continuity remains problematic, again due to an official policy of regular rotation, and to the frequency of transfers resulting from conflicts with local party leaders. By education and style of life, the subprefect is nearly as differentiated from the local population as was the white administrator. Moreover, the authoritarian protocol and military atmosphere which surround the subprefect (he is attired in an official uniform for most public occasions and is usually approached, deferentially, as "mon commandant") enhance the distance between administrator and administered. Paternalistic attitudes remain, too, as evidenced in both conversation and actions. Their French training is responsible at least in part: "the first batch of administrators trained in Abidjan were told that, 'You will have to be their chief, their teacher, and their friend.' "[71]

One might have expected the dearth of reliable intermediaries between the colonial administrator and the villages to have been resolved with the achievement of independence. The Ivorian subprefects have disregarded the artificial chefs de canton for the most part, but alternative linkage roles

71. Staniland, *West Africa.*

at supra-village levels have not been a great deal more satisfactory. The party secretaries-general fill this role in some areas, but they are often themselves in competition with the subprefects and, as discussed, are not always responsive political figures. In other cases the local deputy to the National Assembly may act as an intermediary between the administration and the villages, but his regular field of operations is at a higher level, as an intermediary between the center and his district. The deputy, moreover, often does not really have a popular base. He is selected by the regime rather than any local constituency, and his "election" is on a single national list, which is representative only in a geographic sense. A major gap in political linkage remains at local levels, and here we must turn to the role of local conciliar organs.

The increased administrative penetration of the hinterland since independence has not been matched by a parallel expansion in the activity of local representative councils. Prior to the terminal colonial period, local councils were of no significance in linking popular participation to administrative decision-making. After the war, councils were instituted in the major urban centers, and there were efforts by the terminal colonial regime to activate councils in rural areas. However, the Ivorian regime has done little to exploit the potential of these participatory organs. Existing councils have, in fact, been emasculated.

The largest towns were granted varying forms of municipal status during the 1940s and 1950s, which permitted a degree of self-governing autonomy under an administrative tutelage authority, now located in the Ministry of Interior. Three towns (Abidjan, Bouaké, and Grand-Bassam) became *communes de plein exercice* and could elect their own mayor and council. Six others (Man, Daloa, Gagnoa, Dimbokro, Agboville, and Abengourou) received the novel status of *communes de moyen exercice*, which elect their own council but have an administratively appointed mayor.

This latter status, created in 1955, was to be merely temporary, perhaps for five years, so that a municipality could prove its ability to balance its own budget; then it would be elevated to the more autonomous status of plein exercice. In the meantime, other growing towns were expected to be regularly granted the lower municipal status, from which they too would graduate, and thus the costs and responsibilities of urban development would be increasingly borne by those most directly affected.[72] This process

72. See V. Thompson and R. Adloff, *French West Africa* (Stanford University Press, 1958), pp. 183–86.

has been halted and, in some respects, reversed since independence.

The functions of the municipal councils were conceived very narrowly by the law of 1955, and there have been no subsequent modifications in the Ivory Coast. The only significant authority delegated to a council is discussion of the municipal budget. But this function is severely circumscribed by the limited financial resources at the disposal of the municipalities, the extensive mandatory expenditures over which the council has no control, and the fact that the budget is entirely drawn up by the mayor, who leaves the councillors little opportunity for serious discussion. The effacement of municipal councils, particularly since independence, is evident in the pro forma character of their meetings, a situation the administration apparently encourages. Upon his appointment as prefect of the Man region and mayor of the town of Man, the current incumbent informed the municipal councillors that "we will get along fine here if the council continues to avoid interfering with the actions of the mayor."[73]

No new communes de plein exercice have yet been created, and that status was withdrawn from Grand-Bassam, ostensibly for financial but at least in part for political reasons, in 1965. Studies were completed, and the territorial assembly had enthusiastically approved the creation of eight new communes de moyen exercice in 1957 (Aboisso, Adzopé, Bondoukou, Dabou, Divo, Korhogo, Ferkessedougou, and Sassandra), but the government decided against implementing the legislation. No municipal elections have followed those of 1956 for any of the existing communes (they were scheduled for 1959 and 1965), and council memberships have been seriously depleted through deaths and changes in residence. The municipal council in Daloa was disbanded in 1960 and has yet to be replaced. There has been some public pressure on the government from the National Assembly (and perhaps a good deal more pressure from various interests in private) to deal with these issues. Yet even the new planning orientation to "the participation of the people" in local development avoids any mention of the municipalities.[74] A recent analysis of municipalities by an Ivorian judicial official indicates that the intention of the regime is to

73. My own observations derive primarily from interviews with municipal officials in Man and attendance at council meetings. The citation is from the *Procès-Verbaux* of the Man Municipal Council (18 September 1964). An insightful study of the neglect and potential of communes in the development process in Morocco and Tunisia is Ashford, *National Development*, chaps. 2–3.

74. Several deputies raised these issues publicly following the suppression of Grand-Bassam's communal status, in *Débats de l'Assemblée nationale*, J.O.R.C.I. (1965), no. 5, pp. 22–23. The only official response to such questions, in 1961, was evasive: P. Yacé, *Fraternité* (9 June 1961). On the new planning orientation to "participation," see the citations in note 64 above.

assimilate all arenas of local autonomy to the more directly controlled territorial administrative structure.[75]

Representative councils in the rural areas have been even less effective as participatory organs. During the 1950s the colonial regime did make an attempt to invigorate the old conseils de notables in both function and recruitment. The devolution of some authority over local development planning to these councils, by creating a sphere of financial autonomy through the *taxe de cercle*, was regarded by the governor of the Ivory Coast as an "indisputable success" that ought to be greatly extended.[76] Several proposals to this effect culminated in the provisions of the *loi-cadre* which instituted an indeterminate number and type of councils for rural collectivities," possessing a significant degree of legal and financial autonomy.[77] The Ivory Coast governor insisted that there ought to be "a larger place for the participation of the people in their local councils," and that, henceforth, the "principal role of the *commandants* is to prepare their districts for democratic participation: and the methods to employ are more counsel and guidance than command, even if efficiency must thereby suffer in the short-run."[78] A Ministry of Interior circular three years later, advising local administrators as to the application of the loi-cadre decrees, declared that the clear purpose was to "modify, progressively but as completely as possible, the political and administrative structure of the interior regions and to permit the rural populations at several levels to participate in public life through the creation of responsible organs, charged with the management of their budgets."[79]

The responsibility for implementing this legislation and creating the appropriate councils, however, was left entirely to the new territorial governments. One observer asked pointedly whether the new African regimes would "dare to make use if it."[80] In fact, only Guinea immediately established decentralized rural authorities, though Madagascar and Cameroun

75. See Samille Hoguie, "Structure et organisation communales en Côte d'Ivoire," *Revue juridique et politique* 22, no. 2 (April-June 1968): pp. 371–78. It should be noted that, with few exceptions, communes throughout French-speaking Africa have had their autonomy curtailed or eliminated since independence. See P. Lampué, "Le Régime municipal dans les états africains francophones," *Revue juridique et politique* 22:463–72.

76. Gov. Messmer, "Les Collectivités locales" (November 1954), unpublished ms. I am indebted to Staniland for a copy of this paper.

77. See Montagnat, "Une innovation de la loi-cadre, les collectivités rurales," *Revue juridique et politique de l'Union Française* 12, no. 2 (April-June 1958): 331–36.

78. Messmer, "Les Collectivités locales."

79. Circular, Ivory Coast Ministry of Interior, 2745/I/cab/bc (22 November 1957).

80. Montagnat, "Une innovation," p. 331.

had provided earlier and apparently successful models. More recently, devolution of some decision-making and financial autonomy to various local levels has occurred in a number of French-speaking African states, though the actuality of decentralization probably varies considerably.[81] The Ivory Coast has been particularly reticent in their regard: no "rural collectivities" have ever been constituted, ostensibly for financial reasons but political considerations have been more critical.[82]

At independence, the taxe de cercle and the head tax were eliminated. Thus, the new administrators, lacking any budget, ceased to convoke the conseils de notables for the most part, and they were abolished in 1967. In place of rural collectivities, which were to have elective councils and to be endowed with *personnalité morale*, the Ivorian regime has recently created *conseils de sous-préfecture*. The new councils must be consulted on the disposition of several petty funds collected locally, but its entire membership is ex officio (technical field-agents) or appointed by the subprefect.[83] They resemble nothing so much as the unreformed conseils de notables!

The Ivorian regime has also begun recently to set up *commissions de développement régional* at the level of départements. Their membership is likewise administratively appointed, and their range of autonomous action will be carefully circumscribed at best. Somewhat problematic is the relationship of these new commissions to the already existing conseils généraux at the departmental level. These latter councils, created in 1959 and nationally reelected in 1960 and 1965, have never met officially in any of the regions. They appear and are widely regarded as purely honorific bodies, a not unlikely fate for most, if not all, local conciliar organs in the Ivory Coast.[84]

Neither party secretaries-general nor local administrators seem anxious to see the development of active representative councils at any level, because they might become sources of potential constraint or even competition. Some administrators, however, view the various councils as at least a potentially useful counterweight to the often "difficult" secretaries-general. The role of councils may, indeed, evolve as a situational function of the competition between local government and party officials. Such competi-

81. See Campbell et al., *The Structure of Local Government in West Africa*, passim; and *Revue juridique et politique* (April-June 1968), vol. 22, passim.

82. See my "A Local Perspective."

83. See the J.O.R.C.I. (1967), no. 27. The incentive which financial decentralization can provide for local development has been demonstrated in Ghana and Nigeria. See the contributions of M. Kilson and W. A. Lewis in Foreign Service Institute, *Local Development in Africa* (Washington, D.C., 1967), pp. 19, 32.

84. See "Loi-Plan pour 1967–70," J.O.R.C.I. (1967), no. 37.

tion was criticized at length by national Secretary-General Yacé at the 1965 PDCI Congress, but it is clearly pervasive.[85] This competition has, thus far, been weighted to the advantage of the secretaries-general, at least in the cases of those with the qualifications discussed earlier. Increasingly, as Zolberg has noted, which official dominates may depend on "their relative ability to carry out their assigned tasks and to construct a local coalition to obtain support."[86] In fact, as the older party militants pass on, and as the center's penetrative capacity expands (indicated by the more regular and supervised sous-section elections for the second generation of local party leaders), one can expect continual administrative aggrandizement at the expense of the party.

One might, properly, conclude from the preceding account that the Ivorian center and its localities are not linked into a common arena of public life. Apart from a partially effective administrative penetration, there exist no institutionalized mechanisms upon which the center can rely for information and policy coordination throughout its hinterland and upon which the individual citizen can rely for exerting influence on central decision-making. This is not to say that communication channels are non-existent or entirely blocked. There are a number of "political brokers" at the local level who provide a degree of linkage between center and locality: the local party leaders, the deputies to the National Assembly, the local administrators, and some indigenous chiefs. They operate less as differentiated political and administrative roles than as a highly competitive quartet in most local arenas.

From the perspective of the center such competition is regarded less as a boon because it increases the amount and diversity of information available than as an unassimilable cacophony due to the overwhelmingly centralized nature of decision-making and the lack of regulative processes. Apart from the administration, information flows far less through institutional channels than through personally and ethnically defined relationships.[87]

From the perspective of a local administrator, the competitive situation presents a real dilemma. If he chooses to remain aloof from rival leaders and play a mediating role, he may well surrender strategic initiative to the

85. See Yacé's "Rapport Moral" at the Fifth PDCI Congress, *Fraternité* (1 October 1965).

86. Zolberg, *Creating Political Order*, p. 126.

87. For examples of personally and ethnically defined communication links, see Zolberg, *One-Party Government*, pp. 277–78, 282.

most powerful local figure. If he chooses to actively intervene in local politics and take sides, he may cut himself off from certain groups, or may antagonize an influential party militant. In fact, active intervention is nearly inevitable given the critical local role of the subprefect. The consequences are more often frustration or even transfer than the successful establishment of linkages with all important local groups.[88]

Finally, from the perspective of the citizen, competition between local leaders presents certain obvious advantages in that alternative brokers exist. However, at least the deputy and the secretary-general have usually staked out discrete constituencies which limits and sometimes precludes alternative access for given individuals or communities. Furthermore, only a handful of local leaders possess regular and respected access at higher levels, many are only marginally influential, and some are disregarded altogether. The geographic distribution of differentially influential local leaders is a key factor in obtaining access and benefits, one over which individuals and communities have little control. In other words, what linkage does exist is, in many respects, haphazard, unequally distributed, and not consistently reliable from the perspective of either center or locality. The expansion of the administrative infrastructure is, of course, an effort to deal with this problem based on the needs of the center. Citizen input has been little enhanced, however, because there are no effective representative forums.

A number of factors are responsible for the persistence of linkage problems in the various contexts discussed in this chapter. Administrative linkage has been limited because none of the successive rulers of the Ivory Coast center has been capable of bringing sufficient resources to bear (personnel, communications, finances) to develop structural relationships extending to the village level. The incapacity was primarily a technological (and, more particularly, a logistical) one for the precolonial and early colonial authorities. For the colonial regime at its apogee, the incapacity was, more importantly, political, in two senses. At the local level, the rule of the French commandant rested almost exclusively on force, and thus the "costs" of penetrating a vast hinterland were extremely high. On the other hand, in the competition to obtain resources from the imperial capital, the colonial administration appears to have had relatively low priority beyond that necessary as an adjunct to commercial exploitation. (Needless to say, resources allocated for *African* social and economic needs were an even lower priority.) The independent Ivorian regime, while more potent

88. This analysis derives from discussions of both strategies with successive subprefects in both Mankono and Séguéla.

politically and technologically than its predecessors, has not significantly altered the distribution of resource allocation for local administrative linkage (or, more generally, for local socioeconomic development). The concentration of resources in the Ivorian capital and the immediately surrounding areas is a distinguishing characteristic of this regime.[89]

The persistance of minimal political linkage between Ivorian localities and successive centers appears to have a more summary explanation: authoritarian centers with an uncertain legitimating base are fearful of being overwhelmed by the release of local demands and potential opposition. In spite of the center's need for political linkage with its society, particularly when global development is a regime goal, the instinctual priority of any center is self-maintenance. The Ivorian regime, of course, has maintained itself for a decade now, and it has presided over a remarkable period of economic growth. Yet, as Ashford argues, the key index of regime capability may be its acceptance of "increased involvement in political life [rather] than its more easily specified ability to handle funds, make plans, and market goods."[90] By this measure, the Ivorian regime is not yet a very developed center.

89. See, again, the sources cited in note 57 above.
90. Ashford, *National Development and Local Reform*, p. 300.

# 5

# THE GRASSROOTS
# IN GHANAIAN POLITICS

## Martin Kilson

The problem of the grassroots in Ghanaian politics is, like elsewhere in modern Africa, a matter of how to combine political order with change in authority and socioeconomic patterns of African society. By political order I mean something more than the maintenance of peace: political order is, in its modern dimension, a matter of creating political institutions that are stable and capable of mediating conflicting interests in a manner that does not impede the modernizing functions of other social relations, especially economic relations.[1]

Colonial government in Ghana attempted to achieve political order in local society by grafting on to indigenous authority patterns the colonial oligarchy's conception of the political requisites of modernization.[2] This policy, known as "indirect rule," assumed that political order in a situation of forced colonial modernization of Iron Age societies required a high measure of continuity in authority patterns. Some measure of African authority was needed to mediate normal traditional social relations while these relations were slowly modernized under colonial overrule.

But indirect rule faced a major practical problem: how to determine when an African society subjected to colonial socioeconomic change was ready for modern rather than traditional political patterns. As Ghanaians moved out of traditional society and entered modern social relations as mine workers, cash-crop farmers, moneylenders, educated clerks, teachers, and the like they acquired political needs, interests, and ideas that extended beyond traditional patterns. The problem confronting the political system,

1. Cf. Samuel P. Huntington, *Political Order in Changing Societies* (New Haven: Yale University Press, 1968), pp. 20 ff., passim.
2. The best account of the system of native authorities or native administration in Ghana is K. A. Busia, *The Position of the Chief in the Modern Political System of Ashanti* (London: Published for the International African Institute by Oxford University Press, 1951).

both at the center and on the periphery, was how the needs of these new men were to gain articulation and satisfaction.

Although this problem was central to local politics in Ghana throughout the colonial era, it prevailed in different contexts between the period of full-fledged colonial rule and the period of decolonization. In the latter period (1946–57) many more Ghanaians were involved in modern social relations; for example, by the early 1950s one-fourth of the population was literate. Second, native authorities were being stripped of their modern political functions and replaced by elected local councils. Third, at the center, the colonial oligarchy of European officials and technicians was being replaced by Ghanaian new elites. This change entailed enormous consequences for local politics and for their relationships to the center.

Although the new elites initially acquired power on the basis of representative principles, they soon acquired the monopoly of coercion and force which had been formerly the preserve of the colonial oligarchy. This allowed the new elites, more than other segments of Ghanaian society, to impose their own definition of the center-periphery relationship on the polity. Their supremacy was also facilitated by their access to the central bureaucracy, especially to those government agencies that regulate basic economic activities like the marketing of cash crops.

Yet the periphery was not without some leverage in relation to the center. Since a large part of Ghana's productive wealth in the post-World War II era has been in the hands of men in local society (especially those involved in cocoa production), this afforded groups at the periphery of the polity at least a basis for bargaining with the center.[3] Furthermore, the typical Ghanaian is a rural dweller, and despite some involvement in modern society he remains within the purview of traditional relationships and values. Local interest groups were, therefore, capable of countering the central elites' influence over local society by manipulating parochial norms and relations—tribal, religious, regional, and so on. Inasmuch as the central elites are of diverse traditional origins, the capacity of local interest groups to manipulate parochial forces is of no mean political importance.

Institutionally, the center-periphery relationship in Ghanaian politics was, from the early 1950s onward, mediated in several ways. First, field units of central government departments like public works, agriculture, labor, and local government, mediated technical relationships between the center and the periphery of the political system. Second, political parties also mediated political interests between the center and the periphery.

3. See Walter Birmingham, ed., *A Study of Contemporary Ghana* (London: A. Allen and Unwin, 1966), vol. 1.

Third, local government (of which there were three types of councils—local, district, and municipal) mediated the center-periphery relationship. Unlike both the central bureaucracy and political parties, local councils, at least in theory, were biased in favor of interests at the periphery of the polity. Precisely how this worked out in practice constitutes one of the crucial issues of grassroots politics in Ghana and elsewhere in Africa.

The normative attributes of the mediating institutions have been of primary importance. The values of political actors or interest groups and the wider culture of which they are a part condition the thrust and modality of political institutions in emergent African politics. More specifically, political factors shape the manner in which political institutions set boundaries—that is, the way in which they place, or fail to place, minimal functional limits or boundaries on the behavior of political actors and interest groups.

In emergent politics political institutions may be seen as displaying a poor definition of boundaries.[4] More than in mature modern systems, the sacred or nonsecular constituents of sociopolitical relations are poorly distinguished, functionally speaking, from the secular. Above all, the political uses of sacred constituents of group interaction are ill-defined; there are few rules, norms, and habits in regard to what mixture of secular and sacred constituents of group interaction is allowable. This situation complicates in turn the definition of both mutual and divergent interests of competing groups and structural levels (e.g., center versus periphery) in the polity.

Thus, in Ghana and elsewhere in Africa no small part of the problem of the institutionalization of political order is a "boundary problem." This may be illustrated by the Ashanti nationalist subplot, known as the National Liberation Movement (NLM) in the mid-1950s. Although the NLM was in a basic sense a secular affair, stemming from the key position of Ashanti in Ghana's cocoa industry and endeavoring to give Ashanti greater leverage over the politics of cocoa, the NLM was also a sacred movement. Its operative raison d'être was linked to the historic role and status of traditional Ashanti; its élan derived more from this link with glorified Ashanti past than from the secular fact of Ashanti's large contribution to Ghana's economic life.[5] Insofar as the typical Ashanti, though

4. Cf. G. Almond and J. S. Coleman, eds., *The Politics of Developing Areas* (Princeton: Princeton University Press, 1960).

5. On the historical position of Ashanti in Ghana and West Africa, see Ivor Wilks, "Ashanti Government," in Daryll Forde and P. M. Kaberry, eds., *West African Kingdoms in the Nineteenth Century* (London: Published for the International African Institute by Oxford University Press, 1967). For a view of the link between

a participant in modern social relations to some degree, was still enmeshed in traditional values that shaped self- and group-identity, modern Ashanti politicians seeking support in the mid-1950s could hardly ignore this fact.

This situation posed a major dilemma for the central government. A response to the purely economic or secular factor in the Ashanti nationalist subplot would not be satisfactory unless it overlapped with the sacred element. Politically, this would have entailed major concessions from the central government, bordering on a veritable constitutional reorganization of the Ghanaian polity as inherited from the British.[6] Of course, it does not follow that if the Ashanti leadership of the NLM had functionally distinguished the secular and sacred elements in their demands, the central government, consisting of an alliance of largely southern ethnic groups (Ga, Fanti, Nzima, Akwapim, Ewe) would have accepted them. But the ramifications of whatever decision the central government arrived at would have been much less in regard to center-periphery relationships. As it happened, the negative response of the central government to NLM demands—a largely coercive response—was received in Ashanti not merely as a rebuff to their secular demands but as an attack on sacred Ashanti— on its pride, virtue, and past glory.

The succeeding decade of Ghanaian politics was plagued by the central government's decision in the Ashanti nationalist subplot. In Ashanti itself the central government was often unwilling to allocate to dissident local councils the financial and technical resources they required, not merely because the councils were dissident but because the Ashanti might interpret concessions from the center in sacred terms. When the central government did make political concessions to Ashanti, they were often dysfunctional: for example, requests from Ashanti interest groups to break up local councils into smaller units were often granted by the central government, especially at the height of the Ashanti nationalist subplot in 1956–58, and later from 1963 onward. In short, the boundary problem has been a major factor affecting the institutionalization of political order both between the center and periphery, and in local society proper.

---

traditional Ashanti and the NLM, see Justice Sarkodee Adoo, Gold Coast, *Report of Committee of Enquiry . . . into Affairs of the Kumasi State Council and the Asanteman Council* (Accra: Government Printer, 1958).

6. For demands emanating from the Ashanti nationalist subplot, which called for a federal system, see Gold Coast, *Report of Select Committee on the Federal System of Government and Second Chamber for the Gold Coast* (Accra: Government Printer, 1955).

## THE LEGACY OF PRE–WORLD WAR II LOCAL
## ADMINISTRATION

The system of "native authorities," the statutory structure of local administration before World War II, was low in its capacity to service the modern needs of the rural masses whose taxes underwrote the system.[7] It was equally low in its capacity to provide popular political participation. Only in the late 1930s, after nearly two generations of experienced colonial overrule, was an attempt made to integrate rural commoners (e.g., cocoa farmers, traders, moneylenders, semiliterate clerks) into the native authorities. Popular participation occurred not through but in opposition to the native authorities: articulate elements in rural society frequently rioted against and sporadically attacked the native authorities because of their restrictive and inefficient features. Participation as an institutionalized form of grassroots politics had to await the end of World War II.

One profound consequence of the prewar system of local administration was that it made a variety of modern resources available to traditional elites. Traditional rulers derived comparatively large incomes from their role in native authorities. Chiefs were also enriched through cocoa farming, a function that their position in native authorities facilitated. In this fashion chiefs came to be among the wealthiest groups in local society at the end of the war. With the rise of competitive party politics after the war, their wealth proved an important asset.

Second, the system of native authorities provided chiefs with a network of relationships, both modern and traditional, which were readily convertible into political instruments of a broader kind. Postwar political parties were able to draw upon the network of relationships which chiefs built up under British superintendency, and chiefs derived a not insignificant advantage in consequence.

Third, the prewar system of native administration virtually guaranteed chiefs a position in postwar local government. Many chiefs further utilized their wealth to provide superior education for their offspring.[8] Thus, by

7. I treat in detail this and other issues discussed in this summary appraisal of the legacy of native authorities in my *Chiefs, Peasants, and Politicians: Grassroots Politics in Ghana 1900–1960's* (forthcoming). See also Busia, *Position of the Chief*, passim.

8. Such use of modern wealth by traditional rulers in Ghana was, in fact, prevalent in the late nineteenth century, and the larger sources of wealth consequent upon full-fledged colonial rule from 1900 onward merely broadened this trend. A study of the traditional kinship ties of the modern educated leaders of the Aborigines' Rights Protection Society, the first Ghanaian anticolonial organization founded in 1898, and the

the end of the war a sizable segment of the most highly educated members of the new elites had kinship ties to chiefs. New elites of this type acquired a major role in the initial constitutional formulation of postwar local government, and the proposals that issued from their findings were not unfavorable to traditional rulers.[9]

## THE STATUTORY STRUCTURE 1951–63

### The Structure

A more dialectical comprehension of the structure and dynamics of grassroots politics in postwar Ghana is obtainable if we view them in terms of the special influence exercised by chiefly groups. This same vantage point of observation will also put in sharper relief the problem of institutionalizing political order in the center-periphery relationship.

The formal demise of the system of native authorities occurred in 1951 when the new Local Government Ordinance provided for full-fledged executive local government through the three types of local councils mentioned above. The numerous local councils had a two-thirds majority of elected members (each serving two-year terms). One-third of the membership was reserved for traditional rulers, mainly paramount chiefs, elected through traditional procedures dominated by their peers. This provision, among others with a traditional bias, had its origin in the so-called Coussey Commission Report on the constitutional structure of postwar decolonization.[10] Though the membership of the Coussey Commission was dominated by new elites, many of them—especially the leading figures like Dr. J. B. Danquah and E. Akufo Addo—had kinship ties to traditional rulers and displayed marked sympathy for chiefly membership of local councils.[11]

Local councils were also required to finance the postwar variant of native authorities, called state councils (later traditional councils), whose

---

National Congress of British West Africa, founded in Accra in 1920, shows that the majority were related to traditional rulers. See La Ray Denzer, *The National Congress of British West Africa* (M.A. Thesis, University of Ghana, 1965). See also David Kimble, *A Political History of Ghana, 1850–1928* (Oxford: Clarendon Press, 1963).

9. See, for example, Gold Coast, *Report of the Select Committee of the Legislative Council Appointed to Make Recommendations Concerning Local Government in Ashanti* (Accra: Government Printer, 1951).

10. See Gold Coast, *Report to His Excellency the Governor by the Committee on Constitutional Reform, 1949* (London, 1949).

11. There were forty members of the Coussey Commission, thirty-one of whom were new elites and nine paramount chiefs.

functions were limited to customary matters like marriage, inheritance, and ritual. This requirement proved burdensome for the numerous local councils with a limited taxable population. When compared to the costs of maintaining the staff of local councils, the payments to traditional bodies were sizable: for example, in the 1955–56 fiscal year, these payments in the Eastern Region amounted to £41,142, compared to £77,962 for the staff of local councils (mainly the council clerk, the chief executive officer).[12] Payments to traditional councils also proved sizable when compared to expenditure of all local government councils in 1955–56 on public works like feeder roads and market facilities; these expenditures in Eastern Region totalled £77,053.

Chiefs' influence in the structure of postwar local government was also evident in the policy of organizing local councils along the lines of territorial jurisdiction of former native authorities. Commenting critically on this practice, a special commissioner of inquiry into local government remarked in the mid-1950s that "a chief whose area of authority coincides with an existing local council feels that if it is joined with its neighbour his status will in some way be affected. There is still a deep rooted feeling . . . that areas of local government and traditional authority must coincide. . . ."[13] This situation prevailed at the commencement of postwar local government in 1951 when 185 local councils were instituted, many of which coincided with traditional authority jurisdictions. Hence, local councils were susceptible to the special politics of traditional interests, involving issues like inheritance, chiefly succession, and land litigation. Their staffs necessarily became involved in these issues, thus consuming time, energy, and resources required for facing modernizing tasks. Moreover, insofar as many former native authorities were small in population, the new local councils defined along traditional jurisdiction proved poor in taxable resources, and thus in development capacity. For example, in Ashanti over half of the local councils were in the 3,000 to 10,000 population range and their expenditure under the administration head was normally twenty to thirty percent. Councils in the 15,000 to 20,000 population range were able to pare down administrative costs to around twelve percent expenditure, but only local councils with a population of 40,000 upward got administrative costs down to functional proportions—about three percent.

Subsequently, small councils spread through the political fragmentation

12. See Ghana, *Local Government Financial Statistics, 1955–56* (Accra, 1958), p. 14.
13. See A. F. Greenwood, *Report of the Commissioner for Local Government Enquiries* (Accra: Government Printer, 1957).

of larger councils. Appeals from traditional groups for such fragmentation were legion in the 1950s, and many were granted by the central government. Thus by 1954 there were 204 local government bodies (mainly local councils) and by 1957 there were 282, of which 252 were local councils, 26 district councils, and 4 municipal councils. This process reached absurd proportions in Ashanti, the center of cocoa production, which had 80 local councils and 10 district councils serving a population of 740,000.

THE DYNAMICS

In the years 1951–57, when traditional groups were manipulating particularistic forces in order to fragment larger local councils, the dominant political party was not, surprisingly enough, controlled by that segment of the new elites which was tied by kinship and outlook to traditional authority patterns. The Convention People's Party (CPP) was controlled instead by men of commoner background who gained access to new elite roles less because of their formal education—which was normally not more than that of upper primary and secondary school—than the personal drive they displayed for modern mobility.[14] If anything, this segment of the new elites had a natural inclination to oppose traditional rulers rather than facilitate their political machinations in local society. Why, then, did the leadership of the CPP acquiesce in the structural fragmentation of local government bodies in the 1950s?

Apart from the role of the "boundary problem," the CPP's policy toward the fragmentation of local councils was one of sheer political opportunism. In face of keen competition from the main opposition parties in the 1950s like the United Gold Coast Convention, the National Liberation Movement, and the United Party, the CPP, seeking support in hinterland localities where vestiges of chiefly influences persisted, resorted to any method that helped maintain it in power. Allowing traditional rulers and their supporters to fragment local councils was one such method. This policy enabled the CPP either to win some traditional rulers to its side or to set one faction of traditional rulers against another as they competed to break up large local councils, thereby reducing the likelihood that chiefly groups would unanimously back the opposition. Although the fragmentation of local councils positively weakened their capacity to fulfill local government services, the CPP accepted this as a price it was willing to pay in

14. The best account of the kind of self-made men who formed the CPP is in David Apter, *The Gold Coast in Transition* (Princeton: Princeton University Press, 1955). See also Philip Foster, *Education and Social Change in Ghana* (Chicago: University of Chicago Press, 1965).

order to disorient the opposition. Furthermore, the CPP assumed it could deal with possible negative popular reactions to inefficient local councils.

In 1960–61, by which time the CPP regime had become effectively authoritarian, the government attempted to redress the earlier fragmentation of local government bodies. An expatriate special commissioner in the Ministry of Local Government, Mr. A. F. Greenwood, almost single-handedly persuaded the CPP government—or more precisely, President Kwame Nkrumah—to amalgamate small, financially weak local councils. The economies of scale offered by such a policy were real, and there was even the prospect that discontented popular forces in rural society might be appeased in consequence.[15] Thus in 1961 the 282 councils that existed at independence were reduced to 50; few councils had less than 50,000 population.

This reorganization was, however, shortlived. By 1963 the CPP was experiencing a multifaceted crisis, one dimension of which was a marked decline in its legitimacy—never very firm anyway—and a consequent fear of popular disaffection.[16] How could this situation be neutralized or, better still, reversed? Of course, the CPP, now a largely authoritarian regime (e.g., free elections to local councils had ceased in 1959) was not contemplating a return to competitive party politics as a means to recapture its popular support. This would have meant, after all, at least the distribution to the rural populace of greater rewards in the form of government subventions to the revenues of local councils; it was precisely the fact of party competition in the early 1950s which induced the CPP government to assist significantly the finances of local councils.[17] Furthermore, even if a return to competitive party politics had occurred, the impending financial crisis, consequent to the decline in world cocoa prices, seriously restricted the CPP government's capacity to reward supporters in the localities.

15. From author's interview with A. F. Greenwood, special commissioner on local government, summer 1962. Mr. Greenwood believed that the declining world market price for cocoa, which government revenue began to reflect in 1960, lent support to his proposal to reorganize local councils in order to gain economies of scale. See his *Report of the Commissioner for Local Government Enquiries*, passim.

16. For a skeptical view of the legitimacy of the CPP, see Jack Goody, "Consensus and Dissent in Ghana," *Political Science Quarterly* 83, no. 3 (September 1968): 337–52.

17. For example, grants-in-aid by the central government to local government was twenty-three percent of local revenue in 1949–50, the year before local councils were inaugurated, but by 1955 such aid was forty-two percent of local revenue (£ 2,690,840). Central government education grants to local government were almost nonexistent in 1949–50, but represented thirteen percent of local revenue by 1955–56.

Thus restricted in its political options, the CPP government, apprehensive of the kind of popular dissidence which it had itself effectively articulated for political ends in 1948–51, turned for support to traditional rulers—the very group against whom the CPP had risen in the early 1950s. Curiously enough, there is no evidence that the CPP leadership ever seriously weighed the question of the capacity of traditional rulers to stave off a possible resurgence of popular discontent; it appeared to take as an article of faith that they could do so.[18] Be that as it may, in turning for support to chiefs, the CPP regime paid a price: traditional rulers, sulking from the reorganization of small councils into larger ones under the Greenwood Reforms of 1960–61, requested return to the status quo ante in local government.

The CPP government, which was never seriously committed to the Greenwood Reforms nor cognizant of the conditions of political order at the grassroots, agreed to this request. Beginning in 1962 there ensued an extensive refragmentation of the large local councils established in 1960–61. By 1965 the number of local councils had increased nearly threefold; there were now 139 councils in local government (115 local councils and 24 urban and municipal councils). At the time of the military coup d' état in February 1966, there was every prospect of further fragmentation.

## A THEORETICAL NOTE ON THE INSTITUTIONALIZATION CRISIS

The CPP government's response to the problems of local politics in the years from 1962 onward was something more than political opportunism. Structural crises in emergent African societies force men, willy nilly, back upon their primordial habits and beliefs.[19] One such belief is that traditional authorities, the natural repository of society's well-being, exercise a special capacity to turn chaos into order.[20] Modern African elites are not, moreover, fully free of such beliefs; and insofar as a sizable section of the population, even in a comparatively developed state like Ghana, rely on traditional rulers for many of life's needs (religion, ritual, marriage, interpersonal adjudication) it is not unreasonable of African politicians to turn to chiefs for support in crisis situations. I am not suggesting, of course, that all crisis situations confronted by African political elites evoke this atavistic reliance upon traditional authorities. It is largely

18. From author's interviews with regional and district organizers of CPP, summer 1968. It is noteworthy that the official propaganda and ideology of the CPP contained little or no evidence of the crisis in local politics in the early 1960s.

19. Cf. my *Political Change in a West African State* (Cambridge: Harvard University Press, 1966), pp. 267–80, passim.

20. Cf. Lucy Mair, *Primitive Government* (Baltimore: Penguin Books, 1962).

in those crisis situations where the legitimacy of leadership and the political mechanisms linking them to the masses are put in question. Thus in structural crises entailing the legitimacy of leadership, African regimes display a deeply rooted propensity to vacillate between secular and sacred criteria of political choice. This situation is indicative of a larger problem: the poor definition of political boundaries between the secular and sacred constituents of political processes. Indeed, not infrequently, the need for such a distinction is not even perceived by political actors. This was, I think, very much the case in regard to the CPP regime in the years 1962–65, despite the regime's ostensible dependence upon radical or Marxist secular criteria of political choice.

The political upshot of this situation is that both mutual and divergent interests of competing groups in emergent African polities lack an operational delimitation of their real needs as opposed to their sacred or ideal needs. Without such a delimitation, permitting a functional though dialectical interplay of mutual and divergent interests, an emergent polity cannot easily institutionalize political order. Instead, instability and breakdown vie for ascendancy in such emergent polities. Moreover, the governing elites vent their political frustration by acting-out the trappings or surface dimensions of institutionalized political order. Extensive and often bizarre ideological activity is associated with this process, lending the illusion that the capacity to institutionalize political order is within reach of the system, whereas in fact it is not. The CPP regime proved particularly adept at this during the years 1962–65, the period of failure to institutionalize political order at the grassroots and between the center and the periphery of the political system.

## THE PARTY STRUCTURE 1958–65

### THE STRUCTURE

At independence the CPP was organized at the grassroots for two purposes: first, to muster votes for elections; second, to control the allocation of local services and other resources through party, paraparty, and government instrumentalities. For the central leadership mustering votes was the uppermost concern. This situation, however, changed dramatically as the CPP regime acquired authoritarian characteristics from 1959 onward.

Some writers on Ghanaian politics have claimed that the CPP was a well-organized party at the local level in the late 1950s, but there is little evidence to support this contention. Fieldwork observation in 1960, interviews with party officials, and perusal of party records lead me to the conclusion that the CPP had the minimum local organization in the late 1950s, albeit adequate for election purposes.

Evidence relating to local party finance tends to support this viewpoint: the national headquarters of the CPP provided around £200 per month to the Regional Executive Committees for distribution among constituency branches in the immediate postindependence period, an amount hardly indicative of large-scale party organization at the grassroots. Evidence relating to party membership also supports the "minimalist" view. Party records of membership, probably of questionable reliability in any case, are not available for the late 1950s; but for the year 1962 the records show 392,114 card-holding members of the CPP (in a total population of 7,000,000). Finally, evidence relating to the CPP's electoral support between 1950 and 1957 equally supports my view: In three general elections during this period the CPP won the votes of no more than thirty to forty percent of the registered voters, or between fifteen and twenty percent of the adult population.[21]

It was only from 1961 onward that the CPP obtained a rather large organization in local areas, and thus fairly extensive contact with the masses. It was, furthermore, in this period that the CPP lost its status as a political voluntary association competing with similar associations for popular backing: it was now an agency of the state and equipped with authoritarian powers.[22] Beginning in 1961 the constituency branch of the CPP was dissolved and replaced by village and town branches. These branches, of which there were many hundreds, were run by a secretary and an executive committee. The village and town branches of the party also possessed a paragovernmental status, insofar as they were used as the basis of village and town development committees which functioned as primary units of local government.[23]

Above the village and town branches was the district organization. In 1960 there were some 82 districts headed by the same number of district commissioners; but by 1963 the number of districts and commissioners stood at 155 (Accra Region, 7; Eastern Region, 18; Central Region, 21; Western Region, 17; Volta Region, 16; Ashanti Region, 22; Brong-Ahafo

21. See Dennis Austin, *Politics in Ghana, 1946–1960* (London: Oxford University Press, 1964), passim.

22. Cf. Henry Bretton, *The Rise and Fall of Kwame Nkrumah* (New York: Praeger, 1967).

23. See Ghana, *Administrative Instructions to Village, Town and City and Municipal Ward Committees* (Accra: Ministry of Justice—Local Government Section, December 1962).

Region, 12; Northern Region, 19; Upper Region, 23). The district commissioners, now party rather than civil service officials, performed some administrative functions, including overseeing and often dominating local councils; but they were mainly the eyes and ears of the party at the grassroots, as well as chief coordinators of party activities at the district level.[24] Each district had, in addition to a commissioner and his staff, a District Executive Committee composed of local party stalwarts and run by a district secretary and a district education secretary.

Finally, above the district was the regional organization, headed by a regional commissioner and his staff, partly ad hoc in composition, consisting of civil servants. Like the district commissioner, the regional commissioner was a party rather than a civil service official, and he held quasi-cabinet status. In his party functions, the regional commissioner was aided by a regional party secretary, a regional education secretary, a regional propaganda secretary, and regional organizers responsible for paraparty agencies like the Trades Union Congress and the United Ghana Farmers Cooperative Council. From 1964 onward, these regional party officials formed a Regional Working Committee which regulated all party affairs in the localities.

Apart from the formal party organization at the grassroots, the CPP possessed an extensive paraparty organization. Typical of a paraparty organization was the United Ghana Farmers Council Cooperatives, founded in 1953 as the main instrument for organizing party support among cash-crop farmers. Data on the structure and membership of the UGFCC in the 1950s are unavailable; but data for the early 1960s show that it was organized in 1,077 villages, embracing 1,109 farmers' cooperatives and enrolling 41,097 members.[25] In this period the UGFCC was a well-equipped paraparty bureaucracy, deriving most of its technical and financial resources from the government, including a legal monopoly of domestic cocoa marketing.

Other paraparty organizations, equally funded by the CPP government, were the Trades Union Congress (TUC), founded in 1953, the National Council of Women (market women mainly), also founded in the early 1950s, and the Young Pioneers, founded in the early 1960s. The TUC was the most important of these paraparty organizations. It had no more

24. See Ghana, *Responsibilities of District Commissioners, Councillors and Officers in Urban and Local Councils* (Accra: Ministry of Justice—Local Government Section, 27 August 1960).

25. See Ghana, *The United Ghana Farmers Council Cooperatives: The General Secretary's Report, 1962–63* (Accra, n.d.).

than 50,000 members in the early 1950s, but claimed 154,000 after independence. By the early 1960s the TUC enjoyed a government-backed monopoly in labor activity, with responsibility for exercising the party's will among organized workers.

Thus, in the early 1960s the CPP through a combination of party and paraparty structures possessed a local organization which left few areas of the hinterland untouched. But the nature of this organization, which derived its legitimacy more from government than from the citizenry, makes it rather difficult to describe it as participatory. Neither the principles of organization underlying the postindependence structure of the CPP at the grassroots nor the intent of the leaders who conceived the structure permit one to characterize it as participatory. What, then, lay behind the postindependence structure of the CPP, and what were the dynamics of its behavior?

### THE DYNAMICS

The party and paraparty structures at the grassroots of Ghanaian society in the period 1958–65 functioned more in behalf of the center than the periphery. The reasons for this were twofold: first, the difficulty of delineating the operational or functional boundaries between the center and periphery of the system led the central government to act in ways detrimental to the modernizing needs of the localities; second, the pattern of contest for leadership roles at the center caused the central government to manipulate the localities for its own ends. More specifically, the CPP regime faced a perpetual current of claims from secondary and tertiary leaders or functionaries for leadership roles, and perquisites deriving from these roles, at the center. In attempting either to neutralize or resolve this conflict, the CPP regime organized the localities in a manner that provided leadership outlets for secondary claimants.

### *The Boundary Problem*

As noted earlier, what I call the "boundary problem" is the result of the inability of political actors in emergent African polities to distinguish functionally the secular and sacred criteria of political choice and action. We have already described the Ashanti nationalist subplot in the mid-1960s as an illustration of this problem, particularly as it affected center-periphery relationships. Another instance of the boundary problem, as it affected center-periphery interactions, occurred in the late 1950s when the CPP regime confronted an effort by traditional rulers in the Akim

Abuakwa traditional area (Eastern Region) to checkmate the party's influence.

Akim Abuakwa, once the most powerful native authority in the Eastern Region, proved a difficult area for the CPP to penetrate throughout the 1950s. The traditional rulers in Akim Abuakwa, led by the powerful Paramount Chief Nana Ofori Atta II, used their influence to rally opposition to the CPP in the general elections in 1954 and 1956.[26] Though they failed to defeat the CPP in the several constituencies in Akim Abuakwa, the candidates (both of whom had kinship ties to chiefs) backed by the chiefs held the CPP to marginal victories.[27] Following the 1956 general election, the outcome of which guaranteed that the CPP would be the governing party at independence, the chiefs in Akim Abuakwa attempted to interfere with the functioning of the local councils and other government institutions. Through the use of their ascriptive authority, they sought to reduce the political effectiveness of the CPP-controlled local government and hoped to undermine the legitimacy of the regime.[28]

Once again, the CPPs response was largely coercive. Furthermore, the coercion was neither specific in regard to its source (that is, the central government was not the sole agency of coercion) nor functionally limited. Rather it was diffuse in origin and broadcast in thrust: all levels of the CPP participated in the coercion and few segments in Akim Abuakwa, traditional or not, escaped its wrath. Rationalizing or functionally coordinating this pattern of response by the center to dissident local pressures proved well-nigh impossible, assuming such rationalization was considered desirable, which is doubtful.

Moreover, tensions and frustrations that characterized the contest for leadership roles at the center inevitably found expression in the center-periphery dispute in Akim Abuakwa—as they did too in the center-periphery dispute in Ashanti. All sorts of party figures (CPP legislators,

26. See Austin, *Politics in Ghana*, pp. 272–73, 318–19.

27. The candidates backed by Akim Abuakwa chiefs were Dr. J. B. Danquah, a lawyer and brother of the predecessor of the reigning paramount chief, and W. Ofori Atta, an educator and son of the predecessor to the reigning paramount chief. In 1956 Danquah lost by only 600 votes. Interestingly enough, one of the CPP's main candidates in Akim Abuakwa in the general elections of 1954 and 1956 was, like the opposition candidates, a kin of traditional rulers. He was Aaron Ofori Atta, a half-brother of W. Ofori Atta, the opposition candidate. He is said to have politically deserted his class because of unequal treatment from his father, Paramount Chief Nana Ofori Atta I, when a child.

28. See Ghana, *Report of Commission Appointed to Inquire Into Affairs of the Akim Abuakwa State* (Accra: Government Printer, 1958).

party organizers, paraparty functionaries, district commissioners) who were dissatisfied with the attention they received from the center, took out their frustrations in the context of the Akim Abuakwa dispute.

Invariably, such behavior by party and government officials threatened the institutionalization of political order in Akim Abuakwa. Peculation was a frequent feature of these officials' behavior. Dysfunctional interference in the affairs of local councils was rife. All of this was, moreover, sanctioned by the inability of the central leadership to distinguish between the secular and sacred components of its conflict with Akim Abuakwa— and vice versa. Eventually, the central government stripped the paramount chief of Akim Abuakwa of his symbolic (sacred) titles and ruled that only the president, Kwame Nkrumah, could use them. This last act by the government is symbolic of a profound need of conflicting groups in African states to strip each other of both their secular and sacred attributes of power—a by-product, as it were, of the boundary problem.

Thus, the central government's dispute with Akim Abuakwa further elaborates the range of the problem of institutionalizing political order in Ghanaian politics, and by extension elsewhere in Africa. Above all, competing groups in emergent African polities fail to recognize that the creation of political order is, at bottom, a practical and secular matter: it requires functionally specific skills, techniques, procedures, and special habits. Moreover, it is, functionally speaking, value free: for example, institutionalized political order is found in ideologically divergent industrial societies like Soviet Russia and the United States.[29]

Indeed, the value-free or ideologically neutral aspect of institutionalized political order is the feature of the modern polity least understood by elites in emergent African polities. They act out fierce attachment to the formal, official values or ideologies associated with the different variants of institutionalized political order in industrial societies (e.g., capitalism, socialism, communism) but lose sight of the functional criteria of political order. In Ghana, this pattern occurred to an extreme degree in the CPP era and plagued every aspect of the center-periphery relationship, grossly impeding the establishment of political order.

## The Leadership Problem

The organizational growth of the CPP in the years 1958–65 was related more to the pattern of leadership conflict and tension at the center than to the needs of the populace in local society. There were several levels of

29. Cf. Zbigniew Brzezinski and Samuel P. Huntington, *Political Power: USA/USSR* (New York: Viking Press, 1964).

conflict among political leaders in the CPP during the party's authoritarian phase (1961–65). One level of tension concerned the endeavor of the central leadership (itself made up of largely self-made new elites who possessed not much more than secondary education) to incorporate upper-status Ghanaian new elites (men of university education and often claiming high-ranking traditional kinship) into the government. The upper-status new elites possessed the superior professional and technical skills, without which no modern government could operate. While the CPP leadership recognized this, secondary echelon leaders were not easily persuaded. They hankered after leading government posts and the perquisites associated with these posts, irrespective of their lack of professional and technical skills. They considered their contribution to the political success of the CPP ground enough for claiming government jobs. And, indeed, these secondary and tertiary functionaries in the CPP could hardly be ignored: they, after all, provided key links with popular forces like workers, market women, and cash-crop farmers.

Thus the social basis of the pecking order of leaders within the CPP regime was a major source of conflict and tension. The central leadership had to find a way to satisfy the ambition of secondary echelon leaders for national posts.[30] Its solution was to transform the network of voluntary associations (trade unions, farmers, cooperatives, market-women associations) that provided the party much of its election support in the 1950s into paraparty institutions, or what I have called elsewhere tributaries of mainstream party power.[31] No doubt such formal reorganization of voluntary associations into tributaries of party power—officially called "Party Wings" or "Ancillaries"—was hazardous: the tributaries might attempt to usurp the power of the mainstream. Yet it had its advantages as well: the tributaries would, it was hoped, not only satisfy the political ambitions of thousands of secondary and tertiary party functionaries, but extend the center's links with the periphery—a goal of no mean importance to a one-party regime.

In transforming institutions like the Trades Union Congress, the United Ghana Farmers Council Cooperatives (originally the Ghana Farmers

30. This ambition of secondary echelon leaders in the CPP for national roles was long standing. It appeared prominently during the period of free elections, 1950–57. For example, in the general election of 1954 the central committee of the party confronted some 1,005 claimants for the 104 seats in the legislature. When many of these claimants, nearly all secondary party functionaries, persisted and stood for election as "independents," the central committee expelled 81 of them. See Austin, *Politics in Ghana*, pp. 210, 217–25.

31. See my *Chiefs, Peasants and Politicians.*

Marketing Cooperatives), and the National Council of Women (mainly women traders) into tributaries of mainstream party power, the central party leadership utilized the coercive and regulatory powers of the government, as well as its financial and technical resources. Thus the government endowed the TUC and the UGFCC with a monopoly in labor organization and cash-crop marketing in 1958 and 1961, respectively; and they had government funds to provide posts for thousands of functionaries. For example, the UGFCC employed over 3,000 politically relevant functionaries like regional officers, district officers, marketing officers, depot officers, and secretary receivers.[32]

The manner of establishing the paraparty tributaries was, moreover, positively harmful to the modernization process at the grassroots. In particular, the monopoly given paraparty agencies undercut existing voluntary associations in local society and discouraged their further growth. At the time the UGFCC obtained a monopoly over cocoa marketing in 1960–61, independent marketing cooperatives such as the Ghana Cooperative Marketing Association and the Ashanti-Brong-Ahafo and Sefwi Cooperative Organization were responsible for marketing thirty percent of Ghana's cocoa.[33] After 1961 these and many other independent organizations were dismantled, bringing to near standstill one of Africa's richest experiences in the development of voluntary associations.[34]

Moreover, the central government did not impose effective accountability on the monopolistic position of the paraparty organizations at the grassroots. This left the localities helpless in face of the corruption and malfunction that often characterized the activities of the paraparty agencies. For example, an audit inquiry disclosed the illegal sale in 1965 by a field official of the UGFCC of 1,856 cartons of gammalin (meant for distribution to farmers) valued at G£ 7,424.[35] Another inquiry into the same paraparty agency remarked that "farmers often referred to the opulence of (UGFCC) Secretary Receiver."

It was alleged that these officers who earned £G 180 per annum owned cars, trucks, buildings, etc., and often supported as many as three wives. We saw some Secretary Receivers owning Mercedes Benz cars, Peugeots cars, and

32. See Ghana, *Report of the Committee of Enquiry on the Local Purchasing of Cocoa* (Accra: Government Printer, 1967), p. 137.

33. Ibid., p. 6.

34. Cf. David Brokensha, *Social Change at Larteh, Ghana* (Oxford: Oxford University Press, 1966), pp. 69–79. See also Immanuel Wallerstein, *The Road to Independence: Ghana and the Ivory Coast* (The Hague: Mouton, 1964).

35. Ghana, *Special Audit Investigation Into the Accounts of the United Ghana Farmers Council Cooperatives* (Accra: Auditor-General, 1966), p. 28.

transport trucks. . . . Farmers, particularly in the Ashanti Region complained about levies of from £G 50 to £G 100 demanded from them by some senior members of the Council including Opanyin Kwame Poku, National President . . . before agreeing to establish societies in their villages. . . . Opanyin Kwame Poku . . . was alleged to have demanded £G 40 and a sheep before officially opening any of the many new sheds of the Council.[36]

Such behavior on the part of functionaries in paraparty agencies had a predictable effect on the local populace: it demoralized large segments of the masses and spawned alienation, thus distorting the popular drive for modernity. For example, anthropologist informants reported a growth in local areas in the 1960s of witch-finding cults and other neotraditional religious activities, which invariably entailed major demands on peasants' and workers' incomes.[37] The smuggling of cocoa into Francophone African states was another popular reaction to alienation. This began in earnest in 1964, and though figures of cocoa smuggling are not available for the last years of the Nkrumah regime, figures for 1966, the first year of the military regime, are twenty percent of the cocoa crop, valued around G£ 12 million.

Thus, the expansion of the local organization of the CPP in the years 1958–65 was a response to leadership tension at the center of the regime, not to popular desires for greater participation. Not only did the new party and paraparty structures not extend effective participation to the grassroots, but these structures positively harmed the modernizing potential of the grassroots and thus the capacity to institutionalize political order. Paraparty agencies like the TUC, UGFCC, and the Young Pioneers (formed in 1961 with a monopoly over youth organizations) were particularly detrimental in this regard. And so were party organizations proper, whose expansion in the years 1961–65 was also a response to leadership tension at the center.[38] Local party officials at all levels (village, town, district, and region) were widely corrupt; one regional official spent G£ 3,000 of party funds to cover personal debts.[39] The interference of district and regional party officials into the work of local councils often distorted their operations; and the allies of the CPP in many local councils

36. *Report of the Committee of Enquiry on the Local Purchasing of Cocoa*, p. 20.

37. For earlier instances, see H. deBrunner, *Witchcraft in Ghana* (Kumasi: Presbyterian Book Depot, 1959), pp. 163–71.

38. Cf. David Apter, "Ghana," in James S. Coleman and Carl Rosberg, Jr., eds., *Political Parties and National Integration in Tropical Africa* (Berkeley: University of California Press, 1964).

39. Ghana, *Convention People's Party: Report of Special Audit Investigation* (Accra: Auditor-General, 1967).

often played havoc with local government finances.[40] Popular alienation from politics, entailing the spread of cynicism and demoralization among the masses, was the outcome of the CPP regime's behavior at the grass-roots. It was a most perplexing legacy to the military regime that came to power in February 1966 and to the civilian government of several years later, neither of which found a political formula conducive to the institutionalization of political order in local Ghanaian society. Indeed, the new civilian regime under Dr. Kofi Busia is, alas, repeating the policy of the Nkrumah regime of relying on traditional rulers at times of structural crisis. Karl Marx once remarked that history repeats itself only twice, first as tragedy, second as farce; this is not an exaggerated characterization of the Busia government's policy of placing traditional rulers in a strong articulating and aggregating position in local councils while doing little to clarify functionally the boundary between the sacred and secular constituents of politics in the polity. *Plus ça change, plus c'est la même chose.*

## CONCLUSION: A THEORETICAL SUMMARY

No case study can ever really prove anything general. But with the aid of theoretical analysis of the "middle range," a case study might generate more general principles of description and analysis. This is what I have sought to do.

I first defined local politics in Ghana as a problem of the creation of political order, by which I mean the establishment of political institutions and relationships that are stable and capable of mediating conflicting or competing interests in a manner that does not impede the modernization role of other social relations, especially economic relations. I then proffered a theoretical analysis of the barriers to the institutionalization of political order at the grassroots of Ghanaian politics and between the center and periphery of the system.

I employed a minimal conception of the boundary problem in emergent political systems—namely, the poor delineation of and distinction between

40. For example, an audit of the Kumasi City Council, whose revenue was G£ 1,749,771 in 1964, shows that it executed 20 contracts in 1964 worth G£ 37,231 without requesting tenders, as required by law; purchased 5,000 bags of cement from a private firm at cost per bag much greater than if it had purchased from the government's Ghana National Trading Corporation; issued advances to staff for personal consumption totalling G£ 33,907 (the figure was G£ 82,245 in preceding year); and expended G£ 29,132 on beautifying the private home of the council's chairman. Ghana, *Annual Audit Report on the Accounts of the Kumasi City Council for the Year Ended 31st December, 1964* (Accra: Auditor-General, 1965).

the secular and sacred constituents of political choice and action. This concept was applied to the conflict between the CPP government and the Ashanti National Liberation Movement in the mid-1950s in order to illustrate the mechanics of the problem of institutionalizing political order in Ghanaian local politics. I later elaborated the dialectics of the institutionalization crisis, conceived as a boundary problem, in a description of the dispute between the CPP government and traditional forces in Akim Abuakwa in the late 1950s.

In accounting for the overall pattern of structural change in local government in the 1950s and the 1960s, I took for granted that the unresolved boundary problem distorts all efforts at structural change in emergent polities. I therefore based my analysis on the empirical fact of gross opportunism in the political choice of the CPP regime, and on a conception of African political behavior in the context of structural crises which assumes an atavistic inclination to resort to primordial political props (e.g., chiefs).

But the connection between the boundary problem and political opportunism is apparent: failure to distinguish functionally between the secular and sacred constituents of politics lends a certain laxity to political behavior. For the process through which political actors and institutions arrive at a functional delineation of the secular and sacred constituents of political action is, willy-nilly, a disciplinary experience: it endows political actors with a certain rigor of perception and thus of choice.[41]

In this situation, political choices that fail are seen and related to as failures: seldom is an effort made to turn patent failure by ideological sleight of hand, as it were, into apparent gain or victory. To do so is to confuse illusion with reality; and, of course, it is precisely this penchant for a politics of illusion, so widespread in emergent polities in Africa and Asia, that lends an additional distinction to our conceptual understanding of a modern and emergent polity. The politics of illusion is certainly not unknown to modern polities; but there are always major political actors who recognize it for what it is, and through such recognition can work for the ascendancy of political realism. Until this situation obtains, to one degree or other, in emergent African polities in general and Ghana in particular—and there is alas no blueprint for bringing it about—these polities will never be modern.

41. Cf. Max Weber, *The Protestant Ethic and the Spirit of Capitalism* (London: G. Allen and Unwin, 1930).

# 6

# ATTEMPTS TO CHANGE THE MARRIAGE LAWS IN GHANA AND THE IVORY COAST

## Dorothy Dee Vellenga

One of the more fascinating by-products of the rapid changes occurring in African states is the intensified public debate on the relations between the sexes. Political independence added a new dimension to the debate. At one level, it prompted a gracious Kenyan minister to remark in Parliament that "our women in Kenya today look more beautiful and well-dressed than they were before independence."[1] But in a more fundamental sense, independence put African governments in the position of being bombarded by various groups seeking a revamping of marriage laws and, in general, led to more governmental action in matters affecting the family. A casual perusal of Ghanaian newspapers before and after independence shows a shift in orientation from the preindependence emphasis on the roles of the traditional state councils and the churches in regulating family matters to the new postindependence demands on party and Parliament.

Governmental and party leaders, also, regardless of their ideological leanings, seemed to accept the need for taking some initiative on these matters. Examples can be cited referring to the two nations being compared here. Thompson mentions that at the 1959 conference of the PDCI, the emancipation of women and the abolition of the "matriarchial system" were discussed along with "the future of the Franco-African Community and Africanization of the Civil Service."[2] In Ghana, the Programme of the CPP for Work and Happiness published in 1962 included a section

---

1. Ronald Ngala, Kenya's minister of cooperatives and social services, as quoted by Ali Mazrui, "Miniskirts and Political Puritanism," *Africa Report*, vol. 13, no. 7 (Oct. 1968).
2. Virginia Thompson, "The Ivory Coast," in G. Carter, ed., *African One-Party States* (Ithaca, N.Y.: Cornell University Press, 1962), p. 278.

125

on marriage and a statement on the responsibility of the state in these
matters.[3]

The process which translates such concerns from rhetoric and debate
to governmental action affecting behavioral patterns and vice versa is a
process for which it is difficult to find well-worked-out sociological models.
One of the problems in tackling this is that on a subject as intimate as
sex and the family, the opinions that people express in private may take
on a different guise in public where more steretoyped, dogmatic views
are aired. Bott has pointed out this contrast in her intensive study of
twenty London families. In comparing their private views with those that
emerged during some public group discussions, she mentions that in
public "One frequently expressed view was that the family as an institution
was less stable and secure than it had been in the 19th century and
needed moral strengthening and support. This contrasted markedly with
the research families, nearly all of whom said they thought the modern
family was better than the Victorian family."[4]

Another problem is the extent to which people see the state as having
legitimate and moral authority to deal directly with such problems. The
whole question of the legitimacy of the state is, of course, a serious one
for new nations, but its role in marital matters can also arouse considerable debate in countries with longer traditions of nationhood.[5] Associated
with this is the extent to which a government can actually muster the
machinery to enforce its edicts. Zolberg refers to these problems in speaking of the role of the party-states of West Africa in attempting to affect
the "sphere of norms and regulations relating to personal status." He
observes that "the regime is concerned with extending its authority in
this direction by making laws that will affect these activities, but of course
there is a vast difference between the staking of a claim to do so and the
genuine operation of allocative authority."[6]

Despite these difficulties, it is a useful exercise to look at the nature of
the public debate on such topics as the status of women and the reform
of marriage, divorce, and inheritance laws and to trace the response and

---

3. *Programme of the Convention Peoples' Party for Work and Happiness* (Accra:
Government Printing Office, 1962).

4. Elizabeth Bott, *Family and Social Network: Roles, Norms and External Relationships in Ordinary Urban Families* (London: Tavistock Publications, 1957), p. 28.

5. See, for example, the discussion in the United States surrounding the Moynihan
Report as chronicled by Lee Rainwater and William Yancey, *The Moynihan Report
and the Politics of Controversy* (Cambridge, Mass.: M.I.T. Press, 1967).

6. Aristide Zolberg, *Creating Political Order: The Party States of West Africa*
(Chicago: Rand McNally, 1966), pp. 132–33.

actions of the government to groups advocating such reforms. It is also possible to obtain some measure, albeit a limited one, of the effectiveness of the government in these areas by examining local court records and the records of administrative agencies associated with such reforms.

If one considers the passing of national laws as an example of one phase of the process of translating debate into action, both Ghana and the Ivory Coast provide interesting case studies. A marriage, divorce, and inheritance bill was debated in Ghana for two years (1961–63) without being passed. After two more years of discussion and modification the Maintenance of Children Bill was made law in 1965. In the Ivory Coast a new Civil Code was passed by the National Assembly in October 1964 after about four years of preparatory activities. This code covered many of the same areas debated in Ghana—the definition and conditions of marriage, the grounds for and procedures for divorce, the custody of children and provisions for inheritance.

It may be assumed that many of the problems faced by the two countries are similar regarding contemporary changes in the lineage systems which characterized the traditional family patterns. Both countries have been engaged in a cash-crop economy for decades with its attendant effects on the lineage system as a land-owning entity.[7] Both societies might have been expected to have experienced somewhat similar restrictions on the ability of lineage heads to arrange the marriages of their members and to provide access to the fruits of an emerging status structure based more on education and occupation than ritual rank and inherited status. Although the assumption of similarity needs to be tested, it seems to emphasize that some other explanation must be sought in the different responses of Ivory Coast and Ghana to similar problems arising from changes in a family system based on lineage organization.

One tentative suggestion of the present chapter is that although Ivory Coast has succeeded and Ghana failed to pass a comprehensive Civil Code with a marked Western orientation, the latter country has developed more intermediary structures combining traditional and "modern" aspects which over the years have had more of an "evolutionary" effect on family organization. For example, in Ghana, the sessions of the local Presbyterian churches have adopted methods for settling marital and family disputes which are somewhat similar to those of traditional courts. The Department of Social Welfare in its administration of the Maintenance of Children

7. The adaptability of a lineage to such an impact should not be underestimated, however. See Polly Hill, *Migrant Cocoa Farmers of Southern Ghana* (Cambridge: Cambridge University Press, 1963).

Act has set up Conciliation Committees which function in similar fashion to traditional methods of arbitration. Further, the local courts themselves have retained some traditional characteristics. The outcome of decisions made in such settings may differ from those of a traditional chief's tribunal, but the methods are familiar ones to the participants. It was the representatives of some of these "intermediary groupings" such as the churches and some legal groups who were able to organize to stop the passing of the marriage, divorce, and inheritance bill in 1963.

Whether such piecemeal progress actually has more effect on patterns of behavior than a radical upheaval is a fundamental problem for theorists as well as policy makers. Myrdal states this problem succinctly in his *Asian Drama* regarding the comparative merits of a gradual transitional change in values as opposed to an abrupt "conversion" type of resocialization:

> One fundamental question then becomes whether it is more difficult to cause a big and rapid change . . . than a small and gradual one. This is, in another and more appropriate sense, the problem of revolution versus evolution, posed as a policy choice. Through our study we have grown more and more convinced of the realism of the hypothesis that *often it is not more difficult, but easier, to cause a big change rapidly than a small change gradually.*[8]

It is difficult to say where Ivory Coast stands in comparison to Ghana on this scale. One writer has suggested that "circumstances peculiar to Ivory Coast and to its conquest have made France's policy more inimical there to the survival of native institutions than elsewhere in the Federation [of French West Africa]."[9] A comparison has been made between French and British colonial practice at the local level regarding the administration of customary law. Phillips states that:

> The distinction between *tribunaux indigènes* (in the French sense) and the purely African "native courts" is of great importance in connection with the enforcement of legislative measures of reform which involve the overriding of indigenous law and custom—the former system being obviously more effective for this purpose.[10]

He elaborates on this in another article.

8. Gunnar Myrdal, *Asian Drama, An Inquiry into the Poverty of Nations* (New York: Pantheon, 1968), p. 115.

9. Virginia Thompson and Richard Adloff, *French West Africa* (London: George Allen and Unwin, 1958), p. 119.

10. A. Phillips, *Survey of African Marriage and Family Life*, International African Institute (London: Oxford University Press, 1953), p. 189.

The fact that the courts exercising jurisdiction in proceedings arising out of customary marriages are conducted by administrative officers enable a much closer control to be maintained over such matters than is usual in the British territories.[11]

Other writers, however, have suggested that there was not that much difference between the two policies and that the attempts of French authorities to modify customary law were almost uniformly ineffectual.[12]

These views cannot be systematically examined since the present writer's field work has been initially confined to Ghana.[13] However, we shall attempt to contrast the Ghanaian materials with secondary sources from the Ivory Coast in an attempt to develop a more adequate comparative perspective.

## GHANA: THE HISTORICAL BACKGROUND

It is, of course, not sufficient to confine an analysis to the postindependence period. We must look first at some of the areas where the sharpest conflicts developed between traditional concepts of the family and the notions introduced by the missions and colonial authorities. Marriage seems to have been a particularly vexing problem, and this is the area which will have to be examined in some detail. To quote Sarbah, "The customary law relating to marriage is very simple, but by some inexplicable process it is a stumbling block to the foreigner."[14] To demonstrate some of this confusion, the Akan will be used as an example of a traditional society. They are the largest ethnic group in Ghana and also constitute a sizable minority in the Ivory Coast. Although the term "Akan" covers a number of subgroups, they have certain cultural patterns in common: namely, matrilineal inheritance to property and office and a hierarchial state structure. The following discussion is not intended to be representative but illustrative. The mission group to be considered is the Basel Mission—later the Presbyterian Mission—which had its greatest impact in some of the Akan areas in Ghana.

Among the Ashanti, Rattray commented on the comparative lack of ritual in marriage. He felt that "the Ashanti looks on marriage as being

11. A. Phillips, "Recent French Legislation Concerning African Marriage," *Africa* 22 (1952) :69.

12. Cf. chapter 7 in this volume.

13. The field work was sponsored by grants from the American Association of University Women and the African Women's Program of the United Methodist Church.

14. John Mensah Sarbah, *Fanti Customary Law* (London: William Clowes and Sons, 1904), p. 41.

only the natural consequence" of birth and puberty rites—both of which were surrounded by more ceremony.[15] There were, however, definite rights and obligations associated with marriage. Fortes stresses that the conjugal relationship is "envisaged as a bundle of separable rights and duties rather than as a unit of all-or-none ties."[16] Some of these rights and duties are set forth by de Graft Johnson.[17] The wife had rights to maintenance for herself and children, to care during her illnesses, and to sexual satisfaction. The husband had to obtain her consent if he wished to take a second wife, and he had to treat all his wives equally. The husband had legal paternity to all the children born of the marriage and had the right to the sole enjoyment of his wife as a sexual partner. If she committed adultery, he could sue for compensation from the adulterer and claim paternity of any child conceived in adultery. The wife was bound to perform certain domestic and economic duties, but the husband could neither restrict her liberty or arbitrarily decide the place of conjugal residence. He had no rights over her property.

The procedure establishing such rights and duties involved an agreement between families and a series of presentations of drinks and money to the girl's family by the boy's family. This was usually done after a boy had expressed interest in a particular girl. This process would be spread over a period of time because it involved investigations by both families into the background of the other and discussions within the family on the advisability of the alliance. In the area in which I was conducting field work, the series of payments were divided roughly into two, both given by the boy's family. The first involved an introductory fee or drink and an engagement fee which was again divided into several portions and distributed among the girl's family. This was considered as binding on the couple: they had committed themselves to the marriage. The second payment, involving what the Ghanaians refer to in English as dowry, could be paid at the time of engagement or later and apparently put the final seal on the marriage.

Traditionally, there were variations on this form of marriage. In the form which was known as *asiwa* a man might ask for the daughter of a close friend while the girl was still a child. Over the years he would give

15. R. S. Rattray, *Religion and Art in Ashanti* (London: Oxford University Press, 1927), p. 76.

16. M. Fortes, "Kinship and Marriage among the Ashanti" in Radcliffe-Brown and Forde, eds., *African Systems of Kinship and Marriage* (London: Oxford University Press, 1950), p. 280.

17. E. V. C. de Graft Johnson, "Marriage Laws of the Akan of the Gold Coast" (Ph.D. dissertation, University of Leeds, 1954).

gifts to the family and after her puberty ceremony, would take her as a wife.[18] In other cases where a father would arrange a marriage for his son with the daughter of a close friend or in cross-cousin marriage, which was considered preferential among the Akan, the marriage payments might be minimal or dispensed with.[19] Concubinage was also a recognized state. Here gifts might also be given, but one test of the nature of the relationship was whether the gifts had gone directly to the woman or through her family. A gift given to the woman herself as a token of love was termed *apede*.[20] Regardless of the amount exchanged, if the family did not consider the couple as being married, then it was not a valid marriage according to customary law; conversely, even if only a token amount was given, but the families recognized the marriage, it was deemed valid. Brokensha in referring to marriage in Larteh, Ghana, remarks that:[21]

Many aspects of marriage are not governed by rigid principles, but rather by elastic rules of expediency, where in each case a number of variables must be considered. There are no absolute rules which can be applied to all situations, and sometimes the rules may conflict with each other: they justify rather than regulate conduct, although they do provide a wide general framework of permissible actions.

It appears that one of the effects of the missions was to attempt to telescope these various forms of marriage and their consequences into a single system applicable to all members of the new Christian community. If one takes the Basel Mission in Ghana as an example, its attempts to create new communities governed by rules of their own provide an interesting study of the problems encountered in attempting to codify customary family law. The colonial administrators were less concerned with the matter and generally tried to avoid the issue except when forced to make decisions by frustrated district commissioners, chiefs, or zealous

18. In the course of my research it became clear that this type was one of the first to be discarded and is rarely, if ever, practiced now since most girls when they come of age refuse such a marriage, and the family is obliged to pay back all the gifts previously given.

19. E. V. C. de Graft Johnson, "Marriage Laws," p. 64.

20. One court case which I encountered revolved around whether such a gift made in the presence of the girl's mother amounted to a marriage payment which could be recovered upon divorce. The woman claimed it was *apede*, whereas the man claimed it was part of the marriage payment. The court upheld his claim. (Akwapim Court, 1930.)

21. David Brokensha, *Social Change at Larteh, Ghana* (Oxford: Clarendon Press, 1966), p. 221.

missionaries. It was, however, the missions who first came into direct conflict with the traditional authorities over these matters.

While it is easy to denigrate the influence of the missions on an issue such as polygyny, their importance in creating a new status of persons cannot be denied. This had consequences which often ran counter to what they were attempting to do. One of the more interesting encounters between mission and traditional authorities was over the issue of *ayefare*, the compensation or satisfaction paid by the offender to a husband when his wife had committed adultery. This fee was set according to the status of the aggrieved husband and again illustrates the importance of a traditional tribunal looking at each case individually rather than having a set penalty. The flexibility here was rather limited, however, in that there were agreed amounts depending on the man's place in traditional society. Rattray mentions that "a table of damages, if correct, would give us a valuable if indirect method of arriving at a correct table of precedence in the Ashanti Court in ancient times. . . ."[22] The table shown in Danquah's book on Akan laws and customs lists twenty-eight statuses in Akim Abuakwa for which a fee in gold and sheep was stated.[23] In 1928, the fees varied from £ 3.12.0 for an ordinary citizen to £ 16 for *amantoo-mmiensa-adikrofo* [the chiefs of the Council of Three Counties]. If the husband was not from Akim-Abuakwa but from another state, the fee was £ 2.8.0. In former times, the death penalty was imposed for an adulterer who had seduced the wife of a paramount chief. It was felt that there was no way of satisfying a chief; one could only attempt to "pacify" him by spilling blood, now achieved through the slaughter of many sheep. As another State Council put it, "when a Chief's wife is committed, there is no fixed satisfaction in law and the amount that arbitrators would fix for the adulterer to pay is termed a pacification, for the adulterer is deemed to be incapable of satisfying a chief."[24] Here it is evident that adultery at the chiefly level of society is considered a crime with religious implications— an offense against the ancestors—whereas at the level of a commoner it is less reprehensible. The closeness to the ancestors seems to be the differentiating factor.

Danquah regards *ayefare* as "an institution of no little importance." Indeed, if one reads some of the early histories of the southern Gold

22. Rattray, *Religion and Art*, p. 86.
23. J. B. Danquah, *Akan Laws and Customs and the Akim Abuakwa Constitution* (London: George Routledge and Sons, 1928).
24. Secretary for Native Affairs, file no. 1383/31, "Native Customary Law Relating to Marriage in Akyem Bosome Division" (23 December 1930).

Coast written by Africans, one can see its significance at a state level in the eighteenth and nineteenth centuries.[25] Many of the wars which broke out between states had as their overt justification an offense against a chief's wife. The symbolic importance of this institution of *ayefare* in the status structure of traditional society was largely ignored by the colonial authorities. Danquah writing in the late 1920s felt that "such an offense as criminal intercourse with a Chief's wife" had as yet "received no adequate notice in the regulations made by the British Government for the jurisdiction of our chiefs."[26]

The obvious abuses which could accompany such an institution were what most impressed the Basel missionaries. In their attempt to set new standards for the Christians, they tried at first to make the fee as high as possible. Noel Smith mentions that the Twi Synod in 1909 set it at £ 15 for Christians.[27] One can imagine the havoc this must have caused if a commoner, on becoming a Christian, had his adultery fee almost quintupled to a level higher than that paid by most traditional state officials. In the Akim-Abuakwa schedule of fees quoted by Danquah in 1928, the only new status which had been added to the traditional ones was that of "Volunteers from the Gold Coast Regiment." Apparently these recruits were looked upon as having done a service for the state and "as a mark of appreciation for such valuable service the Okyeman Council distinguished them from their other noncombatant brethren by raising their ayefare fee from £ 3-12-0 to £ 7."[28] The Basel Mission eventually settled on £ 5 as a fee for its members. This was still higher than that paid by a commoner and was rejected by most of the traditional courts. An attempt was made by the churches, however, to keep such cases within the jurisdiction of the church. In one case recorded in the minutes of a local Presbyterian church session, a member had first taken his case to the chief's tribunal, and it was later put before the church presbyters. He received his fee of £ 5 from the adulterer but was fined 10s. for "sending a congregational case to the Tribunal."[29] This is just one example of how the churches sought to create an alternative code for Christians which set them apart from their non-Christian brethren.

25. See, for example, Carl Reindorf, *The History of the Gold Coast and Asante* (Basel, 1895) and E. Samson, *A Short History of Akuapem and Akropong* (Accra, 1908).
26. Danquah, *Akan Laws*, p. 90.
27. Noel Smith, *The Presbyterian Church of Ghana, 1835–1960* (Accra: Ghana Universities Press, 1966), p. 97.
28. Danquah, *Akan Laws*, p. 178.
29. Presbyterian Session Records, January 1940.

The involvement of the church session in hearing such cases was looked upon with uneasiness by both traditional authorities and colonial administrators. One DC in 1930 wrote a memo to the provincial commissioner concerning such "ecclesiastical" courts in the Akwapim area and expressed the fear that the practice "may seriously undermine Government's policy of rule through the chiefs."[30] The mission heads also disparaged the practice but could do little to control it. The assumption by the churches of judicial powers was one of the bones of contention expressed by Nana Ofori Atta I in his famous memorandum to the Presbyterian Synod in 1941. Among other complaints, he stated that:

> We do not wish to guess the reason for your Church prescribing the amount of *ayefare* or adultery fee payable between members of your church which is in excess of the amount the native customary law recognises. What the basis of your calculation is, I do not profess to know; but it does not seem to us anything befitting the sacred or holy moral principles for which the Church stands. In these circumstances, we would respectfully suggest for consideration that the recognised medium of remedy obtainable at the Divorce Court or Tribunal, as the case may be, be left alone. It would be a case of rendering unto Caesar the things which are Caesar's—a secular custom with a secular remedy.[31]

The same process of giving the Christian a new status in society could also be seen in terms of marriage and divorce procedure and provisions for inheritance. However quasi-legal the methods of the church might be, the missionaries had, from the beginning, felt the need for some kind of governmental backing and put pressure on the colonial administration to enact a Marriage Ordinance covering these matters. This was to protect Christians who desired to enter into a binding monogamous form of marriage, but it would not at the same time outlaw customary marriage. According to Dr. Ekow Daniels the colonial authorities were initially reluctant to enact such an ordinance. He says that "the Colonial Administration of the Gold Coast at first took the view that the marriage laws and family life of Ghana should not be disturbed or brought into line with modern developments."[32] A select committee of the British House of Commons had recommended in 1865 that nothing should be done to encourage the inhabitants to lean on British help. The courts in the Gold Coast held that

30. Secretary for Native Affairs, 1072, case no. 41/1930, "Ecclesiastical Courts."
31. Memorandum to the Synod of the Presbyterian Church of the Gold Coast by the State Council of Akyem Abuakwa (11 July 1941), p. 20.
32. Ekow Daniels, "Towards the Integration of the Laws Relating to Husband and Wife in Ghana" prepared for the Conference on Integration of Customary and Modern Legal System, at the Institute of African Studies, University of Ife, Ibadan, (24–29 August 1964), p. 35.

weddings celebrated in a church were subject to customary law until an 1884 decision that concerned a couple who had been married in a church and who had clearly intended (in the eyes of the judge) to contract a Christian monogamous marriage. The petitioner in this case wished a divorce on grounds of adultery and cruelty and was granted it on those grounds. In that same year, the Marriage Ordinance for Christians was passed. The provisions of this ordinance were so strict regarding inheritance and divorce that the missions later sought to modify it. In 1909 the Twi Synod of the Basel Mission sent a "Resolution to Facilitate Divorce" to the governor of the Gold Coast asking that the procedure for divorce be made less stringent and stated that "As polygamy is still customary in this colony and the step to monogamy costs rather much, people are always inclined to fall back again into their old state. As now the obtaining of a legal divorce is nearly impossible it will in many cases directly lead back into polygamy."[33] The ordinance was modified, but the present writer found that sixty years later, some people in the rural areas still believe that divorce under the ordinance is virtually impossible and that inheritance is governed entirely by British law (whereas after the changes one-third of an estate is allowed to devolve under customary law).

Although there was a time when the Basel Mission obliged its ministers and catechists to marry under the ordinance, even this requirement has been relaxed and the majority of Presbyterians now marry under customary law and then have the marriage blessed in the church, making an agreement to abide by church discipline.[34]

In this case also the ordinance created a situation in which Christians acquired a new status in the total society. This meant a corresponding increase in dowry. A study was done by a group of teachers in 1938 to analyze the expenses associated with thirty-four marriages. They listed forty-one items of expenditure for "A Teacher in one of the Coast Towns on his Marriage."[35] The cost of marriage under the ordinance was estimated at £ 156.1.0 and the cost under native custom at £ 68.19.0, both extremely expensive, but the ordinance being *more than double* that of the customary. Even without the ordinance, the difference between the dowry among

33. *Christian Messenger*, vol. 4, no. 1 (31 January 1909).

34. In a town in Akwapim where over 58 percent classified themselves as Christians, only 2 out of 396 married women had been married under the ordinance; 33 had been married in church and 346 by customary law. P. T. W. Baxter and D. Brokensha, eds., *Pilot Survey of Tutu*, Child Development Research Unit (Univ. of Ghana) occasional paper (September 1961).

35. *Marriage and Debt: The Report of a Discussion Group of The Teachers' Refresher Course* (Achimota: Achimota Press, 1938), p. 7.

Christians and non-Christians is marked. In one of the towns I investigated in Akwapim, the dowry for a Christian was estimated at being almost three times that of non-Christians. (The definition of Christian and non-Christian, however, often means educated vs. illiterate.)

Thus, what appear to be parallel systems of legal marriage in Ghana constitute in reality more of a hierarchy. In fact, one often hears people refer to "legal" marriage, meaning ordinance marriage as opposed to customary marriage. Women married under customary law express the desire to be a "wedded" wife or a "Mrs." (Under customary law marriage, the woman usually retains her own name and is referred to as Miss or Madam, although Christians may adopt Mrs.) There is much more security for the woman under an ordinance marriage. Divorce has to be effected through a court action rather than through a family council, and if her husband dies intestate, the wife is entitled to two-ninths of the estate. Under customary law, the husband's successor, who traditionally should have found a new husband for the widow, may now deprive her of any benefit from her husband's estate.

Furthermore, customary marriage is not recognized as marriage for certain important purposes. Until recently, for example, the Ministry of Education provided a gratuity for married teachers, but one had to be married under the ordinance to qualify. The Catholic Church does not recognize customary marriage for its members, considering it concubinage, but it is in the anomalous position of recognizing it as valid for non-Catholics.[36] So, to paraphrase Orwell, all marriages are legal, but some of them are more legal than others. As recently as 1959 an MP made the query in Parliament as to when the government would consider recognizing customary marriage in Ghana. Mr. Mate Johnson replied that "the Laws of Ghana already recognize customary marriage and I would refer the honorable member to the provisions of the Marriage Ordinance (Cap. 127)."[37]

## CONTEMPORARY SOCIAL PROBLEMS IN GHANA

In Ghana, people do not live in isolated sectors of the society—one traditional, another modern (if, indeed, they do anywhere)—but in increas-

36. Frans J. Verstraelen "Catholic Missionaries, Marriage and Family Life in Ghana: A Socio-Historical Study (1880–1960) with special reference to the Coastal Akan" (M.A. Thesis, Institute of African Studies, University of Ghana, Legon, June 1969).

37. Ghana, *Parliamentary Debates*, first series, vol. 16, series 1959–60 (20 July 1959), col. 722.

ingly interconnected spheres. One individual is confronted with a variety of behavioral patterns. An increase in one's resources does not necessarily mean a movement from one way of life to another but can often mean an attempt to expand one's choices to include all. A similar pattern probably prevails in the Ivory Coast. As Clignet observed in his study of plural marriages in the Ivory Coast, the findings "led us to suspect that urbanization and modernization do not necessarily change the values and norms of African individuals but increase their resources and enable them to multiply the choices that they can make with regard to styles of life."[38] Thus, individuals may be involved in several forms of marriage at once. This is strikingly illustrated by a test case which came before the Supreme Court in 1959. This concerned an Accra man who had three children under a customary marriage. This marriage was dissolved, and he married another woman under the ordinance. Of the issue of the second marriage only one child survived. While he was married under the ordinance, he cohabited with another woman and had ten children by her. After his wife died, he married the third woman (Shang) under customary law and had the marriage blessed in a Presbyterian church. The man died intestate, and the son of the ordinance marriage claimed that he was the only lawful child and was entitled to two-thirds of the estate, which goes to the family under the ordinance. In a lower court his claim was upheld, but the widow Shang appealed on behalf of the larger family to the Court of Appeals. This court, recognizing the customary marriage, determined that she was his legal widow and was thus entitled to two-ninths of the estate. The three children by his first marriage were legitimate children and thus entitled to share, with the son of the ordinance marriage, four-ninths of the estate. The ten children of the defendant (Shang) having been born when their father was still married under the ordinance were illegitimate and thus not entitled to a share in the four-ninths. The one-third of the estate which was left to be distributed under customary law, however, would devolve under the provision of the Osu community of Accra which is patrilineal and thus all three sets of children would share in this portion of the estate.[39]

Such choice of styles of marriage is obviously more open to men than to women. The double standard was implicit in the traditional Akan system in which *ayefare* combined with polygyny meant adultery for men and women was very differently defined. The ambiguity concerning the legality of customary marriage as compared to the ordinance enabled a man to

38. R. Clignet, and J. Sween, "Social Change and Type of Marriage," paper read at American Sociological Assn. (September 1968), p. 24.

39. *Ghana Law Reports* (Accra: General Legal Council, 1959), pp. 109–11.

begin the customary procedures, fail to complete them, and then escape the consequences. Children born of such a union would not be considered illegitimate but for all practical purposes were the concern of the mother. Women's claims for maintenance in a customary marriage, however, were and are supported by the local courts. Whereas in earlier times men would desire to establish the validity of a customary marriage in order to collect adultery fees, it is now primarily women who want the validity of the customary marriage imposed in order to be maintained. An interesting index of this shift is provided by Brokensha's analysis of the matrimonial cases which came before the local court at Larteh. A summary of his data is presented in table 1.[40]

TABLE 1
MATRIMONIAL CASES AT LARTEH

| Type of Case | 1913–15 | 1945–58 |
| --- | --- | --- |
| Maintenance | 3 | 49 |
| Seduction and adultery | 51 | 7 |
| Divorce | 3 | 22 |
| Other matrimonial | 23 | 28 |
| TOTAL | 80 | 106 |

This betokens the emergence of women as an organized force in Ghana. In 1953 the Federation of Ghana Women was formed.[41] It was the brain-child of Dr. Evelyn Amartefio who was its general secretary until its de-mise in 1960. The aim was to combine the various women's groups into a federated structure to give women a stronger voice. They undertook a number of philanthropic projects, but high on their list of priorities was an attempt to oblige the government and chiefs to "legalize customary marriage" and look into inheritance practices. It is noteworthy that their overt aim was not necessarily to abolish polygyny but to hold men respon-sible for their wives—all of them. Underlying this, no doubt, was the feel-ing that by so doing men would find "proper" polygyny too much of a burden, and genuine monogamy might emerge. The terminology they used—"to legalize customary marriage"—is also interesting, the impli-

40. My analysis of cases for the years 1930 and 1960 at Akropong, also in Akwapim, show the same trend (see appendix this chapter). The change in emphasis could also be affected by the change in the composition of the court. The early courts were presided over by chiefs and councillors, whereas the later ones were headed by a panel of three or, after 1958, by a single lay magistrate. The chiefs might well be expected to lay more emphasis on the collection of adultery fees.
41. The following information is taken from interviews, attendance at meetings held to revive the federation in 1969, and newspaper clippings from 1953–59.

cation being again that customary marriage was somewhat less than legal and needed state recognition to make it more binding.

One of the fruits of their effort was that in 1959 an Inheritance Commission was appointed to look into the customary provisions for inheritance to see how they might be modified. One aspect of this had been stressed by the federation—the need for some kind of protection for wives and children when the husband and father died. Although this problem was stressed particularly in regard to matrilineal inheritance, it could also arise under a patrilineal system, at least as far as the wife was concerned.

The Inheritance Commission was headed by Justice Nii Amaa Ollennu, an acknowledged authority on the customary law of inheritance in Ghana. There were also representatives from the protestant churches and the Catholic church as well as from the Federation of Ghana Women. After receiving memoranda and hearing reports on the inheritance practices of the different tribes in Ghana, the commission wrote their report. This was where the women's representative parted company with the rest of the commission and refused to sign the final report, apparently feeling that the recommendations to be made would not really protect wives sufficiently. The report was never published and is now virtually unavailable.

It was soon after this in 1960 that the federation was disbanded by the government and the National Council of Ghana Women took its place. Although the federation had insisted that it was nonpolitical, it was difficult in the atmosphere in Ghana at that time to maintain neutrality, and one leader observed that the federation had been accused by some of the CPP women activists of being UP oriented. The National Council of Ghana Women was formed as a political wing of the party. At this time, however, the CPP had not worked out any clear policy regarding family matters and ensuing events caught it somewhat off guard.

The next stage in the process was stimulated by a peculiarity of the Marriage Ordinance in Ghana. The penalties for plural marriage were not included in the ordinance itself but were part of the Criminal Code. Under this code, bigamy was committed if one contracted two marriages under the ordinance without an intervening divorce. This was punishable by seven years in prison. It was an offence but not bigamy if one married under the customary law and then married a different person under the ordinance without divorcing the first (punishable by five years in prison) or if married under the ordinance, one married a different person under customary law (punishable by two years in prison).[42] Considering this

42. "Matchet's Diary," *West Africa* 45, no. 2278 (28 January 1961) :95.

last provision, Allott states that "the restriction merely represents the attitude of Western or Westernized legislators or judges; and there appears to be practically no prosecutions under the Criminal Code for this sort of offence."[43] In February 1961 an attempt was made in Parliament to amend the Criminal Code so that these actions would constitute civil rather than criminal offences. Parliamentary discussions and statements in the press indicate that most people thought that the effect of this amendment was to completely outlaw polygyny. What the amendment would have done was to oblige people to follow one form of marriage completely—that is, either the customary form which could be polygynous or marriage under the ordinance. Violations of this would draw a maximum of three years imprisonment with or without a fine. All that the new amendment would have implied was that the penalty was uniform rather than five years for one offence and two for the other. However, since there was acceptance of evasions on the restrictions on contracting customary marriages after an ordinance marriage, the fact that the situation was being forced into the open may have contributed to the misunderstanding.

In the heated discussion that took place in Parliament, only one man came out in favor of monogamy, and he was a former Christian minister. Even the women MPs seemed worried about outlawing polygyny. One said that "The ratio is one man to nine women. Therefore, I see no reason why one man should be forced by law to marry only one woman. If that is done, the rest of our womenfolk will find it very difficult to get married with the result that many of them will become prostitutes."[44] This misperception about sex ratios resulting from misunderstanding of the census seemed widespread and the point also was raised by another woman MP.

The minister of justice, Ofori-Atta, closed the discussion in Parliament by explaining again what the amendment was supposed to cover and then went on to summarize what he thought the discussion had indicated about the feelings of the MPs concerning the confusion between the different types of marriage. He noted:

Now my impression from the points raised in this House is that the honorable members want one type of marriage . . . in short, marriage law should be so modernized as to suit our tradition and that foreign systems of marriage, namely having to marry one wife and one only should be done away with and that the Marriage Ordinance should be modified in such a way as to allow anyone in this country to marry one or more than one wife if he chooses. In the

43. A. Allot, *Essays in African Law* (London: Butterworth, 1960), p. 214.
44. Republic of Ghana, *Ghana Parliamentary Debates* 22, no. 4 (13 February 1961) :64.

circumstances, if we have to register marriages, it means if you have married more than one wife, you have to register them all.[45]

The position of the Convention Peoples Party on marriage was still not clear at this time. Around this time the party paper the *Evening News* did publish two articles "Polygamy or Monogamy—Which is Which?" The writer begins one of them with the following statement: "Of late, much has been talked and is being talked about the legalization of either monogamy or polygamy. At present the two forms of marriage are in vogue, but a section of the people thinks that the time is up for the Government to abolish polygamy and legalize monogamy alone."[46] This statement was at variance with the tenor of Parliamentary debates and suggests a potential source of conflict.

## THE PROCESS OF REFORM

The discussion aroused by the amendments to the Criminal Code helped expedite the formulation of proposed legislation in the Ministry of Justice, and in May 1961 a White Paper was published which set forth some proposals for a marriage, divorce, and inheritance bill. Comments were invited from everyone and suggestions were to be addressed to the Ministry of Local Government.

The White Paper, after some preliminary statements, suggests that the interpretation placed upon the new provisions in the Criminal Code of 1960 was unfortunate and continues,

. . . there is no indication at all under the law in the old Chapter 9 nor in the new Criminal Code to give the impression that polygamy is being abolished. But it has not been in vain. It has focussed attention on the subject and has provoked a vigorous discussion as to a formula whereby the essence of customary law marriage could be preserved and indeed blended into a marriage law for all citizens of Ghana instead of the present state of affairs in which two parallel systems of marriage law operate.[47]

The essence of the first section on marriage is that a man is to register one wife:

This would take the form of entering the name of that wife in the books of the Marriage Registry thus according public recognition to the wife so reg-

---

45. Ibid., p. 71.

46. S. K. Boateng, "Polygamy or Monogamy: Which is Which?" *Evening News* 3 (29 March 1961) :2.

47. Republic of Ghana, *White Paper on Marriage, Divorce and Inheritance* (Accra: Government Printing Office, 13 May 1961), p. 4.

istered. If a man registers a wife and marries or has issue with another woman this will not constitute an offence nor will the latter action constitute grounds for a divorce. If the man dies intestate, only the registered wife will be entitled to have a share of his property in accordance with the rules governing inheritance. Any other woman with whom a man has children will not be entitled to any inheritance under the law; but her children will be entitled in the same way as the children of a registered wife.[48]

A woman married under the ordinance would be considered a registered wife.

The provisions for divorce introduced in the White Paper would be modeled mainly after customary procedures in that, after petition for divorce by a husband or wife to any High Court judge, circuit judge, magistrate or Local Court magistrate, the official would appoint an ad hoc panel of four to arbitrate on the case. It was stated that the hope was that reconciliation would be the first aim and divorce would be the last resort.

Part III of the White Paper was concerned with inheritance. The different systems of patrilineal and matrilineal succession and the laws obtaining under the ordinance were mentioned. The White Paper stated that under the proposed law the surviving spouse (the registered wife or husband) would inherit one-third of the property and all the children of the deceased regardless of their mother's status would receive the remaining two-thirds of the estate. Estate here referred only to self-acquired or privately held property. None of the property would devolve under customary law where the deceased left both a spouse and children. If there were neither, then the parents would be next in line.

The reactions to the White Paper were confused. Party symposia were held by CPP study groups to discuss the proposals; houses of chiefs in various areas met and had the provisions of the White Paper presented to them; church leaders commented on it; the press published the results of interviews by roving reporters; leaders of women's organizations expressed their views.

In regard to the marriage provisions, some people saw them as favoring polygyny whereas others saw them as encouraging monogamy. What aroused much concern on the part of many women was that if such a law were enacted there would be no system under which a woman could contract a legally binding monogamous marriage since the ordinance would be superseded by this new law.[49] The secretary of the National Council of

---

48. Ibid.

49. This view was expressed forcefully to the National Council of Ghana Women by Justice Annie Jiagge ("Lecture to the Ghana Council of Women on the New Proposals on Marriage, Divorce and Inheritance," mimeo, n.d.).

Ghana Women expressed fears about the possible encouragement of polygyny implied in the bill and considered it:

> . . . an assault on Ghanaian womenhood. Men will be mischievous when polygamy is legalized and there would be no peace in homes . . . ; there should be a law making a man responsible for the proper upkeep of any child he has with any woman. This would discourage men who had children with many women but neither care for the children or their mothers. These are ruining the careers of many promising girls.[50]

Other women found the registration of only one wife distasteful. The fourth wife of a carpenter stated that she was "not so happy that only one woman should be registered. I suggest that none of us be registered at all. We all love our man equally and are all happy."[51]

A Ghanaian law student made the following comment:

> Since by implication a woman with whom a man is having children but who is unregistered can be registered by another man, it is clear that the only legally recognized marriage is the registered one. All other supposed marriages will not improve the status of the woman beyond that of girl friends. But the provisions of the Act do not adequately protect the registered wife. It is true that she alone is the wife and entitled to some interest in the husband's estate if he died intestate, but what about her rights as regards any intention on the part of the husband to bring his girl friends into the matrimonial home?[52]

A draft bill was published in May of 1962. The major change from the White Paper was that men were now allowed to register all their existing marriages within a certain time limit.

By 1962, however, the party had written up its "Draft Programme for Work and Happiness" in which the following statements were made:

> Our marriage laws are at present a mixture of our own indigenous forms and the system existing in advanced industrial nations which we inherited through colonialism. The new circumstances which have been created by a changing socio-economic pattern and the popularisation of education with its increasing movement of people from village to town and subsequent break-up of clan life, makes the polygamous system of marriage inappropriate. New forms of life are breaking up old loyalties. Moreover the Party stands for complete equality between the sexes and complete equality is, strictly speaking, incompatible with polygamy.

50. "What the People Say About the New Proposals," *Ghanaian Times* 4, no. 996 (19 May 1961), p. 3.

51. "Move to Protect Ghanaian Children Welcomed," *Evening News* 4, no. 1009 (3 June 1961) :1.

52. Obed Asamoah, "Proposed Legislation on Marriage, Divorce and Inheritance in Ghana," unpublished paper written for seminar in African Law, Columbia Law School (1962–63), p. 22.

The Party believes that there should be only one form of marriage and that is monogamy. It recognizes, however, that existing polygamous marriages will not disappear with the enforcement by law of monogamy. Hence there can be no legal or social discrimination against children in the form of illegitimacy which is completely alien to our African custom. The State's responsibility in the new social order will be to all children and not merely those from monogamous marriages.[53]

This statement of the party contrasted with the views of many of the MPs. This ambivalence is nicely illustrated by the conflicting statements of the party secretary of education in reacting to the White Paper. In the morning paper the *Ghanaian Times* of 6 June 1962 he is quoted as follows:

Whether we like it or not, polygamous marriage is widely practised in the country because of the predominance of our rural population over urban inhabitants. If a unified system is to be devised then the majority's practice should prevail. . . . If a future generation should think that monogamy was ideal and ought to be enforced, that would be the social conception of that time.[54]

In the evening paper *The Evening News* of that same day he denied the last part of the above statement and came out with a more "progressive" formulation.

Ghana's Socialist objective was equality of both sexes—one man, one woman . . . with the increase in equal educational facilities for both boys and girls and provision of full employment under the leadership of the dynamic C. P. P. coupled with an effective campaign explaining our socialist objectives on this matter, polygamy would disappear.[55]

The bill went through three versions, mostly involving changes in the way an estate should be divided and by June 1963 was ready to be introduced again. At this stage, however, there was a fully mobilized opposition to the bill. The Sarbah Society, a group of leading legal experts, drafted a memorandum criticizing its implications, and they were primarily concerned with the effect it might have on customary law regarding inheritance.[56] The churches also drafted last minute letters to the MPs asking them to drop the bill; one of their arguments being that it was too much opposed to customary law and that "while we believe

53. *Programme of the CPP*, p. 34–35.

54. "All Married Women Must be Registered—C. P. P. Study Group," *Ghanaian Times*, 4 (5 June 1961) :1.

55. "Secretary Denies Report," *Evening News* 3 (5 June 1961) :4.

56. Sarbah Society Memorandum on Marriage, Divorce and Inheritance Bill (mimeo, n.d.).

monogamy is better than polygamy, we also believe polygamy under
Ghana Customary Law is very much better than concubinage.[57]

It was on the receipt of the Sarbah Society memo that the minister of
justice moved in Parliament that the bill be deferred indefinitely and in
June 1963 the matter was dropped.

A Law Reform Committee continued to meet sporadically until the coup
in 1966. An attempt was made to draft two separate bills—one on marriage
and one on inheritance—but they were never placed before Parliament.
The NLC did not issue any decrees directly affecting marriage law, although under a decree calling for general revision of the laws of the country, some committees have been working on the project, particularly in
regard to divorce law. But nothing has been presented to the public, and the
mantle now falls on the new civilian government.

## REFORMS IN THE IVORY COAST

We can now look briefly at the provisions of the Ivorian Civil Code and
make some comparisons regarding the way in which the legislation was
handled in the two countries. The Ivorian Civil Code covers the following
areas: registration of family names, registration of birth, marriage and
death, conditions and procedures for marriage, divorce and separation,
provisions for the assignment of paternity to children born within and out
of wedlock, provisions for adoption, rules on succession and wills, and
finally transitional measures.[58] The latter specify a two year grace period
for most of the provisions. The "dowry" (bride wealth) was, however, to
be immediately abolished, although symbolic gifts could be voluntarily
exchanged. The penalty for imposing a dowry was to be a minimum of six
months' to two years' imprisonment and a fine.

The provision abolishing the dowry was probably most representative
of the radical break with tradition. Two stipulations on marriage, aside
from the abolition of the dowry, were particularly important. First, no
polygamous marriages were to be allowed in the future—all present ones,
however, would be recognized. Second, under the new code provisions are
made for husband and wife to share specific kinds of property in common,
although for existing polygymous marriages each spouse would hold property separately. The rules of succession intestate stipulate that, first of all,
all the children of the deceased inherit equally; if there are no children,

57. Presbyterian Church of Ghana, Mimeographed letter on Marriage, Divorce,
and Inheritance Bill (29 June 1963).
58. "Le Nouveau code civil," *Fraternité*, vol. 6, no. 286 (16 October 1964).

then by a complicated system of classification the property goes through four groups (including sisters and brothers and parents) before going to the remaining spouse.

In the Ivory Coast there appears to have been much more behind-the-scenes work before the legislation for the new code was actually introduced to the National Assembly. Reference is made in some sources to a three to four year campaign by the party beginning around 1961 to educate the masses to accept the new provisions.[59] In 1963 Philippe Yacé, president of the National Assembly and secretary-general of the PDCI, mentioned in his address opening the first ordinary session of the assembly that the bills regarding the provisions of a new Civil Code affecting dowry, inheritance, and so on were being taken from the Bureau politique of the party and the Ministry of Justice and being placed before the deputies in the National Assembly.[60] It was not until September 1964, however, that the bills were actually submitted to the assembly and passed. In the Ivory Coast, then, the party and the government, having taken the initiative from the beginning were not caught in the midst of the controversy as in Ghana.

The churches also played a different role in the two countries. The Catholic tradition of emphasizing social legislation is seen in the Ivorian situation. The Archbishop of Abidjan Mgr. Bernard Yago had headed an Anti-matriarchal Committee for a number of years and upon the passing of the Civil Code sent a congratulatory cable from the Vatican where he was attending the council.[61] In Ghana, however, the churches played a more negative part. After their experience with the difficulties arising from the Marriage Ordinances, one gets the impression that many felt that legislation was not an adequate answer. Furthermore, the relations between the party and the churches at the end of the Nkrumah era were hardly such as to encourage cooperative effort. In both countries, the virtual absence of organized Muslim participation in the debate is to be noted.

The press also reacted somewhat differently in the two countries. In Ghana there was a lively and vigorous debate, often revealing a lack of communication but always expressive. The long tradition of a "newspaper culture" in Ghana referred to by Zolberg may explain part of this.[62] The

59. See "In Ivory Coast, Respect for the Past, but Eyes on the Future," *Réalités ivoiriennes*, no. 64 (May 1967), p. 1.

60. "Le Discours du Président Philippe Yacé" *Abidjan-Matin*, no. 3546 (25 April 1963), p. 6.

61. "Appui sans réserve de la hiérarchie catholique," *Fraternité*, 6 no. 287 (23 October 1964), p. 3.

62. Zolberg, *Creating Political Order*.

Ghanaian papers had the equivalent of a "Dear Abby" column whereas the Ivory Coast press had a woman's page that was mostly educational—dealing with unsolicited advice on child care, nutrition, and so on. In Ghana roving reporters had interviews on the proposed legislation, and letters to the editor dealt freely with the topic. As unreliable as papers may be as indicators of political processes, the Ghanaian press, at least, gives an impression of at least some dialogue and debate whereas the Ivory Coast papers suggest a one-way, didactic approach. The Ivorian paper, *Fraternité*, did make one interesting slip, however. When Yacé introduced the new bills into the National Assembly, *Fraternité* in a burst of enthusiasm headlined this by saying "President Yacé announces a veritable social revolution."[63] After the code was passed, Houphouet-Boigny made clear that "concerning the realities of the Ivory Coast situation, it is an evolution that is operative and not a revolution."[64] In an extensive parenthetical note, the editor of *Fraternité* explained how they were using the phrases "social revolution" in the earlier headline. Thereafter, "evolution" was the term that was used.

## CONCLUSIONS

It will take far more investigation to determine which country has been more "revolutionary" in its approach. We might make some brief comparative comments on just one area—the position of women—since it was the women of Ghana who played a prominent role in the beginning of the post-independence moves. In Ivory Coast, they seem to have been less vocal as an organized force.

Although on the surface, the Ivorian Code seems to be a step forward for the women in the suppression of polygyny and the elimination of the dowry, a closer look suggests that in application, the code may not be so favorable. In the elaborate provisions it makes for the filiation of children born out of wedlock and adultery, the implications are that it provides for a form of polygyny similar to that existing in Ghana. The Ghanaian situation was taken into account in the provisions of the marriage, divorce and inheritance bill in which, although one wife was to be registered henceforth, all the man's children were to be recognized as legitimate. In Ghana the other women would have been second wives, whereas in Ivory Coast,

63. "Le Président Philippe Yacé annonce une véritable révolution sociale," *Fraternité* 6, no. 280 (4 September 1964), p. 5.
64. "Evolution normale et non révolution," *Fraternité* 6, no. 285 (9 October 1964), p. 1.

presumably, they are considered concubines or mistresses. One wonders, however, how much difference there would have been in practice. The "outside women" would seem to be at a similar disadvantage. If one considers that polygyny in one form or the other is going to persist in that part of Africa for some time, the more pragmatic concern of some Ghanaian women that men should be made responsible for *all* the women by whom they have children is as feminist in its way as the demand for genuine monogamy.[65] In one conference in Ghana, a woman speaker deplored the urban form of polygyny—the girl friend system—in which the man settles down with the recognized wife and tosses off an occasional few cedis to the girl friend who may have borne him several children.[66] The sympathy here is as much for the neglected girl friend as the betrayed wife.

In the provisions for inheritance, the Ivorian Code puts the wife at the bottom of the list of inheritors. This is a position which Ghanaian women would hardly have been expected to support where strengthening the position of a wife in matters of inheritance was one of the major aims for which they were fighting.

Finally, there is one more item which may be at the crux of the entire transition from a lineage system to a conjugal system of marriage. This concerns the provisions for common property between husband and wife. This is an item which I feel no Ghanaian legislator, man or woman, would touch. In Ghana (as it was expressed in one Supreme Court case),[67] very few husbands let their wives know their total income. This separation of incomes can, however, also benefit the wife who is free to control and invest her capital in her own way. Even some of the most militant women I interviewed are very ambivalent concerning this idea of a common budget. Some women attribute the continued viability of their marriages to the very fact that they have *not* pooled their resources. With the wife's and husband's relatives making differential demands regarding school fees for

65. This is not to say that monogamy is not the ideal. I have yet to meet a Ghanaian woman who is enthusiastic about polygyny; but there seems to be considerable cynicism about the possibility of any law being able to affect the practice directly—at least as long as most judges and magistrates are men.

66. Notes taken at the Home Science Association Conference, Univ. of Ghana, Legon (31 March to 2 April 1969). Cedis are the national currency.

67. The Judge said: "In this country the overwhelming majority of husbands both illiterate and educated (including salaried husbands) do not disclose their incomes to their wives and children. They do not make any specific periodic payments to their wives and children for their maintenance—they pay everything themselves—their own private outgoings, rent, the wives' dresses and other necessaries, food and drinks, children's school fees and clothing, etc." [Ghana Supreme Court, written judgements delivered during the period January-June 1963 (Civil), civil appeal no. 89/62 (10 April 1963)].

siblings, funeral contributions, and so on, one can easily see how a total community of property could create considerable difficulty. It has its links with all the other problems mentioned—inheritance, care of children outside the marriage, not to mention other wives. The churches have tried to lay emphasis on the importance of a common family budget, but have achieved little success. In a report from one church group which had gathered during Christian Home Week to discuss the topic of the common budget, the following discussion was recorded:

. . . various persons gave their views about this subject. While some contended that this practice is uncommon in Africa according to our various customs of inheritate [sic] others spoke in its favour. According to reports very few couples practice this common budget. This controversial subject brought Mr. A. to his feet as to how WILL conferring inheritage should be made by husbands before their death . . . the senior Presbyter urged the gathering to take the matter seriously and asked the Catechist to enquire from the Christian Council of Ghana whether the subjects according to the programme should be adopted by Christians or whether they are to be left at the discretion of Christians.[68]

It remains to be seen how many Ivorian couples will adhere strictly to the new provisions. If they do, this aspect of the law could well be the most revolutionary part of the entire attempt to impose a conjugal form of marriage on the mosaic of lineage patterns in the society. Whether it is a revolution that will benefit the wife is another question.

So the age-old battle continues. And in the question of the extent to which such problems can be tackled by the state, the new nations of Africa will provide us with a wide array of comparative examples.

## APPENDIX

A comparison of matrimonial cases coming before the Native Tribunal of the Omanhene of Akuapem (3 October 1930 to 23 October 1931) and the Akwapim Local Court (January 1960 to December 1960).

68. Christian Council file on reports from Christian Home Week, 1968, Committee on Christian Marriage and Family Life, Accra, Ghana.

| Nature of the Case | 1930–31 | 1960 |
|---|---|---|
| *Cases Arising outside of or prior to a Valid Marriage* | | |
| Seduction of an unmarried girl | 0 | 5 |
| Claim for return of money spent on pregnancy | 0 | 1 |
| Claim for maintenance for pregnancy | 0 | 4 |
| Breach of contract of marriage | 0 | 7 |
| Order for marriage to take place | 0 | 1 |
| Damages for slander against lover | 0 | 1 |
| TOTAL | 0 | 19 |
| | | |
| *Cases Arising within a Valid Marriage Excluding Divorce* | | |
| Claim for completion of marriage payments from daughter's husband | 1 | 0 |
| Claim for adultery fees or damages for seduction of wife | 12 | 2 |
| Claims against accomplices in seduction of wife | 4 | 0 |
| Claims for interference with wife but not to point of seduction | 2 | 0 |
| Claim against wife for living with another man without divorcing plaintiff | 1 | 0 |
| Claim for maintenance for wife and children | 0 | 11 |
| Incest | 0 | 1 |
| TOTAL | 20 | 14 |
| | | |
| *Suits for Divorce or Cases arising from Dissolution of Marriage* | | |
| Divorce | 1 | 5 |
| Claim for return of dowry | 5 | 2 |
| Claim for custody of children | 1 | 1 |
| Claim for recovery of property from spouse | 0 | 4 |
| Suit against resumption of marital relations with divorced spouse | 2 | 0 |
| Cancellation of divorce | 0 | 1 |
| TOTAL | 9 | 13 |
| | | |
| *Miscellaneous* | | |
| Claim for payment of an arbitration award or a court award in a matrimonial case | 3 | 1 |
| Damages for slander or interference arising from a dispute between a man and woman | 3 | 1 |
| TOTAL | 6 | 2 |
| TOTALS | 35 | 48 |

NOTE: All cases taken from the court record books for the time periods indicated.

# 7

# THE MODERNIZATION OF LAW IN AFRICA WITH PARTICULAR REFERENCE TO FAMILY LAW IN THE IVORY COAST

## Alain A. Levasseur

Do you know of any people who have created a totally new civil code that was drafted without attention to previous practices? . . . Never before has a people undertaken the dangerous venture of breaking away suddenly from all that had civilized them, and of remolding their entire existence. . . . In a virgin field one can mow down with indifference all that stands in the way. But when the land is cultivated, then it is necessary to pull out those parasitic plants which stifle the growth of the useful ones.[1]

Man's receptivity to everything that affects his senses and feelings depends upon a natural state which varies and evolves with his sociological, economic, political, and religious environment. Hence, the instruments and tools suitable for government of one society are not necessarily adequate for government of another. Law, which is the instrument of government par excellence, can contribute to the harmonious development of human government only if legislators remember that law is made for man, rather than man for law. A legal system which did not come to grips with social realities would fail in its function of carrying a society forward.

This is where Africa must prove its wisdom and determination. Whatever Africa, facing a modern world, is striving for, its success in achieving these goals is conditional upon the modernization of juridical institutions. In an emerging nation the political element of the law prevails over social traditions because the law is being placed in the service of a social revolution whose aims are the essential givens of the law. Faced with the necessity of modernizing juridical institutions at a time when Africa must sacrifice some of its deeply rooted traditions in order to meet technical demands, the governing elites have, in fact, a limited choice of strategies if they also take into consideration the social realities onto which the law is being grafted. The experiences of the continent's new states thus provide jurists with an ideal subject for reflection and patience.

1. From the speech delivered by Portalis to the French legislative body in presenting the Civil Code of 1804.

There are, in my opinion, two ways of bringing up-to-date the juridical institutions of a social group. The first possibility consists in making a drastic change in the foundations of the law by undermining the very basis upon which the society rests. Since many of the traditional African institutions such as brideprice and rules concerning contracts derive from the agricultural aspect of African societies, a change from an agricultural to an industrial type of society would eventually provide more suitable foundations for the creation of modern juridical institutions and ultimately lead to modifications in the legal system itself. But Africa cannot afford to wait, because time works against its efforts and its capabilities. Thus African countries have no choice but to elect the second way of modernizing their juridical institutions—namely, by superimposing a new legal system over the existing social structure. There are historical precedents for making this choice.[2] However, Africa does present a peculiarity which one must stress: where the French jurists commissioned by Napoleon drew largely from the traditional laws of southern and northern France, the codifiers at work in the new French-speaking African states are not inclined to borrow very much from their own ancestral and traditional law. They view this law as the reflection of a type of society, of family relationships, which they, together with political leaders, more generally, have condemned as incompatible with the creation of a modern society.[3]

Having chosen the second strategy, lawmakers are faced with a further dilemma: should they borrow a ready-made code or legal system from abroad, or should they create their own? Each method has its own costs and benefits. The main advantage of borrowing is the extreme simplicity of the method. There are once again historical precedents for the successful "export" of the French Civil Code, the B.G.B., or the Swiss Code.[4] However, African societies are so drastically different from the ones whose legal systems are available for borrowing that the question arises whether these laws, which were fashioned to rule and govern the particular society in which they were elaborated, will function in the same manner when transplanted to an alien culture. Or will the receiving society reject the transplant?

The problem may be put as follows. In the societies from which Africans are likely to borrow, the law presents itself as a tool in the hands of the

2. For example, the Code Napoleon or French Civil Code of 1804; the Code of Turkey of 1926.
3. See, for example, the statements made by President Habib Bourguiba. Speech delivered on 13 August 1965 for the "journée de la femme tunisienne".
4. However, no definite conclusion can be drawn because the importing countries—such as Japan, Greece, and Brazil—revealed different social and cultural conditions.

governing authorities to facilitate changes and adaptations in society; it is therefore the expression of a superior need for justice felt in the social body and made manifest by its jurists. In this way it escapes the charge of being solely the product of authority, thus gaining in prestige and dignity. By contrast, in an emerging nation the law is the instrument of a "policy" elaborated and defined outside its social context; it is an instrument, above all, for promoting social progress and for nation-building, with special concern with the following goals: to aid economic development by destroying those obstacles found in the field of private law;[5] to create and foster a sense of national entity so that each citizen can consider the law as being his creation; to fit meaningfully into the general framework of the laws of surrounding states. Under these differing conditions, the imported body of laws runs the risk of remaining a foreign body unable to fit the local social conditions and to enlist the sympathies and wills of the people in preserving *l'esprit de la loi*.

The alternative is to create their own code of laws. The costs and benefits of this second option are the reverse of the first. On balance, wisdom would appear to be on the side of the elaboration of a new body of laws made up of local traditional customs fecundated by the principles of modern law as learned from comparative foreign experiences and the acceptance, in some particularly touchy matters, of the principle that for a certain time the old rule and the new rule may have to coexist. But whichever option is chosen, it must be remembered that a legal rule, in order to be accepted, must be based upon the context of the society which it serves. This does not mean that it must coincide completely with the state of that society at the time of its elaboration since, if it did, it would soon be outdated because social evolution is a continuous process. A body of law, whether borrowed or created *de novo*, must anticipate this element of change and adaptability; but it must not be too far ahead of the society lest a gap be created between the letter of the law and the society it serves. In order to achieve this difficult equilibrium, the law reformer must lean heavily upon the sociologist.

Nowhere are the difficulties discussed so far more critical than in the field of family law. Because this sphere of law affects most intimately the entire population of a given country, because rules governing the family are closely related to religion and to the most valued aspects of culture, any intervention from above, especially if it is foreign-inspired, is regarded with suspicion. Yet, a high priority is usually attributed to reforms in this

---

5. Such as, for example, too broad a concept of the family or the traditional system of land tenure.

sphere because they are regarded as a sine qua non for the modernization of the law as a whole, as well as for modernization of the society more generally. How has the Ivory Coast performed so far? Is the family law that is being elaborated a wise, just, and workable combination of the past and the present? Although innovations are so recent that it is difficult to fully evaluate their effects, we can make a beginning toward the understanding of the critical process of legal reform by analyzing the first steps Ivorian leaders have taken along this path.

## THE IVORY COAST CIVIL CODE OF 1964

The elaboration of a national body of civil law for the Ivory Coast is a risky venture when one considers that some sixty languages are spoken in the country and that customs, including rules regarding the family, often differ greatly from one group to another.[6] For various reasons, the French had generally accepted this state of affairs and did not significantly interfere with diverse customs and traditions. They had allowed customary law to govern the law of persons among the local populations and had granted to customary tribunals the power to hear appropriate cases.[7] When the Ivory Coast received its full independence and became a sovereign state, however, the existence of so many local customary systems of law was perceived by the country's leaders as an obstacle to unity and to the exercise of new responsibilities. In particular, its economic development had reached such a high level compared to the general situation in former French Africa that Ivory Coast authorities felt obliged to acquire a body of laws designed to foster the transformation of social conditions in keeping with the requirements of economic growth. There is, behind this perceived necessity, an implicit acceptance of the notion that economic goals define which social patterns are most desirable.

The ten bills passed by the Ivorian National Assembly in the area of personal law in 1964 thus constitute a bold reform.[8] As the analysis below will indicate, the Ivory Coast has rejected, to a large extent, the idea that

6. There is a definite differentiation between the western part of the country (faithful to the brideprice system), the eastern part (where the matrilineal system prevails), and the northern part (strongly attached to polygyny).

7. See Alliot, "Les Résistances traditionnelles au droit moderne dans les Etats d'Afrique francophone et à Madagascar," in *Etudes de droit africain et de droit Malgache*, p. 235.

8. The bills were passed on 7 October 1964 and published in a special issue of the *Journal officiel de la République de la Côte d'Ivoire* (27 October 1964).

its contemporary legislation should reenact indigenous family laws. On the contrary, the new legislation is based on the European concept of the family, in keeping with Durkheim's theory whereby the matrimonial (conjugal) family represents the last and final step in the evolution of social structures. At first glance, the new laws could thus be viewed as a revolutionary instrument which must either succeed or fail in toto. However, in fact, the feeling of moderation, which is characteristic of the Ivory Coast leadership's approach to social modernization, pervades the new legislation as well. Having recognized that brutal social reactions might be provoked by a rigorous and unimaginative enforcement of the laws, the drafters have provided hardly any means whereby officials might be punished for nonenforcement of the new laws. Instead, they have anticipated that pressures for the enforcement of the new laws will stem from social and economic change.

These various themes are revealed in the statements by Ivory Coast officials concerning the purposes to be achieved by the new laws. Discussing the need to eradicate the commercial features of bridewealth, the minister of justice stated in October 1964, for example, that "the woman must give her own consent and the spouses must no longer impoverish themselves for the benefit of the parents. This is the price that has to be paid to ensure the social and economic development of the country."[9] Others have stressed the need to overcome a system of "disguised slavery," whereby women were "goods to be sold to the highest bidder."[10] Underlying this commitment to an improvement in the status of women is the belief that this is a prerequisite for further development.[11] The process of legal reform is also connected with the task of nation-building and of state-building. Intervention by national authorities in the sphere of the family is required in order "to erase the hundreds of customs that fasten regionalism and tribalism on our beautiful Ivorian land."[12] The state asserts its presence by becoming, through the public registrar, a necessary party to the formation of every new legal family. Finally, illustrating the spirit of moderation and compromise referred to above, officials also indicated that even while building a new family through law, the African family must be

9. Mr. Nanlo Bamba, "Le Président Houphouet-Boigny commente sur la grande réforme de la société ivoirienne," *Fraternité* (2 October 1964).

10. From an interview with an Ivorian citizen, Mr. Bertin N'Guessan (October 1964).

11. Mr. Gon Coulibaly, Ivorian representative. See *Fraternité* (9 October 1964).

12. Mr. Achy Jérome, Ivorian representative, in a speech to the assembly, October 1964.

preserved: "We must not destroy it under the pretext of evolution. . . . Nothing is eternal on this earth, everything evolves, and we seek not a revolution but an evolution . . . ."[13]

## FORMATION OF THE MATRIMONIAL FAMILY

In a manner similar to that prevailing in the days before the promulgation of the Code of Justinian, the lineage structure of Ivory Coast society and the predominant importance of the group had resulted in a marriage which was primarily a contract concluded between two lineages. This had as a consequence the fact that the family group was not only envisaged as a present fact, but also as continuing from the past into the future. The lineage was the fundamental unit of the Ivorian society within which the individual, as a juridical entity, was merged. Under the pressure of new economic forces, the lineage has increasingly ceased to be the basic unit. The ambitions and perspectives of the Ivorian leaders follow the modern tendency that seeks to transform the corporate lineage system into a society of a conjugal type. If the new law is in advance of its time, it follows, nevertheless, a pattern imposed by the natural evolution growing out of the importation of a modern type economy. From this standpoint the new family law of the Ivory Coast has introduced essential rules concerning the celebration of marriage, thereby giving a new outlook to the Ivorian family.

### The Ceremonial Aspect of Marriage

Marriage has become a matter of great concern to the state, which intervenes to substitute itself for the influence that the corporate lineage system exercised previously. It manifests itself in the fact that only the state can give binding and legal force to marriage,[14] whereas under former legislation a marriage performed according to customary law, which excluded any interference from the state, was perfectly valid. The intervention of the state is motivated by the necessity to keep control of the *état civil* [civil status] of each individual and to make sure that the

13. President Houphouet-Boigny, speech to the assembly, October 1964.
14. Law 64-375, 7 October 1964, on marriage:
    Art. 18. "Marriage is necessarily performed by a public registrar [*officier de l'état civil*]."
    Art. 19. "Only the marriage performed by a public registrar can have legal effects."
    Art. 20. "No minister of the church can proceed to the religious ceremonies of marriage without being entitled to do so by the presentation of the certificate described in art. 28 of the civil ceremony."

requirements for a valid marriage are met. Marriage having become a status, the latter can be granted only by a public authority invested with the power to act in the name of the state. The celebration of the wedding before the public registrar (*officier de l'état civil*) will make it very easy to prove its legal existence. Marriage being thus clothed with a formal aspect, the legislator has laid down essential conditions under which it can be contracted.

*Consent of the spouses.*[15] The laws of modern legal systems stress the necessity for the consent of the spouses. The new Ivory Coast laws endorse this basic principle, which is but one manifestation of the triumph of individualism. "Emancipation of man and woman has appeared to us, indeed, as being first of all manifested by the free disposal of oneself in the choice of the spouse or in the refusal of the state of marriage itself";[16] "On marriage rests the existence of the family: It is the reason why marriage can happen only through the manifestation of the will of the future spouses to marry. . . . Marriage being a personal act, consent to marriage must also be personal. There is no marriage where there is no consent."[17] Consent requires that the spouses be able to express their will quite freely. Therefore the minimum age of marriage is of great significance in those societies where the parents could previously decide on the marriage of their children before they had reached the age of puberty or even before they were born. Puberty, in its physiological sense, is no longer the decisive referent, but rather a kind of intellectual maturity which is supposed to be reached at the age of twenty for a boy and eighteen for a girl.[18] This provision of the Ivorian law insures that a young girl will be mature enough to choose for herself and, in some cases, that she will not have to interrupt her studies for the purpose of marriage.[19]

*Abolition of the brideprice.* Article 20 of Law 64-381 abolishes the traditional institution of the brideprice,[20] which was a method of proving

15. Law 64-375, Art. 3: "Each of the future spouses must give his personal consent to his marriage. . . ."

16. Lazéni Coulibaly, "Les Traits principaux du nouveau droit ivoirien de la famille," *Revue juridique et politique* 21 (1967):82.

17. Gon Coulibaly, in *Fraternité*.

18. Law 64-375, Art. 1: "Man under twenty, woman under eighteen cannot contract a valid marriage. However, the President of the Republic can grant a waiver for serious cause."

19. "I had, right then, started regretting my early marriage seeing my studies being 'prematured' [sic]. . . . I claim that justice be done. I could have become someone had I kept going on studying." (Request for a divorce by a young woman from the area of Korhogo.)

20. "By way of exception to the statement of paragraph 2 of article 1, the institution

the existence of a marriage as well as a basic element of its formation. Some identified it with a manifestation of love, others with a means of compensating the efforts made by the parents in the education of their daughters. But the extraordinary rise in the amount of brideprice current in some areas of the Ivory Coast and its purely speculative and onerous features vested it with a commercial element. As a result, the institution was blamed for making men obsessively concerned with the expenses they had incurred and, hence, for viewing their wives primarily as valuable chattel. It was also blamed for contributing to the exodus of youth from rural areas where they could not compete with older, wealthier men in acquiring wives. With the new law, bridewealth was no longer useful as an instrument to prove the existence of a marriage since registration has become mandatory; and as an element in the formation of a marriage it had become an instrument of control and command in the hands of the parents who could easily overrule the sentiments of their children. Whereas several countries have fixed a maximum amount to the brideprice,[21] the Ivory Coast decided to abolish it altogether, giving to the law an immediate effect and listing a number of penalties against infringers.[22]

## PROTECTION OF THE NEW CONJUGAL FAMILY

It followed from the adoption by the Ivory Coast government of a new modern conjugal concept of the family, implying a fundamental equality between man and woman, that the monogamous marriage was to be the rule.

---

of the dowry, which consists in the payment to the benefit of the person having authority over the future bride, by the future bridegroom or the person having authority over him, of material advantages as a condition to the realization of the traditional marriage, is immediately abolished."

21. For example, Art. 3 of the Law 62-17 of 3 February 1962 of the Republic of Mali has fixed a maximum of 20,000 malian francs for a young girl and 10,000 for a widow.

22. Law 64-381 of 7 October 1964:

Art. 21. "Will be sentenced to six months to two years imprisonment and to a fine equal to twice the value of the agreed promises or of the things received or claimed, without the said fine being inferior to 50,000 francs, any person who, in violation of the provisions of the preceding article, will directly or through the means of a third party, whether the marriage took place or not:

1. have required or accepted offers or promises of dowry, required or received a dowry

2. have made offers or promises of dowry or surrendered to earnest requests aiming at the payment of a dowry."

Whereas under customary law the husband enjoyed the right to repudiate his wife, modern Ivorian law, following French practice and in view of the legal equality between spouses, gives the right of divorce to both parties. However, in adjusting this equality to the necessity of maintaining a degree of cohesion in the conjugal family, the law has conferred upon the husband a superior position so far as the control of the family is concerned; thus the hierarchical organization of the family is preserved.

## The Institution of the Monogamic Marriage

It is beyond doubt that the possession of many wives will remain for many years the ideal of numerous Ivorian males: "All aspire to polygamy. . . . A man cannot be considered as glorious unless he has several wives."[23] Yet the Constitution of Ivory Coast, which proclaims equality between man and woman and grants women the right to vote, conflicts with the spirit and the practice of polygyny, which allows the man to have the leading role in the family, while his several wives share whatever power the female side of the marriage possesses.[24] When abolishing this institution, the Ivorian Assembly took a realistic and conscious decision, which formally guarantees equality between sexes.[25] This bold decision, which does not, however, make Ivory Coast a pioneer in the field,[26] was tempered by other features of the law. First, in the whole law on marriage, there is no provision stating any penalty of any kind against those who would violate the new rules.[27] The only sanction provided by law is that of the absolute nullification of a marriage celebrated in contravention of Article 2 of the law.[28]

A second feature is justified by the peculiarities of the country: the drafters of the code have tempered the principle of the prohibition of polygyny by granting rights to a natural child and by allowing, with

23. Denise Paulme, *Une société de la Côte d'Ivoire, hier et aujourd'hui: Les Bétés.* (Paris: Mouton, 1962).

24. Constitution of Ivory Coast, Art. 6: "The Republic shall ensure equality before the law to all without distinction of origin, race, sex or religion. It shall respect all beliefs. . . ."

25. Law 64-375, Art. 2: "No one can enter a second marriage unless the preceding marriage has been dissolved. . . ."

26. Tunisia, for example, had already abolished polygyny.

27. Law 64-375 of 7 October 1964.

28. Art. 31: "Must be annulled, those marriages celebrated: (1) In contempt of the rules laid down in articles 1, 2 (paragraph 1), 3 (paragraph 1), 10 and 11 (paragraph 1)."

the consent of his spouse, the acknowledgment by the father of a natural child born to him by any woman outside the marriage contract.[29] This provision corresponds to the traditional view that any child must be made part of a family. Today, in the Ivorian society these provisions are unanimously approved, the men saying that they are willing to accept any child from their wives provided they are given a kind of compensation in having the right to "legalize" the fruits of an excusable misconduct.[30]

## *Divorce*

In France, since the Law Naquet reinstated divorce in 1884, divorce has become a kind of sanction imposed on the guilty spouse: a spouse, to obtain a divorce must bring evidence of a serious wrong by the marital partner. French law, therefore, had laid down a restricted number of causes that can justify a divorce. Despite this restrictive element of the law of divorce, the number of divorces has been increasing steadily and has become a remedy. It has as its effect the breaking up of the conjugal family, the basic cell of European societies, and the leaving of the children in a psychological, moral, and social situation that may hamper their full development. Given the very different African concept of family, divorce does not destroy the family since the latter transcends the individual personality of its members. It would effect a transfer of protection over the wife and her children, and a change in the holder of the patria potestas. The Ivory Coast, once more, breaks away from the customary law.[31] In the opinion of some, divorce is quite conceivable in the light of customary law because all that matters is the "patriarchal" family, which cannot suffer from the dissolution of the conjugal family.[32] In the opinion of others, divorce was not admitted by custom and should

29. Law 64-377, Art. 22: "Acknowledgment by the father of the child born out of an adulterous commerce is valid . . . only with the consent of the spouse. . . ."
    30. Law 64-377:
    Art. 1. "The child born during wedlock has, as his father, the husband. However, the latter may disavow the child, if he can prove that during the period that ran from the 300th to the 180th day before the birth of the child, he was either because of his absence or because of some accident, in the physical impossibility to cohabit with his wife."
    Art. 2. "The husband will not have the right to disavow his child by alleging his natural impotency; he will not have the right to do so even for the motive of adultery, unless the birth had been hidden from him, in which case he will be allowed to put forward any fact that would prove he is not the father."
    31. Law 64-376 on divorce and separation.
    32. This mentality may offer an explanation for the extreme fragility of the African marriage.

not be recognized by the new law. They argue that the increased number of divorces is due to the liberal evolution that tends to free the woman from the control of her family or the authority of her husband.[33] This laxity of mores has largely contributed to the weakening of the matrimonial bond on which the conjugal family is based.

If divorce has been admitted by the Ivorian legislators the strict rules that govern its grounds and procedures show quite plainly that it is tolerated but not favored.[34] Divorce can be granted only for reasons listed by the code, which are not those usually recognized by customary law. These reasons are basically the same as those laid down in the French code.[35]

Procedures are designed to discourage divorce actions. Following a first mandatory conciliatory hearing, the judge can impose a second one to be held within six months. It is hoped that a couple will resume their conjugal life after the judge has disclosed to them the full extent of the consequences that might flow from a divorce.

### Prominence of the Male

If the new family law of Ivory Coast has thought it proper and just to lay down the basic principle of equality of rights between husband and wife, this ideal has not been pursued to its logical conclusion. Equality between husband and wife does exist at the stages of formation and dissolution of marriage, but the intermediary stage is not based on the same principle. In the traditional family, customary law emphasizes the rights of the husband over his wife and, conversely, the duties of the latter towards the former. The new law deals in great detail with the "rights and duties" of the husband, his prerogatives and their counterparts being summed up in this strong sentence: "the husband is the head

33. See Jean Binet, *Le Mariage en Afrique noire*, in which the author shows that the great majority of divorce cases are filed by women.

34. Lazéni Coulibaly, "Les Traits principaux."

35. Law 64-376 on divorce and separation:

Chap. 1,

Art. 1. "Judges may grant divorce or separation from bed, at the request of either spouse
1. for adultery of the other spouse;
2. for excesses, cruel treatment or outrages of one of them towards the other;
3. when the spouse has been sentenced for facts casting a slur on honour and consideration;
4. for desertion of family or matrimonial domicile.
Whenever these facts make their living together or the upholding of the matrimonial bond insupportable."

of the family."[36] He has the choice of the family's residence,[37] he administers his own personal movables and immovables, those of the community and those of his wife.[38] The drafters of the Ivorian Civil Code have considered that a merger of the patrimonies is necessary to the unity of the family. The matrimonial regime, that of community of movables and immovables,[39] was intended to create common pecuniary interests between husband and wife: the prosperity of the family will benefit both of them. However, this prosperity of the family will depend essentially on the husband as head of the community,[40] which phrase is understood in a very broad sense.[41] Therefore, the principle of full capacity of right recognized to the wife[42] may be deprived of any content considering that she has no real power and very few rights.[43]

This new organization of the family secures its unity by substituting the idea of hierarchy to that of division of burdens; it stresses, legally, the autonomy of the small family, freed from any obligation to refer to the authority of the elders. . . . The effect of the community of movables and immovables is to create a conjugal association in which the bonds of marriage should prevail psycho-

36. Among the many articles of Law 64-375 we can quote:
   Art. 58. "The husband is the head of the family. He exercises this function for the common interest of the household and the children.

   "The wife contributes with the husband in ensuring the moral and material leadership of the family, in providing for its maintenance, in raising the children and helping in their settlement.

   "The wife takes the husband's place as leader of the family if he is unable to express his will because of his incapicity, of his absence, of his remoteness or of any other cause."
   Art. 67. "The wife can have a job separate from her husband's, unless the latter opposes.

   "If the opposition of the husband is not justified by the interest of the family, the wife can be authorized by the judge to disregard it."
37. Law 64-375, Art. 60.
38. Law 64-375, Art. 77.
39. Law 64-375, Art. 68.
40. Law 64-375, Art. 69.
41. Art. 71: Law 64-375, "Are community property, the earnings and incomes of the spouses and all the movables and immovables they acquired subject to payment during marriage. Are also community property the movables and immovables received or inherited jointly by both husband and wife."
42. Law 64-375, Art. 61, provides: "The wife enjoys the full capacity of right. The enjoyment of this capacity is limited only by law."
43. See J. Emanié, "Les Droits patrimoniaux de la femme mariée ivoirienne," *Annales africaines* 85 (1967): 126.

logically over the bonds by blood. Husband and wife are bound for better or worse.[44]

## THE SURVIVAL OF THE AFRICAN FAMILY

Twice, during the colonial period a serious threat hovered over the African family: in 1939 the *décret Mandel* had enacted a regulation of marriage between *indigènes;* in 1951 the *décret Jacquinot* had tried to lay down rules governing some aspects of marriage (especially the bride-price). Both failed completely in their purpose. The African family managed to survive until the day of independence, resisting very forcefully the strong winds of integration and cultural assimilation. Did this resistance suddenly wane between 1960 and 1964? Did the legislators of 1964 sign the death warrant of the traditional family? In fact, the new laws have not carried the traditional African family to its grave, not only because of its resiliency, but because the Ivorian leaders, stressing "an evolution and not a revolution," intended all along to preserve many of its features. The flexibility of the provisions of the laws warrants their efficiency on the one hand as concerns marriage, on the other hand as concerns the fate of children.

### As Regards Marriage

Alongside the many provisions of the law concerning legal marriages, Article 47 leaves the door open to a union that would not satisfy the formal  requisites of the law but would nevertheless produce the same effects as if the marriage had been contracted according to the letter of the law.[45] The facts that may be invoked by a man and a woman to avail themselves of the status of spouses are not very stringent; hence it is likely that many youths will have their first experience of conjugal life under the protective and understanding mantle of Article 47.

Ivorian law has also introduced the concept of putative marriage. By means of this fiction a man and a woman are given the benefits of a legal

---

44. E. Abitbol, "La Famille conjugale et le droit nouveau du mariage en Côte d'Ivoire," *J.A.L.* (1966) : 141, 151.

45. Law 64-375 on marriage:

Art. 47. "The possession of the state of spouses is established by an adequate meeting of facts that imply the existence of the matrimonial bond. The most important of these facts are:

—that the man and woman bear the same name

—that they consider themselves as husband and wife

—that they are accepted as such by the family and in society."

marriage, although in the eyes of the law they were never married.[46] Article 41 of the law on marriage makes the putative marriage a general consequence of nullity, whenever the spouses act in good faith; Article 43 further stipulates that the bad faith of the parents cannot have any effect on the condition of the children who remain "legitimate" despite the retroactive effect of the nullity of their parents' marriage. There is no doubt that the "African family" will find in these provisions ways to insure its comfortable survival. This is all the more true since African custom has usually accorded a child born of unlawful union or even of adultery a situation very similar to that of legitimate children.

### As Regards Children

Traditionally, marriage was justified in relation to procreation. For many, polygyny was more a means of becoming the father of several children than an institution to which they were strongly attached. Woman, considered as an individual, a human being, had little room in the African customary law of marriage. The enactment of laws governing the conditions of a valid marriage led to the definition of the conjugal family and consequently to the logical necessity to specify a different legal status for the children born of lawful wedlock and for those not so born, with the former having rights that the latter should not share. Once again, however, tradition has weighed very heavily among the considerations of the drafters of the code. They have multiplied the means of proving one's filiation so as to maintain the rights that customary law vested in the children. The situation of the legitimate child raises no difficulty since his status is defined by the maxim "Pater is est quem nuptiae demonstrant."[47] Proof of their filiation by natural children is governed by a set of rules that combine precepts of customary law and norms of modern law with the result that the natural child benefits from a happy "seasoning" of laws. Vis-à-vis the maternal family, proof of filiation results from delivery of the child from the mother's womb. Paternal filiation will result either from acknowledgment by the father or by decision of the court.[48]

46. It is surprising to notice that none of the articles on nullity (whether absolute or relative) refer back to Articles 18, 19, and 20 on formalities of marriage. Is it to say that a marriage cannot be annulled on the ground of non-fulfillment of the requisites laid down in these provisions? Obviously not. To decide otherwise would be to hold that the new law on marriage has changed very little in the traditional law of marriage.

47. Law 64-377, Arts. 1 and 3.

48. Law 64-377, Art. 19: "Filiation of children not born of lawful wedlock is

The adulterine child is also given the right to bring an action in court to have his filiation established.[49] Moreover, the father can acknowledge his adulterine child with the consent of his wife; and should the wife be initially reluctant, "the judge may exercise pressure on her to win her consent."[50]

Once they are given a filiation that fits the law, all these children, whether they are legitimate, natural or adulterine, enter the family and enjoy the same rights. The Ivorian legislation makes no difference among the types of filiation and rules that "children not born out of marriage, whose filiation is legally established enjoy the same rights as legitimate children."[51]

The result of this complete assimilation of natural and adulterine children with legitimate children is to maintain the African tradition of community, as well as to preserve polygyny. Indeed, the lawful wife will be forced to accept by her side the existence of unions which, despite their unlawfulness, will beget children to whom the law will grant the same rights as to her own children. The African family is not dead; beneath the mark of modernity, one can easily identify its familiar features.

## CONCLUSION

The Ivorian government has attempted to satisfy one of its main concerns to endow a young nation with a modern code drafted with an eye to African realities. The new laws triumphed on paper; will they also triumph in the society at large? Much depends upon the criteria we use for evaluating their success. It is necessary to stress, once more, that the purpose of these laws is not to produce a drastic change in society today, but, more modestly, to sow the seeds of the society of tomorrow. This was President Yacé's thought when he said that:

The rules which govern relations between individuals, that is to say private law, are far behind the existing economic and political structures; if this lag were to become greater, it would curb economic development. Why this delay? Because, in this sphere, we have remained attached to our ancestral customs. This is not a charge against our customs; but one must admit that existing customs, even though they were an obstacle to the unity of the rules governing

established as regards the mother by the fact of birth. . . . Vis-à-vis the father, proof of filiation can result only from acknowledgment or from decision of the Court."

49. The situation of the adulterine child is governed by Law 64-377, Arts. 21 to 23.

50. Lazéni Coulibaly, "Débats sur les communications de MM. Coulibaly et Vangah," *Revue juridique et politique* 21 (1967) : 102.

51. Law 64-377, Art. 29.

relations between individuals, were, with reference to the stage of evolution of our country, a survival of the past and a hindrance to progress. Unless we can provoke the enthusiastic support of the Ivorian masses, the work that marked the second extraordinary session of the National Assembly, instead of standing as a monument matching our aspirations, will appear finally as a brilliant but short-lived adventure.[52]

Several years later, we have the great advantage over President Yacé of being able to evaluate this "monument" on the basis of some information concerning the impact of the Civil Code in the country at large. In the absence of adequate government reports and of reliable independent research on the subject, however, we can rely only on a few clues. A survey conducted by the Jeunesse Ouvrière Chrétienne among nearly four hundred youths aged thirteen to twenty-five in 1967 revealed that many of them had never heard of the Civil Code; among those who had, many indicated a continued preference for marriage according to customary law; the most favored aspects of the code concerned the establishment of a community of property between husband and wife, and the abolition of brideprice.[53] Although inconclusive, this information suggests that even among relatively educated youths reached by a Christian organization, the code's impact was severely limited. Ivorian officials themselves expressed doubts concerning the impact of the legislation discussed in this chapter. Although one can continue to hope that the country will achieve some success in transforming its legal system, it may well be that the Ivory Coast, by refusing to compromise more than symbolically with customary law, has tried to do too much too soon and has entered into the realm of "fantasy law."

52. From the speech delivered by Philippe Yacé, president of the Ivorian National Assembly, 9 October 1964.
53. From the editorial of *Fraternité* (1 September 1967).

# 8

# THE MODERNIZATION OF LAW IN GHANA

## Beverley Pooley

The focus of this chapter is on the legal order in Ghana since independence in 1957. First, I shall consider efforts which have been made at formal levels to change legal norms and practices with a view to harmonizing dissident provisions and precedents—mostly of a technical nature.[1] These I will refer to as "housekeeping matters"; most legal systems undergo a continuous process of reform at this level. There are, however, a number of reasons for investigating this aspect of legal modernization in Ghana with special care.

Next, I propose to examine those changes which have been introduced in order to effectuate the dramatic shift of policy articulated during independence, particularly in the economic sphere. Here, our principal concern will be with the absence of innovation. Instead of a spate of radical legislation, necessary for putting into effect the dramatic changes necessary to realize postindependence goals, one finds a significant gap.

This area of silence extends to the field of academic work and concern. Whereas political scientists, economists, social psychologists, and other behavioral scientists have examined with unusual fervor the impact of independence and its sequelae, very little indeed is to be found in the legal literature to reflect this in comparison with, for example, the enormous annual literature on the responsiveness of law to social policy in the United States.

I shall address myself, therefore, to the advances actually made and, more importantly, shall offer some rationales for legal passivity.[2]

---

1. "Technical" is used here in a very wide sense, with which some would be in disagreement. Reforms in the law of contract, or of the procedure to be adopted in the case of intestate succession, are here regarded as "technical" matters.

2. Not so universal a phenomenon as might popularly be supposed. The growth of the private limited liability corporation in the nineteenth century to effectuate pressing economic goals represents a remarkable effort of legislation and judicial inventiveness.

I shall then describe some administrative law problems and, finally, make brief mention of the unhappy history in Ghana of constitutional protection of civil liberties. Before embarking on any of this, however, I would like to make some general observations regarding legal research in Ghana.

In any society it is wise to heed the principal warning of the American realist school of legal thought, namely, that substantial differences may be discernible between law in action and law in the books. In a society which has developed with sufficient freedom from outside interference and domination for a unitary system of law to have evolved, the differences between what the lawbooks say ought to happen and what does in fact happen are sufficiently startling for "the law" to fall into some disrepute.

Further, it is a trite observation that when a group in society feels the law is wrong, or is right but not followed or enforced, that group's obedience to the law lacks several of the principal normal stimuli to conduct its affairs in accordance with the law. If the law is regarded principally as a source of trouble, it is unlikely to be either followed or resorted to as a means of finding redress. If, however, the law is thought of as providing a number of benefits, it will find a measure of acceptance both substantively and as a means of societal problem-solving.

I make these somewhat shallow observations in order to point up some of the initial difficulties we find in conducting any kind of legal research in Ghana. The colonial legal system was primarily one which might be seen by the ordinary individual as causing a good deal of annoyance and distress, and thereby aroused antipathy, while providing few concomitant compensations. It taxed, enforced criminal restraints, and imposed a number of other disagreeable duties upon the populace without visibly giving a fair return. Since the colonial power was obviously unrepresentative of the indigenous population, the law lacked one of the principal ingredients of legitimacy, that is, the consent of the governed. Further, the colonial formal legal system did not purport to regulate all aspects of life. Customary and, to a much lesser extent, religious laws had far more visible and day-to-day impact upon life, were more responsive, had greater legitimacy and a far greater consensual element.

To the extent that attitudes forged during the colonial period extended into postindependence Ghana, the whole formal structure of the independent legal regime, not visibly dissimilar from its predecessor, might legitimately be supposed to be operating in a cloud-cuckoo-land, substantially divorced from and unknown to the majority of citizens. The party framework of the CPP undoubtedly played some role in involving the people in the process of government at least to the extent of informing them of new government proposals for legislation. In some areas (notably the area of marriage and divorce) an informed and restive citizenry was able fundamentally to change legislative proposals. However, a number of false starts in programs which required the active participation of significant segments of the population indicate that the government may not have been well informed as to the acceptability of its proposals,[3] even if it also showed that, up to 1963 at least, the government was to some degree responsive to popular agitation against its proposals.

A nonacceptance, for the reasons presented above, of the relevance and legitimacy of the activity of the legal structure can, of course, cause unrest which takes the form of unlawful violence. It can also, and this is even more important for our purposes, cause a more or less constant resort to extra legal norms (i.e., norms exterior to the formal legal structure) both for everyday conduct and for the resolution of disputes. Again, to the extent that one can assume a degree of alienation on the part of the population from formal legal institutions even after 1957, one must assume that the statute book inaccurately reflected not only the accepted norms but also the actual practice of some segments of Ghanaian society. The whole uncertain edifice of statutes and judges, attorneys and court reports reflected an exotic British value system and modus operandi.

The obvious conclusion is that one should not confine one's inquiries to a study of this possibly irrelevant excrescence, but investigate further to discover to what extent the basic norms under which both the colonial and independent regimes operated were in fact accepted or successfully imposed. We have hardly any information, alas, on a host of matters which would be crucial to such an undertaking. We can give some tentative conclusions as to the effect of legislation upon the activities of two smallish groups which are at once more readily visible than most and whose activities are more likely to be the object of legislative regulation, namely, businessmen and civil servants. While the impact of the legal system on these groups is of prime importance in the economic sphere, it must be admitted that in other areas of social concern we are able to show very little in the way of a quantifiable relationship between the formal legal structure and actual behavior.

3. See, for example, the compulsory savings plan abandoned in 1963; Ghana, Compulsory Savings (Abolition) Act, Act 196 (1963).

## THE COLONIAL LEGACY: GHANA'S LEGAL SYSTEM IN 1957

A detailed analysis of the British colonial legal system in Ghana and the forces which created and sustained it does not, unfortunately, exist; and no attempt will be made here to provide anything more than a few didactic observations—any or all of which might be legitimately questioned.

The colonial system was naturally modeled on the British example, but differed from it in several important particulars: Constitutionally, the position of the colonial subject was quite different from that of his British counterpart. Further, many of the basic sources of rights, duties, and so on, were in documentary form (Orders in Council, etc.); and the possibility, therefore, existed that, since the interpretation of written instruments has long been held to be a proper exercise of judicial authority, the courts might have played an important role in the development of constitutional ideas and policies (as they have in the United States) rather than leaving such matters to the legislative or executive branches— as has been the case in Britain, where the formulation and interpretation of constitutional notions is not derived from documentary sources but rather from a variety of political and social instincts for which activity the legislative and executive branches can legitimately claim some suitability.

It is perhaps appropriate to emphasize that in a British colony the powers of government were typically in the hands of civil servants who played a role markedly different from that which the civil servant in England normally plays, except insofar as is possible to see the Gold Coast administrator as a dutiful servant of the Colonial Office, administering programs devised by politicians and imposing them upon a population whose interests it was not necessary for him to consult. Colonial administrators in fact assumed far wider powers,[4] formulated and initiated policy themselves and consulted the interests of at least some sections of the local community.

The basic formal law in 1957 consisted of: "The Common Law, the doctrines of equity and the statutes of general application which were in force in England on the 24th day of July, 1874."[5] Further, "native law or custom" so far as it was not "repugnant to natural justice, equity, and

---

4. See, for example, Ronald E. Wraith, *Guggisberg* (London: Oxford University Press, 1967), an account of the strongly independent governor of the Gold Coast in the 1920s. See also Geoffrey Bing, *Reap the Whirlwind* (London: MacGibbon and Kee, 1968), pp. 284–88.

5. The Courts Ordinance, Laws of the Gold Coast, 1951, cap. 4, s. 83.

good conscience, nor incompatible either directly or by necessary implication with any ordinance for the time being in force" applied in certain
circumstances.[6] As has been pointed out, this definition makes it appear
that the normal everyday law to be applied was English law, or a variant
of it, with local customary law being applied on rare, unusual occasions.
In fact, the opposite was the case. Customary law would always govern,
between Africans at least, disputes concerning customary land and customary marriage, divorce and devolution of property. Further it may
perhaps be surmised that in fact, if not in law, a good many crimes and
most civil wrongs were dealt with by customary procedures, whatever
jurisdiction the colonial courts may have claimed.

The English common law in 1874 was, of course, strongly influenced
by laissez-faire notions of the nineteenth century. In contract heavy
emphasis was placed on bargain and agreement, there being little legislation (other than in the labor field) to delimit from social or economic
perspectives the legal power of contracting parties. Subsequent legislation
and case law in Britain went some way to mitigate the hardships which
flowed from this attitude. None of these later modifications applied in
the Gold Coast, however. Company law was modernized in England; so
was the law relating to property and a number of other basic matters.
No corresponding legislation was to be found in the Gold Coast. Thus, in
1957 the case and statute law of Ghana was out-of-date and more politically
responsive to nineteenth century thinking than was that of England; even
worse, only that part of the total *corpus juris* which had been produced
by the Gold Coast legislature and courts could possibly be said to have
been framed with the needs of the people of the Gold Coast in mind.

Some have averred that the colonial legislation was produced by the
merchant class in the Gold Coast to serve their own interests. There can be
little doubt that the commercial interests which dominated the gold,
diamond, and cocoa markets and those who depended upon the colony's
government for concessions and similar indulgences were anxious to make
their voices felt, and were successful to a large degree. On the other hand,
the interests of the Colonial Office and the merchants were not always
coincident, particularly on matters of taxation.

Generally speaking, therefore, the formal (as opposed to the customary) law at the time of independence was British in origin, out-of-date,
even by British standards, and generally reflected the interests of the
dominant British group in the colony—the merchants. Customary law had

6. Ibid., s. 87 (1).

reacted to and attempted to absorb a number of legal devices introduced by the common law—the lease, the mortgage, the pledge, and so on. However, the principal factor in the development of customary law during the colonial period probably lay in the fact that interpretation and articulation of customary law lay in the hands of the colonial judiciary, at least at the appellate level, where sweeping precedents were forged. Not only were such judges initially wholly inexpert in the law which they were supposed to be applying and interpreting; their judgments became binding precedents for the future. Understandably, the result tended to be chaotic, the flames of confusion being fanned by an indigenous fondness for litigation —especially in land matters.

Lastly, the personnel of the law were, to a man, British trained. No Ghanaian had received his basic legal training outside England and no Ghanaian law school existed.

Lawyers, required by the nature of a common law system to look to precedents, tend to become by virtue of this necessity a conservative group. While the novelty of this assertion is less than breathtaking, it is perhaps important to realize that lawyers whose intellectual and professional underpinnings were strongly linked to the preservation of the British system (and whose natural professional conservatism was further emphasized by wealthy aristocratic origins in many cases) would not react favorably to, still less initiate, ideas which would professionally invalidate their qualifications and experience.

## DEVELOPMENT SINCE 1957

### HOUSEKEEPING; IMPROVING THE CAPITALIST SYSTEM

Following the grant of independence the new Ghana National Assembly was initially concerned with a number of statutes which were an essential consequence of independence, such as the Nationality and Citizenship Act[7] and the Immigration Act.[8] Shortly afterwards, however, we find the Hotel Proprietors Act[9] modifying the common law liability of innkeepers, the Hire Purchase Act[10] regulating installment purchases (substantially similar to earlier British legislation on the subject),[11] the Law Reform (Civil Wrongs) Act[12] again making earlier British legislation applicable

7. Act 1 (1957).
8. Act 15 (1957).
9. Act 20 (1957).
10. Act 55 (1958).
11. Gold Coast Hire Purchase Act, 1938 (1 & 2 Geo. 6, c. 53).
12. Act 12 (1959).

in Ghana.[13] This concern with modernizing Ghana law—to make it more like British law—continued after the Republican Constitution in 1960. We have the Contracts Act[14] and, perhaps most extraordinary of all, the Administration of Estates Act in 1961,[15] which provides rules (again, founded on the British model) to be followed by the personal representatives of deceased persons and which seems to ignore the fact that the overwhelming majority of all "estates" in Ghana are dealt with by customary procedures under which no one would dream, for example, of putting notices in the *Ghana Gazette*.[16] Other examples could be found of post-independence legislation, the purpose of which was to bring Ghanaian law more in line with British law, however dysfunctional this might seem to be with the needs of Ghana. Clearly, there has been little effort in this area to cast off the heavy burden of British tradition and to seek to fashion new legal imperatives responsive to the Ghanaian circumstance.

Indeed, if one attempts the unusual task of taking the postindependence volumes of legislation and glancing through each successive act, one feels that the new legislature has exactly the same preoccupations and attitudes as its predecessor, except that it perhaps is a little more attuned to the distant tinkling clamor of Oxbridge and London academic lawyers. The only conceivable indicium of revolutionary government are measures like the Emergency Powers Act,[17] which could, however, easily have been the product of the colonial administration.

Taking the period 1957–60, one is surprised not so much in the apparently unquestioning adoption of some British technical legal reforms, but rather (as in the case of the dog which didn't bark), to find hardly any legislation which might be characterized as the product of an effort to reduce the priority accorded to private decision making and to magnify the legal impact of government decision making, especially in the economic sphere.[18]

13. Gold Coast, The Law Reform (Miscellaneous Provisions) Act. 1934 (24 & 25 Geo. 5, c. 41) ; The Law Reform (Married Women and Tortfeasors) Act, 1935, (25 & 26 Geo. 5, c. 30) ; and the Law Reform (Contributory Negligence) Act, 1945 (8 & 9 Geo. 6, c. 28).

14. Ghana, Act 25 (1960).

15. Ghana, Act 63 (1961).

16. See, for example, s. 53 (1) of the Administration of Estates Act—note 15, above.

17. Gold Coast, Act 28 (1957).

18. There was, of course, no shortage of legislation having to do with economic matters. Again most was either reenactment, sometimes with minor variations, of British legislation such as: The Bills of Exchange Act, No. 55 (1961) ; the Bills of Lading Act, No. 42 (1961) ; the Exchange Control Act, No. 71 (1961) ; the Merchant Shipping Act, No. 57 (1961) ; the Sale of Goods Act, No. 137 (1962).

After 1960, as will be seen below, the statute book reflects a growing concern for the introduction of new policies of governmental regulation of industry and management of a number of enterprises. The attention given earlier to technical matters aiming at improvement of the applicable common law perceptibly wanes. In part, these earlier housekeeping measures may be ascribed to the reforming zeal of expatriate lawyers in the Parliamentary draftsman's office of the attorney-general's department, who initiated and drafted the legislation. Perhaps as time went on there was also an awareness of the surrealism inherent in such measures. If so, there is little evidence that this awareness prompted the further reflection that if the legal system were to be more attuned to the realities of Ghanaian life, a fundamental restructuring of the legal order and the assumptions upon which it was based should be undertaken as a matter of urgent priority.

### Building the Policy Structure: The Legislative Program 1957–66

It is pertinent to observe initially that the predominant means by which we suppose social and economic change to occur is by enactment of a legislative program geared to new aspirations and goals. This is not to assert important changes cannot occur by other means; indeed, the less responsive the legal order is to the "real world" the more hesitant one should be to infer the direction and scope of social change from a study of positive law. Here I would emphasize that just as the colonial legal structure was basically irrelevant (because unresponsive) to the daily life of most Ghanaians, the postindependence structure retained a good deal of this artificiality. Whether a change occurred in the attitudes of people towards the law, its relevance and legitimacy, its functionaries and its effectiveness during the postindependence period has not been empirically established. The purpose, form, and content of some of the legislation already referred to may give rise to some doubts. However that may be, it remains important to examine some of the policy implementing legislation in the economic field, for the purpose of much of the legislation was to affect the behavior of only a very small segment of the population, a segment one might well assume to be especially responsive to positive law, namely, businessmen and civil servants. As has been pointed out, we have a little more information concerning the effectiveness of legislative devices for controlling the activities of those two groups.

Whatever Marxist rhetoric may have been propounded by President Nkrumah and his supporters, the fact remains that he at all times resigned himself to the prospect of a significant private sector in Ghana's economy.[19] Economic plans not only projected the sustaining and nurturing of existing private investment, they depended for their efficacy on attracting a sizeable share of additional capital investment. The extent to which the government was supposed ideally to regulate from economic and social perspectives the operation of expatriate corporations is not at all clear. Again, if one looks for a flexible set of standards ranging from conduct required by law of expatriate corporations through a range of measures ending up with conduct prohibited by law, one finds that most governmental endeavors are clustered at the extreme poles. A set of flexible intermediate controls, in matters of taxation, employment of local labor, repatriation of profits, availability of import licenses, and so on is not to be found.[20] A comparison with the comparable provisions in Francophonic countries would perhaps be instructive here.

Ghana, at any rate, followed the simple pattern of granting tax holidays and prescribing a set series of other inducements, leaving the government with little apparent maneuverability with respect to the direction in which it wanted private capital to be diverted, or with respect to the integration into the government investment policy of a number of other policy concerns, such as training and employment of Ghanaians, the decentralization of industry, the location of import substitution industries and the like.[21] There seems little reason to suppose that these provisions actually induced expatriate businessmen to invest in Ghana, for foreign investment has been consistently below expectation and probably (I lack the competence to make a judgment here) has been below the levels attracted by other countries more or less similarly situated. Whenever any particularly large investment seemed to be in the offing, it was clear that ad hoc legal arrangements would be made to effectuate agreement arrived at.[22]

These measures, in the main, sought to regulate conduct by induce-

19. See, for example, Ghana, *Seven Year Plan for National Reconstruction and Development* (Accra: Government Printer, 1964), pp. 39–50.

20. Ghana, Capital Investment Act, No. 172 (1963).

21. See, for example, the Pioneer Industries and Companies Act (No. 63 of 1959) as amended by the Pioneer Industries and Companies (Amendment) Acts of 1960 (Act 28) and 1962 (Act 98), providing flexibility only for a period between five and ten years for a tax holiday; the Capital Investments Act, 1963 (Act 172) (superseding the Pioneer and Industrial Companies Acts) as amended by the Capital Investments (Amendment) Act 1965 (Act 267); and The National Investment Bank Act 1963 (Act 163).

22. For example, the agreement for funding the Volta Dam project and the agreement with Valco, Ltd. (Ghana) with respect to the building and operation of an aluminum smelter in Ghana.

ment: if a businessman acted as desired, benefits would flow to him. The great technical superiority of such a method of influencing behavior is that it is largely self-enforcing. The burden is substantially on the individual to convince the government that he meets the prescribed standard; it is not for the government to show he has departed from it. Regulatory techniques based upon inducements by threat of unpleasant consequences to the delinquent run into enormous enforcement problems. This is not to say that both techniques might not be wrecked by corruption or bureaucratic ineptitude.[23] It may well be, therefore, that the lack of emphasis upon use of the criminal law for divergencies from desired policy goals, such as training and employment of Ghanaians, honest tax-reporting, increasing (in the case of retailers) the percentage of those seeking import licenses—provided that each supposes he has a fair chance of success within the published guidelines.[24] The assumption that businessmen, or other groups, in Ghana actually would prefer such a system is not self-evident. The absence of proper restraints on government officers may well induce a situation in which extralegal (and illegal) techniques become preferable simply because they are most efficacious.[25]

This brings us back to what may be seen as the crucial underlying question, namely, the relevance of positive norms and the aspirations of the legal system. Here, attention must be focused upon the clear inadequacy of the common law system to provide an adequate administrative law structure by means of which disputes between the citizen and the state, or between different organs of the state can be properly adjudicated.[26] The establishment of statutory corporations by statutory instruments under the Statutory Corporations Act of 1961 was an ambitious undertaking.[27] By 1 March 1966 fifty-three state enterprises had been incorporated in addition to twelve joint state-private enterprises or associated companies.[28]

23. See, for example, Ghana, *Report of the Commission of Inquiry into Trade Malpractices in Ghana* (Accra: Government Printer, 1965).

24. In particular, Ghana, *Commission of Inquiry into Irregularities and Malpractices in the Grant of Import Licenses* (1967); popularly known as the Ollennu Commission and herein referred to as such. *Report of the Commission of Inquiry into Trade Malpractices in Ghana* (1965). *Report of the Commission of Inquiry into the Circumstances Surrounding the Establishment of the Cargo Handling Company* (1967). *Report of the Commission Appointed to Inquire into the Affairs of Nadeco, Ltd.* (1966).

25. Ollennu Commission Report, p. 19.

26. See the last section of this chapter.

27. Act 41 (1961).

28. Ghana, *Report and Financial Statement by the Accountant General and Report Thereon by the Auditor General for the Year Ended 31st December, 1964* (1967), para. 181.

After the coup of February 1966 the future management of these corporations presented one of the most severe internal problems facing the National Liberation Council. After extensive discussions with international financial institutions, a holding corporation was established to manage the affairs of nineteen of the industrial state enterprises.[29] The holding corporation is to be run substantially independently of the government, with the exception that the commissioner for industries has the power to give general directions.[30] The decree specifically provides that "it shall be the duty of the corporation to conduct its affairs on sound commercial lines, and in particular, so to carry out its functions under this decree as to insure that its revenues are sufficient to produce on the fair value of its assets a reasonable return. . . ."[31] A similar trend can be noticed in the establishment of the Electricity Corporation of Ghana.[32] This corporation is not subject to general policy directives from the government except insofar as the government may secure such control by virtue of its power to appoint members of the board, and to grant or deny loans to the corporation. Whether such independently established corporations will be able to withstand the impact of civilian government with their integrity unimpaired is perhaps doubtful; it is difficult to see how a responsible government could refrain from prescribing general policy directions for so important a public utility as the distribution of electricity, still less with respect to the very large sums of public money involved in the industrial state enterprises.

Other important developments during the Nkrumah period which deserve mention are the trio of statutes modernizing Ghana's corporation law. The Incorporated Private Partnerships Act of 1962[33] was enacted pursuant to the recommendations of the Gower Report.[34] Although the Gower Report was persuasive in showing the utility of a device of this nature, there seems little evidence thus far that private entrepreneurs in Ghana have resorted to it in any great numbers. The Companies Code of 1963,[35] provides an up-to-date framework, more advanced in many ways than the corresponding provisions in Britain, for the orderly governance

29. See the Ghana Industrial Holding Corporation Decree, NLCD 207 (1967).
30. NLCD 207 (1967), s. 15.
31. NLCD 207 (1967), s. 9 (1).
32. The Electricity Corporation of Ghana Decree 1967, NLCD 125 (1967), as amended by NLCD 239 (1968).
33. Act 152 (1962) as amended by the Incorporated Private Partnerships (Amendment) Act of 1963, No. 214 (1963).
34. Commission of Inquiry in the working and administration of the present company law, *Final Report* (1961).
35. Act 179 (1963) as amended by Act 214 (1963).

of the affairs of private corporations; this too, was recommended by the Gower Report. Finally, the Insolvency Act,[36] which had largely been the creation of another Commission of Inquiry[37] having many interlocking provisions with the Companies Code and the Incorporated Private Partnerships Act, produced a reasonably modern and efficient method of dealing with bankruptcy problems, an area of the law which the colonial administration had left in a state of disastrous disarray.

An experimental device, whereby a government corporation was to acquire shares in private corporations, presumably for the purpose of insuring adequate representation, and perhaps control, on the part of the Ghana government, resulted in the enactment of the Ghana Holding Corporation Act of 1958.[38] For various reasons, including an increasing shortage of government capital for this purpose, the experiment was abandoned and the Act repealed in 1962.[39]

The whole question of government regulation of the labor market is not one which can be readily investigated by a study of legislative enactments, for the TUC was regarded as the industrial arm of the Convention Peoples Party, and it is clear that substantial restraints upon the effectiveness of collective bargaining were imposed not only by statute but by political persuasion. The Industrial Relations Act of 1958[40] and the Industrial Relations Act of 1965[41] established a framework for collective bargaining, negotiation, and conciliation of a fairly comprehensive nature, although substantial grounds for doubt exist as to whether the workers really had any basis for pursuing remedies against the opposition of the CPP.[42]

After the coup, the National Liberation Council appointed an Industrial Awards Review Committee with wide powers to confirm or deny awards[43] and further made it a criminal offence to instigate or incite strikes or lockouts or any other industrial disturbances for the implementation of any

36. Act 153 (1962).
37. *Report of the Commission Appointed to Inquire into the Insolvency Law of Ghana* (1961).
38. Act 45 (1958).
39. Ghana Holding Corporation (Repeal) Act, No. 120 (1962).
40. Act 56 (1958).
41. Act 299 (1965), as amended by NLCD 189 (1967).
42. See Henry L. Bretton, *The Rise and Fall of Kwame Nkrumah* (New York: Praeger, 1966), pp. 76–78, for a sweeping condemnation of the government's activities with respect to the labor movement of the Nkrumah period.
43. Industrial Relations Act, 1955 (Amendment) Decree, NCLD 189 (1967), s. 1 (1).

award which was to be reviewed by the committee.[44] If Ghana's critical economic condition requires a wages policy which goes beyond the mere enactment of a minimum wage, then clearly a more sophisticated structure than that which is at present afforded will be necessary.

Finally, attempts to control prices, by virtue of the Control of Prices Act 1962 were bolstered,[45] and more widespread criminal sanctions for improper activities on the part of retailers provided by the Control of Prices (Amendment) Act of 1965.[46] Their efforts clearly failed to be of any substantial effect during the last year of Nkrumah's government, tremendous price increases of basic foodstuffs being one of the principal stimuli to Nkrumah's final ouster. Again, it is necessary to reflect on the circumstances of Ghanaian life; the retailing of goods, especially foodstuffs, is not in the hands of a small number of easily controllable supermarkets. Rather, it is in the hands of a very great number of petty traders, most buying their commodities on credit and selling in small quantities at locations close to the people throughout the country. Effective price controls, therefore, are not going easily to be imposed unless very great efforts are spent in the enforcement of this particular law, or unless the methods of food distribution and retailing are substantially changed.

ADMINISTRATIVE LAW DEFICIENCIES

The common law, throughout most of its growth, handled problems posed to the king's judges by commoners; its principles were developed to cover what we now call private law. In the one great area of state concern, criminal law, the ambiguous position of the judiciary has long been evident. Paid and appointed by the state, the judge has to try a case between the state and the individual. To some extent, the jury system and the efforts to establish an independent judiciary have helped to overcome what seems an anomalous situation in many common law countries. It may be doubted whether the same effect has been achieved in Ghana: juries are not used to the same extent as in the United States in criminal cases. Some cases of interference with the free judiciary (albeit accomplished constitutionally) have cast doubt upon the judiciary's true independence from government.

Equally important over the last 100 years in all common-law countries has been the gradual accretion of government's role in society in general, but particularly in economic matters. This raises the questions: Who is to

44. Industrial Relations Act, 1965 (Amendment) Decree, NCLD 189 (1967), s. 3.
45. Act 113 (1962).
46. Act 298 (1965).

decide a dispute between the government and an aggrieved citizen who believes he has been wrongly denied a pension, or a passport, or an import license? Or who is denied permission to build a factory on his land, to employ non-unionists, to set his own wages or prices? The judicial power in some of these areas, in contrast to the United States where it was constitutionally created, cannot operate as successfully as it does in the private area; the government has virtually unlimited resources with which to support its case; has control over most of the pertinent facts; and the most important decision makers may be beyond the reach of the judicial arm. Here the clash between the judicial power, on the one hand, and executive and legislative power, on the other, is at its most evident, even where constitutionally the government cannot actually exclude the jurisdiction of the court.

In Britain, the situation is, of course, far more heavily weighted in favor of the government. British notions of due process do not stipulate a judicial review of executive acts; Parliament can, and regularly does, totally exclude the judiciary from trespassing upon executive areas of decision making by legislatively prohibiting the courts from entertaining a suit in those areas. Consequently, in British practice the only form of appeal from the decision of a civil servant or his minister lies through political action by having the matter raised by a member of Parliament.

This attitude was reflected in the Ghana constitutions, both of 1957 and 1960. No constitutional requirement of due process existed and thus there was no means by which the court might examine executive and administrative decisions. If a society believes that some outside discipline over such decision making is necessary and if the total cost of such a system can be borne, then means must be found for providing some kind of relief. It may be that the regular judicial machinery, because of its expense, delays, and relative lack of expertise, is ill-fitted for such a supervisory role. Certainly, there were political considerations during the Nkrumah regime which would have militated against increasing the power of the judiciary, especially in such delicate areas. The French *Conseil d'Etat* has been favorably and somewhat enviously regarded by Western comparative lawyers as being a device superior to anything thus far suggested in the common law system for the resolution of these problems.[47]

However this may be, there is an evident need for rationalizing executive decision making, whether a judicial or some other kind of adjudicatory body is used. In this connection, the proposals of the recent constitu-

47. See Charles J. Hamson, *Executive Discretion and Judicial Control* (London: Stevens, 1954).

tional commission are of interest,[48] since they envision a constitutional framework which will give the judiciary substantial oversight of administrative decision making.

One might perhaps raise a reservation with respect to these proposals: Concern with the rights of the individual and the defense of these rights against encroachment has caused Western lawyers to focus their attention in administrative law matters upon a confrontation between government and the individual. The Ghanaian proposals reflect this concern. However, in reality, the questions most pressing for resolution tend to be those in which different instrumentalities of government[49] whose interests sometimes clash (all the more so in any system in which the public sector is large and diverse) can have their disputes solved rationally by a process in which the interests of the different parties are articulated and subjected to unbiased scrutiny.

Let us take, for example, the case of the statutory corporation. Large sums of government money were directly invested in the economy by means of this device, which bore a certain deceptive resemblance to ordinary private corporations: It was a legal entity, could sue and be sued, had a board of directors and an initial authorized capital.[50] It was typically established by government enactment (an act, a legislative instrument, or executive instrument) which somewhat resembled the articles of incorporation of a regular company. The functioning of a statutory corporation, however, differs quite sharply from its private counterpart. Office holders in a private company are controlled, in part at least, by shareholders and creditors. If, for example, they fail to produce annual reports, or use the assets of the corporation for improper purposes, other private parties (shareholders and creditors) are likely to intervene through judicial means, if necessary, to protect their interests. The state plays a more or less passive role unless actual fraud is involved, and even then, the state is largely dependent upon information given to it by aggrieved persons. In other words, the conduct of officers of private corporations is not governed simply (or, in some matters, at all) by the law—there are other effective control devices.

In the case of the statutory corporation, the Board of Directors is not subject to periodic re-election by shareholders; creditors of the corporation

48. "Proposals of the Constitutional Commission for a Constitution for Ghana" (Accra: Government Printer, 1968), especially paras. 511 and 512.
49. The term is here used as broadly as possible so as to include, by way of example, the University of Ghana, the State Electronics Products Corporation, and the Ghana Commercial Bank.
50. For example, the State Distilleries Corporation Instrument, L.I. 391 (1965).

are unlikely to be able to influence the corporation effectively; and such control as was statutorily to be exercised by the relevant minister[51] or the president[52] does not appear to have been effective in persuading officers of the statutory corporation to carry out even basic duties provided for by law. The auditor general, for example, regretfully announces in his 1965 report that "audited accounts of some of the organizations are still not available because the accounting offices have failed in their duties of preparing necessary accounts for the auditors. In future, government will have to take strong measures against the chief accountants of all state agencies who, for no reasonable cause, fail to submit annual accounts within the prescribed period."[53] Ex post facto control of a criminal nature hardly seems to be the best solution for the basic problems posed by the auditor general. Nor can the boards of the statutory corporations concerned have been wholly innocent in the matter. Some administrative body, with wide-ranging powers of inquiry, hopefully with a good deal of bureaucratic experience and expertise (as in the case of the *Conseil d'Etat*) might be able to effectively resolve these disputes arising within the bureaucracy itself; for, it should perhaps be stressed again, a substantial sector of the economy is in public hands and tight political control (even if this were thought wise) has hardly ever been effective in Ghana.[54]

Another suggestion advanced by the constitutional commission, namely, the creation of an ombudsman,[55] might help in this direction. The rather wide-scale borrowing of this Swedish device (in Great Britain, New Zealand, and a number of American states) shows that Ghana is not unique in the common-law world in facing a problem which the accepted range of legal instrumentalities do not effectively solve. The chief defect of the ombudsman device, for our present purposes, is that his is generally an investigatory and reporting role. Even here, he is ordinarily concerned with disputes between the citizen and the state. The principal need in Ghana, it is here asserted, is for the swift investigation and resolution of disputes within the government apparatus itself. One of the early by-

51. See, for example, State Distilleries Corporation Instrument, L.I. 391 (1965), part XI.

52. See, for example, State Pharmaceutical Corporation Instrument, L.I. 409 (1965), part XIV.

53. *Report and Financial Statement by the Accountant General and Report Thereon by the Auditor-General for the Year Ended 31st Dec. 1964* (1967).

54. See "Government Proposals in Regard to the Future Constitution and Control of Statutory Boards and Corporations in the Gold Coast" (Accra: Government Printer, 1956), pp. 8–9.

55. "Proposals of the Constitutional Commission for a Constitution for Ghana" (1968), p. 494.

products of such a system might be the formulation of more comprehensive and effective guidelines within which official action should be taken.

Here again, the statutory corporations afford an illuminating example. Albeit that the motive for creation of one particular corporation might have been one of a number of possible stimuli (import substitution, provision of a subsidized service, the employment of labor, distribution of industry, and creation of a domestic supply of strategic materials, etc.) the Board of Directors were nowhere given a clear mandate in the enactment establishing the corporation as to which of these goals the government had in mind, and the importance of the original goal in contrast with, let us say, the goal of profitability.

### JUDICIAL PROTECTION OF CIVIL RIGHTS

The broad generalization may initially be offered that in postindependence Ghana whenever there has been a clash between the imperatives of economic advancement on the one hand, and egalitarianism on the other, the former has always triumphed. The International Commission of Jurists declared at a congress held in New Delhi in 1959 that ". . . the Rule of Law is a dynamic concept . . . which should be employed not only to safeguard and advance the civil and political rights of the individual in a free society, but also to establish social, economic, educational and cultural conditions under which his legitimate aspirations and dignity may be realized. . . ."[56] This somewhat surprising statement goes beyond our immediate concerns, but it may be helpful if it serves to focus our attention (and if I may speak somewhat parochially, I refer here particularly to lawyers) on the fact that the term "civil rights" might (and maybe should) be used to denote a much wider range of opportunities than those which we are customarily used to seeing litigated in the courts, such as the right to vote, to speak and write freely, to be free from arbitrary arrest, and to be provided with the opportunity to state our case before we are punished in some way by the state.

If all this is considered, it is clear that government efforts in the sphere of education, both for children and adults, in decreasing unemployment and raising the standard of living, in diversifying the economy to provide

56. International Commission of Jurists, *The Rule of Law in a Free Society: Report on the International Congress of Jurists* (Geneva: International Commission of Jurists, 1959), p. 3. For a most perceptive analysis of the troublesome concept of the "Rule of Law" and its relevance and application to a range of developing African nations, see Robert S. Seidman, "Law and Economic Development in Independent, English-speaking, Sub-Saharan Africa," *Wisconsin Law Review* 1966, no. 4 (fall 1966) : 999–1070.

a wider range of job opportunities, to improve health services, to improve communications and so on, can properly be said to have improved, though not spectacularly, the social, economic, educational, and cultural conditions under which the ordinary Ghanaian lives.

However, with that in mind, I shall now address myself to those rights and immunities which the citizen enjoys against his government and which are (successfully) protected by the legal order.

## The Colonial Heritage

The one universal primary concern of colonial government was the maintenance of law and order. However, unrepresentative, and in large measure despotic, it was liable to make egregious errors with respect to the motivations and purposes of political agitators.[57]

Preventive detention, control over all reading matter introduced into the colony, and other restrictions on political freedom were part and parcel of the colonial system. The writ of habeas corpus was, of course, available to secure the deliverance of anybody held without authority; but it provided no relief to anyone held, even without trial, under valid legislative authority.[58]

## Development after Independence

The Emergency Powers Act of 1957[59] provided that upon the declaration of a state of emergency, the governor general might make regulations providing for the detention of persons, and the deportation and exclusion of persons from Ghana,[60] entering and searching any premises,[61] and for amending any law or suspending the operation of any law.[62]

57. A Commission of Inquiry in 1948, for example, said of Nkrumah, ". . . he appears while in Britain to have had Communist affiliations and to have become imbued with a Communist ideology which only political expediency has blurred. In London he was identified particularly with the West African National Secretariat, a body which had for its objects the Union of all West African Colonies and which still exists. It appears to be the precursor of a Union of West African Soviet Socialist Republics. . . . Mr. Nkrumah boldly proposes a programme which is all too familiar to those who have studied the technique of countries which have fallen victims of Communist enslavement." Dr. J. B. Danquah is described as "a man of very great intelligence but [who] suffers from a disease not unknown to politicians through the ages and recognized under the general name of expediency." Gold Coast, *Report of the Commission of Inquiry with Disturbances in the Gold Coast* (Accra: Government Printer, 1948), paras. 68, 71, and 74.
58. See, for British practice, Liversidge v. Anderson (1942), A.C. 206.
59. Act 28 (1957).
60. Emergency Powers Act, No. 28 (1957), s. 5 (1) (a).
61. Emergency Powers Act, No. 28 (1957), s. 5 (1) (c).
62. Emergency Powers Act, No. 28 (1957), s. 5 (1) (d).

In mid-1958, the National Assembly passed the infamous Preventive Detention Act[63] which provided that a citizen of Ghana might be detained without trial for a period not exceeding five years if the governor general was satisfied that such detention was necessary "to prevent that person acting in a manner prejudicial to—(a) the defense of Ghana, (b) the relations of Ghana with other countries, or (c) the security of the State."[64] Startling though such legislation may appear to American eyes, it should be borne in mind that similar, if not more drastic, legislation had existed during the colonial era in Ghana, and, indeed, during World War II in Britain itself.[65]

The following year saw the enactment of the Offenses against the State (False Reports) Act,[66] which made it a criminal offense, carrying a possible punishment of imprisonment up to fifteen years, for any person to communicate to another" . . . any false statement or report which is likely to injure the credit or reputation of Ghana or the Government of Ghana, and which he knows or has reason to believe is false . . ." It was, further, specifically provided that "it shall be no defense to a charge under this section that the person charged did not know or did not have reason to believe that the statement or report was false unless he proves that, before he communicated the statement or report, he took reasonable measures to verify the accuracy of the statement or report."[67]

Attempts to challenge the Preventive Detention Act in the courts met with failure,[68] and there can be little doubt that such wide-ranging legislation could be used by the government not only to repress undesirable forms of political activity but also to put a severe damper on political discussion and any form of criticism. One closely associated with the Nkrumah government both at the time of the passage of the Preventive Detention Act and afterwards, Mr. Geoffrey Bing, has conceded, in a general defense of the Act, that "no doubt also among the political detainees were a number of persons who had done nothing wrong but who were there through personal intrigue and victimization."[69] Government powers were

63. Act 17 (1958).
64. Ibid., ss. 2 & 4.
65. See Liversidge v. Anderson (1942), A.C. 206.
66. Act 37 (1959).
67. The Offenses against the State (False Reports) Act, No. 37 (1959), s. 2 (3).
68. In Baffour Osei Akoto and Others v. The Minister of the Interior and Another (Civil Appeal No. 42/61) the Supreme Court held, following British precedent, that it was not permitted, in a habeas corpus proceeding, to inquire into the reasonableness of the minister's decision to detain.
69. Bing, *Reap the Whirlwind*, p. 272. For a more hostile view, see Bretton, *Rise and Fall*, pp. 56–60.

further strengthened by the Criminal Code Amendment Act of 1960,[70] the Emergency Powers Act of 1961,[71] the State Secrets Act of 1962,[72] the Preventive Detention (Amendment) Act of 1962,[73] the Foreign Travel (Exit Permits) Act of 1963,[74] and the Preventive Detention Act of 1964.[75]

While there can be no doubt that the effect of this legislation was gravely to hamper if not extinguish individual freedom and self-expression, a plausible case for tight security measures could be made.[76] Whether under the colonial power, during the eight years after independence, or under the National Liberation Council, the fact is that there have always been substantial restraints on political activity in Ghana. The National Liberation Council, while repealing the Preventive Detention Act, and releasing persons detained under it, nonetheless found it necessary to enact the Protective Custody Decree[77] shortly after taking office. This decree provided that persons named in it might be taken into custody and detained for such period as the National Liberation Council might determine. Subsequent legislation, such as the State Security Decree, 1966,[78] the Prohibition of Rumors Decree, 1966,[79] and the Criminal Procedure Code (Amendment) Decree, 1966,[80] made substantial inroads on freedom of speech and movement; the Preservation of Public Peace Decree, 1966,[81] prohibited "the formation or operation by any person of any political party"[82] and "all activities whatsoever likely to assist in the formation or operation of a political party. . . ."[83] Whatever the provisions of the current constitution with respect to constitutional guarantees of individual freedom, the history of both pre- and post-independence Ghana justifies some skepticism as to whether the protection of full political freedoms can withstand the impact of assertive, but (maybe justifiably) apprehensive governments.

70. Act 5 (1960).
71. Act 56 (1961).
72. Act 101 (1962).
73. Act 132 (1962).
74. Act 212 (1963).
75. Act 240 (1964).
76. In particular, see Bing, *Reap the Whirlwind*, pp. 270–77.
77. Protective Custody Decree, NLCD 2 (1966).
78. NLCD 119 (1966).
79. NLCD 92 (1966).
80. NLCD 93 (1966).
81. NLCD 3 (1966).
82. Preservation of Public Peace Decree, NLCD 3 (1966), s. 1.
83. Preservation of Public Peace Decree, NLCD 3 (1966), s. 2 (1).

# 9

# STRUCTURAL TRANSFORMATION VERSUS GRADUALISM: RECENT ECONOMIC DEVELOPMENT IN GHANA AND THE IVORY COAST

## Elliot J. Berg

Even if Nkrumah had not launched his famous challenge to Houphouet-Boigny in 1957, the temptation to compare economic performance in the Ivory Coast and Ghana during the past decade would be irresistible. When two neighboring countries are so similar in social structure, stage of development, and general environmental conditions and opt for markedly different development strategies with very different results, they invite comparison.

The recent economic experience of these two countries has particular interest inasmuch as it raises in clear form certain central issues of general development strategy. Most prescriptions for development policy tend toward one of two polar strategies. One can be called "structural transformation," the other "gradualism." The transformationists tend to emphasize industrial development more than agriculture. Within agriculture they emphasize capital-intensive, often large-scale schemes aimed at fundamentally changing the technology and organization of peasant life. They see little hope in the export sector as an engine of growth and emphasize reduction of dependence on the outside world. Distrust of the market mechanism, a large role for the state in mobilizing and managing resources, and a low tolerance for inequalities in income distribution tend to be typical of their world view.

The gradualists tend toward the opposite position in all these respects. They emphasize outward-looking growth and the potentials of the export sector, focus on peasant agriculture, the importance of individual incentives and the use of the market. They are more kindly disposed toward private capital, both foreign and domestic, and give a smaller role to the state in the development process. They are rather more concerned with efficiency and growth than with equity in income distribution.

This classification, of course, involves some oversimplification. Few writers are unalloyed transformationists or gradualists, and few countries pursue wholly consistent sets of policies of one or the other polar types. What makes Ghana and the Ivory Coast so nice a comparison is that the recent development strategies of the two countries fall so much into the two categories—Ghana's economic policies under Nkrumah being very much transformationist in orientation, the Ivory Coast's being very much gradualist. In Nkrumah's Ghana, at least after 1960, priority was given to import-substituting industrialization, capital-intensive, state-managed agricultural development, the reduction of external dependence, and the Ghanaianization of the economy. Socialism was proclaimed to be the guiding ideology, and the public sector was given the leading role in economic expansion. The Ivory Coast, on the other hand, has had policies focused on the development of agriculture, with much attention to peasant agriculture and the export sector has been regarded as the main source of growth. Policies of fiscal orthodoxy have prevailed, and the role of the state has been restrained. The Ivory Coast has kept and even intensified its ties with France and its dependence on foreign capital and skill.

There is not much question about the relative economic performance of the two countries during the recent past. From 1960 through 1965 gross output probably rose by six to seven percent a year in real terms in the Ivory Coast, while it rose by two to three percent in Ghana. Output per capita was about the same in Ghana at the beginning of 1966 as it had been in 1960, while it had risen by some four percent a year in the Ivory Coast. The Ivory Coast remained in internal and external equilibrium during these years; internal prices rose by about three percent a year; consumer prices were some seventeen percent higher in 1966 than they had been in 1960. Export earnings nearly doubled between 1960 and 1965, and the Ivory Coast enjoyed an easy balance of payments position throughout. In Ghana, consumer prices in the beginning of 1966 were seventy-five percent higher than in 1960, and this understates the extent of inflation since, among other reasons, most goods were unobtainable at any price. From 1961 on, there were foreign exchange shortages and exchange controls, with the extent of external imbalance growing larger over the period; by the beginning of 1966 the manufacturing, agricultural, and transport sectors of the economy were operating well below capacity because of scarcities of imported inputs. In the industrial sector, manufacturing value added in the Ivory Coast grew by over twenty percent annually between 1960 and 1965, a faster rate than in Ghana. Nonagricultural recorded employment grew between 1960 and 1967 at a compound rate of over seven percent annually in the Ivory Coast, more than twice as fast as in Ghana between 1960 and 1965.

By all the obvious measures, therefore, the Ivory Coast has been one of the truly star performers in the less-developed world, and Ghana one of the really catastrophic failures. A simple-minded observer looking at the numbers might be led to conclude that there was something wrong with the general strategy or particular policies pursued in Ghana under Nkrumah, and something very sound in Ivory Coast policies. So homely a conclusion seems to be unacceptable to many writers, however. This is no surprise, for the ideological stakes are very high. Writers of a structural transformationist persuasion, in particular, feel compelled to explain the Ghanaian failure without at the same time compromising the general validity of the transformationist diagnosis and strategy of development. The Ivory Coast performance also requires some explaining, since on the surface at least it appears to be an overwhelming validation of gradualist ideas.

This explains the peculiar tenor of much that has been written about the Ivory Coast and Ghana experiences. One finds in the two or three main published pieces a number of propositions:

It has been argued that different public policies had relatively little to do with the divergent performance of the two countries. This is the thrust of a recent article by Eshag and Richards.[1] These writers conclude that the fall in cocoa prices after 1958, the greater importance of cocoa in Ghana's economy and a tax structure which made public revenues peculiarly dependent on cocoa prices, are the major factors explaining Ghana's poor performance and the different rates of growth in the two countries.[2]

---

1. E. Eshag and J. Richards, "A Comparison of Economic Developments in Ghana and the Ivory Coast since 1960," *Bulletin of the Oxford University Institute of Statistics* (December 1967), pp. 353–71.

2. This is the general tone of their article. Their language is guarded throughout: "It may be argued with some justification, that what initiated the divergence in the paths of economic development of Ghana and the Ivory Coast was the difference in the impact of changes in external demand, notably the fall in the cocoa price, on their economies. Given the important differences in the pattern of production and export of the two countries and their dissimilar structures of taxation, over which neither of the two Governments had control at the time of independence, and given the developments in export prices, which were similarly beyond their control, the Ivory Coast could not but enjoy more favorable conditions for growth and stability than Ghana" [ibid., p. 356].

"This argument, although valid in itself, is rather incomplete. The unfavorable course of external demand for Ghanaian exports could reasonably account for the slowing down of the rate of growth of production and income in that country. But it cannot *fully* account for the economic and political instability. . . . For this the Gov-

In the opinion of a number of commentators, the Ghanaian strategy between 1960 and 1966 was essentially correct, though its execution was bad and certain "errors" were made. Reginald Green, for example, mentions in an earlier version of his contribution to this volume, "gross underestimation of the time span between fixed investment and GDP growth, . . . overdependence on supplier credit, . . . overestimation of GDP growth in the early years of the plan," the wrong assumption that civil servants understood and had accepted the need for discipline, and excessive negativism in the economic civil service.[3] As areas of "ineffective or irrational implementation," he mentions, "disastrous agricultural policy and programming," poorly coordinated industrialization, inefficient capital and manpower allocation, unsound external finance, loss of financial control, misuse of funds, and incompetence.[4] He, nonetheless, apparently does not believe that these were fundamental, for he states that "Ghana's deteriorating performance and to a significant extent the 'unsoundness' of her 1961–1965 international economic and financial policy stemmed directly from world market conditions for her exports" [ibid., p. 4], and elsewhere states that despite some weaknesses in the Ghanaian strategy, "these would not have been fatal if either the export proceeds had remained buoyant or implementation had been less woefully inept in critical areas" [ibid., p. 6].

There is a systematic pooh-poohing of the Ivory Coast achievement and a downgrading of the role of sound policy in accounting for that achievement. Thus the Eshag-Richards article and the Green paper contain oblique statements, generally without specific evidence, that after all, Ivory Coast policies have not been all that much better than were Ghanaian policies. Eshag and Richards, for example, in discussing capital expenditures, say that "information on capital investments is rather incomplete in both countries, but particularly in the Ivory Coast" ["A Comparison," p. 366]. So they say nothing further about Ivory Coast investment programs ex-

---

ernment's economic policy, in particular its budgetary measures, must be held largely responsible. The main criticism of government policy in Ghana concerns the rapid expansion of public outlay in a period of deteriorating terms of trade and of stagnating production" [ibid., p. 371].

What this seems to say is that external factors beyond Ghana's control largely explain its poor growth performance, while government policy partly accounts for the economic and political instability of the 1960s.

3. R. H. Green, "Ghana and the Ivory Coast, 1957–1967: Reflections on Economic Strategy, Structure, Implementation and Necessity," paper presented to 1967 meeting of African Studies Association, pp. 29–30.

4. Ibid., p. 40.

cept to comment in passing that "as in Ghana, part of this expenditure could not be justified on rational social and economic grounds" [ibid., p. 372], leaving the impression that resource misallocation was probably not on a much different scale in the two countries. Reginald Green mentions "hap-hazard industrialization" in the Ivory Coast ("Ghana and the Ivory Coast," p. 33), but his criticisms (ibid., p. 32) turn out to be directed at the Ivory Coast strategy itself, on the a-priori grounds that growth based on exports and foreign capital inflow cannot last but a few years more, so that "rapid strategy alterations are needed" in the Ivory Coast (ibid., p. 41).

A related common attitude toward the Ivory Coast is rather more amusing: this is the view that it was easy to do what has been done in the Ivory Coast. Thus, Green says: "Export centered, neo-laissez faire, substantially foreign financed, and dominantly foreign technically staffed and managed economic growth is certainly the simplest for a government to oversee. If fiscal orthodoxy and pragmatic caution are added the likelihood is that what is attempted will be largely accomplished but that a good deal less than what would have been possible will be attempted" [ibid., p. 32]. The tone of the Eshag-Richards article is that the robustness of the Ivory Coast economy is due to the fact that government in the Ivory Coast did not have to do all the unpleasant things that the Ghanaian government was forced to do, such as impose higher taxes and exchange controls. Samir Amin, in a recent volume on the Ivory Coast, asserts that the Ivory Coast "miracle" is not really so miraculous; other countries in Africa did the same in the past (he cites the ex–Belgian Congo, Ghana, and Nigeria), and seems to attribute it to the existence of unused land.[5] Green takes a similar position. The biggest difference between the Ivory Coast and Ghana, he argues, was that the Ivory Coast has unused land and underutilized labor, as well as assured high-price markets for its output in France, while none of this was so for Ghana by 1957. The Ivory Coast in 1957 was in these crucial respects more like the Ghana of 1900 than the Ghana of 1957.[6]

A slightly different "explanation" of differences, related to all of the above, is much simpler; it has all been a matter of "luck." The Ivory Coast has been in good export crops, while Ghana was in a bad one.[7]

5. Samir Amin, *Le développement du capitalisme en Côte d'Ivoire* (Paris: Les Editions de Minuit, 1967).
6. Green, "Ghana and the Ivory Coast," pp. 9–10.
7. See, for a crisp expression of this widely held view, "The Ivory Coast Picture," *West Africa* (14 December 1968), pp. 1480–82.

Finally, there is in much of the writing about the Ivory Coast a strong emphasis on what are regarded as the "unhealthy" aspects of Ivory Coast growth; continued and even deepening dependence on the outside world for capital and skill, inadequate attention to manpower development and an unequal distribution of income. Samir Amin even concludes his book by stating that the Ivory Coast is really a case of "growth without development," apparently because the proportion of "urban income" going to foreigners has not changed over a decade or more of rapid growth.

Not all of these propositions can be appraised in this chapter, though some of them will be specifically considered, and I hope to show that most of them are wrong, irrelevant, or unconvincing. The main point argued here is that Ghana's failure is the failure of a development strategy, the structural transformation strategy, while the Ivory Coast success is genuine and confirms the appropriateness of a gradualist strategy for small countries at early stages of development.

## WHAT HAPPENED IN GHANA?

### THE DIMENSIONS OF ECONOMIC FAILURE

The impact of the Nkrumah years on Ghana's economic development was little short of catastrophic. Only some aspects of the catastrophe can be considered here.

The rate of growth of aggregate real output first slowed down, then fell to less than one percent in 1965, as can be seen in table 1.

TABLE 1
GHANA GROSS NATIONAL PRODUCT, 1957–66

|  | 1957 | 1958 | 1959 | 1960 | 1961 | 1962 | 1963 | 1964 | 1965 | 1966 |
|---|---|---|---|---|---|---|---|---|---|---|
| GNP, millions of G£ current prices | 368 | 389 | 443 | 473 | 504 | 542 | 595 | 673 | 795 | 890 |
| constant (1960) prices | 392 | 388 | 443 | 473 | 488 | 514 | 528 | 543 | 547 | 555 |
| Rate of increase |  | −1 | +14 | +7 | +3.2 | +5.3 | +2.7 | +2.8 | +.7 | +1.5 |

If a rate of growth of population of 2.5 percent annually is assumed (as Ghana's Central Bureau of Statistics assumes), then per capita GNP in 1965 and 1966 was about the same as it had been in 1960.[8]

8. Some observers claim that the population is increasing by as much as 3.5 percent per annum, in which case, of course, per capita growth would have been comparatively less. See J. C. Caldwell, "Population Change," in W. Birmingham, S. Neustadt, and

These figures do not look particularly shocking. But by themselves they give only the gentlest hint of Ghana's performance. To get their true meaning it is necessary to note the tremendous effort that was made during these years. Between 1960 and 1965, investment as a proportion of GNP was very high by less-developed-country standards. In 1965 it reached twenty-two percent of GNP. The result of all this "investment," however, was the meager increase in total output shown in table 1[9]. This investment effort, moreover, was by itself enough to explain growth of the order shown in the national aggregates. That is, heavy and rising budget expenditures in conjunction with public investment that was being financed through short-term contractor or supplier credits provided injections of income which, with their consequent multiplier effects, was bound to have some effect on rates of growth of GNP. This is not "real" growth in the sense of a permanent increase in the income stream or productive capacity of the economy. It is a peculiar kind of growth, inherently temporary, unless the investment expenditure in question creates additional capacity to produce.[10] Investment in Ghana during this period was not, for the most part, of this output-generating type. Although development expenditures and supplier credit financed projects continued to grow after 1963, their effects on output were slight; output growth was being restrained by other developments in the economy associated with the high level of public expenditure such as the acute balance of payments disequilibrium, with the attendant shortages of consumer goods, imported raw materials, spare parts, and farm inputs. The main point is that aggregate output rose only by some fourteen percent between 1960 and 1965, and per capita output was stagnant, and that this modest increase is explainable in large part as the short-term income rising effects of the high rate of heavy public expenditure and externally financed investment which occurred during this period.

---

E. N. Omaboe, eds., *A Study of Contemporary Ghana: Vol. II, Some Aspects of Social Structure* (Evanston, Ill.: Northwestern University Press, 1967), p. 109.

9. To give some idea of orders of magnitude involved, between 1960 and 1965, it can be inferred that somewhere in the neighborhood of G£ 700 million were invested in fixed capital formation. This is the sum of current price gross fixed capital formation estimates in the latest version of the national accounts, plus an estimated G£ 100 million in supplier credit financed capital investment installed during the period but not paid for (and hence not included in the budget or in the national accounts). Output in real terms (constant 1960 prices) increased by some G£ 70 million between 1960 and 1965. The capital-output ratio implicit in these figures is extraordinarily high.

10. This is a point that has been frequently stressed by Wolfgang Stolper, in informal discussions with the author.

The real income of large sections of the population, and particularly the economically relevant portion (those most fully in the money economy) declined drastically. Private consumption expenditure apparently rose by only four percent in aggregate, between 1960 and 1965, whereas population (assuming a minimal 2.5 percent annual increase) increased by 13 percent—implying a nine percent drop in average per capita real consumption during these five years. Specific income-earning groups suffered even sharper falls. Urban wage earners, for example, received little in the way of increases in wage rates; between 1958 and 1966 there was only one change in the minimum starting rate of unskilled government labor in Accra, which is the key wage rate in the wage structure; this was a rise of some five percent in 1960. Base rates then remained unchanged until 1967. Consumer prices, meanwhile, approximately doubled between 1960 and 1965. This means a day's unskilled labor brought in slightly more than half the real income in 1965 than it had yielded in 1960. Other indicators of wage changes give a rather less precipitous, but still substantial fall in real wages. The index of average earnings of African employees in the private sector (which covers employees in firms with more than ten workers, and includes only straight-time pay) shows a rise of twenty-six percent in average money earnings between 1960 and 1965, which means a fall of about thirty-three percent in general real earnings. Real incomes of cocoa farmers also fell substantially as producer prices declined throughout the period.[11] Since so many cocoa growers also grow their own foodstuffs (which make up more than half of the weight of the urban consumer price indices) the real income decline experienced by cocoa growers cannot be easily measured. That their terms of trade (ratio of unit prices paid to cocoa farmers to prices of consumer goods bought by cocoa farmers) declined by at least twenty-five percent between 1960 and 1965 seems a reasonable guess.[12]

There occurred during these years an extraordinary rapid dispersal of national liquidity and a heavy mortgaging of future income. At independence Ghana's external assets totalled over G£ 160 million, or about

11. The effective price paid to cocoa growers fell from 80s. a load in 1955–57, to 72s. in 1957–59, 60s. in 1959–61, 54s. in 1961–63, 50s. from 1963–65, and 40s. in September 1965.

12. It should be noted however, that aggregate cocoa farmer revenues were higher throughout the 1960s than they had ever been, due to larger crops. Also, the Cocoa Marketing Board cushioned the fall of prices throughout the period of declining world prices, and the farmers as a group were probably beneficiaries of transfers from the board throughout these years. The Marketing Board ran deficits in every year after 1960, these amounting to over G£ 35 million, or almost 20 percent of the total payments to cocoa farmers during the years 1960–65.

$450 million. These were largely gone by 1963, and were virtually at zero by 1965. In addition, and of much greater consequence, heavy borrowing, mainly of the relatively short-term supplier credit type, left the country in 1965 with foreign obligations of some G£ 190 million in external debts, of which G£ 150 million was the result of supplier credits. In nine years the Ghana government thus spent almost $900 million in foreign exchange. The debt service requirements which would have been required in 1966 and 1967 had there been no coup and no debt rescheduling, would have amounted to twenty-five percent of foreign exchange earnings—an unsupportable proportion. As the *Economic Survey* of 1966 notes: "It was evident that Ghana would have defaulted on her external payments."[13]

Another way to measure the achievements, or lack of achievements of the Nkrumah years is to measure them against the goals of the regime. One version of some of those goals can be found in the "Seven Year Development Plan (1963–1969)." It is hard to know what to make of this document. On the surface, it is not credible; too many of its targets are clearly impossible, the product of unfettered imagination. So the cynic's natural assumption about it is that nobody knowledgeable, either inside or outside of Ghana, took it seriously. Yet there appear to be some observers who did, in fact, take it at face value. Reginald Green, for example, in an article which was written in 1965,[14] argues that Ghana's plan reflects a correct transformationist strategy and was essentially a sound and realistic document.

The plan is unusual. It is virtually a text of applied economic analysis and policy . . . as well as a detailed blueprint of policies, projects and their implementation.

The clear expression of economic programs as a function of national aspirations is matched by a sober—if perhaps optimistic—calculation of what can be achieved and what are the real resource constraints on development. As a result the plan *is* a serious force both in the political drive behind its implementation and the fact that its fulfillment—at least to, say, 80% of output and 80–90% of input targets—is attainable, barring radically unfavorable foreign sector influences.[15]

In fact, many of the targets of the "Second Development Plan" were practically impossible, the policies and projects required to attain them were most sketchily indicated, and the actual decisions taken on investment

13. Ghana, Economic Survey (Accra: Government Printer, 1966), p. 26.
14. R. H. Green, "Four African Development Plans," *Journal of Modern African Studies* 3, no. 2 (August 1965) : 249–79.
15. Ibid., p. 253.

and other development expenditure had, in any event, little to do with
what was in the plan. Agriculture, for example, was one of the key sectors
in the plan; it was allotted G£ 68 million, or almost twenty percent of total
planned public investment during the period 1963–69. One indication of
the lack of connection between what the plan said and what actually happened is the fact that the state agricultural sector during the first two years
of the plan spent at a rate far exceeding its allocation in the plan, and
development expenditure in activities affecting private small holders was
far below plan allocations.[16] With respect to output targets in the plan,
those fixed for public sector agriculture turned out to be five or ten times
greater than output probably attained in 1965–66. In the State Farms
Corporation, only in rubber, rice, and oil palm were as much as half
of the 1965 acreage targets met; for the other crops, achievement was ten
to fifteen percent of the targets fixed by SFC to meet the development plan
targets. And this is to say nothing of the costs involved.[17]

Reduction in "dependence" on the outside world was another objective
of Ghanaian policy under Nkrumah. The concept of dependency is ambiguous; its extent is difficult to measure, and it is of limited meaning if
considered apart from other factors, such as rates of growth of output or
income. By some possible indicators Ghana did reduce its dependency
during the Nkrumah years. The geographical concentration of its foreign
trade was diminished, a larger share taking place with the communist
countries.[18] Also, as a result of nationalization and public sector investment in directly productive activities, a rather larger proportion of total
economic activity came under direct Ghanaian control, and less private
foreign control. The trend toward Ghanaianization of personnel, which was
marked before 1960, accelerated, particularly in the public sector.

These indicators of reduced dependency, however, should not be exaggerated. Ghana remained tied to its export sector and even more dependent
on cocoa than before, since most of its minor exports either stagnated or
diminished. Most of its exports still went to the noncommunist countries.
The shift in ownership of the means of production to the state was minor;

16. See below, p. 208.
17. See H. Miracle and A. Seidman, "State Farms in Ghana" (Land Tenure Center,
University of Wisconsin, 1968), for a relatively sympathetic discussion. An example
related to agriculture is to be found in the cattle targets of the plan. The public sector
target for beef and mutton in the plan was 4,000 tons annually by 1969–70. This implied an annual slaughter of 32,000 head of cattle, and a public sector cattle operation
amounting to 150,000 head. This is approximately one-third of the total cattle population of the country in 1964, as estimated in the 1964 Agricultural Census. In 1964, the
state livestock herds actually totalled under 2,000 head.
18. Cf. Green, "Ghana and the Ivory Coast," pp. 16–17.

over eighty percent of the manufacturing sector in 1965 was still in foreign private hands. Ghanaianization did not mean, nor could it mean, self-sufficiency in skills and experience; expatriates remained plentiful and continued to dominate the managerial and technical heights of the economy.[19]

Moreover, by at least two possibly meaningful indicators it can be argued that Ghana in 1965 was more dependent than she had been in 1960. First, import dependency was greater than before. In the 1963–65 period imports were roughly twenty-four percent of GDP (measured in constant prices), as against twenty-two percent in 1957–59. The composition of imports had changed, with more investment goods and raw materials and less consumer goods. But this, as Latin American experience has abundantly demonstrated, and the 1965 Ghana experience confirms, only makes the economy more vulnerable to balance of payments difficulties, since there is no longer any "fat" to be cut out of the import bill, while domestic manufacturing is heavily import-dependent.

Second, Ghana was becoming more, not less, reliant on external financing for its development expenditure. Gross domestic savings in 1957–59 exceeded gross public investment; by 1963–65 very little of gross investment was being covered by domestic resources. In the public sector, less than fifteen percent of budgeted investment expenditure in 1963–65 was financed out of government savings.

The legacy of the Nkrumah policies had been such that much of the period since the coup has been taken up with simply picking up the pieces. The rescheduling of the debt alone dominated most of the first year, and inquiry into the affairs of the state enterprises went on for longer. The general administrative disorder characterizing the last years of Nkrumah's rule could not be improved quickly; the first postcoup years showed that stronger budgetary discipline and expenditure control would not be imposed overnight.

Any calculation of the costs of Nkrumah's missteps should take these factors into account: part of the price of failure, and a substantial part, is the future growth because of the need to deal with the errors of the past. Not many new fences can be built when so many old ones must be mended.

19. In 1965 there were an estimated 800 expatriates at work in the civil service, over 500 of them teachers. Another 600 were in state enterprises. There were also some 500 technical assistance experts in the country. The secondary schools depended heavily on foreigners for their more qualified staff, most of the university graduates teaching in the secondary schools were foreigners.

## WHY DID IT HAPPEN?

Measured by its objective achievements, the Ghanaian economic effort since independence and especially between 1962 and 1965, was clearly unsuccessful. About most of this there is no dispute. There are differences of opinion, however, about how to explain what happened. It was noted earlier that some commentators have stressed external factors—notably the decline in cocoa prices during the first half of the 1960s—as a central factor accounting for the evolution of the Ghanaian economy between 1960 and 1965.[20]

The decline in the price of cocoa on world markets is not altogether without relevance. Average realized prices in 1959–61 were less than eighty percent of the average price in 1954–56, and in 1962–65, only sixty-three percent. Since cocoa provides some sixty percent of Ghana's export earnings, these price movements had adverse effects on the level of export earnings and the terms of trade (the ratio of average prices per ton of exports to average price per ton of imports).[21] The problem was aggravated, as has been emphasized elsewhere, by the fact that Ghana in 1969 was not only highly dependent on cocoa export duties (which provided thirty-seven percent of total revenues), but that the revenues were highly elastic with respect to changing prices of cocoa.

The external factors made growth more difficult in the period 1960–65 than it might otherwise have been. But the impact was not very great, and they can in any event hardly be made the strategic factor in an explanation of Ghana's economic evolution. First of all, export earnings from cocoa were actually on a slightly rising trend throughout the period 1957–65; in the 1960s increases in volume balanced the declines in price. Nor did overall foreign exchange earnings decline significantly—they rather stagnated.[22]

---

20. Eshag and Richards, "A Comparison," pp. 4–5.

21. With 1954–56 taken as 100, Ghana's terms of trade averaged 81 in 1959–61 and 61 in 1962–65.

22. Average earnings from export of cocoa beans was G£ 67 million in 1958–60 and G£ 68 million in 1963–65. Total merchandise exports averaged G£ 112 million in 1959–60 and G£ 113 million in 1963–65. It's hard to know how Eshag and Richards could write of a "drastic decline" in export earnings after 1958 (p. 310). With respect to the trend of cocoa prices, it is worth mentioning that while prices in the 1960s were lower than in the 1950s, they were still relatively high by longer-term standards; compared with their 1948–50 level, for example, cocoa prices were relatively high in the 1960s. The overall terms of trade were better throughout the 1960s (with the exception of 1965), than they had been in the late 1940s.

Second, the behavior of exports cannot be viewed—as it so often tends to be viewed—as entirely exogenous, evolving independently of domestic policies. No country can maintain an overvalued exchange rate, price and tax policies which discourage exports, and generally neglect its export sector and then expect to perform well anyway. Ghana's policies were not so obviously antiexport sector in these respects as some other countries.[23] The export sector however had low priority, and government policies affected it adversely in a variety of ways. Government's emphasis on the state agricultural sector reduced the availability of labor in cocoa and in other lines of production, for example.[24] Allocation of import licenses seems to have given low priority to the smallholder agriculture. Cutlasses, for example, were scarce in 1964 and 1965, insecticides were in short supply, and capsidicides were completely unavailable in 1965. The general restrictions on consumer imports stimulated smuggling of cocoa and other agricultural output to neighboring countries.[25] Most significant perhaps is the neglect of minor exports and the absence of signs of any real effort in diversification of agricultural exports. In fact, government policy was a major factor explaining the reduction in timber exports.[26]

Finally, there are few countries that do not experience shifting fortunes in their external accounts, and this is true of rich as well as poor, industrial as well as agricultural countries. These changing fortunes require adaptations in economic policy, including sometimes, temporary reductions in desired rates of economic expansion. Ghana is no exception to this rule. She had access neither to the foreign exchange nor to the domestic resources to initiate the kind of development spending under-

23. The volume of cocoa exports in fact doubled over the period. But this was mainly the result of the past planting and, in the bumper year 1964–65, marvelous weather.

24. Cf. M. Miracle and A. Seidman, *Agricultural Cooperative in Ghana* (Land Tenure Center, University of Wisconsin, 1968) for comments on labor scarcity.

25. Between ten and thirty thousand tons of cocoa each year are said to have been smuggled out of Ghana during the period 1960–65.

26. In 1960 the Ghana Timber Marketing Board was created, with a monopoly in the buying and export of logs. Its operations were disastrous to the industry, resulting in failures to deliver abroad, frequent marketing breakdowns, difficulties in quality control and long-term damage to Ghana's position in the world timber market. The board was disbanded in 1962. But the industry remained very heavily taxed, and its costs were further affected by transport regulations and costs. Moreover, faced with depletion of Ghana's traditional export species, government nonetheless retained an old law prohibiting the export of a good, well-known species (Odum), despite the recommendation of the forestry technicians; the repeal of this law would have helped maintain Ghana's timber exports.

taken after 1961.[27] To say that adverse developments in the export sector "explain" the course of Ghana's economic development is therefore an extremely misleading way of looking at the problem.

It suggests a parable. Suppose that one summer a man's house burns down. He decides he will not build a new house like the old one, but a geodesic dome instead. He does not know much about geodesic domes, which turn out to be more complicated and expensive than he thought. He therefore does not finish the dome, and that winter he freezes to death for lack of shelter.

Now if a stranger were to be told upon inquiry at the funeral, that the man froze to death because his house burned down the summer before, he might think it a queer kind of answer. Yet this is in effect the answer we are given about Ghana by those who stress cocoa price and export earnings as the source of Ghana's poor performance between 1960 and 1965. Very little of what happened was due to "structural forces" beyond Ghana's control. Ghana was no more "forced" to undertake the policies she did undertake than the man in the story was "forced" to build a geodesic dome instead of a house. In the face of given resources and other environmental constraints, the Ghana government adopted a development program and economic policies which led to disaster.

The first and most general error of strategy was to attempt too much and, particularly, to throw on the state too much of the responsibility for organizing the development effort. Government economic activity and the size of the development effort increased sharply after independence. As compared with an average annual rate of increase of government expenditures of three percent in the five years preceding 1957, government expenditures more than tripled (in current prices) between 1958 and 1965 —an annual rate of increase of about seventeen percent. While all categories of expenditure reflected the growing public sector role, development expenditures rose most rapidly. Government annual capital expenditures increased from G£ 13 million to G£ 71 million during these years, or at an annual rate of about twenty-four percent. Recurrent expenditures rose more slowly—by fifteen percent annually. But as we have seen, gross domestic product was rising at an appreciably slower rate—ten percent annually in current prices. An increasing share of total national expenditure was therefore being channelled through the public sector. Public consumption expenditure as a proportion of GDP rose from eighteen percent in 1957–58 to twenty-five percent in 1965; budgeted capital invest-

27. Nor did she have information or knowledge of what specifically was to be done, but this it not the point here.

ment as a proportion of GDP increased from 3.4 percent to about 9 percent; government employees as a proportion of the recorded wage-labor force rose from about half to about three-quarters.

The true rate of expansion of public sector activity is even greater than is suggested by these figures. The budgeted expenditures exclude expenditures of statutory corporation, foreign public-aid, and—most significantly —public investment undertaken through suppliers' credits. There exists no consolidated public sector budget or complete public sector accounts for three years, and ambiguities and inconsistencies in the generally poor data make it impossible to say with any precision just what the level of public investment was during these years.[28] Taking probable levels of completed supplier-credit financed programs into account, the proportion of total gross fixed capital formation which took place in the public sector was probably between seventy to eighty percent; in 1957–58 it had been about twenty-five percent, in 1960–61, about forty-five percent.

As a result of the expansionary government role, aggregate rates of "investment" were at extremely high levels relative to most other less developed countries and relative to Ghana's past performance, despite the fact that private investment fell off. Measured in constant prices (1960), gross domestic fixed capital formation averaged twenty percent of GDP during the six year period, 1960–65, reaching almost twenty-two percent of GDP in 1965. This compares with a 1955–57 average of about sixteen percent.[29]

Government revenues also rose very substantially during these years— from G£ 60 million in 1957–58 to G£ 142 million in 1965, or an annual rate of increase of about thirteen percent. Revenues grew faster than GDP between 1957–58 and 1965, and were eighteen percent of GDP in 1965 as

28. To give some idea of the relative importance of supplier-credit-financed programs in total public-sector activity, according to informal and unofficial estimates made in Ghana the value of supplier-credit projects installed during the year 1965 amounted to some G£ 28 million, while budgeted capital expenditure was G£ 71 million.

29. Use of constant prices here reveals one of the major difficulties of analyzing the Ghanaian data for this period. If current prices are used for the same measures, quite a different picture emerges; the ratio of gross capital formation to GDP, for example, is in constant prices about the same as it was in the latter half of the 1960s (16 percent). This is due to the differential movement of prices in an inflationary open economy. Prices of consumer goods rose much more than prices of investment goods, which were mostly imported. (The import content of investment in Ghana is about 50 percent). Between the mid-1950s and 1965 consumer goods prices appear to have risen by less than 20 percent. Because of these differences, the constant price GDP data gives a more meaningful idea of the way resources were used than does the current price series.

compared to sixteen percent in 1957–58. The major increase occurred after 1962, as government sought additional revenues to match its soaring expenditures; between 1960 and 1962, the ratio of government revenues to GDP was only about fourteen percent.

This tax collecting achievement was remarkable, especially since the government at the time made fundamental changes in the structure of the tax system, reducing the importance of export duties and increasing import duties and direct taxes.[30]

Despite the strong revenue-raising effort, however, expenditures continued to increase at a faster rate, and budget deficits persisted and widened. The fiscal years 1957–58 and 1958–59 were the only years after independence in which surpluses were registered. After a small deficit in 1959–60 (G£ 6 million, or about eight percent of budgeted expenditure) the deficits rapidly became more sizeable, growing to G£ 25 million in 1960–61, or about twenty-three percent of budgeted expenditure, G£ 50 million in 1962–63 (thirty-seven percent of expenditure), and G£ 39 million in 1965 (twenty-four percent of budgeted expenditure).

Until 1965 government revenues grew rapidly enough to cover increases in current expenditure. But they could not provide the savings necessary to finance the even more rapidly growing development expenditure. Government savings fell in absolute terms from highs of G£ 20 million in 1957 and 1958 to an average of under G£ 6 million in 1960–64. (They rose to over G£ 25 million in 1965, following the introduction of new taxes.) Government savings as a proportion of government development expenditures fell from over 140 percent in 1957 and 1958 (i.e., government savings exceeded development spending), to an average of only 13 percent in the five years 1960–1965.[31]

The acceleration of development spending begun after independence clearly could not be sustained with the level of financial and physical resources at the disposal of the Ghana government. Until 1961 the government covered gaps in its financial resources by drawing on the considerable foreign asset position it had built up in earlier years. After 1961–62, how-

30. Cf. Eshag and Richards, "A Comparison." The cocoa export duty was the biggest revenue earner in 1957–58 accounting for about 37 percent of total revenues; by 1965 it yielded only 7 percent of total revenues. Import duties brought in one-third of total revenues in 1956, as against about 25 percent in 1957–58. A sales tax introduced in 1965 fell mainly on imports, raising to 47 percent the approximate yield from import duties. Given the fact that changes of this order of importance were introduced in a short period, it is hard to see how the tax structure can be called a "structural" element, as Eshag and Richards suggest it to be.

31. In 1963 and 1964 only 6 and 9 percent of budgeted investment expenditures was covered by government savings. In 1965 it was 45 percent.

ever, this was no longer possible—the reserves were almost gone—and the main source of resources became budget deficits financed through the Central Bank. Internal debt of the government grew from G£ 39 million in 1960 to G£ 204 million in 1965. Massive deficit financing of this magnitude had relatively limited effects on domestic prices at first. Between 1957 and 1960 consumer price index rose hardly at all; between 1960 and 1963 it rose only by five percent annually. But the pace picked up in 1964 and 1965, when the annual rises were seventeen percent and forty percent, respectively. Between 1957 and 1965 the consumer price level approximately doubled, but the the major part of the increase occurred in the last two years.

The behavior of prices is clearly related to what was happening in the balance of payments. Until 1961 deficit financing had little impact on prices, in part because the deficits were not large relative to total expenditures, money supply grew relatively slowly, and real output was growing (at a rate of about five percent annually between 1958 and 1961) and, most important, because the run-down of foreign reserves allowed imports to siphon off inflationary pressures.[32] By the end of 1961 this was no longer possible and import controls were imposed, consumer imports in particular being particularly curtailed.[33]

Without external reserves, with export earnings not rising at a rate sufficient to provide foreign exchange for the investment program planned by the government and with government determined to go ahead nonetheless, it was necessary to resort to foreign lending. In part because there was a mutual lack of interest between "legitimate" foreign capitalists and the Ghanaian government (except for the Volta Project) and in part because government had few well-developed programs and projects for submission to conventional aid-giving institutions (i.e., outside of the East European countries), supplier credit arrangements became the major form of foreign borrowing. By 1965, and mostly between 1962 and 1965, credits amounting to at least G£ 150 million had been established in this way; supplier credits financed most public sector investment expenditure after 1962.

What these aggregate figures boil down to is this: in the early 1960s, when government's external assets were disappearing and export earnings were rising very slowly and foreign private investment was shrinking, the

32. Imports rose by 47 percent between 1957 and 1961, to a level of G£ 145 million. They then remained constant at an average of about G£ 126 million annually between 1962 and 1965, rising again (by 28 percent) in 1965.

33. In 1961–62 alone, external assets were drawn down by G£ 24 million.

Ghanaian government undertook a massive investment program designed to "transform" the economy. The program was financed by large and growing budget deficits and heavy foreign borrowing. In terms of real resources, government mobilized a growing share of output for its program by heavy taxation, by compression of real consumption through deficit financing, and by mortgaging future income through foreign borrowing.

The excessive size of Ghana's development program affected—one might even say predetermined—the outcome in various ways. It could not be done first of all, without shutting off the economy, without exposing it, that is to say, to permanent crisis in the balance of payments. While this is in some quarters regarded as necessary and desirable even where it is not inevitable, it creates profound difficulties, and in the Ghana case was one of the main factors in the disorganization of the economy after 1962.

While export earnings increased slowly after 1957, imports grew tremendously; they averaged forty-three percent more in 1963–65 than in the late 1950s, and at the same time, invisibles grew rapidly. The current account deficit in the balance of payments soared—from an average of G£ 12 million in the late 1950s to an average of G£ 50 million in 1963–65. As already noted, the deficit was financed mainly by run-down of foreign assets and utilization of suppliers' credits. Despite this massive foreign exchange expenditure of about $900 million in nine years (excluding private capital movements and conventional foreign aid), the balance of payments remained under steady pressure after 1961, when exchange controls were imposed. This had far-reaching consequences. It exposed a highly open and fairly complex economy to the uncertainties and inconveniences of exchange controls, particularly import licensing. Exchange controls in most less-developed countries seem to bring in their wake certain almost inescapable results: irrational allocation of import licenses, particularly the tendency to award too few licenses for raw materials and spare parts; favoring of the public as against the private sector; and the opening up of rich possibilities for corruption. All of this happened in Ghana. The economy suffered periodic scarcities of raw material inputs and spare parts, particularly in 1965. According to some observers in Ghana at the time, something like seventy percent of the total manufacturing capacity of the country was unutilized in 1965 because of lack of inputs and spares. A similar informal estimate is that in early 1966 over one-third of the trucks in the country were out of operation for the lack of parts.[34]

34. Between 1960 and 1964 the number of registered trucks actually declined from 13,500 to 13,000. New truck registration also declined, from 2,871 in 1960 to 2,209 in

Export licensing did seem to favor public sector activities, whatever their share in output in a particular sector. It appears, for example, that the state-owned portion of the manufacturing sector, which accounted for only seventeen percent of gross manufacturing output, received half the foreign exchange allocated in 1965 for raw materials and spare parts used in manufacturing.[35] This would help explain the extraordinarily high degree of unused capacity in manufacturing in 1965.

Finally, that much hanky-panky accompanied import licensing has been suggested by official inquiries conducted during the Nkrumah years.[36] Its extent was probably greater than indicated in the Abraham Report, given the high rates of profit, the extreme politicization of decision-making in general, and the limited control capacity of the government.

There is a second sense in which the size of Ghana's program was excessive; it put impossible strains on the country's limited stock of administrative and organizational capacity. It created in the civil service, demands for wholly new abilities, especially in the areas of project selection and evaluation, and the management or supervision of state productive activities. It led to extremely long lags in the completion of projects.[37] It made the tasks of coordination and control infinitely more difficult and created a general environment conducive to disorderly decision-making.

The point is simple but basic and deserves to be underscored. A large increase in the size and character of the tasks imposed on a weak administrative system does not simply mean that capacity to perform declines marginally. Rather it tends to set into motion forces that erode the whole decision-making machinery and destroy the capacity to execute and control.

Finally, the Ghana program was too big for the existing state of knowledge about the economy, where specifically it should go and how it should get there. Accumulated research on subsoil and soil resources, on crop suitability, on raw material potentials for local processing, on suitable tech-

---

1964. The total of new trucks registered during this five year period was 11,000. Ghana, *Economic Survey* (Accra: Government Printer, 1964). This should be compared with the Ivory Coast, which had about the same number of new truck registrations between 1960 and 1964 (10,200), but whose total truck population was 21,600, almost twice as large as Ghana's.

35. John Esseks, "Economic Decolonization in a New State of Africa: Ghana, 1957–1966," unpublished paper. This author cited an interview with Bank of Ghana officials for this estimate.

36. Cf. Ghana, *Report of the Commission of Enquiry into Trade Malpractices in Ghana*, Abraham Commission (Accra, 1966).

37. Between the signing and completion of projects during these years, lags of four years were normal, five years common.

nologies and scale—very little of this kind of information existed. But these are precisely the kinds of information needed to generate sensible projects and programs and give any public sector development program of a directly productive kind a chance for success.

Ghana had virtually no closely studied projects for public sector execution, nor was much done to develop them. Even in the best of administrative circumstances the proportion of unstudied projects and programs in the total development effort would have risen sharply as the size of the program increased. In Ghanaian circumstances of the early 1960s, where the shelf of projects was so bare, the capacity to fill it so limited, and the degree of administrative control so tenuous, a rapid deterioration of the quality of investment as the size of the investment program increased was a near certainty.

In addition to trying too much too fast and hence creating external imbalance, overloading the state far beyond its administrative capacity and extending the range of state activity far beyond the limits of detailed knowledge of what was to be done, there were specific errors related to priorities. Industry was given too much emphasis, and agricultural policy centered too much on large scale, state-run schemes. This contributed to misallocation of resources on a massive scale.

The government's determination to push industrial development and to do so through the public sector is symbolized by the share of total investment allocated to industrial development in the "Seven Year Development Plan." Out of a total planned investment of G£ 475 million between 1963–64 and 1969–70, twenty-three percent was given to industry and mining, mostly to industry.[38] Even more to the point is the behavior of actual budgeted expenditures. In the 1950s government development energies were oriented toward provision of infrastructure and social services. In 1957–58, for example, roughly forty percent of central government development expenditure was devoted to the transport and communications sectors. After 1962 these accounted for only about fifteen percent of the total. The biggest increases took place in industry and agriculture, and in both sectors it was direct participation in production that was mainly involved. Development expenditure on industry and mining was about six percent of total development spending in 1957–59, and close to twenty percent in 1963–65; this, it should be recalled, is exclusive of the externally financed portion of supplier credit projects.

A book could (and should) be written about the industrial development

38. Ghana, *Seven Year Plan*, p. 34.

effort. It is enough to note here that a considerable share of the total resources spent on industrial development resulted in white elephants of an unhappily pure type, and much of the rest was of doubtful viability. The outstanding examples of white elephants are the well-known cocoa silos, which probably cost G£ 10 million, and the cocoa processing mills (at Tema and Takoradi) of the state Cocoa Products Corporation (another G£ 10 million) cannot yield a net return over cost or even net gain in foreign exchange, except under exceptional and unlikely conditions in the world cocoa market.[39]

There is not enough information available to determine what proportion of the total industrial investment made between 1960 and 1965 has the potential to produce a reasonable rate of return. There are enough examples of doubtfully viable projects to suggest, however, that it is not high.[40] It is probable that something in the neighborhood of G£ 50 million was put into industrial investments which will either be shut down, operate with subsidies for long periods, or show very small rates of return, even were the most charitable shadow prices put on inputs and foreign exchange.

39. The profitability of processing cocoa depends on finding markets for cocoa butter and the relative prices of cocoa beans, cocoa butter, and (to a lesser extent) cocoa cake. In neither respect is there much hope for the Ghana industry. World supply of cocoa butter is abundant so marketing prospects are not bright. But more important, the price relationships between beans and butter would have to evolve in a most unlikely way for the substitution of butter for bean exports to be profitable. A quick example should make this clear.

A ton of cocoa beans is processed into approximately 40 percent butter, 40 percent cake, and 20 percent waste. The average price ratio between beans and butter has been about 1:2.4 in recent years. If this ratio falls to about 1:2.2 it does not pay to export butter; the value of the processed product is less than the value of the raw beans. Now the bean-butter price ratio is particularly sensitive to the price of beans; at a low bean price it is relatively high, since processing costs are a greater proportion of total costs. Even with bean prices at low levels, as in the early 1960s, the bean-butter price ratio was unfavorable to Ghana; in 1963–65, Ghana cocoa butter sold at a price giving a ratio below or near the 1:2.2 level. Ghana would have been better off in terms of export earnings and value of output if during these years the beans had been exported unprocessed. Since cocoa prices have been rising, the bean-butter price ratio has become increasingly unfavorable to cocoa processing.

These unfavorable conditions would create difficulties even if Ghana's plants were low-cost and well managed. In fact, the average capital cost per ton of capacity in the two recently built plants is more than ten times greater than the plant of the preexisting West African Mills, Ltd.; and their management does not seem distinguished. Yet the West African Mill has required heavy government subsidies and operated much below capacity in most years before 1962.

40. Some of these are a pharmaceutical plan (G£ 7 million), a tannery (G£ 1.5 million), a dry dock (perhaps G£ 7 million), a good storage scheme (perhaps G£ 3 million), assorted food processing and construction materials, plants (marble, furniture, boatyard, glass, and other unprofitable and problem-ridden industries) representing an undetermined investment.

Similar and even more costly policy errors and misallocation of resources occurred in the agricultural sector. The smallholder sector was
ignored, harassed, disfavored in agricultural policy, while the state farming sector was given (or took) an increasingly large role in the effort to expand and diversify agricultural output. According to the plan the private
farming sector which was responsible for virtually all agricultural output,
was to receive some attention. Out of a total planned agricultural investment of G£ 68 million for 1963–64 to 1969–70, almost half (G£ 32 million) was to be spent "on central services and other activities on behalf of
the private farmer" [Seven Year Plan, p. 75]. By 1965, however, it was
clear that the actual allocation of expenditure would be very different than
what was in the plan. It appears from the budget, for example, that services
for private farmers were being expanded very slowly, far slower than the
rate implied in the plan; by the end of 1965 only G£ 2 million had been
spent on these services, out of the G£ 32 million allotted for the whole plan
period. The State Farms Corporation, meanwhile, had spent during the first
two years of the plan G£ 7.5 million, or most of its total seven-year-plan
allotment of G£ 9.2 million. The Workers' Brigade was allotted G£ 4.5 million in the plan, but had managed to get G£ 3.3 million by 1965. The
United Ghana Farmers Cooperative was allotted G£ 2.9 million; its actual
allotment in the budget is not known, but it is known that the UGFC had
contracted for more than G£ 5 million in supplier credits up to 1965. The
State Fisheries Corporation spent in the first two years, G£ 2.6 million,
while its total allocation in the plan for seven years had been G£ 3.6
million.

While the state farming sector got most of the money, it produced very
little in the way of output. As indicated earlier, the State Farms made deri-
sory progress toward meeting most of the output targets set for it in the
plan. The Workers' Brigade apparently did not do much better.[41] Though
their time was short, there was very little in their performance to indicate
much potential for improvement. Both organizations fell prey to the policy
pitfalls so common in state agricultural efforts. They could not resist fancy
machinery, and so imported (mainly under supplier credits) a consider-

41. For example, the public-sector output target in the plan for 1966–67 was 41,000
tons for maize, 14,000 tons for rice, 48,000 tons for yams, and 21,000 tons for plantains.
Actual outputs in 1965 of the State Farm Corporation were 800 tons of maize, 1,200
tons of rice, 800 tons of yams, and 400 tons of plantain. The Workers' Brigade claimed
to have produced in 1965, 2,000 tons of maize, 1,000 tons of yams, and 3,000 tons of
plantains. These figures may be imaginary, but even if not, they still mean that virtually no progress had been made toward meeting public-sector food crop targets in the
plan.

able number of tractors and other equipment. Nor could they resist political pressures to employ workers who had friends in the right places. As a result, their payrolls soared. These factors, combined with a host of particular technical problems, and the scarcity of good management, meant that the state farming experiences with the possible exception of tree crop plantations, were largely a waste of money and manpower.

At the same time that resources were going to the state farming sector the private farmer was neglected or discouraged. The extension service, never particularly strong, languished. Credit facilities were made available through the UGFC, and the politicized allocation of credit undoubtedly caused grievances in some farming quarters. Difficulties and scarcity of truck transport created problems. The disappearance of imported consumer goods reduced farmer incentives to market output. There was apparently some reallocation of farm labor to state farming operations, which paid better than the traditional farming sector.

Cocoa farmers saw the subsidies on sprayers and insecticides diminish to nearly nothing in 1965. They also had to deal with the UGFC buying monopoly, which apparently had especially wide effects in creating grievances.[42] Encouragement (subsidy) for replanting in cocoa ceased.

These policies go a long way toward explaining the failure of Ghana's agriculture during these years. Food output lagged; this is the general view in Ghana, and tends to be confirmed by the fact that locally produced foodstuff prices rose faster than any other component of the consumer price index. By 1965 local food prices had risen 100 percent as compared to 1960; in 1965 alone the rise was 13 percent.

The true reasons for Ghana's poor performance under Nkrumah, then, are that the wrong policies were adopted, which is to say the wrong strategy, since the policies involved are for the most part an inherent part of a transformationist strategy. The analysis could stop here. Or it could be pushed a step further, and the question raised: why were these unsuitable policies and programs adopted? One could, after all, conclude that it was wicked or incompetent men, not policies, that led Ghana down the primrose path. In my view, this would be an incorrect conclusion. It was not Nkrumah's vanity or folly that was Ghana's sorrow. It was rather a matter of wrong ideas about how to develop a small, open, plural economy at a relatively early phase of its evolution, and in particular a lack of understanding of the kinds of constraints that are imposed on development strategies by size, politics, administrative capacity, and many other factors. I will

42. Cf. Miracle and A. Seidman, *Agricultural Cooperatives and Quasi-Cooperatives in Ghana, 1951–1965* (Land Tenure Center, University of Wisconsin), pp. 35–36.

focus here only on one of these constraints—the administrative, partly because Ghana provides such a storybook case of a general phenomenon in this area.

Given a short-handed, competent, and professionalized civil service on the one hand, and a political leadership anxious to push development faster on the other, certain inevitable problems can be anticipated in any less developed country. The technicians and civil servants tend to take a long time studying proposals, and to be unenthusiastic about most of them on technical or economic grounds—as they normally have good reason to be. For this reason, and perhaps also because of the incompetence of existing administrative agencies, political leadership responds by administrative short-cuts, and by setting up new and hopefully more responsive administrative units. One result is that administrative coordination, never very well developed to begin with, becomes immensely more difficult. Procedures for decision-making take on an increasingly ad hoc character. Available trained and experienced people are spread over more administrative units, increasing the need for coordination while the capacity to coordinate declines. The incentive to coordinate also declines. When the system loosens to the point where ministries and a large variety of state corporations and agencies are able to make budget and foreign aid commitments without much screening and control at the center, everything goes up for grabs. Any ministry which doesn't do as its less finicky public sector counterparts are doing will fall behind in budget allocations, in personnel, in status. Under the worst assumption about motivation, there are pockets to be lined by these activities. Under more benign assumptions, each minister or statutory corporation head identifies his task with the forward progress and welfare of the country.

Along with a proliferation of agencies, administrative shortcutting, the decline of coordination and communication within the public sector, and a growing disorderliness of decision-making there occurs a deterioration of budget capacity and expenditure control. Many of the new functions and programs of administrative units have not been properly budgeted for; there are new activities for which the usual "incremental" type budget submissions are inadequate. The ministries and other agencies do not in fact know how much new programs will cost. Many often guess wrong. If as in the French and British tradition the Ministry of Finance keeps a tight rein, there will be gross confusion at the operating level and little will get done. In response to pressure for action, the Finance Ministry tends to relax its control, and the operating ministries are free to run. The loss of control at the center is aggravated when statutory bodies and ministries are given authority to make aid agreements, credit commitments, and technical assistance arrangements. At this stage the treasury is presented with faits accomplis.

In these dynamics of administrative breakdown, outside forces come to play a crucial role, in particular the promoters, wheeler-dealers and machinery salesmen who offer "supplier credits," and for whom the most appropriate name is "carpetbaggers." These are usually peculiarly gifted men, highly resourceful, unscrupulous, persuasive. When necessary, they grease local palms. Often it is not necessary. They point to the development plan and tell the local people: "We can do that for you, and finance it as well." The economic or technical suitability of the projects they peddle is not their concern.

Now if the local administrative structures were such that these proposals could be carefully and properly evaluated, the damage from supplier credit deals might be limited. But in fact few less-developed-country administrations are capable of this kind of screening. Weakly staffed, uncoordinated, short of well-prepared projects, and unwilling or unable to go through the hard, often long work necessary to get conventional financing, most responsible officials leap at the chance to get something through supplier credit arrangements. Each proposal gathers powerful allies as it matures, until, having reached a certain stage it becomes terribly hard to stop, even when the planning organization or the treasury tries to stop it.

All of this means that any substantial development effort anywhere in the less-developed world runs the risk of falling out of control, and this is especially likely when the ideological focus underlying the effort is strongly disposed toward industrial development, for then almost any proposal of an industrial type falls on receptive ears.

Ghana's experience fits nicely into this general schema. One of the symptoms of the kinds of conflict just outlined was administrative proliferation. By 1965 Ghana was an administrative jungle. There were thirty-one ministries. Statutory corporations were scattered all over the place. It is not certain that at any one time anyone knew just how many there were. Key operating ministries were cut up periodically, their functions divided, then shuttled back and forth. Agriculture was the best example; between the old ministry, the State Farms Corporation, the United Ghana Farmers Council, the Agricultural Wing of the Workers' Brigade, and twenty-five other agencies, lines of authority were hopelessly tangled, coordination inexistent, and personal access to political figures more important in decisions than technical or economic issues.

Now the absorption of these new administrative units and the coordination of all the new functions of the public sector would have been a Herculean job even if there were lots of trained people available, little politicization of decision-making and firmly established institutions for making considered economic decisions. But though Ghana was much better endowed with manpower and with a good civil-service tradition than most African countries, these demands were too heavy. Nor were there in fact that many trained people to be called upon. To take the example of agriculture again, the total output of post-secondary-level professionals in agriculture was twenty people in 1960; throughout 1960–65 the total outflow of graduates with agriculturally-oriented training was in the neighborhood of 100. Yet of a total of 287 approved professional posts (agronomists, engineers, economists, etc.) in public-sector agriculture in 1965, only 67 were filled; and even more striking, 900 out of 1,500 subprofessional posts were empty.[43]

That the administrative machinery in Ghana could not absorb a massive increase in state activity should have been evident to anyone who spent any time in the country. The history of pre-1962 planning exercises, for example, was not reassuring. As early as the 1957–58 "Consolidation Plan" the difficulties of holding to any rationally considered expenditure plans became apparent.[44] Evidence of the buoyant spending propensities of the ministries and the limited control at the center became much clearer during the "Second Development Plan" (1959–64). Planned expenditures were set at G£ 26 million annually. By 1961, actual expenditures reached G£ 43 million, and the direction of expenditure bore little relation to the plan.[45]

Even more ominous and obvious was the evidence of looser budgeting. Supplementary estimates, indicating inadequacies in expenditure plans at

43. Ghana, Ministry of Agriculture, *Training Schools for Staff, Workers and Farmers* (1965).

44. The 1957–58 Consolidation Plan, for example, allocated G£ 500,000 for air transport and G£ 600,000 for water transport between 1959 and 1961; actual expenditures were about five times as much—G£ 3.9 million for air and G£ 3.1 million for water. (D. Scott, "Growth and Crisis: Economic Policy in Ghana, 1946–65," Ph.D. Dissertation, Harvard University, 1967, p. 88).

45. Ibid., p. 92. The transport and communications sector investment, for example, was set in the plan at G£ 29 million for five years. In less than two years G£ 39 million had been spent. The plan had G£ 1 million in it for ships, 0.5 million for aircraft; 3.5 for airport improvement. Actual investments committed (including supplier credits) were G£ 7.5 million in the first year of the plan (1959–60) and G£ 17 million in the second year. Only a few months after the plan was issued (in January 1960) a supplier credit arrangement was signed for purchase of eight merchant ships at a cost of G£ 7 million against a plan allocation of G£ 1 million.

the ministerial level, became increasingly important. In 1961–62 and again in 1963–64 budgetary affairs became sufficiently muddled that it was necessary to extend the fiscal year. The supplementary votes became a bigger proportion of total spending—about twenty percent in 1961–62 and 1962–63. Development expenditure supplementaries in 1959–60 and 1960–61 were fifty percent of those years' development budgets.

All of these were straws in the wind, strongly suggesting that budgeting procedures were weakening, expenditure controls loosening, with ad hoc commitments becoming more frequent. And all this was before the big push of the transformationist "Seven Year Plan of 1963–64."

In truth, it seems that after 1962 the lid had come off. Even such screening and evaluation procedures such as had existed, withered. Coordination between ministries and within the public sector virtually disappeared. Some of the indications of these developments have already been mentioned—notably the heavy overspending of the state agricultural sector. But they were not alone. Education, which is almost always a runaway ministry, was overspending at a rate of about thirty percent on capital budget, and had hopelessly underestimated recurrent costs.[46] The Ministry of Industries had in two years probably surpassed the seven year total of G£ 109 million allotted in the plan for industry and mining.

The loss of control over economic decisions, in combination with the presence of supplier-credit peddlers and an ideological receptivity in government to any kind of industrial project or any project which might reduce dependence, explain why so many wasteful investment decisions were made during these years. These decisions were almost all made without proper analysis or evaluation, and in many cases with no evaluation at all.[47]

By 1965 there was clearly an accelerating rate of deterioration in administrative control, and an increased degree of disorderliness in decision-making.[48] The pressure of supplier credit salesmen and other promoters

46. The plan said recurrent education costs would rise to about G£ 33 million (in 1962 prices) by 1970 from their 1963 level of G£ 15 million. They hit G£ 28 million by 1965. (Since teachers' salaries, the biggest element of recurrent costs, had not risen except for incremental increases, the rise in 1962 prices was probably not much different from the current price increase.)

47. It is common knowledge in Ghana, for example, that the Cocoa Marketing Board and other relevant agencies never knew the details of the cocoa silo project until after it was approved. Nor is it clear that they knew about the cocoa processing factories.

48. It is not easy to give a systematic picture of how much things had fallen apart in Ghana. Some examples (culled from various issues of *West Africa*) give some of the

was growing, and the Ghanaian capacity to resist was weakening. This can be seen in the rash of irrational commitments made in 1965 and the fact that nobody in government knew exactly what commitments were being made. According to some informal estimates in Ghana there were at the end of 1965 some G£ 50 million in industrial projects which were then at a stage of near-completion. But new agreements had been approved for about G£ 40 million more, and another G£ 75 million were in the works. Very few, if any, of these new projects had been analyzed for technical or economic feasibility.

At the same time most of the state enterprises were operating in free-wheeling fashion. Accounting information was very rare; in 1966 many of the state enterprises could provide records only up to mid-1963, and those records were often unreliable. While commitments were being made at every turn, and prices rising at an accelerated rate, and while effective controls over public resources slipped, and balance of payments restraints were dislocating the economy—at this time the government insisted on submitting an even bigger budget for 1966 than the year before. Another year of Nkrumah's rule and policies might have inflicted shattering damage on the Ghanaian economy—far worse even than the years 1962–65. It may after all have been a secret recognition that the Ghana economy

---

flavor of the situation. The State Farms took land by force in parts of the Eastern and Central regions. They were obliged to hire 10,000 workers after the reorganization of the agriculture ministry. Decision-making was highly centralized, with enormously long delays in answering requests from the field. There was evidence that taxis used State Farms as filling stations and tractors were frequently used for shopping trips. There are even reports of individuals buying tractors with loans from the development bank, and using these as taxis. According to some officials 80 percent of the tractors were inoperable in very short periods (580 crawler tractors had been ordered from Yugoslavia and 1,500 wheeled tractors from Czechoslovakia). There were no cranes to lift abandoned tractors onto trailers, and only a few trailers were available anyway. The Asutsuare sugar scheme involved location in an area whose soils seem unsuitable for cane, and which is in any event without water. Between project recommendations from technicians (where they existed) and actual projects there was little relationship. For example, a UN-WHO team recommended a water and sewage scheme for Accra costing a maximum of G£ 6.5 million. The actual project signed with a West German firm was for G£ 9.5 million. The civil service had recommended a G£ 1.9 million road between Accra and Tema; this was changed to the G£ 4 million Accra-Tema Motorway. The Bolgatanga airport is believed to have cost G£ 6.5 million, though nobody seems to know, since it was a secret Defence Ministry Project built with Russian technicians and supplies; it has a swimming pool and lavish barracks. The tannery is located in Bolgatanga, the meat processing plant in the Volta Regime; it is unclear whether transport costs will make hides from the meat plant too expensive for profitable use.

had run the string out which led the president to Peking and a quiet life in Conakry.

## THE IVORY COAST RECORD

To turn from Ghana to the Ivory Coast is, in terms of the aggregate figures on economic performance, a move into another world, a world of dazzling economic expansion. Some of the numbers are in fact staggering. In the eight years 1958–65, total GDP (including subsistence agriculture) in the Ivory Coast increased by 125 percent in money terms, or an annual rate of increase of almost fifteen percent. Monetized GDP rose even more dramatically, from 87 billion C.F.A. francs to 201 billion. These are current price figures. There are no official constant price GDP data for the Ivory Coast, so the rate of expansion of real output must be guessed at. Samir Amin, in his recent study, estimates that real output grew seven to eight percent annually between 1950 and 1960, and eleven to twelve percent between 1960 and 1965. His estimates are twice as high for the 1960–65 period at a semiofficial figure of six to seven percent.[49]

Table 2 lists a number of indicators which suggests the magnitude and character of the Ivory Coast's recent growth. They are magnificent numbers, matched by few countries in the world during the past decade. There is certainly no African country that has had growth of such speed and breadth. A few points deserve emphasis:

Growth has been largely export-propelled. Between 1958 and 1967 export earnings grew at a compound rate of eleven percent annually. Current account surpluses have allowed growth of external reserves and ease in the balance of payments.

Industrial development has also been rapid. Value added in manufacturing has grown by twenty percent a year since 1958; the volume of turnover in manufacturing has grown by about forty percent a year between 1960 and 1967. Manufacturing value added as a percentage of money GDP grew from about 6.5 percent to 9 percent between 1960 and 1965. Although part of this manufacturing growth derives from replacement of Senegal in local and neighboring markets, this is probably a minor part.

49. Amin cites a lecture given at the IBRD in 1964 by Father J. L. Fyot, *La Planification du développement en Côte d'Ivoire* (Amin, pp. 108–266). The basic problem aside from the large range of error possible in the underlying data, is the variability of prices of agricultural output, which makes the behavior of any real GDP series in an agricultural economy highly dependent on the choice of the year. Eshag and Richards (table 7) gives an estimate of about 10 percent annual growth of real GDP in the Ivory Coast between 1960 and 1965, but the origin of their deflator is not indicated.

## TABLE 2
### Ivory Coast Economic Indicators, 1958–67

| | 1958 | 1959 | 1960 | 1961 | 1962 | 1963 | 1964 | 1965 | 1966 | 1967 |
|---|---|---|---|---|---|---|---|---|---|---|
| GDP at market prices (billions of current C.F.A. francs) | 127 | ... | 155 | 173 | 183 | 208 | 250 | 248 | | |
| Money GDP (billions of current C.F.A. francs) | 101 | ... | 114 | 132 | 136 | 163 | 204 | 201 | | |
| Per capita C.F.A. francs | 28,000 | ... | 30,000 | 35,000 | 34,000 | 40,000 | 48,000 | 46,000 | | |
| Exports (billions of current C.F.A. francs) | 32 | 35 | 39 | 47 | 48 | 57 | 75 | 74 | 77 | 80 |
| Gross fixed capital formation | | | | | | | | | | |
| Private | 5.7 | ... | 9.9 | 14.1 | 15.5 | 19.0 | 24.2 | 25.8 | 23.0 | |
| Public | 5.2 | ... | 10.3 | 11.5 | 11.2 | 11.3 | 18.2 | 18.1 | 17.0 | |
| Gross investment as percent of GDP | 11.3 | ... | 13.9 | 16.8 | 11.9 | 15.6 | 19.3 | 17.5 | | |
| Gross investment as percent of money GDP | 14.3 | ... | 19.1 | 21.9 | 16.0 | 20.0 | 23.9 | 21.6 | | |
| Gross domestic savings total | 24.5 | ... | 30.3 | 31.4 | 27.5 | 44.5 | 63.1 | 54.3 | | |
| Percent of GDP | 21.8 | ... | 19.5 | 18.3 | 15.0 | 21.4 | 25.2 | 21.9 | | |
| Percent of money GDP | 24.3 | ... | 26.8 | 23.8 | 20.2 | 27.3 | 30.9 | 27.0 | | |
| Central government | | | | | | | | | | |
| Revenues | ... | ... | 23 | 28 | 31 | 33 | 43 | 47 | 45[a] | |
| Savings as percent of revenues | ... | ... | 28 | 28 | 22 | 21 | 34 | 34 | | |
| Industrial production (mfg.) | 5.2 | ... | 7.8 | 9.2 | 10.2 | 12.5 | 15.1 | 18.8 | | |
| Turnover | ... | ... | 12.7 | 16.7 | 19.7 | 25.6 | 31.6 | 40.5 | 51.4 | 60.6 |
| Consumer price index (Abidjan; February 1960 = 100) | ... | ... | 102.8 | 114.1 | 112.4 | 112.4 | 113.9 | 117.0 | 122.0 | 124.0 |
| Electric power consumption (thousands kwh) | 35 | ... | 57 | 77 | 102 | 131 | 158 | 189 | 242 | 280 |
| Road mileages (km) | | | | | | | | | | |
| All-weather | | | 8,700 | 10,700 | 18,600 | | | | | |
| Other | | | 8,000 | 15,000 | 15,000 | | | | | |
| Number of licensed vehicles (thousands) | 14.9 | 19.7 | 23.7 | 34.4 | 36.9 | 44.5 | 52.8 | 61.9 | 70.5 | 80.2 |
| Private autos (thousands) | 7.3 | 9.9 | 11.5 | 15.5 | 19.0 | 23.8 | 28.1 | 33.3 | 38.0 | 43.5 |
| Trucks (thousands) | 6.6 | 8.4 | 10.3 | 12.8 | 14.3 | 16.2 | 19.1 | 21.6 | 24.4 | 27.0 |

a. Estimate

Most of it comes instead from the increased size of the Ivory Coast market and the fact that a relatively large share of Ivory Coast manufactures are exported to industrial countries.[50]

Government revenues have grown faster than GDP; government's share of total GDP in 1965 was almost twenty percent, and of money GDP about twenty-three percent. At the same time government consumption (not shown in the table) has grown comparatively slowly, so that saving as a proportion of total revenue has grown from twenty-eight percent to thirty-four percent between 1960 and 1965. Budget surpluses out of current revenues have provided an extraordinarily high proportion of total investment —about two-thirds between 1960 and 1965.

The physical indicators in the table give a picture of an economy undergoing extensive change. Paid employment in the nonagricultural modern-sector occupations has grown from 92,000 to 129,000 (by forty percent) in six years, and the overall increase in employment opportunities throughout the economy has been far greater; there are no usable figures on the growth of paid employment in peasant agriculture, the biggest sector of the economy, which has expanded fast during these years. Electricity consumption has increased at a rate of about twenty-five percent a year. Something like a minor transport and mobility revolution is suggested by the fast expansion of road mileage and the number of vehicles.

Because there is not much argument about the fact that judging from the aggregates, the Ivory Coast record is brilliant, the most useful way to proceed here is to consider the criticisms which have been raised about the Ivory Coast.

As noted earlier, there is a strong tendency to downgrade the Ivory Coast's performance on the grounds that it has been "easy." Thus Amin says that it has been a matter of simply applying a known and simple technology through "extensive plantation agriculture" in the presence of unutilized land and labor from outside the country. Other countries have done the same; he cites in various places Senegal, Southwestern Nigeria, Ghana, the Belgian Congo. Reginald Green equates the Ivory Coast in 1957 with Ghana in 1900, on roughly similar grounds.[51]

It should be said, with respect to this argument, that the fact that other countries have had comparable growth, even if true, hardly detracts from the Ivory Coast record. It shows that if the right things are done, early-

---

50. About one-third of manufacturing output is exported, of which most (about three-quarters) consists of processed foodstuffs (tuna, pineapple, soluble coffee, etc.) to industrial countries.

51. See above, n. 6.

stage economies can grow very fast. In fact, however, there are distinctive aspects of the Ivory Coast growth. As Amin himself notes, it has occurred a good deal faster than the other countries he cites, and along a broader front; only the early expansion of the Ghana cocoa industry is comparable, but here too the pace was slower and more specialized. The Congo is not relevant because it was not a peasant producer economy, as the Ivory Coast essentially is.

It is worth recalling the physical quantities involved in Ivory Coast agricultural expansion. In 1950–54, an average of about 60,000 tons of cocoa and the same amount of coffee were marketed. For the period 1962–63 to 1966–67, little more than a decade later, coffee purchases averaged 212,000 tons and cocoa 122,000. Moreover, some five percent of the cocoa crop was produced by expatriate plantations in the early period; these have since disappeared (the expatriates turning to bananas and pineapples). The Ivory Coast in 1968 has the potential to produce close to 300,-000 tons of coffee and 150,000 tons of cocoa. This is in a country of four million people. In Western Nigeria, less than a decade ago, only about 175,000 tons of cocoa was produced, in an area containing about ten million people, and cocoa was the only export crop of significance. Ghana, with a population of eight million, produced some 250,000 tons of cocoa annually in the 1950s, and virtually no other export crop. The Ivory Coast, therefore, in a much smaller country, has in only a few years built up a cocoa and coffee base larger than the most advanced economies of West Africa had a decade ago. And in addition it has a big timber and banana industry, and is diversifying into pineapples, rubber, oil palm, and other crops, as well as into light manufacturing.

It may be "easy" to expand peasant production of three crops when the technological knowledge, the land, and the labor are there to do so. But it does not seem to happen everywhere, even where conditions seem particularly appropriate; Guinea is one clear case. One of the main reasons it does not happen is that policies are unsuitable, as is so obviously the case in Guinea.

The unutilized land and labor issue is not altogether relevant. With respect to labor, both Ghana and the Ivory Coast have for a long time relied on foreign migrants from the savanna countries of the north (Upper Volta and Mali, mainly) for a substantial proportion of their agricultural labor force. Ghana historically was the first to use these workers, and in the 1950s competed well with the Ivory Coast for them. Since then, the Ivory Coast may have bid away part of Ghana's migrant work force, but this was due to its rate of expansion and hence opportunities. Ghana had a highly elastic labor supply at its disposal, just as the Ivory Coast did.

The land issue is more complicated. It is probably true that the forest areas suitable for tree crops were by the mid-1950s more fully occupied in Ghana than in the Ivory Coast. But "land" is not the absolute constraint implied in this argument. The Ghana government, had it been so disposed, could have expanded its program for replanting with high yielding Amazon seedlings (a program it had dropped by 1965) and there are other ways to substitute other inputs for land in cocoa production—capsid control, for example—another program which received declining attention by the Nkrumah government. Presumably suitable areas might have been freed for other crops. The Ghana government chose not to take this line of approach.

It is sometimes suggested that the quality of investment in the Ivory Coast has not been much better than in Ghana.[52] The first thing to be said about this is that if it were true, then something odd is going on which can explain all that growth. The unsuitability of Ghana's investment program quickly showed up—in declining rates of growth of GDP, balance of payments problems, unutilized capacity, and demands for subsidization by state enterprises and corporations. There are few comparable signals in the Ivory Coast. If in fact the ratio of investment inputs is compared, the orders of magnitude indicate the sharp difference involved.[53] Ghana was "investing" a larger share of gross output than the Ivory Coast during this period, but getting far smaller increases in output from it.

But there is more to it than this. The Ivory Coast, by virtue of the strategy option it has chosen, has certain built-in safeguards against massive resource misallocation. It has first of all maintained a strong technical assistance contingent in its civil service, which has presumably allowed for a relatively high level of effectiveness in that respect. But more important, it has reduced the possible areas of error and the costs of errors when made, in a variety of ways. One way is by leaving directly productive activity to the private sector. The proportion of private to total investment in the Ivory Coast was much higher than in Ghana throughout the 1960s,

52. Cf., Green, "Ghana and the Ivory Coast"; Eshag and Richards, "A Comparison."

53. No attempt is made here to use capital-output ratios in a systematic way because the data are too bad and the concept itself so dubious. With deflation procedures favorable to Ghana, and using total 1960–65 gross fixed capital formation as the input and the change in GDP between 1960 and 1965 and the output, the Ghanaian capital output ratio is in the neighborhood of 6–8, the Ivory Coast ratio about 2.

despite the Volta project.[54] Although investment inducements do introduce misallocation in the industrial sector everywhere, including the Ivory Coast, these are minor compared to what can and often does happen in state productive projects. Moreover, the place of the carpetbagger, though growing, has been distinctly smaller in the Ivory Coast than in Ghana. Of the total public sector investments in the Ivory Coast between 1960 and 1965 which amounted to about 100 billion C.F.A., only about 12 billion were supplier-credit financed. This can be assumed to mean that overall investments were of lower cost and higher quality, by definition.

Finally, a significant share of investment in manufacturing has been in export-oriented industries, and this creates some presumption that they do not involve serious resource misallocation. It is when import substituting industry is involved that all bets on efficiency are off."[55]

There have, of course, been some mistakes involving misallocation. Supplier credit obligations have grown; while a total of 12 billion C.F.A. was paid for such projects in 1960–65, another 7 billion was obligated in 1967, though at that time the government was aware of the problem, and announced its intention to resort to them only for emergency projects for which conventional financing could not be found.

Legitimate doubts can also be raised about some major expenditures recently committed. The big San Pedro project, involving a major port and road development in the undeveloped southwestern part of the country does not seem to have been adequately studied. The cost will probably be close to 6 billion C.F.A., almost 4 billion of it to be provided through supplier credits. The big hydroelectric project on the Bandama River (probably costing 20 billion C.F.A. francs) appears to be of even more doubtful priority; there appear to be much cheaper alternatives for production of power, both in terms of foreign exchange and total cost, gradual expansion of thermal capacity, for example, or use of power from the Volta grid in Ghana. Nor is any substantial agricultural impact foreseeable. That project is nonetheless going ahead, with a recent United States EX-IM loan of $35 million.

While all of this indicates the existence of probable resource misallocation, it also indicates the limits placed on it by the Ivory Coast general

54. Out of total investment, roughly two-fifths was public in the Ivory Coast, three-fifths in Ghana.

55. According to Ivory Coast Ministry of Planning estimates, out of a total of 18 billion C.F.A. invested in manufacturing by 1966, one-third was in export industries, and another 4 billion C.F.A. in industries which produce partially for export.

development orientation. There are important differences between a dubious hydroelectric project and a bad investment in a directly productive state enterprise; the latter will probably make continuing claims on the future flow of recurrent revenues far in excess of the original investment. By avoiding direct state involvement in productive activities, the Ivory Coast has eliminated the greatest source of possible misallocation. Also, the Ivory Coast is able to finance its "mistakes," if mistakes they are, on relatively more favorable terms, presumably for political reasons. It is better, after all, to waste grant money, or even six percent money, than it is to waste twelve percent money, if wasteful decisions cannot be avoided. (With grant money or low interest money, of course, investments of low yield become worthwhile.) It is not irrelevant that the Ivory Coast received, in the 1960–65 period, some 15 billion C.F.A. in grants from the French and EEC aid agencies, or fifteen percent of its total public sector investment; it received another 9 billion in long term loans under favorable conditions, and some 10 billion in other transfers including technical assistance. There were in addition some 12 billion C.F.A. in committed but unspent grants in the pipeline in 1967.

Another general criticism of the Ivory Coast pattern of development is the great dependence on foreigners and foreign resources which it entails.[56] It is certainly the case that there is a much stronger foreign presence (especially French) in the Ivory Coast than in Ghana. The number of foreign residents has grown rapidly since independence; there are now said to be more than 30,000, and their influence is pervasive in the private sector and strong in the civil service. There are even elements of white settler atmosphere in the country, as there have always been.

While the foreign presence is particularly visible in the Ivory Coast, and may have peculiar social aspects, the simple and basic question is: can any country as small, as undeveloped, and as short of capital and skill as African countries generally are, have much development without heavy

---

56. See the letter from a Nigerian in *West Africa* (4 November 1967), p. 421: "How has the Ivory Coast's prosperity benefited the common man? Are the French not the very life and wire of most of its industries? How rapidly are nationals being trained to take over? Is the true foundation of the economy really Ivoirian? Admirers of the 'miracle' should answer these questions. Economic prosperity more beneficial to foreigners than to nationals is more to be feared than admired. Liberal capitalism is not African, and will not thrive in Africa unless nurtured by Western capitalists. The N'Krumah style has been sabotaged, and saboteurs are busy in Guinea and Tanzania, which are seeking a truly African economic system. . . . The Ivoirian 'miracle' is a sham."

use of foreign factors of production? There is no way out of this problem, except to sacrifice growth for greater national "control."[57]

It is not self-evident, moreover, that dependence is greater in the Ivory
Coast than in Ghana. The Ivory Coast has a sounder, more diversified,
more solidly based economy, one precondition for independence. It is less
dependent on external resources for its public development expenditure,
most of which it finances out of current revenues.[58] Its public finances,
including its external debt position are relatively healthy. Foreign creditors, including the IMF, are far from the door. France has great influence,
but must also tread lightly as French stakes there are now large.

The main point, however, is that there is no escape from dependency.
Industrialization based on import substitution leads to an even more acute
form of reliance on the outside (the industrial structure becoming dependent on continuing flows of imported inputs), and completely inward
looking growth is not feasible (even if its desirability should be granted)
for small countries at beginning phases of modernization. What the Ivory
Coast has done is openly embrace its economic reliance on the outside,
and exacted a price for it: preferences in Europe, aid flows, technical assistance on relatively good terms, private investment and the export market
that often accompanies it.

The distribution of income in the Ivory Coast is another source of
speculation and suspicion. It is said to be highly unequal both geograph-
ically and socially. Amin has tried to study this in some detail, and his
results are worth attention. He says that regional income differences are
"extremely great," within the southern half of the country as well as
between North and South. The North had in 1965, twenty-seven percent
of the rural population, according to his figures, and an average money
income of 2,400 C.F.A. per capita. The South, with the rest of the rural
population, had average income of 14,000 C.F.A.[59] Whether these are
"extremely great" or not, depends upon the measuring rod used. It would

57. Amin raises this point, presumably to destroy it, but he never really comes
back to it, restricting his discussion to pointing out the "limits" of this type of growth
(pp. 270 ff.).

58. Total central government investment was 78 billion C.F.A. between 1960 and
1965, and total investment, including public corporations and supplier credits, was
about 100 billion. Of this, 59 billion came from recurrent budget surpluses, and 7 billion was self-financed out of current revenues of public corporations. This means that
two-thirds of total investment during these years came from budget surpluses or current
earnings of corporations—a remarkable achievement in a poor country with a high
rate of investment.

59. With respect to these figures as to most others in this book, it is not easy to
know how they were derived, since Amin refers the reader to his thesis for details.

be a peculiar place where there were no differences in regional levels of development as measured by income levels.[60]

It is not obvious that these differences are bigger than in the rest of West Africa, for example. Moreover, the differences here are exaggerated, since they exclude nonagricultural income, and the North has probably benefited most from growth through the emergence of greater wage earning opportunities in the South. The fact that the relative size of population in the North has declined from thirty-four to twenty-seven percent of the total in fifteen years, and that absolute numbers of people there have, according to Amin, declined by ten percent in these years, suggested that this has been important.[61]

The most significant thing about regional income differences, as portrayed in Amin's book, is how much change they show in the rural areas. Only one-third of the rural population is now in "isolated and stagnant" zones, as compared to sixty percent in 1950, and the real cash income of the northern villager has, according to Amin's figures, doubled in fifteen years. Nor do Amin's figures even show such enormous inequality leaving out the isolated zones, which are shrinking fast, the differences seem rather modest for a country whose growth is recent and whose regions are very unevenly endowed. In the "ordinary plantation zone," half the rural population receives about twenty-five percent of the total rural income, and a "privileged" region around Abidjan, with ten percent of the population gets eight percent of the income. His data also show that ordinary planters in the South and cereal growers in the North have had faster growing incomes since 1950 than farmers in the better-located privileged regions of the country. The conclusion on the regional distribution of income that emerges from this study is that growth has affected a

60. There is considerable misunderstanding about regional inequalities in development in general, signified by a frequent implicit assumption that they are "bad" and ought to be done away with. This is obvious nonsense. The Mojave Desert can be made to bloom, perhaps nearly as the San Bernardino Valley blooms, but it would probably be at considerable cost in real income to the economy as a whole. There are two main economic questions to ask about regional differentials in development: is there any reason to think the poorer region is lagging because of lack of attention or discrimination in the allocation of development efforts; and if income differences are big, why don't people move? If the answer to the first question is negative, then there is no a priori economic reason to regard regional inequality as "bad"; to the extent that it induces migration of people, it is "good." It may be necessary for social or political reasons to attach weight to regional equality. And if people can't or won't move there are social reasons to give the region special attention. But from the point of view of economic development, the best answer to regional inequality is usually for people to move from poor to rich regions.

61. The question of how these figures were generated, however, is troublesome.

large proportion of the rural population, and has narrowed income differences appreciably.

With respect to class or "social" income distribution, Amin asserts that profound social differentiation has appeared, and he refers to the "20,000 rich planters who exploit almost one-fourth of the land, employ almost one-third of the laborers and enjoy incomes of about 400,000 CFA francs a year."[62] On close examination of the data presumably underlying this statement, however, it turns out that there is really little hard information on size of holdings or average incomes, and that all the estimates are derived by making heroic "assumptions" (such as about the number of laborers available). More important, the procedure by which he reaches his conclusions render the figures highly suspect.[63] Finally, his data do not show quite what his statement says they show.[64] They show only what is given in table 3, which is reproduced from his book. When the pro-

TABLE 3
IVORY COAST ACREAGE AND INCOME, PLANTATION ZONES, 1965

| | ORIGINAL RESIDENTS | | | |
| | Small | Medium | Large | Foreign Communities |
| --- | --- | --- | --- | --- |
| Total acreage (thousands of hectares) | 120 | 230 | 230 | 230 |
| Acreage per community (hectares) | 3.0 | 5.7 | 11.5 | 2.2 |
| Wages paid (billions of francs) | ... | 0.8 | 1.6 | ... |
| Income of planters (billions of francs) | 4.8 | 8.4 | 7.6 | 9.3 |
| Income per holding (thousands of francs) | 120 | 210 | 380 | 85 |

SOURCE: Samir Amin, *Le Développement du capitalisme en Côte d'Ivoire* (Paris: Editions de Minuit, 1967), p. 293.

62. P. 277.

63. He assumes, first of all, that size of holding is related to labor available, and since his bigger farmers have bigger families (presumably by assumption) they have bigger farms. He further assumes that laborers receive a fixed salary (2,000 francs a month), which makes income level clearly depend on farm size more than it should, since the majority of migrants are probably paid in shares (one-third or one-half the crop). To top it off, he assumes that all income from holdings should be counted as belonging to the head of family, even though he acknowledges that income distribution within the family is egalitarian. Since the larger income earners have larger families, this is an especially questionable procedure.

64. For example, it is one-quarter of the land in plantation production in 1965 which is presumably held by the "big" planters, not one-quarter of cultivable land. The two-thirds of the laborers refer only to 35,000 laborers; there are surely many more than this employed on African (*originaire*) farms. And the 400,000 franc average income turns out to come from a "linear extrapolation" of his income distribution categories, which do not in fact show any very big holdings or big incomes.

cedures used to reach these figures are taken into account, it is extraordinary how little skewness there is in the income distribution among planters. The famous 20,000 rich planters turn out to be 20,000 (larger than average) families (or "communities"), who are not actually shown in his data and who in any event are said to have an average income per holding of 400,000 C.F.A., or $1,600 a year, and an average holding of about 125–250 acres at most. If the figures in the table are supposed to show inequality of income distribution, they are not very convincing.

There remains a final issue to be considered—the contention that the Ivory Coast's recent growth must soon run out of steam. This is a proposition central not only to criticisms of the Ivory Coast pattern of development but to the whole fabric of structural transformationist ideas.

Amin summarizes the argument admirably. Growth based on extensive export agriculture and light import substituting industry, he says, in the framework of a smaller market, must slow down for three main reasons: (1) the possibilities for continuous and rapid growth of exports of tropical products is limited, both on the production side, which without "intensification" of production methods quickly reaches a ceiling "which is now near," and on the demand side, since export prospects are poor; (2) import substituting industrialization saves little foreign exchange and in fact creates continuing demands for imported raw materials; (3) debt service and repatriation of profits takes a growing share of foreign exchange earnings. He concludes that these are fundamental contradictions in the present strategy, which "if it continues as in the past fifteen years, will result without any doubt [in] . . . first, a slowing down of the rate of growth of exports; second, the maintenance of the rate of growth of imports at a high level; and third, an increase in the relative weight of profit and savings remittances."[65]

Two questions are involved here. First, if it is true, are there more attractive and feasible alternative strategies? And second, is it in fact true?

On the first question, it seems fair to say that Amin presents no satisfactory alternatives. His main specific criticism of Ivory Coast agricultural policy, for example, is that it has not focused enough on foodstuff production, so that food imports have risen almost as fast as GDP. This is the kind of thing that troubles politicians, but why an economist should worry so much about it is certainly not clear. In any event, there is not much possibility for food production to serve as a real growth propellant; evidence elsewhere, for example, indicates that the expansion of produc-

65. Amin, *Le Développement*, p. 272.

tion of protein-rich high-value foodstuffs such as meat, poultry, and dairy products quickly runs into a market constraint.[66] Moreover, a monetized and changing economy can be counted on, with proper encouragement, to respond to rising demands for local foodstuffs. The Ivory Coast experience with rice is revealing in this respect.[67]

Aside from recommendations on turning toward foodstuff production, Amin, like most transformationists, suggests that the only answer is to concentrate on basic industries with large linkage effects. But he recognizes that market size prevents any small country from taking this route, so he ends up with a plea for the creation of "larger economic space"—that is, the formation of larger economic units. Given the fact that few statesmen in West Africa seem to have any genuine interest in the formation of such larger economic units, either West African or larger in scope, Amin's suggested policy turns out to be no policy at all. Whether the Ivory Coast or other countries would at this stage be wise to devote more energy to bringing about economic integration is another issue, which need not be gone into here.

What about the second question—whether export-oriented growth must "soon" run down? One of the reasons given by Amin—the production constraint under existing technology—is clearly not important, given the possibilities of opening new land, a possibility which he admits and which is in fact being realized. Second, even with "extensive plantation" methods, small technological changes can bring large increases in output—pest control, replanting with high-yielding varieties, and so on. So the production constraint is not serious.

Whether exports prospects are "poor" or not is now known. As most economists tirelessly and apparently fruitlessly emphasize, there is no empirical or theoretical support for the widely believed assertion that relative prices of primary product exports have declined steadily in the past

66. Cf., Carl Eicher.

67. A big push is now on in rice production. The effort has been given over to an autonomous body, the Société d'assistance technique pour la modernisation agricole (SATMACI), which is in charge of extension work and personnel. By the end of 1966 SATMACI had almost 1,100 extension workers on the job, spreading information on irrigation techniques, fertilizer use, insecticides, etc. About 100 small irrigation dams have apparently been built already, allowing irrigation of about 21,000 acres of irrigated rice. By 1970 some 50,000 acres are planned, which would bring rice output to 460,000 tons, and presumably self-sufficiency. Government plans to spend 4.4 billion C.F.A. on rice production, mainly in the North, and is getting technical assistance (160 people) for this effort. A relatively high price has also been set for rice. That results may already be coming is suggested by the sharp drop in rice imports in 1967, when only 35,000 tons (paddy) were imported, as against 129,000 tons in 1966. (*Afrique nouvelle*, no. 1083 [9–15 May 1968].)

or will do so in the future. Projections of future market conditions are notoriously unreliable.[68] The issue is largely irrelevant anyway. Even if the price outlook for a given commodity is not optimistic, it will still pay a country to produce it, and expand output, if there are no better alternative uses of resources available to it. It is worth noting that the view that the Ivory Coast's export-propelled strategy must fail because of dim market prospects could have been made at any time since 1950, and probably would have been made by most transformationists.

Recently, it has looked as though the prospective decline was at hand in the Ivory Coast. The rate of growth of exports and GDP markedly slowed during the years from 1965 through 1967. But the economy has surged forward again in 1968, fed largely by good crops and prices for cocoa and coffee, but also by rising outputs of other agricultural commodities.[69]

World markets may not always treat the Ivory Coast so kindly. Export earnings may in fact slow down and then stagnate. What is noteworthy about Ivory Coast policy, and so unusual about it, is that they have not let future uncertainties hinder their diversification efforts, and they have not drawn back from the export sector. They continue to display considerable ingenuity and effectiveness in seeking new alternatives. While oil palm, for example, has been talked about for some years as a likely crop for expansion, most efforts in West Africa have been rather modest. The Ivory Coast to the contrary, has launched a tremendous program of oil palm expansion, which is moving ahead approximately on schedule. This was based on long experimentation by the famous French research organization, I.R.H.O. In fruit production, similarly they have maintained, through the French, the best research operation in West Africa,[70] which has stimulated the development of fruit production and particularly pineapples.[71]

Competition in export markets for primary products may be something

68. Who would have guessed that in 1959 there would be talk of possible future underproduction of coffee on the world market? See *Bulletin de la Banque centrale des états de l'Afrique de l'ouest*, no. 155 (October 1968), p. 17.

69. Banque centrale des états de l'Afrique de l'ouest, "Indicateurs économiques ivoiriens," no. 154 (August–September 1968).

70. The Institut français de recherches fruitières outre-mer maintains about a dozen scientific researchers in two stations. They keep nursery stock and give technical assistance to planters, circulate a journal to all interested agencies and individuals, containing latest research findings around the world, and explore new crop possibilities for the Ivory Coast.

71. In 1961 the Ivory Coast exported 200 tons of fresh pineapple, 4,000 tons of canned, and 3,600 tons of juice. By 1967 the respective exports were 7,700, 7,200, and 26,000.

like war, in which there are only the quick and the dead. The Ivory Coast has so far shown it is one of the quick. So long as it remains on its present path, there is no reason why it cannot continue this way. Meanwhile its economy is being monetized, its people are being educated, its network of social and economic services is growing, the state is extending its influence throughout the countryside, and knowledge about the economy and about what will and what will not work is accumulating. In short, a base is being built for a later stage of development into which the country can move with confidence and competence.

## CONCLUSION

The striking differences in economic performance between the Ivory Coast and Ghana which have been outlined in this chapter are due mainly to the differences in economic policy adopted in the two countries. Ghana under Nkrumah adopted a set of policies, a strategy of development, which fits well into the transformationist category: a rapid increase in rates of investment, a greatly enlarged role for state in mobilizing, allocating and managing resources, emphasis on import-substituting industrialization and large-scale agricultural projects, reduction of dependence on foreign capital. Under these policies Ghana experienced a massive waste of resources, a continual balance of payments crisis and by 1965 economic paralysis due to scarcities of imported inputs, stagnant or declining per capita income. In the Ivory Coast, gradualist policies prevailed, involving a limited role for the state in directly productive activities, export orientation, continued reliance on foreign capital and skill. Under these policies, the Ivory Coast has enjoyed one of the highest economic growth rates in the world, a rapid rate of monetization of the economy; substantial shifts of people out of less productive regions and employments into more productive ones with a consequent rise in average incomes and declines in regional and personal income differentials. The Ivory Coast economy is vastly more productive and flexible now than it was a decade ago. It has made giant steps forward in the establishment of social overheads and private services. It has experienced relative political stability; the decade of survival and economic expansion has almost certainly increased the legitimacy of the state. Foreigners, to be sure, continue to dominate the economy outside of agriculture, but this is changing and will change faster in the future; it is, in any event, part of the price paid, from a nationalist point of view, for the rapid change that has occurred. Gradualism in the Ivory Coast has thus been associated with genuine economic transformation. Transformation-ism in Ghana was accompanied by false steps, misdirected effort, waste, reduced personal income, and a heavily mortgaged future.

As noted earlier, many of the commentators on the Ghana experience emphasize external, accidental, political, or structural factors in explaining what went wrong. They allow the transformationist strategy itself to escape unscathed. Bad luck on cocoa prices, faulty implementation of basically sound programs, incidental errors of judgment or execution, defects of character in the people concerned (foot-dragging civil servants and corrupt politicians), lack of political will—these are given the main explanatory weight.

These kinds of factors may have played some role in determining the speed with which economic dislocation came, and they gave the Ghana experience some of its special flavor. Free spending on inter-African and international political ventures, for example, did come to represent a sizeable drain on public resources and foreign exchange, and incidents such as the massive import of consumer goods for display during the 1965 Organization for African Unity meeting in Accra dealt the economy some sharp blows. But these were hardly fundamental. The basic elements were the disintegration of the economic decision-making system, the loss of control over expenditures, the generalized administrative muddle and pervasive politicization that made rational screening, evaluation and control of programs and projects next to impossible. Public sector decision-making simply fell out of control. This occurred within an ideological framework which shaped specific policies—that growth via the export sector was no longer possible for Ghana, nor desirable even if possible; that industry is the true modernizing force and deserving of high priority; that significant industrial development was possible through import substitution; that large-scale mechanized farming, financed, organized, and managed by the state was not only feasible, but was the preferred path for agricultural modernization. And it occurred in part because there was among Ghanaian politicians, and many of the advisors and others who urged them on from the sidelines, a nearly total lack of appreciation of the extraordinary complexity of effectively implementing even a modest development program. Except for a few civil servants who were soon discredited as "obstructionist" or counter-revolutionary, few voices were raised pointing out the thousand pitfalls awaiting every new venture, even those which seemed plausible, and the extremely feeble capacity of the government to deal with these kinds of problems.

Ghana's failure, then, had little or nothing to do with Nkrumah's personality, or the nature of the Ghanaian political elite, except in a remote sense. Any political leadership imposing a development program of the size and kind that emerged in Ghana, would have faced much the same results. Import-substituting industrialization quickly runs out of steam in a small country, whatever the political complexion of its leadership. And a big public sector development program cannot be effectively administered by government organizations short of trained people, short of experience, short of organizational or bureaucratic competence, short of knowledge about the environment, operating in a heavily politicized atmosphere and an ideological setting rich in half-baked ideas, and all the while exposed to unhappy influences emanating from aid-givers and machinery salesmen of all description.

Nor did cocoa have much to do with the outcome. Even if cocoa prices and earnings had soared, the results would have been little different. In fact, it would probably have been worse. By 1965 the capacity to resist bad programs and projects was weaker than ever; dozens of costly projects of extremely doubtful feasibility had been "approved," most of them under carpetbagger initiative. At the same time the state enterprises and operating ministries were making increasing demands on the recurrent budget. Had more revenues been available as a result of better cocoa earnings, they would most likely have encouraged deeper commitments of an uneconomic kind.

What this analysis implies is that for small countries at early stages of development, there is no viable or feasible alternative to the kinds of policies we have called "gradualist." The formation of larger economic units might open additional options, but there is little evidence of any willingness to move very far in this direction in most of the world. The gradualist strategy involves risks and uncertainties—risks of shifting world market conditions, and risks inherent in close dealings between small, poor countries and powerful foreign interests. It involves a larger, more openly admitted dependence on foreign factors of production, as well as on foreign markets, a condition not especially appealing to most political leaders. But in the historical period in which African (and many other) countries find themselves, where the overwhelming priorities are national consolidation, the development of administrative and social overheads, and the expansion of knowledge about the environment and how to deal with it, gradualist policies have many positive advantages. They cannot everywhere be counted on to produce results so brilliant as those in the Ivory Coast. But they will almost certainly produce better results than any alternative policies, and this may be the most persuasive point in their favor.

# 10

# REFLECTIONS ON ECONOMIC STRATEGY, STRUCTURE, IMPLEMENTATION, AND NECESSITY: GHANA AND THE IVORY COAST, 1957–67

## Reginald H. Green

Reflections on and comparisons of economic strategy, implementation, and change in the Ivory Coast and Ghana over the decade 1957–67 are of considerable importance not simply for understanding and evaluating the politicoeconomic evolution of these two states but also for indicating the potential courses of action open to other African economies and the constraints or requirements these impose. In 1957 Ghana was the least poor and least underdeveloped of Britain's sub-Saharan African colonies, and the Ivory Coast was one of France's most prosperous territories.[1] Both

The author was engaged in teaching and research in West Africa during 1960–65 and has revisited it in 1968 and 1969. He wishes to express his intellectual debt for ideas and discussion to S. H. Hymer, G. B. Kay, J. D. Esseks, A. Seidman, and the Honorable J. H. Mensah but also to add that they are not responsible for the analysis and conclusions in this essay from which each would dissent with varying degrees and levels of vehemence.

Dr. Green is currently economic advisor to the Tanzania Treasury. However, the views expressed are his personal responsibility and are not necessarily those of the Treasury.

An earlier version of this paper was presented at the 1967 African Studies Association Meeting.

1. For general economic descriptions and analyses of Ghana see: T. Killick, E. N. Omaboe, and R. Szereszewski *The Economy of Ghana* (London: Allen and Unwin, 1966) ; Ghana, *The Economic Survey 1967* (Accra: State Publishing Corporation, 1968) ; S. Amin, *Trois expériences africaines de développement: Le Mali, la Guinée, et le Ghana* (Paris: Presses Universitaires de France, 1965) ; J. D. Esseks, "Political Independence and Economic Decolonization: The Case of Ghana under Nkrumah," *Western Political Quarterly* (forthcoming 1971). For the Ivory Coast see M. Miracle, "The Economy of the Ivory Coast" in P. Robson and D. Lury, eds., *The Economies of Africa* (London: Allen and Unwin, 1969) ; S. Amin, *Le Développement du capitalisme en Côte D'Ivoire* (Paris: Editions de Minuit, 1967) ; A. Zolberg, *One Party Government in the Ivory Coast* (Princeton, N.J.: Princeton University Press, 1964), esp. chap. 5; *Banque centrale des états de l'Afrique de l'ouest–1968* (Paris: BCEAO, 1969).

were widely seen as likely candidates for rapid economic growth and development. In any event, they followed what were usually perceived to be radically different politicoeconomic strategies, policies, and styles; and, as a result, their successes and failures (as interpreted by observers) have been widely heralded and interpreted by proponents of a wide array of economic, political, and ideological doctrines, strategies, and systems.[2]

By mid-1967 current price Gross Domestic Product (GDP) in the Ivory Coast and Ghana was apparently in the $250 to $300 per capita range, up from $150 in the case of Ghana and from $125 for that of the Ivory Coast a decade earlier.[3] Both had become high-cost economies—although Ghanaian prices had been distinctly lower through 1963, they were probably slightly higher by 1967—with relative price data suggesting approximate equality in per capita real output or a slight edge to the Ivory Coast, a reversal of the 1957 position in which real per capita output in Ghana was distinctly higher. Ghana was absolutely the larger of the two economies; both in population (8 to 8.5 million) and domestic product ($2.5 billion before, and $1.75 billion after devaluation), it was slightly under twice the size of the Ivory Coast (4.5 million and $1.2 billion). Gross Domestic Product per capita exceeded that of all other independent African states with the exception of three sparsely populated mining enclaves—Gabon, Libya, and Mauretania—and was over twice the average level for sub-Saharan Africa.

Three superficial readings of the 1957–67 record are possible. The first is that both economies developed from a similar initial position and at about the same rate. Neither country pursued a massive, but followed an active, industrialization policy with the Ivory Coast slightly in advance. If one were to accept this view, the major difference in strategy lay in Ghana's achieving this record while exports rose only 35 percent in value to the Ivory Coast's phenomenal 210 percent.

A second reading is that both economies started at the same point but that unwise strategy in Ghana (either from 1957 or after 1960) led to runaway inflation, external imbalance, and economic collapse, whereas a

2. The "discovery" by a number of Ghana's exsupporters that it really was not very different—as exemplified in B. Fitch and M. Oppenheimer, *Ghana: End of an Illusion* (New York: Monthly Review Press, 1966)—is simply another stage in misinterpretation, telling more of the observers than of West Africa. However, rather more similarities than are normally supposed have existed, cf. Amin, *Le Développement* and Jean Due, "Agricultural Development in the Ivory Coast and Ghana," *Journal of Modern African Studies* 7, no. 4: esp. 660.

3. Both figures are before Ghana's 1967 and the Ivory Coast's 1969 devaluations.

cautious pragmatism and adherence to comparative advantage principles (in this case primary export expansion) resulted in a massive success story in the Ivory Coast. In support of this contention, deflated (compared to 1960 prices) GDP growth appears to have been 100 percent in the Ivory Coast with the growth trend rising through 1964 and under 50 percent in Ghana with a steady fall in rates for successive three-year periods.

Finally, it could be argued that economic policy was irrelevant; that results in both economies were determined by a rate of growth of export proceeds which was largely if not totally beyond the control of Abidjan or Accra.[4] During 1957–60 Ghana's growth rate was two-thirds the Ivory Coast's for GDP and one-half for exports. Thereafter, Ghanaian exports stagnated along a declining path to 1966 largely because of cocoa price falls in significant part occasioned by Ghana's own sharply increased production. Meanwhile, the Ivory Coast experienced an export boom based on the opening up of unused land and benefitted from the EEC Association's (and previously, Franc Zone membership's) price stabilization and preferences leading to rising export prices. When the export boom faltered in 1962 and 1965, constant price GDP stagnated or fell. Ivory Coast constant-price GDP per capita did not regain 1964 levels until 1968 in a manner similar to the 1962–64 stagnation of the Ghanaian economy.

Of these readings only the first—ignoring as it does price trends—can be rejected out of hand. Both the second and third clearly contain some aspects of reality. At least in 1964–65 (and possibly in 1966–67 for quite different reasons) Ghana's economic management was markedly unsound. Ivorian errors of comparable magnitude have not occurred in implementation—they may exist in medium-run strategy. On the other hand Ghana's deteriorating performance and, to significant extent, the "unsoundness" of her 1961–65 international economic and financial policy stemmed directly from world market conditions for her exports.[5] Whether the Ivory Coast has made better use of her export boom to lay the foundations for her development in a period of slow foreign exchange earnings growth is doubtful. Related to this, also, is the extent to which Ghana's export stagnation can be attributed to her own policies as opposed to economic market forces beyond her control.

4. This is argued at greater length in E. Eshag and P. J. Richards, "A Comparison of Economic Development in Ghana and the Ivory Coast since 1960," *Bulletin of Oxford University Institute of Economics and Statistics* 29, no. 4 (November 1967): 370–72.

5. cf. D. Rimmer, "The Crisis in the Ghana Economy," *JMAS* 4, no. 1:17–32.

## GENERAL CHARACTERISTICS AT INDEPENDENCE

Even a careful inspection of the economic structures of the Ivory Coast and Ghana in 1957 may suggest near identity.[6] Export/GDP ratios were high; modern sectors were centered on production and manufacturing of exports, import-related commerce and transport, and the production of food, with a few manufacturers for cash markets arising directly and indirectly from export earnings. Institutional patterns were relatively similar: extensive, largely, but not uniformly, probusiness government intervention and growing provision of infrastructure characterized public-sector economic policies and expenditures.[7]

Concentrated foreign controlled oligopoly was pervasive in the large-scale private sector. Middle level business and service firms were largely foreign, with a sizable French element in the Ivory Coast and with large levantine communities in both countries. The Ghanaian middle business-men were somewhat more numerous and stronger. The bulk of African export production came from, at most, ten percent of the rural population and was channeled through combined private-firm/public-board oligopoly structures. Foreign plantation agriculture had been hard hit by the depression of the 1930s in both countries but, while still significant in the Ivory Coast (unlike Ghana), was not dominant.

Institutionally the differences had already begun to widen. Ghana's policy was becoming more interventionist and less predictably private-sector supporting. In money and banking, external reserves, and tariff policy, greater Ghanaian control already existed, and its extension was a prime objective. However, the most basic difference was related to the export sector and the noncommercialized resources readily available for its expansion. The basic pattern of the 1957 Ghanaian economy had developed in the period 1885–1915 with the rise of cocoa to the position of a dom-inant export (the Gold Coast, in turn, became the world's largest pro-ducer).[8] From 1930 through 1945 the economy had been stagnant; the post-1945 boom was within the established economic structure and, in the

6. For a fuller discussion of economic structure and development as used here see D. Seers, "The Stages of Development of a Primary Producer in the Middle of the Twentieth Century," *Economic Bulletin of Ghana*, no. 4 (1963), and R. H. Green, *Stages in Economic Development: Changes in the Structure of Production, Demand, and International Trade* (Khartoum: Bank of Sudan, 1968), also published as Yale Economic Growth Center Paper 125 (1969).

7. cf. Esseks, "Political Independence."

8. See R. Szereszewski, *Structural Changes in the Economy of Ghana 1891–1911* (London: Weidenfeld and Nicolson, 1965).

case of cocoa, was based on improved terms of trade rather than rapid expansion of output. The amount of land and manpower available for increased cocoa production was limited, and the market prospects for selling sharply increased volumes at remunerative prices were none too good although this fact had been clouded by the boom prices of the past decade. Of the secondary exports, only timber, and perhaps bauxite, offered scope for rapid expansion; and no serious export prospect was in sight except for that of aluminum smelted via hydroelectric power.

The Ivory Coast position was radically different. Its export sector had expanded moderately during the 1930s under the *mise en valeur* regime and explosively after the Vridi Canal made Abidjan a deepwater port in 1951. It was blessed with very large reserves of usable land and labor still in the self-consumption (subsistence) sector, either in the territory or neighboring Upper Volta.[9] The build-up of the Port of Abidjan and of road and rail services to it had already led to plantings of coffee and cocoa which were to give rise to subsequent export expansion of timber. Several secondary primary exports, including the long established banana industry, showed definite progress. On the market side the tropical commodity deficit nature of the Franc zone and the determination of France to minimize nonfranc primary product imports virtually guaranteed outlets at remunerative prices for expanded output. In this sense the Ivory Coast in 1957 was rather more analogous to the Gold Coast of 1900 than to Ghana of 1957.

The figures presented in tables 1 and 2 are virtually self-explanatory as to the main aggregative trends in the two economies over the past decade. Ivory Coast development has been based on an increasing share of exports in GDP. Since 1964 export growth has dropped sharply and so has the growth of GDP. Ghana exhibited this pattern only in 1957–60. Thereafter exports actually followed a downward trend to 1966 basically as a result of cocoa price falls in the sense that overall export volume rose. Real domestic product for domestic use rose moderately through 1963, but to a substantial extent this represented not internal market directed and supported development but the income effects of investment paid for out of reserves accumulated during the 1950s. After 1963, falling reserves and tightening external credit conditions, combined with a radical failure of food output to expand even as rapidly as population, choked off growth throughout the economy, demonstrating that 1957–63 had not laid the

9. cf. E. J. Berg, "Real Income Trends in West Africa 1939–1960" in M. Herskovits and M. Harwitz, eds., *Economic Transition in Africa* (Evanston, Ill.: Northwestern Univ. Press, 1964) and Amin, *Le Développement*.

## TABLE 1
### Ghana, Selected Economic Indicators, 1957–67 (in millions of new cedis)

| | 1957 | 1960 | 1963 | 1966 | 1967 |
|---|---|---|---|---|---|
| GDP, current price | 734 | 946 | 1,190 | 1,779 | 1,769 |
| Percent of growth | | 29 | 26 | 50 | −0.3 |
| GDP per capita, current prices (new cedis) | 117 | 141 | 164 | 224 | 217 |
| Percent of growth | | 21 | 16 | 37 | −3 |
| | | | | | (227) |
| Exports, current prices | 183 | 232 | 218 | 191 | 245 |
| Percent of growth | | 27 | −6 | −12 | 28 |
| | | | | | (19) |
| GDP less exports, current prices | 551 | 714 | 972 | 1,588 | 1,524 |
| Percent of growth | | 30 | 36 | 63 | −4 |
| Value added, manufacturing, current price | 30 | 45 | 70 | 110 | 140 |
| Percent of growth | | 50 | 56 | 57 | 27 |
| Percent of GDP | 4.1 | 4.8 | 5.9 | 6.2 | 8.5 |
| GDP, 1960 prices | 781 | 946 | 1,056 | 1,099 | 1,125 |
| Percent of growth | | 21 | 12 | 4 | 3 |
| GDP per capita, 1960 prices (new cedis) | 124 | 141 | 145 | 138 | 138 |
| Percent of growth | | 14 | 3 | −5 | 0 |
| Exports, 1960 prices | 195 | 232 | 285 | 294 | 280 |
| Percent of growth | | 19 | 23 | 3 | −5 |
| GDP less exports, 1960 prices | 586 | 714 | 772 | 805 | 845 |
| Percent of growth | | 22 | 9 | 4 | 5 |

NOTE (table 1): Value added in manufacturing is adjusted to cover primary processing (cocoa butter paste mass manufacture, sawmilling, oil expressing), VALCO smelting, and a rough estimate of artisanal and commercial establishment manufacturing type value added to secure consistency with Ivory Coast data and the general practice of African accounts.

The figures in parentheses with respect to 1967 current price exports indicate what the figure would have been in the absence of the cedi devaluation.

The 1967 constant price GDP figures compared to the current price ones show a significant decline in average price levels relating almost totally to domestic foodstuffs. The reality of the price decline is open to some doubt as the magnitude of the output increase.

## TABLE 2
### Ivory Coast, Selected Economic Indicators, 1957–67 (in billions of C.F.A. francs)

| | 1957 | 1960 | 1963 | 1966 | 1967 |
|---|---|---|---|---|---|
| GDP, current prices | 102 | 139 | 189 | 250 | 266 |
| Percent of growth | | 36 | 36 | 32 | 6 |
| GDP per capita, current prices (thousands C.F.A.) | 29 | 37 | 47 | 56 | 58 |
| Percent of growth | | 27 | 27 | 23 | 4 |
| Exports, current prices | 26 | 39 | 57 | 77 | 80 |
| Percent of growth | | 50 | 46 | 35 | 4 |
| GDP less exports, current prices | 78 | 100 | 132 | 173 | 186 |
| Percent of growth | | 28 | 32 | 30 | 8 |
| Value added, manufacturing current prices | 5 | 8 | 15 | 23 | 26 |
| Percent of growth | | 60 | 88 | 53 | 13 |
| Percent of GDP | 4.9 | 5.7 | 7.9 | 9.2 | 9.8 |
| GDP, 1960 prices | 108 | 139 | 172 | 204 | 198 |
| Percent of growth | | 29 | 24 | 19 | −3 |
| GDP per capita, 1960 prices (thousands C.F.A.) | 31 | 37 | 43 | 46 | 44 |
| Percent of growth | | 19 | 16 | 7 | −5 |
| Exports, 1960 prices | 27 | 39 | 54 | 62 | 58 |
| Percent of growth | | 44 | 38 | 15 | −6 |
| GDP less exports, 1960 prices | 82 | 100 | 118 | 142 | 140 |
| Percent of growth | | 22 | 18 | 24 | −2 |

NOTE (table 2) : All constant price series have been computed by the author. The export component of GDP has been deflated by export price index (checked against volume index) data and domestic component by an average of modern and traditional sector cost of living indices.

The 1967 decline of exports at 1960 prices is confirmed by published data. The decline in the domestically marketed component of GDP is, however, rather puzzling and not subject to direct verification.

foundation for an economy capable of autonomous development only secondarily influenced by export-price and foreign-lending-terms changes. The manufacturing-value-added/GDP ratios for both economies indicate structural change toward processing of exports and domestic manufacturing capacity to meet a substantial share of domestic consumer goods demand, but manufacturing remained a distinctly secondary economic sector even in 1967.[10]

The indicators of external economic dependence (table 3) suggest that, by and large, the Ivory Coast was more externally dependent and that its dependence was more concentrated than that of Ghana in 1957, and to an even greater degree in 1967. However, this pattern is not uniform.

TABLE 3
GHANA AND THE IVORY COAST, INDICATORS OF
EXTERNAL ECONOMIC DEPENDENCE

|  | 1956–58 | | 1965–67 | |
|  | Ghana | Ivory Coast | Ghana | Ivory Coast |
| --- | --- | --- | --- | --- |
| *External Trade* | | | | |
| Percent of GDP | 42.5 | 50 | 25 | 60 |
| Percent of commercialized GDP | 65 | 82.5 | 30 | 75 |
| *Exports* | | | | |
| Percent to leading market | 35 | 60 | 22.5 | 35 |
| Percent to 2d–5th markets | 50 | 33.3 | 47.5 | 42.5 |
| Percent from leading product | 60 | 60 | 66.7 | 42.5 |
| Percent 2d–5th products | 38 | 37.5 | 31 | 50 |
| *Imports* | | | | |
| Percent from leading source | 42.5 | 70 | 27.5 | 62.5 |
| Percent 2nd–5th sources | 33.3 | 16.7 | 33.3 | 20 |
| *Weighted Average Size Trading Partners to National GDP* | | | | |
| Export markets | 50 | 80 | 35 | 70 |
| Import sources | 40 | 80 | 30 | 65 |
| *Foreign Finance* (as percent fixed investment) | | | | |
| Government | 20 | 0 | 66.7 | 40 |
| Private | 50 | 80 | 30 | 65 |
| *High Level Manpower* (percent foreign) | 60 | 80 | 35 | 70 |
| *External Reserves* (as months of imports) | 20 | 2 | 0 | 3 |

10. They are, in fact, below those of Kenya at the same dates and only slightly above Uganda—both economies with a GDP per capita under $100.

Sources: All data have been derived or adjusted from national and international published sources. In the case of Ivorian GDP there are substantial differences among the series, but these do not appear to affect the trend. All price indices and the Ghanaian manufacturing value added are exceedingly fragile.

Note: Ivorian imports from the EEC "Five" were twelve percent in 1957, ten percent in 1964 but have gradually risen since 1965.

Capital dependence includes depletion of official reserves as net foreign finance (and their expansion as a deduction from gross foreign finance). Private sector data are adjusted to take account of investment in tree crops and also reinvested earnings of foreign firms.

Highlevel manpower is roughly defined as professional, managerial, technical, civil service, and educational personnel with post-secondary qualifications or their equivalent in experience.

In computing export concentration, processed forms of a product have been aggregated with unprocessed: for example, coffee and instant coffee; cocoa, cocoa butter, cocoa paste and cocoa mass.

In 1956–58 net transfers (tax receipts less expenditures in the Ivory Coast) to the French West African Federal Budget appear to have exceeded French official capital transfers to the Ivory Coast.

Net external reserves of the Ivory Coast are probably understated by up to one month's imports by exclusion of certain governmental and quasi-governmental accounts. When IMF drawings and similar official short term liabilities are taken in account, Ghana's net official reserve position was negative in 1966 and 1967.

External trade/GDP and commercialized GDP ratios were extremely high in 1956–58 even by the standards of moderate sized developing economies. By 1967 the Ivory Coast ratio had risen relative to total GDP reaching sixty percent, but the rapid commercialization associated with its export-centered development had gone far enough to reduce the external trade/commercialized GDP ratio from over eighty percent to seventy-five percent. The even more radical fall in the case of Ghana is basically the result of the 1960–66 export growth failure.

Concentration of markets for exports and sources of imports has always been greater in the case of the Ivory Coast. However, in respect to exports, very sharp diversification of markets took place toward the United States and the EEC "five". No parallel change occurred on the import-source side, where the price of French personnel and financial aid was a series of formal and de facto agreements to maintain the dominant French position.[11] Ghanaian external-trade-partner diversification away from the United Kingdom and toward a variety of countries, especially, but not solely, the central planned economies, is very marked. On the other hand, diversification of exports made no progress with the

11. cf. R. H. Green and A. Seidman, *Unity or Poverty: The Economics of Pan-Africanism* (Harmondsworth: Penguin, 1968), passim, and T. Hayter, *French Aid* (London: Overseas Development Institute, 1966), passim.

same five products accounting for ninety-eight percent of the total in 1967 and the cocoa share actually going up. In the Ivory Coast, coffee's dominance had been eroded, with cocoa and timber rising to a combined-export proceeds in excess of coffee and secondary exports totalling over twenty percent.

Ironically, both economies' public-sector investment programs were almost certainly more dependent on foreign financing in 1967 than in 1957.[12] This is not, in fact, surprising—the investment goals and ability to raise foreign funds of newly independent states are likely to grow substantially more rapidly than their capacity to generate either domestic long-term borrowing or recurrent budget surplus increases if their pre-independence situation has been characterized by relatively large local resource contributions to public-sector investment. Private-sector dependence has remained high and would be higher still, were the normal investment estimates which exclude tree crop capacity increases used.[13] No really significant African private-medium or large-scale capitalist-entrepreneurial class has yet emerged.[14] There are signs of such a development in Ghana if present government strategies and policy patterns are continued. High level manpower dependence provides the starkest contrast. While Ghana had a head start in 1957, the disproportionate rates of change since then reflect very different priorities. In both countries the foreign dependence rate is higher for managerial (especially senior managerial) and technical posts.[15]

An additional index of foreign dependence might be the adequacy of foreign exchange reserves. Ghana shows a marked deterioration from a very comfortable 1957 position to literally negative net official reserves. The Ivory Coast holds reserves on the order of magnitude of three month's import requirements, but this figure is subject to two qualifications. First, Ivory Coast reserve policy is, in fact, subject to Bank of France control so that reserve use to pursue policies leading to contraction of foreign aid resulting from disagreements with France would not be practical. Second, so long as Franco-Ivorian economic and political relations remain cordial the Bank of France in practice stands ready to provide foreign exchange to bridge short-run gaps.[16]

12. cf. Zolberg, *One Party Government*, chap. 5.
13. Foreign finance is defined to include reinvested profits of foreign firms.
14. cf. Amin, *Le Développement*, passim.
15. However, in 1966 the Economic Commission for Africa estimated that 3,000 of 5,250 engineers and scientists in Ghana were Ghanaians.
16. cf. Hayter, *French Aid;* "The CFA Franc System," *IMF Staff Papers*, 10, no. 3 (November 1963).

## THE APPEARANCE OF DIVERGING STRATEGIES

Ivory Coast economic strategy has been relatively stable and the following themes appear dominant:

There has been rapid export growth, including promotion of improved methods in established areas and territorial expansion. Expansion has also been pursued through emphasis on developing new export crops and on increasing the share of products exported in the processed or semi-processed state. Monopoly crop research, extension, purchase, processing, and selling bodies managed by French public or quasi-public institutions have been used extensively in relation to new export and certain domestic staple crops (e.g., rice). The entire expansion process is dependent on broadening the cash-crop labor base both by greater activity in the southwest, southeast, and northern areas and by labor migration from Upper Volta and the northern Ivory Coast.[17] Finally, the securing of protected, privileged, or tied markets has been a consistent theme of Ivorian policy.

Fiscal orthodoxy has prevailed in viewing sources of public finance as domestic recurrent revenues plus foreign grants. More recently surpluses of the social security system and soft loans have become secondary additional sources.

There has been a neo-laissez-faire interpretation of the proper role of public economic activity as providing infrastructure, tax incentives, technical assistance, and development loans to a dominantly private productive sector. While somewhat more favorable versions of these policies have been applied to Ivorian business and a relatively dimmer view taken of levantine and *petit blancs*, their overall impact has been most advantageous for the larger African export growers, the administrative-cum-business bureaucratic elite, and the large modern sector of foreign firms.[18] Even adjectival forms of socialism have been firmly rejected, and the welcome afforded to foreign investment seeking to enter on its own terms has been made quite explicit, albeit some doubts have begun to emerge even at cabinet level.[19]

17. cf. Due, "Agricultural Development"; Miracle, "The Economy"; V. L. Galbraith, "When Trade Does Act as an Engine of Growth: The Case of the Ivory Coast," to appear in a forthcoming volume from Temple University Press edited by S. Schatz, for fuller discussion of the critical role of low wage, immigrant labor in the Ivory Coast.

18. cf. Amin, *Le Développement*, p. 279.

19. cf. M. Diawara, "From Risk Rewarded by Profit to Investment without Risk," Columbia University Conference on International Economic Development (1970), mimeo.

Close relations with France flow from the preceding points. Protected export markets, substantial foreign grants, and the management, expertise, and capital for modern business-sector expansion have been seen to depend on French approval.[20] The Ivory Coast government has seen its economic interests as best served by being as analogous to an internal French pressure group as possible[21]—a strategy well served by rapidly increasing imports from France as well as by a foreign policy which serves to bolster *la grandeur de la France*. Since 1965 a certain shift has been evident: economic links with Washington and Bonn have been strengthened, partly as a defense against France's decreasing overall aid flow and to increase Ivorian receipts but also apparently to increase general external bargaining room. In at least a few cases, key economic appointments have deliberately been made from non-French sources.

There has been at least an implicit set of principles for distributing gains. The most favored groups are the political, administrative, and technical elites. They have close ties with the small but growing Ivorian modern business community. In the second rank come the local notables who provide the basic support for the PDCI and the core of the larger African export crop producers. The next favored group is organized (and largely urban) labor, which because of its location and structure is always a potential threat and must therefore receive both wage increases and a price control system. The remaining urban and rural majorities receive distinctly less, albeit the urban group does have increasing access to a variety of education and health services, and, in the areas being opened up for export production, substantial gains accrue to a sizeable proportion of the farmers.[22]

Cautious Ivorianization has been practiced even in the public service with initial moves largely at the expense of Dahomeyans and Senegalese.[23] Partly, this is related to doubts about the competence of inexperienced personnel and partly to even greater doubts about their political reliability

---

20. This represents the economic side of the political-economic reevaluation which led the Democratic Party of the Ivory Coast (PDCI) to break with the French Communist Party. For a full discussion see R. S. Morgenthau, *Political Parties in French-Speaking West Africa* (Oxford: Oxford Univ. Press, 1964), chaps. 3, 5.

21. cf. Zolberg, *One Party Government*, chap. 5.

22. cf. Morgenthau, *Political Parties*, chaps. 3, 5; Zolberg, *One Party Government*, chap. 5; I. Wallerstein, "Elites in French-Speaking West Africa," *JMAS* 3, no. 1: 1–33.

23. See Due, "Agricultural Development"; Galbraith, "When Trade," passim; Amin, *Le Développement*, esp. pp. 42–47, 265–82.

given the complexion of francophonic African student politics in both France and Dakar. With the growing realization that well-paid jobs were, in most cases, an effective deradicalization force and that the growth of a more readily controllable university at Abidjan, on the one hand, and increasing pressure from the younger members of the Ivorian elite for promotions that could come only by phasing down the promotions of French personnel, on the other, a more active localization policy has been pursued since 1965. Its most evident symbol is the replacement of Finance Minister Raphael Saller by Konan Bedie and Mohamed Diawara.

There has been a shifting African regional approach with the Ivory Coast's initial aim being to disentangle itself from the old West African Federation both as to fiscal transfer payments and to being a major market for Senegalese industrial exports. Both goals have been achieved—much industrial growth has been at the expense of Senegal. Until about 1964 the rest of the Ivory Coast's African policy was basically political. The Sahel-Benin Entente (with Upper Volta, Dahomey, Niger, and now Togo) was initially a fiscal transfer system to head off the greater Mali Federation scheme, although it has now become viewed as a means of securing a protected and privileged market for Ivorian manufactured goods. In francophonic African regional organizations the Ivory Coast has usually pressed a political line while Cameroun and Senegal have spearheaded the economic approach. To a considerable extent the Ivory Coast's political initiatives in African circles may have been motivated by economic gain potential, but the gains were seen as coming from France not Africa. More recently, Ivory Coast strategy has altered to moderate support of certain Western African economic regional initiatives although those actively supported appear to be attempts to enlarge her industrial export base rather than viable units for overall regional developments.[24]

The dominant characteristic of the strategy is pragmatic caution based on assessments of the possible. On a different plane, the key element in the entire strategy is the successful attainment of export growth. Without it, the entire strategy appears unviable even if regionalization as a route to industrialization were pushed far harder than it has been to date, especially as the rapid buildup of transfers and factor earnings remittance following on expanded private investment now means that an export slump followed

---

24. For a fuller argument for this position see Green and Seidman, *Unity or Poverty;* for a counter position, Galbraith. See also B. Vinay, *L'Afrique commerce avec l'Afrique* (Paris: Presses Universitaires de France, 1968).

by a decline in new capital inflows could very rapidly lead to a serious balance of payments crisis.[25]

In contrast to the Ivorian situation Ghanaian economic strategy falls into three distinct phases. The first and last can most easily be viewed as modifications of the Ivorian. The first, the "Lewis" strategy, was in force from prior to 1957 through 1960.[26]

On the first three points Ghanaian strategy was basically similar to Ivorian, albeit export promotion was not related to preferential market creation. Similarly, while grants were welcomed, foreign finance was not seen as crucial for the public sector. Cordial relations with the United Kingdom were pursued, but a more diversified and independent foreign economic stance was sought. In practice an aristocratic distribution of benefits took place although rather more public services were available to broader groups of the population. Ghanaianization was pursued at a much faster pace, and education at primary through university levels had higher priority. Regional policy tended to become limited to the abortive Ghana-Guinea (later Ghana-Guinea-Mali) protounion and emphasis turned to political and politicoeconomic continental Pan-Africanism because of growing divergences of style (and personal ambitions) between Ghana and its neighbors.[27]

Ghana's postcoup (IMF) strategy is in many respects similar to that of the Lewis period. However, soft loans and/or grants as well as debt rescheduling have received high priority as critical to operating a viable foreign balance polity without sending the economy into a prolonged decline. Ghana's international economic strategy has retained significant elements of diversification and the goal of regaining a base for international economic bargaining and freedom of maneuver.[28] The 1966–69 dependence on IMF and United States approval of economic policy to

25. Because an export growth rate decline would both limit the growth of the market for manufactures and give rise to self-fulfilling doubts about ability to service existing investment, it would be likely to cause a sharp reduction in net private capital inflow.

26. This is not intended to imply that Sir Arthur Lewis forced his proposals into the minds and documents of unwilling politicians. They were during this period accepted by most Ghanaian senior politicians and economic civil servants.

27. cf. J. Mohan, "Nkrumah and Nkrumaism," *Social Register 1967* (London: Merlin Press, 1967), and "Ghana, the Congo, and the U.N.," *JMAS*, 7, no. 3:369–406 passim.

28. This is particularly true of the present finance minister, J. H. Mensah, who was critical of NLC policy as being too cautious and too conciliatory toward foreign lenders.

secure foreign finance has been seen as a necessary but unwelcome interim phase. While Ghanaianization retains a high priority, there have been signs of decreased faith in the ability of citizens to fill certain posts, especially in economic planning and parastatal top management—a trend which may well be reversed under the Busia government.[29] African policy has been overhauled to place higher priority on economic regionalism and the attainment of joint African positions in such bodies as UNCTAD, albeit the 1969–70 expulsion of noncitizen residents cannot be expected to be particularly conducive to good regional relations.

It may be worth noting that the Ivory Coast's and Ghana's first and third strategies seem to imply a fairly definite political pattern—one which did not exist in 1957–60 Ghana. Basically this is the aristocratic (in the Aristotelian sense) blend of Plato's *Republic* and John Stuart Mill which Sir Arthur Lewis propounds as the form of democracy most appropriate to African conditions.[30] Its basic element is regulation of the political and economic system by a self-perpetuating intellectual-administrative-business-chiefly elite in a manner which excludes irresponsible elements from power but maintains broad passive acceptance. This pattern is basically similar to that of the Ivory Coast, but in 1957–60 Ghana it was the National Liberation Movement not the Convention People's Party which advocated it.[31] The National Liberation Council and its method of recreating a civilian political system and the nature and style of Dr. Busia and his Progress Party and government have been very much in accord with the Lewis model.

The form of political organization sketched can be defended—certainly it seems more likely to be an effective frame for economic development that the "democratic charade" of precoup Nigeria[32] or the agony of multiparty systems in which a reversal of electoral preferences—but not a transfer of power—is possible within the system as in Sierra Leone after the last election. However, it is misleading to call such a system "democracy." It surely is not so either in the modern Western meaning of that term or in the wider sense of a political system based on broad participation and mobilization of active support.

29. This is another area in which NLC policy was critized by Mensah.
30. Arthur Lewis, *Politics in West Africa* (London: Allen and Unwin, 1965).
31. cf. Mohan, "Nkrumah"; Rimmer, "The Crisis."
32. R. H. Green, "Nigeria: The Economics of Socio-Political Bankruptcy," *New African* (August-September 1965), and "A Lament for Nigeria," *Mawazo*, 1, no. 1 (1967).

Ghana's second, Mensah-Omaboe, strategy of 1961–65 was radically different:[33]

1. There was to be a dependence on primary exports, to be attained through expansion of domestic and African regional market-oriented production accompanied by absolute (but slower) rises in raw and processed commodity exports to finance growing capital goods and fuel raw material input requirements.

2. Rapid expansion of manufacturing with reduction of dependence on exports as the primary growth stimulus, increasing of export earnings by processing of commodities, and raising average output per capita through widening the sectors using highly productive techniques were seen as primary goals.

3. Radical expansion of the economic role of the state with neo-laissez-faire dropped in favor of comprehensive state economic control and increasingly dominant state (public-sector) ownership in directly productive as well as infrastructural fields was viewed as critical to planned development.

4. Modernization of agriculture with the twin goals of providing adequate growth of food and raw material supplies and of affording a decent standard of living to the rural majority was posited, but the tendency to emphasize large-scale state farms was not (at least in practice) evidently consistent with these goals.

5. Expansion of fixed investment—absolutely and relative to GDP—was sought, based on faith in the power of capital (including infrastructure) to generate short term increases in GDP. Linked to this faith was a parallel conviction that the domestic rate of saving (including that of the public sector) could be stepped up rapidly enough to reduce relative, if not absolute, dependence on foreign investment and loan flows.

6. Attainment of basically national control over key economic decisions was to be achieved via pursuit of the first three themes combined with diversification of foreign economic contacts and promotion of economic regionalism.

7. Rapid expansion of wage employment and steady increases in average earnings per employee was to be made possible by steady upgrading of the labor force productive capacity through both human and physical investment, which—together with the expanded agricultural output—would give rise to the effective demand necessary to allow rapid sustained growth of wages and salaries payments.

33. See Convention People's Party, *Work and Happiness* (Accra: Government Printer, 1961) ; *Seven-Year Development Plan* (Accra: Planning Commission, 1964).

8. Income redistribution was to be based on a more progressive tax system and an incomes and wages policy designed to favor farmers and lower income wages earners combined with a general stepping up of broadly available public services.

9. Continued and accelerated Ghanaianization was planned with substantial expansion of secondary and tertiary education provided to impart the skills necessary for rapid growth of the modern sectors of the economy and the modernization of agriculture while sharply decreasing dependence on expatriate personnel.

10. African economic cooperation and integration, while partly a by-product of political Pan-Africanism, was seen also as a basic political economic goal related to the attainment of successful industrialization and of an economic structure capable of autonomous growth rather than almost totally dependent on rapid export expansion for sustained growth.

In concept this strategy was radical in the sense of seeking structural changes including a rapid decline in external economic dependence. Given Ghana's export position and prospects by 1961 it was not necessarily less realistic or pragmatic in outlook than the Ivorian. Basically this strategy gambled that an economic transformation from an open, export-centered pattern to a quasi-closed, domestic-market-centered form could be attained speedily and efficiently before the level of domestic austerity and external credit constraints reached crisis proportions. The gamble was seen as necessary because the successive export-fueled booms of 1890–1910, 1920–25, and 1950–55, even with reasonably coherent and energetic planning in the latter two cases, had neither created an economy capable of continued advance during export stagnation nor involved the majority of the population in the central modern sectors. There was no reason to expect them to do so in the future without a different internal strategy and set of resource allocation priorities.[34] The rhetoric in which this decision was often cast was rather wild, but the choice itself was a relatively sober and, at least, a potentially rational one.

It is difficult to outline the political patterns consistent with the operation of the foregoing political economic strategy. Given the high degree of sacrifice and austerity required in the absence of major export stimuli and with reduced foreign aid and investment (at least relative to total invest-

---

34. In this context see Rimmer, "The Crisis," on the new strategy as a gamble taken as a result of worsening external economic conditions and R. Genoud, *Nationalism and Development in Ghana* (New York: Praeger, 1969) on it as a means to create irrevocably a new economic base whose timing—and effectiveness in the short run—was altered by the external evolution.

ment), an aristocratic system would encounter grave difficulties in mobilizing and maintaining adequate levels of public acceptance. Although a highly centralized, coercion-based neototal state system might be effective in theory, it is almost certainly not technically possible in Africa today. The final possibility is a mass-support-based system. To work, it would have to include perceived equity in the distribution of gains and sacrifices; fairly broad participation in decision influencing, a substantial degree of government and party decentralization, and at least broad freedom of dialogue and discussion. Rhetorically—but only rhetorically—1961–65 Ghana sought to approximate to the last pattern; the reality was of an increasingly less effective, less honest, and less acceptable elite system.

## GENERAL STRATEGIC DEFICIENCIES

Both of the two basic strategies as presented (fairly explicitly in the case of Ghana II [from 1961 to 1965] but largely implicitly in the other cases) appear to suffer from basic weaknesses quite apart from specific policy, project, and implementation issues. A common one is a quite inadequate realization of the nature, complexity, and magnitude of the tasks involved in securing a sustained, broad front increase in agricultural productivity as opposed to opening up new areas or limited technical change gains in selected export or industrial crops.[35] A second is a failure to see broad policy outlines and major specific policies in respect of the parastatal public, the large scale private, and the small scale rural private sectors as a part of planning no less integral and no less demanding in terms of technical preparation and evaluation for feasibility, consistency, and efficiency than government projects and their preparation.[36] Many of the weaknesses in implementation flow directly from these two failings at the strategy level.

The following other inadequacies appear to be present in the Ivorian strategy:

There was dependence on a continued export boom, when from 1960 onward it should have been evident that an eight to ten percent annual export increase could not be sustained indefinitely unless steps were taken to ensure very rapid shifts from raw to processed farm exports and the rapid development of a regional-market-oriented manufacturing sector in

35. cf. Miracle, "The Economy," esp. pp. 207–16, 233–34.
36. At the microlevel Ivorian research and programming has been better on the whole than Ghanaian but at the price of being almost totally non-Ivorian in senior technical and managerial staff.

the context of a broad West African economic and customs union.

There was inadequate preparation for national market-oriented development, a result of which has been that the Ivory Coast has not laid an economic foundation capable of sustaining development based on domestic and regional market stimuli nor have investment and policy been directed toward attaining that end.

Relatively sluggish Ivorianization aggravates the impact of the preceding points and limits the internal and external flexibility of Ivory Coast policy.

Placid acceptance of continued concentrated external dependence was arguably sound so long as exports and French aid kept rising. However, with both less certain, it now imposes limitations to working out a nationally oriented strategy, maintaining it in external negotiations, and implementing it with Ivorian personnel and technical direction. The point is not that the Ivory Coast sought to continue a neocolonial relation of extreme dependence, but rather that it overestimated the time span over which substantial gains could be secured by operating within it.

Overconcentration in the distribution of gains exists, but as a weakness, it is debatable. To build up Abidjan and nearby rural areas first may have been economically valid; a greater spread of development has begun and appears to be continuing. On balance, however, the criticism appears to stand.[37] Further, the markedly unequal distribution of gains by economic groups and the very sharply skewed income distribution (high by Anglophonic African as well as world terms) appears both unnecessary and inefficient from an economic incentive viewpoint and potentially dangerous from a political one, especially with rising urban unemployment.

Ghana's first strategy was open to the same criticisms except with respect to manpower development. The inherent drawbacks and errors in the context of Ghana II are distinctly different:

1. Gross underestimation of the time span between fixed investment and GDP growth, using one to two years as a rule of thumb for large scale productive investment ventures when four to eight would have been more realistic, was common. When coupled with spending programs based on the projected rather than the actual GDP growth and the tying up of a sum approaching $1,200 million in 1966 in uncompleted projects (twenty percent of total capital stock), this error had far-reaching distorting and inflationary impact.

2. Overdependence on supplier credit flowed from the first. Short term,

37. cf. Miracle, "The Economy"; Amin, *Le Développement*, chap. 3.

high interest credit is usable for rapid pay-off projects assuming foreign exchange can be mobilized. The Seven Year Plan probably implicitly called for two-thirds supplier credit, one-half Western commercial and one-half Eastern governmental and state firm. This was a quite implausibly high level given the investment composition, even had better vetting of individual proposals have been carried out.[38]

3. Overestimation of GDP growth in the early years of the plan resulted from calculating as if the growth rate would leap from its low 1962–64 rate to a much higher level and then remain static. Resource allocations were projected on the basis of instant attainment of that rate of growth implying an instant real resource gap.

4. Administrative as well as political support was assumed to be a non-problem area. It should have been realized by 1961 that Ghanaian political acceptance in principle of sound economic strategy could be anticipated but would be hard to secure in terms of specified projects, policies, and alterations. Given that experience, a strong case existed for a more cautious, loose initial plan to allow greater leeway for subsequent decisions not fully consistent with it and for weaknesses and delays in implementation. Similarly, it was clearly evident that the discipline required for effective planning was neither comprehended nor accepted by most civil servants and state corporation managers and that priority attention was needed in education and institutional reform at this level.[39]

5. The economic civil service did not place enough weight on increasing its preparation and evaluation capacity so that enough sound projects were available to fulfill macrotargets or at least ensure efficient use of available resources. As a result, their answers to economically unsound proposals tended to be flatly negative rather than offering revisions or counterproposals which would have had a far higher chance of gaining political support than a simple "No."[40]

6. Manpower allocation did not fit plan strategy. The logical counterpart to a strategy geared to rapid reduction of external dependence and to expanding the public-sector role in directly productive activity is, surely, a reallocation of manpower and education programs toward the commanding decision-making and operation positions in the large-scale mod-

---

38. See Omaboe's endorsement in chap. 18 of Killick, Omaboe, and Szerescewski, *The Economy of Ghanda,* but also his later critiques in the 1964 and 1965 *Economic Surveys.*

39. cf. Rimmer, "The Crisis," and Omaboe, *The Economy of Ghana,* passim, and R. H. Green, "Four African Development Plans," *JMAS* 3, no. 2: 270–76, on problems of control.

40. cf. Omaboe, *The Economy of Ghana.*

ern sector. This approach was never clearly worked out in principle, much less fully implemented.

7. Inadequate attention was given to distribution issues. On the macro-level the need for austerity and for greater equality in division of gains was enunciated. To limit urban-rural differential growth, a wage growth limited to productivity increases policy linked with price controls was attempted from 1960 onward with some success until late 1964. However, no more detailed policy with respect to the urban sector and virtually none at all with respect to the rural sector was evolved. This failure was a significant contributing factor to the agricultural policy errors leading to virtual stagnation of food production after 1963.[41]

8. Overoptimism was evident as to the rate at which dependence reduction could be carried out. This error probably stems from the first three points and the sixth. It also relates to continued quasi-optimism in respect of medium-run export growth which turned out to be singularly ill-placed, further weakening the external balance position already eroded by heavy short-term borrowing.

In fairness to the Ghanaian economic civil service, it should be noted that the external advisors and internal plan conference participants did not pick out these points as self-evident weaknesses.[42] Ghanaian civil servants themselves identified most in 1963–65, and subsequent failure to act effectively or in time was political, not economic civil service, in origin.

## PROBLEMS OF STRATEGY IMPLEMENTATION

A detailed examination of the quality of economic policy and project formulation and implementation in support of national economic strategy in the Ivory Coast and Ghana cannot be conducted in one essay. At most a few rather sketchy and schematic points can be made.

Ivory Coast implementation has, overall, been better than Ghanaian. By and large Ivorian policy and projects have been consistent with and in furtherance of the strategy outlined above. Equally, the level of competence in implementation and operation has—with some exceptions in the rural sector—been fairly high.

However, this result is partly of the strategy itself. Export centered, neo-laissez-faire, substantially foreign financed, and dominantly foreign

41. Ex–farm prices appear to have fallen or stagnated while the available transport to move food to cities declined in quantity and reliability.

42. The author has talked to several of the consultants and read the transcript of the conference on the plan.

technically staffed and managed economic growth is certainly the simplest for a government to oversee. If fiscal orthodoxy and pragmatic caution are added, the likelihood is that what is attempted will be largely accomplished, but that a good deal less than what could have been possible will be attempted.

Microlevel criticisms can be leveled at Ivorian economic implementation beyond those directly stemming from criticisms of the basic strategy:

Overconcentration—with Abidjan itself as the largest single example—leading to enclavization and thus limiting the spread impact of growth has been endemic. A recurrent problem in low-income countries is to build to standards which preclude quantity provision of the service in question; for example, roads, hospitals, secondary schools.[43] This problem has been particularly acute in Ghana and the Ivory Coast because the illusion that funds really were not scarce has lasted longer. Related to, though separable from, this failing is a tendency to concentrate effort on a few large projects, because they are more dramatic, more interesting to the planner and administrator, more appealing to foreign finance providers, easier to build up into an overall program of some given magnitude, *a fortiori* easier to construct and—hopefully—to run with a limited number of high-level expatriate staff.

Failure to secure a sustained pattern of agricultural development on a broad front springs directly from overcentralization albeit the Ivory Coast has been spared the more dramatic grand scheme failures which litter Senegal and Mali. Output expansion by opening up new areas and/or by publicizing and securing the adoption of marginal changes in production patterns and techniques for a few export crops is a means of securing time to develop a long term set of policies, programs, and institutional reform, not a substitute for them. Basic and applied research (especially outside export crops); development of effective extension services working with local peasant producers; adequately channeled and supervised rural credit; improved processing and storage facilities; alterations in the marketing system to reduce its costs and provide more effective incentives to domestic market-oriented production—all remain inadequate in the Ivory Coast; and, far more serious, none shows much sign of rapid and sustained improvement.[44] There is reason to wonder whether domestic market food production is now increasing at a rate significantly above that of population and for fearing it may fall below it as the high growth until 1965 was

---

43. cf. Amin, *Trois expériences*, passim; R. Dumont, *L'Afrique noire est mal partie* (Paris: Editions de Seuil, 1963), passim; Hayter, *French Aid*, passim.
44. Miracle, "The Economy," pp. 206 ff.

influenced by an opening-up program in a limited northern grain area.

Investment in human capability has been inadequate. This is in part a strategy weakness. But even given that context the quality, quantity, and direction of formal and informal education—for example, *investissement humain* in the latter category—gives rise to doubts. Adherence to established French models (often after their abandonment or revision in France) relatively secondary emphasis on technology at all levels, rigidity in rural involvement programs even when results objectively suggest need for thorough revisions, do not appear to be very efficient routes to rapid human development in the African context.

Industrial sector promotion has been haphazard and unselective. Import substitution against Senegal has accounted for perhaps the largest single chunk of Ivorian industrial expansion over the past decade. This, however, is a virtually exhausted stimulus. Import substitution in selected consumer soft good industries against France may also reach its limit in the next five years.

At least some of the theoretically more "advanced" industries in the Ivory Coast—automobile assembly, for example—are very heavily dependent on imports and achieve substantial "domestic" value added only by quite uneconomic increases in final cost. If—as the Ivory Coast has begun to believe—the basic pattern of industrialization over the next decade or two will increasingly be regional market production, then the initial emphasis on substitution against Senegal may prove less than helpful and provide all too enticing an example for others to follow against the Ivory Coast. Further, the concept of economic groupings with Abidjan as the dominant industrial center becomes open to challenge as a truly viable way of implementing economic regionalism. In the first place, if one is to be a captive market there is some advantage in being tied to a low-cost source. In the second, a handful of microeconomies with low growth rates tied to sluggish export earnings do not really provide the strongest of bases for Ivorian industrial development. This is not to argue that a planned expansion of Ivorian imports of livestock, fish, grain, and cotton could not play a major role in creating a viable regional grouping. It could, and would need to, especially in relation to Mali and Upper Volta.

The Ivorian elite is not self-evidently the most appropriate to spearhead rapid economic development nor have incentives been organized to make it become so oriented. The bureaucratic-political-business bourgeoisie is, with notable exceptions, rather far removed from the Schumpeterian entrepreneur or the successful public-sector development leader. It appears to be basically conservative (in the literal sense), consumption and status oriented, and risk avoiding. The economic justification for the concentration of economic gains in the hands of a small group with these characteristics is decidedly slim whether one uses capitalist or socialist criteria.

The same criticisms albeit less forcefully in respect of human investment and more so in respect of agriculture apply to Ghana over 1957–60. Overall efficiency by 1960 had, in part, declined because the strategy itself had come into discredit, but no alternative had been formulated with policy and project decisions necessarily piecemeal. In addition neo-laissez-faire combined with random marginal industrial promotion led to an almost uninterrupted series of debacles on the part of the Industrial and Agricultural Development Corporations.[45] In fact the average viability of public sector productive activity rose after 1960, but it started from a very low level indeed, and its vastly increased scale made even a reduced level in inefficiency much more aggregatively serious.

The Mensah-Omaboe strategy was in many ways a mirror image of the Ivorian. It certainly was an inherently more difficult one to implement because of its requirements of greater austerity, higher dependence on national personnel, and lesser attractiveness to foreign sources of finance. Further, it radically enlarged the areas of economic responsibility of the state and the planning secretariat—a problem compounded by the failure to create either effective decentralization or specific policy and project decisions where appropriate, or to attain operational coordination and control of basic policy and major project decisions. Finally, precisely because it was ambitious and was formulated in a "tight" plan, it was likely to achieve less than was possible, not by attempting too little but too much. Ad hoc political structures and civil service were created; and by interfering with the plan, adding to it, and (more rarely) emending from it, they turned this probability into a certainty. The following particular areas of ineffective or irrational implementation stand out:

Disastrous agricultural policy and programming with stress on giganticism and technical modernity without reference to economic relevance were pushed to extremes in the state farm program. All the errors cited in relation to the Ivorian strategy were at least equally evident despite proposals for their rectification. This was both narrowly and more broadly a continuation of the colonial heritage. Applied agricultural research was at best spotty and effective extension or rural credit even weaker. At the same time there was great faith in unselective and untested importation of large-scale mechanized techniques—an approach which had already led to total

45. See Killick, pp. 287–93 in Killick, Omaboe, Szereszewski, *The Economy of Ghana.*

British failure in the 1940s at the Gonja groundnut scheme and in pre-depression plantation development efforts.[46] Transport policies and taxation led to rising costs of produce movement and probably increasing profit margins for transporters and buyers. The marketing and distribution system—always rather creaky in the postwar period—failed to cope with the very rapid urban growth after 1957 (especially in Accra-Tema). As a result, urban food prices began to rise sharply after 1962 and skyrocketed after 1964 but grower prices in many cases remained constant, rose slightly, or even declined. Further, the supply of goods to rural areas was particularly hard hit by erratic import supplies and the failure of consumer goods import supply to keep pace with monetary demand growth—a trend which reduced the value of the farmer's proceeds.[47] In this context, neither the failure of food supplies to grow as rapidly as population over the 1961–65 period nor the stagnation or decline in existing secondary agricultural exports (including timber) and the failure of new ones to develop, is very surprising.

Coordinated or selected industrialization was absent despite an overall plan. Bad financing arrangements, failure to recruit adequate expatriate personnel, and often inadequate public-sector management aggravated problems in this sector, but several more basic errors would have caused severe problems even without them.

The state productive sector excluding airways and farms did not turn in by any means as horrendous a record as is often supposed.[48] Similarly the number of utterly implausible ventures begun, while disquietingly high, is not markedly worse proportionately than that in numerous other countries including their private sectors. However, there was apparently no effort to establish priorities for first developing industries which would use, largely, local raw materials nor to develop raw material supplies in cases where this would have been feasible, or, even in some instances, where it was essential as with sugar and bagging. Combined with a lack

46. On state farms see Due, "Agricultural Development"; M. Miracle and A. Seidman, *State Farms in Ghana*, and *Agricultural Cooperatives and Quasi-Cooperatives in Ghana 1951–1965*, papers 43 and 51, Land Tenure Center, University of Wisconsin (1958). On the heritage see R. H. Green and S. H. Hymer, "Cocoa in the Gold Coast: A Study in the Relations between African Farmers and Agricultural Experts," *Journal of Economic History* 26, no. 3 (September 1966), and sources cited therein.

47. Based on findings of a research study by T. Stoches, professor of Agricultural Economics, University of Ghana, 1963–66.

48. In the case of the State Mining Corporation shadow pricing of foreign exchange earnings at a twenty-five percent premium would have resulted in a profit. For more detailed data on individual results see the 1963 and 1964 *Economic Surveys*.

of adequate foreign exchange budget allocations to the industrial sector for fuel, raw materials, and spares this haphazard industrialization "pattern" led both to increasing strains on foreign exchange resources and to underemployment of existing capacity rising to over fifty percent by 1966.[49] Finally, both export processing and theoretically multinational market African plants were set up with utterly inadequate research into market potential, much less with buildup of marketing channels.

Capital and manpower allocation was inefficient. Given the resource constraints evident, by 1963 an absolute reduction in infrastructure investment would have been logical.[50] Existing infrastructure was clearly underutilized. In fact the reverse was attempted. Similarly, given the degree of Ghanaianization and establishment expansion attained in the government and teaching sectors the logical concentration of manpower education, training, and allocation was on the directly productive sector's management and technicians. Shifts did take place but, especially in technical and middle managerial fields, were not of the order of magnitude indicated necessary by the proposed expansion of public-sector directly productive activity.

The strategy's apparent aim of one-third private contractor finance, one-third socialist de facto contractor finance, and one-third international institution or capitalist state soft loans for the public sector and long term foreign investment of perhaps a quarter as much for the private was, as noted above, inherently unsound. The actual result of virtually 100 percent contractor finance (two-thirds private Western, one third socialist) and very little private foreign investment except from retained (blocked) earnings was far worse, especially as it resulted in a debt service burden which tended to grow more rapidly than projected despite the failure of export earnings to provide even the anticipated, much less a higher, debt-carrying capacity base.[51]

Loss of internal fiscal control led to inflation. After 1963, control over recurrent budget expenditure deteriorated alarmingly—at times in estimate preparation, at others in massive overspending. Through mid-1964 local deficit finance was arguably justified as a means to maintain a high level of investment. Price increases, while becoming disturbingly rapid, were largely related to tax boosts, failure of agricultural policies rein-

49. In 1965 E. N. Omaboe estimated the underutilization at sixty-five percent of capacity.

50. Amin made this point forcefully in *Trois expériences*, as a criticism of the draft Seven Year Plan.

51. See *Economic Survey* (1967), pp. 28–31.

forced by bad crops in 1963–64 and again in 1964–65, and the failure of consumer import growth to keep pace with demand.

Consumer import levels rose erratically after 1960, but they did rise, not fall, with 1965 a record year. From the foreign exchange point of view "too little and too late" and *a fortiori* "too incompetent" not "too much too soon" is the appropriate judgment on Ghana's import controls. Late 1964 saw the sudden release of $56 million increased cocoa grower purchasing power at the same time as the radical increase in output shattered the world cocoa market. Combined with an untimely hiatus in import licensing, a continued government deficit financed with the banks, and continued low food deliveries, this massive increase in cash purchasing power with no counterpart in real goods availability was quite enough to set off runaway inflation. In its last months the CPP government made desperate attempts to check inflation through slashes in the cocoa price and in its 1966 budget.

Misuse of funds and incompetence in key places were linked though separable. Corruption in Ghana sprang to a considerable extent from an attempt to secure covert funds for CPP operations of a secret nature first within the country and later internationally as well. On the other hand covert funds tended to become totally intermixed with private funds of those controlling the secret operations—a pattern hardly conducive to acceptable, actual, or seen levels of public probity; even if it did not, in fact, constitute the total diversion of public funds to private purposes, it has been made to appear so by recent investigating committees.[52]

Not surprisingly, the men most willing to act in "managerial" roles in this type of operation were—with a few surprising exceptions—not of great personal honesty or administrative and policy-making competence. The damage they did in policy making and implementation probably far exceeded whatever amount was diverted to the CPP and intermediate pockets plus the additional costs resulting from the "need" to place contracts with those who would cooperate in the form of discounts, commissions, or other kickbacks. A somewhat specialized field of incompetence comprised advisors, information-collecting bodies, and secretariats which provided either laudatory glosses on any idea of the president or senior political figures, even when they were well aware that sharp criticism was more appropriate. They also produced documents which may have represented the author's view of the problem in hand but certainly bore little

---

52. The immediate issue is not the propriety and wisdom of the CPP's uses but whether the diverted funds were to be used for what the CPP leadership considered to be public purposes.

relation to any other known type of reality. Agriculture and regional economic integration were fields in which policy was especially badly warped by this particular form of incompetence.[53]

The rather dismal record of Ghanaian implementation in respect of the strategy followed during Ghana II led a senior Ghanaian economist to remark that day-to-day economic policy decisions appeared designed to defeat government aims rather than implement them. The overall weaknesses especially in respect of overcommitment of real resources were aggravated by the 1960–66 export decline. Responses to this decline tended to decrease rather than increase economic efficiency and rationality. However, while a twenty-five percent export earnings growth from 1963 to 1966 might have averted the worst effects of the failings cited, it would at best only have bought time for their correction. Given the number of false starts at basic implementation reforms from 1961 on, it is not very likely that the 1965 reform and austerity pattern would have been carried out.

NLC policy in respect of controlling expenditure, was publicized but not too effective. The 1966 domestic cash deficit was the highest on record, partly because revenue declines offset much of the fifty percent slash in investment spending partly because—except for economic services—recurrent spending rose above 1965 levels by 1966–67.[54] Unemployment rose sharply but 1966's rate of price increase was clearly below only that of 1965 and perhaps that of 1964 because of continued deficit and a sharp curtailment of consumer goods imports only partly offset by increases of domestic industrial output. The 1967 and subsequent statistics, however, show considerable stability.[55] The greatest errors of commission in the agricultural sector have been halted and examination made to pinpoint the errors of omission. It is not clear—even by 1970—that an effective set of policies is in operation or that agricultural output has shifted to a consistent trend at least equal to that of population growth as reports of serious shortages recurred in 1969.

Cocoa has posed particular problems. Farmer receipts in 1966 fell forty

53. In private a number would agree with criticisms of this type but defend their stance either on the grounds that it was unfair to criticize Africans (inherently a most paternalistic approach) or that praise would "promote socialism" (obviously an absurdity if it prevented correcting errors undermining the system).

54. *Economic Survey* (1967), pp. 115–17. The only period of recurrent budget austerity would seem to have been that when the NLC was operating on the holdover CPP 1966 Budget.

55. The 1967 result flows from a seventeen percent fall in domestic food prices in Accra and perhaps half as much for the country. This result did not seem in accord with the views of consumers as to how domestic food prices had moved during 1967–68 and is a priori suspiciously high.

percent, and 1966–67 showed only a slight recovery. As a result, smuggling, and to some extent nonpicking of cocoa aggravated actual output declines even though grower prices were raised by the new government.

By mid-1967 when price increases were believed to have declined to a bearable level, a thirty percent devaluation was effected to allow higher domestic prices for exports (including cocoa whose price was marked up thirty percent), to discourage consumer goods imports, and to lay a basis for regional-based industrial production at competitive prices. Various tariff and wage rate/cost of living measures accompaning devaluation limited its cost of living effect. At least through 1969, however, inadequate allocations for raw materials and spares continued to hold back domestic manufacturing to a serious extent.

While a moratorium was arranged on debt repayment, it was a relatively brief one and the rescheduling hardly generous—especially considering the volume of export credits and guarantees for dubious contractor finance involved. Aid, apart from IMF credits and US commodity assistance, has not been forthcoming in substantial amounts nor has foreign investment other than the VALCO aluminum smelter.

Certainly the military regime sought to uproot the corruption created by its predecessor. However, a number of scandals, conflict of interest cases, and doubtful transactions with foreign firms (including those with doubtful previous records)[56] raised doubts as to how deep the changes went. Reorganization of economic decision-making tended to mean drastically cutting investment spending and de-Ghanaianizing even when—as in planning—competent Ghanaians were available, a pattern ill-suited to rebuilding morale or long term efficiency.

In short, the NLC over 1966–67—and indeed during its whole period of office—preached an orthodox IMF recovery line and attempted to consolidate. To a degree it did this, but its expenditure cutting was unbalanced and probably ill-selected; its development policies, especially in agriculture, limited and overly cautious; its trade policies ineffective, especially in cocoa where Cocoa Board price realizations from 1966–68 compare very unfavorably with 1958–65 results when set against average world market prices; and its allocation of imports limited industrial expansion.

The Busia government inherited an economy massively restructured and provided with a reasonably good physical and local manpower infrastruc-

56. For a running account of these incidents the best source is the *Legon Observer* published at the university during this period. The Abbott Laboratories and General Ankrah cases are the most notorious but by no means the only ones. A very serious one involved the Cocoa Board.

ture—but also with a heavy debt burden—from the CPP. The NLC contribution has been at best a breathing space with a partial consolidation but little positive action and less long-term politicoeconomic rethinking.

## POSSIBLE REMEDIES

In the short to medium run the economies of Ghana, certainly, and of the Ivory Coast, probably, face severe problems. In the case of the Ivory Coast an interim step-up in exports other than coffee and cocoa combined with success in securing United States, West German, and international institutional public-sector loans and private-sector investment to bolster French flows could well provide half a decade with twenty percent growth in constant price terms giving a breathing spell for working out a revised economy strategy by 1975. However, flat exports and a falling away of private investment giving rise to GDP stagnation and a much more urgent need for rapid strategy alterations remain possible.

Ghana's present need is to complete its reorganization and consolidation as rapidly as possible. If the agricultural-output-lag problem can be surmounted for the interim period through improved transport and opening of new areas, then objective prospects for any well-designed set of policies are fairly bright. Barring another cocoa price collapse—with or without a Cocoa agreement—and given even neutral policies with respect to diamond and gold mining and timber production (all beneficiaries of devaluation), exports in the early 1970s should be running fifty percent above 1966 in foreign exchange terms and rising five to six percent per year.[57] A more rational import allocation system to allow fuller use of existing capacity combined with completion of work in progress on new plants should result in constant price industrial value added over twice that of 1966 as a base.

The overall external debt burden even allowing use or cancellation of its undrawn balance component will remain a serious problem unless a moratorium to, say, 1973 and a fifteen year repayment period at not over five percent interest can be arranged.[58] Certainly, significant net new resource inflows will be required even after 1970, but if the balance of payments and debt repayment situations evolve reasonably well there is

57. VALCO exports of aluminum are estimated net of alumina imports for this projection.

58. While Ghana has now repudiated one of its more doubtful private "investors" claim to repayment, its policy on any general forgiveness of major easing of terms still does not seem very forceful. See "Dr. Busia Defends Ghana's Ban on Aliens," *Times* (4 March 1970), p. 4.

no reason to expect insuperable problems in this respect either on the borrowing or debt servicing fronts.

One of the main dangers in Ghana—and, if exports stagnate, in the Ivory Coast as well—is a loss of will and of self-confidence. Both economies possess natural resource bases, infrastructural facilities, industrial bases, administrative and institutional capacity, and (particularly in the case of Ghana) high and medium level manpower capabilities well above average for developing economies as a group and *a fortiori* for African economies. The attainment of sustained development from these bases will almost certainly require close attention to the following clusters of economic strategy and implementation issues:

In agriculture the basic need is to secure a higher rate of output growth on a broader front, both with respect to a number of farmers' steadily increasing sales and of commodities in which a significant annual growth of production can be expected. Stable domestic prices, viable industrial enterprises, and even moderately buoyant export proceeds are heavily dependent on agricultural sector success.

Requirements fall into two main categories: provision of information to farmers on how to increase output, on the one hand, and, on the other, supporting provision of institutional structures, facilities, and resources to allow them to increase and sell their output remuneratively. African farmer responses in a majority of cases make extension services, backed by actual markets for the products promoted and real economic gains from the new techniques, likely to prove highly effective.[59] The bottlenecks are lack of adequate data on packages of technique changes (dealing with seed, fertilizer, crop pattern, modest improvement of tools, planting time, and tilling) to be promoted, qualitative and quantitative weaknesses of agricultural extension personnel in the field, rural credit which tends to be inefficiently directed and either over- or undersupervised.[60] There has also been a failure to parallel production drives with transport, warehousing and preserving, processing, and marketing institutional policy or project improvements to make use of the increased output economically feasible nationally and economically attractive to the farmer.

A difficulty is that research (on institutions and incentive policies as well as production techniques) and the provision of personnel capable of communicating effectively with farmers will take half of a decade or more to reach acceptable levels even if they are made top priorities now. This difficulty is probably aggravated by the fact that the broad-front improve-

59. cf. Green and Hymer; Due, "Agricultural Development."
60. cf. Miracle, "The Economy," pp. 205–8.

ment approach to agriculture with limited supporting use of large scale ventures (e.g., irrigation in Ghana from the Volta reservoir) and of tractors in special circumstances does not have the glamour or offer the specious promise of "instant solutions" associated with massive "transformation," settlement, state-farm, and similar programs.

Industrialization and economic regionalism are, ideally, interlinked. With poor export prospects, it is essential that an increasing share of domestic demand for manufactured goods be met from domestic production either directly or indirectly through manufactured goods exports. Even in Ghana and the Ivory Coast, the possibilities for pre-export processing of primary products and for viable national market-based substitution against imports will not sustain an industrial growth rate of the needed magnitude (probably twelve to fifteen percent annually) for more than a decade and a half, probably not that long.

The most viable alternative is coordinated regional industrial development. A market area stretching from Senegal-Mauritania through Nigeria-Niger, or even through Togo, would provide a much more adequate basis for industrial development whether public- or private-sector financed. The difficulty lies first in the preparation of industrial plans for the region allocating production in a manner benefitting each participating state and based on feasibility studies for proposed plants. Securing political acceptance of the degree of restraint on national policy required by such a system will, even then, be difficult. Ghana and the Ivory Coast in particular would have to agree that plants which might, in the abstract, best be located in Abidjan or Accra go to the less favored states. Otherwise those states which find no benefits in regional economic integration (a present danger in the Ivory Coast centered Entente), will tend not to join or to withdraw, and at best will not provide very dynamic markets.

Reduction of external economic dependence requires new economic structures which in turn require foreign exchange.[61] Only in the field of high-level manpower localization is a straightforward rapid program possible by itself. Beyond that, intermediate policies can include diversifying trading and resource-providing partners and widening the range of significant exports if viable possibilities exist. The latter include, for example,

---

61. For a fuller exposition see R. H. Green, "Political Independence and the National Economy: An Essay on the Political Economy of Decolonization" in C. H. Allen and R. W. Johnson, eds., *African Perspectives: Essays in the History Politics and Economics of Africa (Presented to Thomas Hodgkin)* (Cambridge University Press, forthcoming 1971).

tinned tropical foodstuffs in the Ivory Coast case and backward (bauxite) or forward (aluminum semifinished products) integration from VALCO —Ghana's new hydrolectric power export industry. In the long term, the creation of autonomous economies in West Africa is integrally linked with regional integration and industrialization.

In at least two senses Ghanaian and Ivorian planning is inadequately comprehensive. First, the formulation of plans is separated from coordination, oversight, and modification of implementation—a procedure well-calculated to making the planning exercise a waste of time. Second, there is a need to secure a coherent set of policies capable of influencing de-centralized public-, as well as private-sector actions along the lines of plan goals.[62] Equally, however, the trend toward concentration needs to be reevaluated. Not all projects or policies can, or should, be run through one central body. Within a general framework (backed by sectoral and regional planning units) there can be room for substantial initiatives. These could usefully include a structure of village-district-region development committees with citizen, as well as technical and interest group members who can provide both broad popular understanding of and participation in planning and a raison d'etre for more effective local government. The failures of planning in Ghana stem not from over comprehensiveness or too much control but from massive lacunae and quite inadequate implementational control. The former weakness, though not necessarily the latter, is even more evident in the Ivory Coast.

Internal and external balance must receive priority attention. Fragile economies and still more fragile planning machines do not cope readily with rapid inflation. Structural change—directly and via its tax finance requirements—will cause all the price increases consistent with orderly economic management under African conditions.[63] Domestic borrowing and investment programs, and also income policies and price incentive schemes, must be viewed in that context. External economic balance— usually the first casualty of internal imbalance (*vide* Ghana after 1958)—

---

62. cf. P. Borel and F. Jackson, "Some Experiences of Planning in Africa," *Development Plans and Programmes* (Paris: Development Centre, OECD, 1964).

63. cf. D. Seers, "A Theory of Inflation and Growth in Underdeveloped Economies Based on the Experience of Latin America," *Oxford Economic Papers* (June 1962). This is not an argument either for making a stable price level per se the be all and end all of economic policy nor for totally eschewing borrowing from the banking system but for a relatively cautious fiscal policy designed to maintain domestic resource supply-demand equilibrium and not exacerbate other upward pressures on prices.

is vital to operational medium-term planning determined domestically and not by foreign aiders and investor-lenders. An economy bereft of external reserves and lumbered with short-term debts is an economy delivered into the hands of its creditors whatever the strategy which led to that impasse.

# 11

# CONVERGENCE AND DIVERGENCE IN EDUCATIONAL DEVELOPMENT IN GHANA AND THE IVORY COAST

## Remi Clignet and Philip Foster

The rationale for comparative studies of educational systems must lie in the attempt to factor out which relationships between schools and society are universal and which are the result of specific and unique historical circumstances.[1] From this viewpoint, Ghana and the Ivory Coast constitute a particularly appropriate pair for comparative analysis since they are societies of a generally similar nature that differ with respect to certain modes of action and relationship.[2] Hopefully in this type of situation we may be able to effect some form of crude controlled comparison; and, by viewing education as a dependent variable, we can attempt to establish what common structural features have led to similar educational outcomes and what distinctive elements have created divergent educational patterns and problems. Moreover, we shall attempt in some measure to indicate whether the patterns of relationship to be discussed can be generalized to other new states in Saharan Africa.

First, with respect to convergent features there are substantial parallels between the two nations in terms of the economic and occupational context within which the schools function. Both areas are wealthy by African standards, and in recent years the upsurge of the Ivory Coast economy and relative stagnation in Ghana has reduced differences in mean income per capita to a minimum.[3] Moreover, the two countries are highly dependent upon the export of a limited number of agricultural commodities,

1. For a review of the rationale justifying comparative studies in the field of educational development see R. Marsh, *Comparative Sociology* (New York: Harcourt and Brace, 1967), chap. 5.

2. See, particularly, S. F. Nadel, *The Foundations of Social Anthropology* (London: Cohen and West, 1951), pp. 223–29.

3. In fact it was estimated that in 1965 the Ivory Coast per capita income was already slightly above that of Ghana. See *Réalités ivoiriennes* no. 50 (November 1968) : 3.

and the proportion of nonagricultural wage earners in the total adult labor force is relatively small in both cases. To be sure, the profile of the occupational structure in Ghana is more "mature" than that of the Ivory Coast; in the latter territory approximately eighty percent of the adult male labor force is involved in farming or fishing as opposed to a Ghanaian figure of roughly sixty percent. Furthermore, in Ghana approximately seven percent of the total male force is classified as working in professional, technical, administrative, or clerical positions as contrasted with a figure of about three percent in the Ivory Coast. Thus, although the occupational characteristics of both territories are generally similar, that of Ghana is less constricted at the summit and is characterized by greater diversity. It is also clear that in both territories the small enclave of paid-wage or salaried nonagricultural employment tends to expand very slowly in relation to demand for access to such opportunities in the modern sector.

As might be expected, Ghana is also the more urbanized of the two states, with approximately sixty percent of its population living in towns with below 5,000 inhabitants as compared to over eighty percent in the Ivory Coast. Furthermore, the Ghanaian urban population is more evenly distributed among a larger number of cities.[4] In both nations, however, there is a markedly greater concentration of urban populations in the southern half of the country where the process of modernization is most underway and where the development of cash-crop farming and other exchange activities has been most marked. In short, the pattern of socioeconomic transition from the forested South to the savannah lands of the North appears substantially the same, and in some measure, these zones tend to overlap with ethnic differentials. There are, furthermore, substantial parallels in the sociopolitical organization of the Anyi-Baoulé peoples of the southern and central Ivory Coast and the institutions of the related Akan who occupy the littoral and heartlands of Ghana. In like manner the Kru groups of the Ivory Coast seem to have a rather similar social organization to the Ewe peoples of southeastern Ghana. In the North, although Voltaic peoples are more represented in Ghana there does seem to be some convergence between them and the peripheral and nuclear Mande

4. For a general review of the consequences attached to variations in the distribution of cities by size see Brian Berry, "City Size, Distribution, and Economic Development," *Economic Development and Social Change* 9, no. 4 (July 1961): 573–87. For a discussion of contrasts between Ghana and the Ivory Coast along these lines see Remi Clignet and J. Sween "Accra and Abidjan, A Comparative Examination of the Theory of Increase in Scale," *Urban Affairs Quarterly* 4, no. 3 (March 1969): 297–324.

of the Ivory Coast in terms of traditional structure. Above all, the two territories exhibit a similar division between a largely Moslem North and a formally Christian South.

This terse introduction serves to highlight some convergences between these countries that have implications for the diffusion of formal education. Yet it is also clear that very real differences exist and these latter are crucial to our understanding of the process of educational development. The most obvious difference, of course, concerns the duration and character of colonial overrule. British influence in the southern Gold Coast increased steadily throughout the first half of the nineteenth century culminating in the annexation of the coastal region in 1874. By the end of the century, indeed, the process of colonial absorption was completed with the final incorporation of Ashanti and the Northern territories into the imperial framework. By contrast, French penetration into the Ivory Coast came generally later and was more spasmodic in its initial impact; a resident in the Ivory Coast was not appointed until 1878—four years after the British had formally recognized their long standing de facto administration on the Gold Coast, while military campaigns against African populations were conducted as late as World War I. In fact, over substantial portions of the Ivory Coast no administration was effectively established until the early 1920s.[5]

It would be tempting, therefore, to interpret subsequent quantitative educational growth in the two areas as merely reflecting a pattern of staggered colonial development with the Ivory Coast consistently lagging behind but following essentially the same course as the Gold Coast. In part, this has been the case, but one other factor of crucial significance for education has been the type of colonial administrative structure established in the two territories. Some reservations must be entertained concerning the attempt to characterize French and British administrative practice in terms of a simple dichotomy between direct and indirect rule. Indeed, earlier French policy in the Ivory Coast was fairly pragmatic in its orientation and was based, at least initially, upon indirect rule through traditional political structures.[6] However, it is true that on balance the French tended progressively to develop more centralized administrative

5. See Remi Clignet and Philip Foster "Potential Elites in Ghana and the Ivory Coast: A Preliminary Comparison," *American Journal of Sociology* 70, no. 3 (spring 1965) : 66–73.

6. For a description of the French style of indirect rule in the Ivory Coast see, P. Atger, *La France en Côte d'Ivoire de 1843 à 1893: 50 ans d'hésitations politiques et commerciales* (Dakar: Publications de la section d'histoire, Université de Dakar, 1962).

structures within the framework of the West African Federation and stronger links with the metropole. By contrast British administration relied to a greater extent on indirect rule (particularly in Ashanti and the Northern Territories) and tended to deemphasize linkages with other areas of British West Africa and the metropole itself. One of our tasks, therefore, must be to discern whether this difference in administrative practice has spilled over into the realm of educational decision-making. We must also attempt to see whether the legacy of this colonial past has more explanatory power than the present in interpreting the course of educational development in the two countries. One cannot, of course, ignore the impact of postindependence leadership, but here considerable caution must be exercised. We are already moving from that phase of study of African political life during which there was a distressing tendency to confuse rhetoric with reality. Early scholarly preoccupation with the ideology of new political elites often obscured the fact that their apparent commitments were not matched by genuine efforts at major institutional change. From this viewpoint, casual comparisons made between pre-1966 Ghana and the Ivory Coast seem essentially stereotypic. Thus Ghana's pre-coup leadership was often characterized as radical and egalitarian in intent and concerned with a major transformation of Ghanaian society while by contrast the PDCI has been regarded typically as cautious, pragmatic, and basically conservative in orientation. It cannot be doubted that there were many differences in political style and approach in the two nations, but we should be led astray if we attempted to interpret the course of their educational development solely in these terms.

The truth is that African leadership everywhere—whatever its ideological hue—conceives of formal education as a major independent variable in stimulating economic and social change. This viewpoint seems no less characteristic of the Ivory Coast of Houphouet-Boigny than the Ghana of Kwame Nkrumah. Moreover, bearing in mind the constraints imposed by the financial disasters of the 1960s there seems little doubt that Nkrumah's political successors are substantially committed to an enlargement of educational opportunities.

In effect, what impresses the observer of the educational scene in most of sub-Saharan Africa is the essentially autonomous quality of educational expansion; schools burgeon in response to popular demand whatever the content of formal educational statements and educational growth seems singularly unresponsive to the well-intentioned efforts of visiting manpower specialists. We submit, therefore, that in both Ghana and the Ivory Coast the crucial factors that have determined and continue to determine educational development are colonial precedents and public demand and expectations which are, in large measure, a response to the changing characteristics of the occupational structures of the two countries. Indeed, in view of their colonial past it could be argued that a PDCI Ghana and CPP Ivory Coast might have produced a comparative educational picture little different from the present one.

In the light of these introductory remarks we can now effect some comparison between the course of educational development in the two territories under the following headings: administrative policy, access to formal education, the content and process of schooling, and the relationship between education and the occupational structure. It need hardly be added, however, that this categorization of content is hardly satisfactory since issues raised under one heading invariably spill over into ensuing sections. These rubrics, therefore, merely constitute a modest series of signposts to guide the general course of the discussion.

## ADMINISTRATIVE POLICY AND PRACTICE— THE COLONIAL HERITAGE

It has already been observed that the basic assumptions governing French and British administrative policy in the two colonial territories tended to have implications for educational development. Both indirect and direct rule had their educational analogues which, so far as administration was concerned, might be generally termed "voluntarism" and "egalitarian centralism."

Although there is evidence that the British administration showed some interest in the provision of a chain of tax-supported schools on the coast in the mid-nineteenth century, the Education Ordinance in 1887 created a system of dual control that was typical of educational practice in the majority of British territories. In effect, the major responsibility for the development of schooling was left in the hands of missions and other proprietary groups or individuals with schools qualifying for government assistance on the basis of what was initially a markedly inadequate system of inspection.[7]

This laissez-faire approach had considerable implications for educational growth. There can be little doubt that it led to extreme variability in educational standards due to the absence of effective quality controls,

7. See Philip Foster, *Education and Social Change in Ghana* (Chicago: University of Chicago Press, 1966), pp. 80–86.

but at the same time it did result in a rapid proliferation of institutions at minimal cost to the central administration. The diffusion of mission schooling, indeed, generally reflected a pattern of public demand for education that was in turn linked to the level of urbanization and the extent of development of an exchange economy among local populations. Thus the second major consequence of the policy was considerable variation in the geographic diffusion of schooling.

Whatever its limitations, it can be asserted that British policy led to a degree of flexibility in the development of what was essentially a low-cost education. Moreover, the absence of any coherent educational plan indicated a reluctance on the part of the administration to control the size of the overall system in relation to the putative demands of an emerging occupational structure. Thus the thrust of educational expansion was never effectively determined by estimates of manpower needs but was in considerable degree, a response to African demand. Clearly, in the later colonial period such demand had far outstripped both government and mission ability to meet it, but the custom of charging fees even at the primary level placed some restraints on mounting pressure and tended to provide educational places to those most willing or able to pay for them.

The assumptions underlying French educational policy in the Ivory Coast provide an interesting contrast. To be sure, in the earlier period the French administration was obliged to rely upon missionary efforts in the provision of schooling. However, this represented a grudging acceptance of an unpleasant necessity rather than, as in the British case, the recognition that missions were the most appropriate agencies for developing the educational system. Support by the French administration for the efforts of voluntary agencies was, to say the least, equivocal, and there was a general assumption that educational provision was substantially a public responsibility. Indeed, the French West African Educational Ordinances of 1903 as amended by the Ordinance of 1924 reveal a distinctive attempt to create a generally coherent structure of education subject to effective central administration—a feature that becomes more evident over time.[8] First, plans were made for the creation of village, urban, and regional schools for Africans (as distinct from a metropolitan-type system designed

8. See Jerry B. Bolibaugh, "Education as an Instrument of National Policy in Selected Newly Developing Nations," *Phase 2: French Educational Strategies for Sub-Saharan Africa* (Stanford, Calif.: Comparative Education Center, 1964), pp. 29–38.

for Europeans and children of mixed descent), whose location was to be determined by the distribution of the local population. Second, clearly defined quality controls were imposed, designed to check the flow of students through different levels of the system. Third, differentiated curricula were to be provided in the light of local conditions and supposed manpower needs. In the context of a centralized federation, the future of the Ivory Coast was conceived almost entirely in agricultural terms. Consequently, local enrollments were to be kept at a minimal level while clerical personnel needed in the administration were to be imported from Dahomey or Senegal where initial demand for education was higher. It is apparent, therefore, that in contrast to the Gold Coast situation, developments in the Ivory Coast were the consequence of more global educational planning. This orientation was obviously very congenial to a small but politically influential group of European *planteurs* who had no counterparts in the Gold Coast.

Two other factors must also be mentioned that characterized French as distinct from British practice. First, emphasis was always placed on the provision of free education for Africans; and, second, language requirements and the need for stricter quality control predicated the greater utilization of qualified and highly paid French *instituteurs* at lower levels of the educational system. By contrast, the British in the Gold Coast relied entirely on African teachers at the primary level, and European personnel were concentrated in teacher training institutions and secondary schools or involved in administration and inspectorial duties.

What implications did these variant approaches have for educational development? It can be advanced that the French as contrasted with the British approach militated against any rapid expansion in schooling. Both administrations were parsimonious in educational matters, but one cannot avoid the conclusion that the British were able to obtain more mileage from their limited educational expenditures through the procedure of "topping-up" revenues derived from mission sources or fees. The result was, of course, the growth of a somewhat ramshackle educational structure of extremely variable quality but one that responded in a general fashion to the thrust of public demand. The French, however, insisted on the development of a more uniform structure subject to more rigid quality controls. This combined with an unenthusiastic attitude toward mission or other private resources actually impeded the quantitative expansion of the schools. Nonetheless, this policy did lead to a system with more uniform standards of somewhat higher quality than that prevailing in the Gold Coast. Although hard data are difficult to come by it is reasonable to assert that it was a high-quality but essentially high-cost system; and, even allowing for the later colonization of the Ivory Coast and its smaller population, it is striking that the figures for primary school enrollment in that country did not reach the Gold Coast 1900 figure for "assisted" schools alone until 1937. Moreover, setting aside the period of World War II, it is apparent that the quantitative disparities in the size of the two systems continued to increase dramatically before internal self-government was achieved in the Gold Coast in 1951 and the direction of educational policy was placed in the hands of African political leadership.[9]

It is suggested here that these colonial precedents have really been the most decisive factors influencing development in the postindependence period. To be sure, the African rulers of the Ivory Coast have had to be somewhat more responsive to the pressure of public demand than their French predecessors while the CPP administration and the present NLC leadership have paid more lip service to the need for "controlled" expansion in the light of manpower projections.[10] To this extent, there has been convergence between the two countries. Yet in the Ivory Coast marked preoccupation with levels of achievement has led to an elaborate examination system at *all* levels, which has resulted in a substantial degree of retardation, class repeating, and involuntary drop-out. We shall return to this point in a later section, but it is sufficient here to note that the more centralized educational structure of the Ivory Coast and the greater deference paid to formal planning has made it possible for the administration to turn off the "output tap" at any point in the system. Vast inputs in the lower primary sector can be reduced to a mere trickle at the secondary level through the manipulation of examinations. Although it can be anticipated that secondary and higher enrollments will increase rapidly in the next few years, it is still apparent that the Ivory Coast's greater willingness to consciously control the rate of educational expansion is in considerable contrast to the more "free-wheeling" approach of the Ghanaians.

9. See Elliot J. Berg "Education and Manpower in Senegal, Guinea and the Ivory Coast" in Frederick Harbison and Charles A. Myers, eds., *Manpower and Education: Country Studies in Economic Development* (New York: McGraw-Hill, 1965), p. 238.

10. See, for example, Ghana, *Survey of High Level Manpower in Ghana 1960* (Accra: Government Printer, n.d.); Ghana, *Second Development Plan 1959–1964* (Accra: Government Printer, n.d.), pp. 35–41; Ghana, *Report of the Education Review Committed appointed by the National Liberation Council* (Accra: Government Printer, 1967), p. 39.

## ACCESS TO EDUCATION

This discussion of policy leads us to a direct examination of the present level of quantitative educational development in the two nations. Table 1

TABLE 1
GROSS SCHOOL ENROLLMENTS, 1965–66 (to nearest hundred)

| Level | Ghana | Ivory Coast[a] |
|---|---|---|
| Primary | 1,137,500 | 353,700 |
| Secondary[b] | 312,700 | 28,100 |
| Technical | 6,700 | 3,800 |
| Higher[c] | 4,300 | 1,900 |

a. Gross population estimates for 1965 are: Ghana, 7,990,000; Ivory Coast, 3,900,000. Age distributions for the younger segment of the population are generally similar. See *La Côte d'Ivoire 1965: Population—synthèse—études régionales 1962–1965* (Abidjan: Ministère des Finances, des affaires économiques et du plan, July 1967), p. 78; Walter Birmingham, I. Neustadt, and E. N. Omaboe, eds., *A Study of Contemporary Ghana: Vol. 2. Some Aspects of Social Structure* (Evanston, Ill.: Northwestern University Press, 1967), p. 30.

b. Figures for Ghana include returns for students in secondary grammar schools, middle schools, and teacher training colleges since these types of institutions are included under the general rubric of "l'enseignement secondaire" in the Ivory Coast.

c. Figures for the Ivory Coast relate to enrollments at the University of Abidjan only, since returns for a small number of students in "les grandes écoles" are not available.

illustrates very clearly the far greater provision of formal schooling in Ghana. If we assume that the five to fourteen age group represents approximately the potential primary school population, then on the basis of projected 1965 population figures fifty-six percent of that cohort is at present enrolled in Ghana and thirty-five percent in the Ivory Coast. What is more striking, however, is the enormous difference at the level immediately beyond the six year primary course; enrollments for the whole five to nineteen age group drop to twenty-nine percent for the Ivory Coast but remain at fifty-five percent for Ghana. To be sure, about eighty percent of students in the Ghanaian secondary sector are enrolled in the less prestigious middle schools as opposed to secondary grammar type institutions, but the former are to be legitimately compared to the *cours complémentaires* in the Ivory Coast whose enrollments are always included in secondary school statistics. It might also be added that so far as the figures for higher education are concerned only a little over one-third of students at the University of Abidjan are Ivorians (an almost identical num-

ber are French), while students at the three Ghanaian universities are
overwhelmingly from that country.

In aggregate, therefore, greater educational opportunity exists in contemporary Ghana accompanied by a lower sex ratio in the student population: girls constitute approximately thirty-three percent of primary
school enrollments in the Ivory Coast and forty-four percent of enrollments in Ghana, and these disparities are even sharper at the secondary
level. It is clear that as aggregate opportunities expand the proportion
of female pupils rises. However, in school systems that are undergoing
rapid expansion there may be short-run reversals of this trend when girls
from educationally privileged categories have to compete with large
numbers of boys from still "underprivileged" groups.

Perhaps more crucial than aggregate access, however, is the question
of internal variation in the extent of educational opportunity by region
and ethnic or socioeconomic background. It should not be necessary here
to stress the extraordinarily salient role played by education in processes
of social mobility and elite recruitment in contemporary sub-Saharan
Africa except to reiterate that where education is in short supply inequality
of access may not be economically damaging, but it can be socially and
politically inexpedient.

If we compare enrollments in the two nations on a regional basis
(recognizing that primary and middle school figures also reflect ethnic
differentials), it is clear that the more centralized control of educational
development in the Ivory Coast has not resulted in a very even diffusion of
educational opportunity. The level of enrollment of the potential primary
population ranges from 9.7 percent in Seguela to 82.4 percent in Binger-
ville while in Ghana by contrast a high of 83 percent is reached in Ashanti
and a low of 25 percent in the Northern Region. Indeed, apart from the
Upper and Northern Regions of Ghana the variation between the remaining areas is not great, but in the Ivory Coast interregional variance is
everywhere more marked. No doubt, disparities must diminish in the long
run as the educational system expands, but the course of development is
by no means unilinear. In other words, short-run differentials may increase rather than diminish in periods of rapid educational development.
This was certainly the case in Ghana in the 1950s when increased enrollments in the North in no way matched southern development with the
result that the proportional differences in enrollment levels became even
sharper.

This raises the crucial question of whether the qualitative expansion of their educational systems will result in the greater "democratization" of educational "life-chances" in the two states. For even if the number of primary and secondary school students drawn from different regional, ethnic and socioeconomic categories increase, the distribution of educational opportunity may remain unchanged or, indeed, become more uneven. This is the kind of question to which we addressed ourselves in our earlier studies of recruitment into secondary schools in Ghana and the Ivory Coast. The empirical findings have been reported extensively elsewhere, but it is worth briefly summarizing them at this juncture.

First, it is apparent that recruitment into this "elite producing" sector is positively correlated with ethnic and socioeconomic background in both areas.[11] In short, the children of more urban families with higher levels of socioeconomic status as measured by paternal education and occupation are proportionally far better represented in the schools than the offspring of rural farmers and fishermen, though it must be noted that the least favored group are drawn from the ranks of urban unskilled labor. We should expect this to be the case in view of the fact that entry is accorded on the basis of academic-type examinations, and there is no reason to suppose that the broad patterns of relationship that appear universally in studies of this type should not appear in the African context.

However, it is equally apparent that in *absolute* terms, patterns of recruitment into both Ghanaian and Ivory Coast secondary schools are relatively open: well over one-third of male students in the senior classes of elite secondary grammar schools in Ghana and almost two-thirds of those in the *lycées* of the Ivory Coast come from rural farming families, and the proportions are almost identical in regard to students whose fathers had never attended school. If it is assumed that entry to secondary school frequently leads to elite membership (however we define this term), then it can still be argued that the schools perform an effective job in recruiting from a wide spectrum of the population.

Nonetheless, in our present comparative perspective this is perhaps a less interesting finding. Ivory Coast pupils are more likely to come from rural areas and have illiterate farming parents than their Ghanaian counterparts, and this difference might indeed have some implications concerning the attitudes of potential elites, but it tells us little about comparative selectivity between the two systems. When students' characteristics are re-

11. See Foster, *Education and Social Change*, pp. 220–59; Remi Clignet and Philip Foster, *The Fortunate Few: A Study of Secondary Schools and Students in the Ivory Coast* (Evanston, Ill.: Northwestern University Press, 1966), pp. 50–91.

lated to adult male population proportions, however, one fact emerges: the selectivity gradient is *steeper* in Ghana with respect to ethnic and urban origin than in the Ivory Coast,[12] though it is more marked in the latter country when paternal occupation is used to classify students. Moreover, ethnic origin is more closely correlated with all other indices of socioeconomic background in Ghana than in the Ivory Coast.[13] This casts doubt on the frequent assumption that as processes of modernization continue, forms of social differentiation operate increasingly independently of one another.[14] We had anticipated initially, in view of the much greater size of the Ghanaian educational system proportional to the potential school-age population, that selectivity gradients would everywhere be less marked and intercorrelations between variables considerably lower than in the Ivory Coast. Our findings were, to say the least, equivocal on this point and lead us to suggest that educational development, at least in the short run, is not necessarily associated with a lessening of differential opportunities. This finding, in fact, is consistent with evidence from Western nations where it has been noted that increases in enrollments in selective secondary schools or at the higher level are not necessarily correlated with greater proportional representation of pupils of working-class origin.

Generalizations derived from these limited investigations must remain very tenuous, but they do raise major questions concerning the role that education may play in the future with respect to social mobility in the new African states. Ghana, in spite of her much higher level of educational development, presents a rather similar recruitment profile to that of the Ivory Coast, and it is reasonable to assert that under certain conditions, secondary and higher education may play less of a role in providing mobility opportunities for a broad spectrum of the population than it will in maintaining a pattern of "self-recruitment" among existing elites. This could occur either when the secondary and higher educational sectors remain relatively small in relation to the potential student population or when the rate of economic growth, and hence the increase in the provision of expanded occupational opportunities, is low. In this context it must be

12. Ibid.

13. See Philip Foster, "Secondary Schooling and Educational Opportunity: Ghana and the Ivory Coast" in Joseph Fischer, ed., *The Social Sciences and the Comparative Study of Educational Systems* (Scranton, Penn.: International Textbook Company, 1969), pp. 221–39.

14. For a critical evaluation of such assumptions see Clignet and Sween, "Accra and Abidjan."

noted that although both nations are now committed to a policy of giving priority to the expansion of secondary education, Ghana is undergoing a period of marked economic difficulty, while the severity of selection and promotion policies in the Ivory Coast system might ultimately lead to greater educational inequalities.

These observations bring us back full-circle to the initial remarks that we made concerning "universals" in the educational situation in sub-Saharan Africa. Whatever immediate educational tactics are pursued, most governments will have to accept the fact that schooling will remain in short supply in the foreseeable future. Under these conditions the task of creating some measure of equality of educational opportunity is a formidable one, and it is likely, in fact, to conflict with strategies designed to maximize the possible economic benefits of educational investments.

Ghana and the Ivory Coast face similar problems in the latter context. Both countries have multitrack postprimary systems that are intended to enhance the "efficiency" of the educational system in relation to manpower needs. But it is quite obvious that parity of esteem does not exist between different types of postprimary schooling since these do not provide equivalent opportunities for access either to higher education or to prestigeful and remunerative employment. One might speculate whether increased structural and curricular differentiation leads to a greater degree of social inequality in terms of access to various forms of postprimary education. This situation—typical of many Western multitrack systems—has not yet arisen in either country. There *is* evidence that certain very elite Ghanaian secondary institutions recruit from a more restricted segment of the population than the more run-of-the-mill grammar schools, and there are also slight variations in the ethnic and socioeconomic background of Ivory Coast students in the *lycées* as opposed to those in technical or agricultural institutions.[15] Although these differentials are, as yet, not great in magnitude there is always a possibility that the elaboration of multitrack systems at the secondary level (apart from their questionable economic contribution) will lead to increased social rigidities and perhaps diminish educational opportunities for segments of the student population.

In summary, neither expansion in the size of educational systems nor flexibility in their structure ensures that inequality of educational opportunity will diminish; Ghana's position in comparison with that of the Ivory Coast demonstrates that this is a considerable oversimplification.

15. See Remi Clignet and Philip Foster, "La Prééminence de l'enseignement classique en Côte d'Ivoire," *Revue française de sociologie* 7 (1966):32–47.

## THE PROCESS OF EDUCATION

Discussion of educational differentiation brings us directly to the whole question of the content of the educational process and the curriculum of the schools. There has been a considerable amount written on the curricular problems of sub-Saharan Africa, but most of it is largely polemical or hortatory in nature.[16] Thus, in the case of the Ivory Coast and Ghana, although we have some data on patterns of access to schooling, we have nothing of comparable value concerning the cognitive, attitudinal, or occupational outcomes of alternative kinds of educational curricula. In this situation matters concerning curricular change become a happy hunting ground for education ideologues (who are never in short supply), and at present all that can be done is to attempt to indicate what constitutes the main area of current controversy. Initially, we must be careful to distinguish (at least conceptually) between issues concerning the substantive content of formal curricula and those relating to educational methods. Regarding the latter, it is reasonable to suppose that serious studies of the early cognitive and affective development of Ivory Coast and Ghanaian children would have considerable implications for the character of the learning situation in the classroom.[17] It is noteworthy that in Ghana and the Ivory Coast there has been concern with "Africanization" of the curriculum but little with Africanization of teaching methods. In the absence of meaningful research on this latter issue the ensuing discussion will concern itself with the question of formal structure and curriculum content; in essence this centers largely on the issue of identity between metropolitan and local systems.

One facile observation that is often made concerning the development of French and British educational policy in the colonies is that the former was largely "assimilationist" in its objectives and stressed the expansion of schooling along essentially metropolitan lines while the British were concerned largely with the development of educational systems that were "culturally adapted" to the African environment. The situation was far more complex than this, and a considerable gap often existed between official policy statements concerning education and the actual evolution of the systems themselves.

16. For a recent example of literature of this genre see Abdou Moumouni, *Education in Africa* (New York: Frederick A. Praeger, 1968).
17. A pioneering study in this context is John Gay and Michael Cole, *The New Mathematics and an Old Culture: A Study of Learning among the Kpelle of Nigeria* (New York: Holt, Rhinehart and Winston, 1967).

French policy, in particular, was subject to considerable change in its objectives; these were in turn determined by radical and egalitarian views that predicated the export to the colonies of metropolitan education in toto and a more conservative stance that stressed the advisability of adjusting local systems both quantitatively and qualitatively to local conditions. Indeed, one of the surprising features of French efforts was that in many ways they foreshadowed post–World War II developments in educational manpower planning.[18] Besides placing quantitative constraints on educational development in order not to overproduce a supply of educated individuals who could later find employment, the French were also involved with the development of agricultural and vocational curricula that hopefully might check the drift from the land to growing urban centers. The cynic might note that a great deal of current educational controversy in sub-Saharan Africa revolves around precisely the same issues with little indication that any lessons have been learnt from previous educational experiments.

As we have noted, the French West African Educational Ordinances of 1903 and 1924 attempted to establish a system of graded schools with adjusted local curricula; and, in particular, the effort to develop the *écoles rurales* underlined an intent to provide schooling of an essentially non-metropolitan variety. Indeed the first *lycée* established in Senegal in 1928 was only created to accept Europeans and those Senegalese who enjoyed full citizenship status; an academic institution of this type was not established in the Ivory Coast until after World War II. Moreover, the famous Ecole William Ponty, established in Senegal to train medical assistants or teachers and attended by selected Ivory Coast pupils, had no educational parallel in metropolitan France. In short, in virtually no respect did the pattern of education as it evolved in the prewar Ivory Coast resemble the metropolitan system in either structure or content, neither was it articulated in any sense with academic secondary or higher education in France. For the French *planteur*, in particular, vocational and agricultural education was to be preferred to the academic *lycée*; and in only one feature, the stress upon French as the medium of instruction at all levels, could it be asserted that Ivory Coast education was "assimilationist" in intent.[19]

British policy in the Gold Coast was also paradoxical in its outcomes. First, it has been noted that the type of educational organization that

18. Berg, "Education and Manpower," p. 240.
19. Even in this case French colonial educators had some hesitation concerning the use of French in African schools. See D. Bouche, "Ecoles françaises au Soudan 1884–1900," *Cahiers d'études africaines*, 22, no. 6 (summer 1966) : 228–67.

emerged in colonial times was not effective in placing constraints on the quantitative outputs of the system although there were plenty of warnings from the mid-nineteenth century onwards of the dangers of creating a group of educated unemployed. Neither did British policy seem to be particularly effective in controlling the actual content of school curricula. Emphasis in most educational documents throughout the late nineteenth and early twentieth century was on the provision of basic elementary education in the "three Rs" and training in elementary industrial arts or agriculture.[20] The inclusion of manual subjects in the curricula of the schools was to be stimulated through the provision of special per-capita grants; and, indeed, before World War I the Basel Mission, in particular, had developed a very extensive system of industrial and agricultural training. Certainly, during this earlier colonial period there was little enthusiasm for the development of postprimary academic-type education, and this was associated with a general view that metropolitan education was not suited to local Gold Coast conditions.

In practice, however, the schools tended to develop along increasingly academic lines largely as a result of African pressures. In the view of educated Africans, educational parity with the metropole was the real issue; academic schooling provided an essentially vocational education that gave access to the most remunerative and prestigeful jobs within the emerging colonial occupational structure. Moreover, it provided opportunities (however limited) for a minority of Africans to proceed to higher studies in the United Kingdom. It is not surprising therefore, that the first academic secondary schools created in the Gold Coast were the result of African and later missionary enterprise while government made only a relatively late entry into the field in 1923 with the foundation of Achimota College. The fact is that repeated government emphasis on the need to provide a system of education in the Gold Coast that was adapted to local conditions in terms of structure and curriculum had little effect on the actual growth of that system. By 1939 a growing number of academic-type primary and senior primary schools was capped by a small number of highly selective secondary grammar institutions, the latter providing access to metropolitan universities or certain higher-level studies at Achimota. By contrast, the system of technical education continued to languish, and agricultural or manual training in the schools had virtually disappeared.

Thus by 1939 the paradoxical outcomes of educational development in the two territories were quite clear. The French in spite of their formal

20. See Foster, *Education and Social Change*, pp. 80–90, 148–71.

stress on assimilation and identity as the basis of colonial policy had succeeded in producing a system of education on the Ivory Coast that did *not* resemble that of France in terms of objectives, structure, or curriculum. Nor was this system articulated in any meaningful way with the structure of higher education in France. The British, by contrast, had created a reasonable facsimile of metropolitan education in the Gold Coast notwithstanding an "adaptive" approach to educational matters that was in part derived from political theories of indirect rule. To be sure, there was a stress on the use of vernacular languages in the lower classes of the primary school, but the curriculum became progressively more "Anglicized" as pupils moved up through the system. Most important, the secondary schools were linked to the system of higher education in the metropole through the employment of examinations acceptable to British universities.

Since 1945 the course of development in both countries has led to a greater parallelism emerging between local and metropolitan systems, and in the Ivory Coast this process has been particularly striking but entirely predictable. As we have seen, African opinion on educational matters counted for far less in French territories than in the British, and it was not clearly articulated until the Brazzaville and Dakar conferences of 1944. More important than the demands for the mass development of primary education made at those conferences was African stress on the need to replicate the French system of education in colonial areas and, above all, to abolish the *écoles rurales*.[21]

It cannot be argued, however, that African success in pressing these issues led to any immediate radical transformation of education in the Ivory Coast. Although the *écoles rurales* disappeared, French administrators were neither enthusiastic about increasing the amount or improving the quality of postprimary academic education. To be sure, a *lycée* was opened in Abidjan and four *écoles primaires supérieures* were converted to *collèges* but the enrollments of students in academic secondary studies only rose from a little over 1,000 in 1948 to 3,000 in 1955.[22] Primary schooling fared better, with an increase from 23,000 to 69,000 over the same period, but the cynic might well remark that in the first decade after World War II the administration was making little effort either to instruct the mass or create an elite.

The political entente between Houphouet-Boigny and Francois Mitterand in 1952 and, later, the *loi cadre* of 1956 really marked the major turning points in the development of the system. From that period on

21. Bolibaugh, "Education as an Instrument," p. 46.
22. See Clignet and Foster, *The Fortunate Few*, p. 41.

major efforts have been focussed on the creation of an educational structure which largely replicates that of metropolitan France. This is not to imply that there has been a totally unthinking transfer of metropolitan institutions to the Ivory Coast. For example, it was originally hoped that the curricula of the *cours complémentaires* created in the late 1950s would vary with the economic conditions prevailing in different parts of the country. However, this objective was not achieved since the aspirations of African students to enter the higher levels of the secondary system tended to maintain a standardized academic curriculum in institutions in the first cycle of postprimary studies. Serious efforts are also underway to effect curricular change in the schools. The *Service pédagogique* has for some years been adapting French materials for use by African pupils while the number of textbooks designed specifically for Ivory Coast conditions is increasing. The introduction of new curricula in Afro-Asian history and geography has now been effected, and attempts are being made to overhaul the educational content of other major subject areas.[23]

In spite of this, it is quite apparent that the system of education in the Ivory Coast is still modelled more closely on that of France than it was in 1939. The actual attitudinal or behavioral outcomes of recent curricular changes will be, of course, extremely difficult to assess, but it might well be asked whether these are significant as the fact that the objectives and structure of the system are essentially metropolitan in origin. Moreover, it is plausible to suggest that innovation is more difficult at the higher reaches of the system. Curricular changes can be effected in the primary schools for the simple reason that the significance of the latter as an instrument of mobility is declining. The secondary schools and universities, however, control access to elite status and occupational opportunity, and it is at this level that pressure for parity with the metropole in terms of content and standards is most evident. Moreover, it is questionable whether radical transformation is possible in a system where over thirty percent of students at the *baccalauréat* level are expatriates and where the practical direction of educational policy is still largely in the hands of French administrators.

Ghanaian development in recent years would suggest, however, that the special circumstances of continued French domination in the Ivory Coast do not explain the latter country's continued adherence to metropolitan educational norms and practices. For all practical purposes educational

23. See Avigdor Farine, *The Development of Education in Three Francophone Countries: Ivory Coast, Dahomey, and East Cameroon* (Ph.D. Dissertation, University of Pittsburgh, 1967), pp. 60–81.

planning in Ghana has been firmly in African hands since the early 1950s. Autonomy in matters concerning primary schooling was always substantial, but in recent years external control over the form and content of secondary and higher education has been achieved through the supervision of most subject testing by the West African Examinations Council and the elevation of local higher institutions to full university status. By contrast with the Ivory Coast, therefore, Ghana has remained relatively free of *direct* metropolitan influence over her educational development.

In spite of this, Ghana's educational achievements over the last decade and a half have been largely quantitative and have not involved any major restructuring of the system; the colonial educational heritage bequeathed the nation has remained virtually intact. The Accelerated Development Plan of 1951 paved the way for an enormous increase in the provision of schooling but did little about the structure or content of the educational process. To be sure, existing senior primary schools were rechristened middle schools (as if some change in name could lead to a transformation of their function) while day secondary schools were created to supplement the activities of the boarding institutions that were so much a feature of British policy. These were hardly radical innovations, and one cannot but reach the conclusion that in the decade and a half that succeeded the plan the underlying assumption of most educational policy has been to enlarge the system but do relatively little else.

As in the Ivory Coast, various attempts at the africanization of the curriculum have been made, particularly in the area of the social studies, but here also change has been more easy to effect at the lower levels of the system. But even in the primary and middle schools the intense competition for entry into secondary institutions places a premium on the mastery of English and mathematics with a consequent atrophying of emphasis on other subjects.

In summary, whatever claims can be made concerning Nkrumah's radicalism in the political sphere, there can be little doubt that Ghanaian educational policy up to 1966 was fairly conservative in its approach to problems of structure and curriculum. Attempts were made during the sixties to utilize the schools as agencies of political socialization, but these efforts were a dismal failure and testify to the resilience of colonial traditions of education. Ghana's experience in this regard, therefore, underlines the difficulty of mobilizing educational systems in the pursuit of political objectives.

In short, the history of structural and curricular developments in both Ghana and the Ivory Coast show striking similarities. In both cases African

opinion has been crucial in pushing educational systems closer to the
metropolitan model on the assumption that the definition of a "good" education must be universal. There are significant differences, however, between the two countries. Convergence between metropolitan and local
systems began much earlier in Ghana, and the circumstances under which
this convergence took place were somewhat different in the two nations.
In Ghana the sensitivity of schools to African demands was determined by
the organization of the system itself. In the Ivory Coast, by contrast, the
response to African pressure was essentially a matter of political expediency: the choice was either to assimilate individuals into a common community dominated by France or accept the consequence of separatist
nationalist movements.

## THE SCHOOLS AND THE OCCUPATIONAL STRUCTURE

We have so far discussed the nature of the inputs into the educational
system and the educational process itself but have not yet examined what
happens to the outputs of the schools. Every self-respecting African state
has, of course, a national manpower plan that in some way attempts to
relate both the quantity and characteristics of educational outputs to the
estimated future needs for middle and high-level manpower. It is not our
intention here to question the adequacy of current manpower planning
techniques except to note that the initial anxiety that educational outputs
could not meet manpower needs is now being replaced by a series of warnings concerning the limited "absorptive capacity" of African economies.
There is, indeed, some evidence to suggest that what looks like a damaging
shortage of manpower can become an embarrassing surplus in a very short
period of time.

In this respect, Ghana and the Ivory Coast face similar problems. It is
apparent that in most of the states of sub-Saharan Africa economic development is not correlated with any substantial increase in employment
within the modern exchange sector of the economy; opportunities for full-
time wage or salaried employment grow extremely sluggishly. On the other
hand, educational outputs (particularly at the primary level) are increasing rapidly. This leads in turn to the phenomenon of mass unemployment
among primary school-leavers which has been evident in Ghana for some
years and is now reaching considerable proportions in the Ivory Coast.[24]
This unemployment is likely to be characteristic of all "enclave" economies

24. Ibid., p. 54.

where a slowly growing modern sector is associated with a rapid expansion in population and schooling. There is little that educational systems can do about this: in most areas government must respond to public pressure for schooling while, as we have noted elsewhere, changes in the school curriculum in the direction of agricultural studies will have little effect in stemming the flow of ex-pupils looking for employment in the urban centers. In fact, of course, a growing proportion of these can be expected to return to agricultural activities after a hopeless search for urban or non-farm jobs, but at present most African nations will have to accept the fact that unemployment or underemployment among school-leavers will be a feature of their societies for some time to come.

It is now increasingly recognized, however, that this kind of problem is not confined to the lower levels of the educational system. We do not suggest that the products of secondary or higher institutions will not find employment, but they will be obliged increasingly to accept positions that do not conform to their expectations. This can occur in any society where the occupational currency of a given level of education is declining, but what is critical in the African context is that radical restructuring of expectations may have to take place over relatively short time spans. In very general terms this is true of Ghana and the Ivory Coast, but there are two specific features that differentiate these countries in this context.

First, we have already alluded to the greater control that is maintained over the volume and quality of school outputs in the Ivory Coast. Clearly, the use of selective examinations is a feature of the educational system of both countries, but their frequency and impact are very different. The use of formal selective techniques begins far earlier in the Ivory Coast and is a major feature of the primary school system. The reliance upon annual assessments results in extremely high rates of retardation and wastage: the average number of repeats per class was thirty-one percent in 1964 while over two-thirds of all pupils repeat at least one class during their primary school careers. Moreover, out of any 1,000 pupils who commence first grade only 510 reach the sixth and final year of primary schooling and of these about forty percent gain the primary school leaving certificate (C.E.P.E.).[25] Beyond this, entry to the secondary level is only gained through an examination which is, in fact (if not in theory), a competitive *concours*.

Figures of comparable accuracy concerning retardation are not available for Ghana, but a general principle of automatic annual promotion for

25. Ibid., p. 44.

primary students is accepted, if not uniformly applied, and rates of repeating are probably low. Wastage is still extensive but is much less evident in Ghanaian than Ivory Coast schools, and it is not the result of the rigid use of annual evaluations. Further, access to middle school is not through examination, and the first major hurdle the Ghanaian child must face is the Common Entrance Examination for secondary school that is normally taken after some eight or nine years of schooling.

A similar situation prevails at the postprimary level. Here, well over thirty percent of secondary students repeat one class or more in the Ivory Coast, and rates of attrition are extremely high. The "weeding out" functions of annual assessments are supplemented by major examinations at the end of the first and second cycle, and the severity of the selection process was most evident in the *baccalauréat* examinations of 1968 when only fifteen percent of candidates (about one-third of these French) were successful. Above all, the pass level in examinations can be adjusted on a sliding scale to meet anticipated educational places or manpower needs.

In Ghana, by contrast, the Middle School Leaving Certificate is gained by about seventy percent of entrants for this examination, and in the secondary schools rates of attrition and retardation are generally low except where student financial difficulties occur.[26] The General Certificate of Education examinations at the "Ordinary" and "Advanced" level are also organized in a different manner to the BEPC or *baccalauréat* examinations in the Ivory Coast: certificates are awarded on the basis of individual subject passes, and in 1966 the mean rate of passes by subject was forty-two percent at the Ordinary level while only twenty percent of candidates met total failure at the Advanced level.[27] Finally, the rate of examination passes is not subject to any manipulation in terms of available educational facilities or putative manpower estimates.

In short, the Ghanaian schools maintain a reasonable flow of students through the system: over 50,000 pupils sat for the Middle School Examination in 1966, almost 9,000 for the Ordinary G.E.C., and just under 1,000 for the Advanced level G.C.E. Correspondingly in the Ivory Coast in 1965 only about 3,000 pupils were eligible to sit for the BEPC (or its equivalent) in the *troisième*, and less than 1,000 for the first and second *baccalauréat*. The corollary of this latter situation is that the system is fantastically expensive: each student who finally gains the *baccalauréat* costs

26. See The West African Examinations Council, *Annual Report for the Year Ended 31 March 1967* (n.d.), p. 17.
27. Ibid., pp. 55, 67.

$14,000 and each BEPC holder, $5,000. Although comparable estimates are not yet available for Ghana, costs are undoubtedly far lower.[28]

It can be argued that, so far, the Ivory Coast has been more successful in regulating school outputs than Ghana with the implication that unemployment or frustration among school graduates is less evident. It seems highly unlikely, however, that current policies can be maintained in the face of mounting public pressure for schooling and increasing dismay at the high rates of failure in the system. In effect, the Ivory Coast has merely delayed the impact of employment problems and has paid an extremely high educational price for so doing. In one other respect, moreover, the Ivory Coast is far more seriously placed than Ghana. In 1965 expatriate personnel occupied over eighty percent of places in the administrative and technical cadres and almost sixty percent of all supervisory positions. In Ghana Africanization became a serious issue in the 1950s, and by 1965 virtually all senior personnel in the public and a substantial number of those in the private sector were locally recruited.

Although continued French domination of senior positions can be justified in terms of general efficiency and productivity in the Ivory Coast, it is increasingly evident that serious tensions have been created between the administration and younger Ivorians who perceive themselves as qualified to assume administrative and supervisory positions. The continuation of control of outputs and the placing of a ceiling on opportunities for educated Ivorians may produce a tense situation. To be sure, it can be expected that there will be increasing competition for high and middle level jobs among qualified Ghanaians, but at least the task of Africanization has been tackled perhaps to the country's long term benefit.

To supplement these general observations, we have some empirical materials concerning the vocational attitudes of students in the postprimary systems of both these countries and some fragmentary data concerning the actual pattern of occupational recruitment. Detailed tabular presentations of this material are available elsewhere but at the risk of some oversimplification we can reiterate the major findings.[29]

Secondary-school students in both countries are generally unrealistic concerning their chances of continuing their education beyond their present level of studies. In terms of their hopes of continuing and their actual expectations of so doing there is a failure to recognize the constraints

28. Farine, *Development of Education*, p. 53.
29. See Foster *Education and Social Change*, pp. 259–91; Clignet and Foster, *The Fortunate Few*, pp. 114–73.

imposed in terms of available educational opportunities. To be sure, both the aspirations and expectations of students concerning their academic future are mediated in some measure by their socioeconomic background and their perception of their own academic competence, but the overwhelming conclusion must be that students have an inflated set of aspirations and expectations concerning their educational life chances.

As we might expect, occupational aspirations are also couched at a high level, and there is a remarkable similarity in the profile of attitudes as between the secondary school students of both countries. In general, considerable emphasis is placed on entry to scientific, technological, and medical or allied occupations while about one-quarter of all students wish to enter teaching. However, these patterns of aspiration do not reveal any interest in middle-level technical posts or work in primary schools. In other words, technical or teaching jobs are generally desirable only if students can obtain access to them at a relatively high level.

Even if individuals are unrealistic in terms of their overall perception of the opportunities available to them, they may have a more sober view of the kinds of jobs they can obtain with a given level of education. Thus, when students were asked what kinds of jobs they expected to enter if they were unable to continue beyond their current level of secondary schooling, a very narrow range of responses emerged, and primary-school teaching and clerical work tended to figure largely in student expectations. What was striking, in fact, was the considerable correspondence between these student attitudes and the actual pattern of occupational recruitment as revealed by follow-up data on previous cohorts of secondary-school graduates. These latter materials revealed substantial recruitment into teaching and low-level clerical work whereas only a trickle of former students entered occupations that could even be broadly defined as technical in nature. Indeed, in the case of the Ivory Coast it was apparent that the products of vocational institutions (*Centres d'apprentissage*) are less successful than their counterparts in the academic schools in obtaining adequate employment related to their previous training.

It can be suggested that the findings described here might be reproduced in most contemporary sub-Saharan states. Although education might still remain the "royal road" to occupational success, the payoff to it can decline rapidly in the first few years after independence. Students are reluctant to evaluate realistically their own educational and occupational opportunities but, yet, perceive that the occupational returns to a given level of schooling are declining. Moreover, where government remains overwhelmingly the largest single employer in the modern sector and the growth of new opportunities is relatively slow, then it is plausible to assume that the fit between occupation and education may become increasingly tight with a larger proportion of secondary-school pupils finding that primary-school teaching is the major outlet open to them. In short, the educational system will become increasingly the major consumer of its own middle-level products. Finally, regardless of the precise content of occupational choices, the overwhelming preference of students in both countries for urban employment may exacerbate the gap in levels of development as between the urban centers and their rural hinterlands.

## CONCLUSION

We can now attempt to view some of the specific observations made in this chapter in the light of a set of more general propositions—for it is evident that the purpose of any comparison in the social sciences is to establish the necessary and sufficient conditions under which sets of relationships among selected social phenomena hold true. These relationships may take a variety of forms:[30] (a) *Replications*—In this case we are concerned with establishing that similarities in the general political and socioeconomic characteristics of selected societies are associated with corresponding similarities in the characteristics of their educational institutions. (b) *Universal generalizations*—Here one might demonstrate that certain features of schools remain the same in spite of substantial variation in the institutional matrices within which they function. (c) *Contingency generalizations*—In this context, the purpose of the investigation is to establish that political and socioeconomic contrasts are accompanied by parellel differences in educational institutions. (d) *Specifications*—Here the strategy is to indicate that the relationships between the schools and their institutional environment may be mediated by the operation of certain intervening variables (historical, cultural, or structural).

We have tried to isolate examples of such variant forms of relationship in the previous pages by using a crude form of "controlled" comparison. This is possible because Ghana and the Ivory Coast exhibit broad parallels in terms of their physical, ethnic, and socioeconomic profiles; but, at the same time, they differ with respect to certain features. These latter features which have been treated as "independent variables" involve duration of exposure to modernizing influences; the form of political organization in colonial and postcolonial periods and the *rate* of change that has occurred

30. See Marsh, *Comparative Sociology*, p. 41.

within a specific time period. As we have seen, our dependent variables are (1) the administrative organization of education, (2) the pattern of access to schooling, (3) the content and process of education, and (4) the articulation between the schools and the occupational structure.

We can now draw attention to the various forms of relationship generated by our comparison and speculate in some degree about their universality.

First, at the most general level, we suggest that the educational development of the new nations is more influenced by antecedent than by present political, economic, and social structures. In short, the current level of economic development or contrasts in the style of contemporary political leadership provide less satisfactory explanations of the similarities and contrasts in the educational structures of Ghana and the Ivory Coast than do convergences and divergences in their earlier colonial experience. This underlines the need to undertake diachronic rather than synchronic comparisons in the study of education in the new nations.

Second, we can look at our independent variables in succession and identify the kinds of relationships which accompany them. Our first independent variable is "exposure to modernizing forces," operationally defined in terms of the size and maturity of the educational system. Examples of contingency generalizations in this case are that variations in the extent of the system of schooling are systematically associated with variations in (1) the sex ratio of the student population, and (2) the stage at which maximal selectivity in ethnic or socioeconomic terms actually occurs. With less mature systems maximal differentiation will occur at the lower rings of the educational ladder but as the system expands, selectivity is progressively deferred.

An example of universal generalization is that the relative size of the educational system does not affect (at least in the short run) the proportional representation in selective secondary schools of certain socioeconomic subgroups such as urban unskilled manual workers. In short, the expansion of educational opportunities is not necessarily correlated with greater "democratization" of the educational system. This can be regarded as an illustration of "specification."

If we take our second independent variable, namely degree of centralization, we can suggest the following propositions: (1) the more centralized a system the less variation there is likely to be in the quality of educational facilities (e.g., student teacher ratios, teaching standards, etc.) ; (2) as the degree of centralization of the system increases the influence of ethnicity per se on access to secondary schooling decreases; (3)

more centralized systems are less responsive to demands for structural or curricular change as well as to pressures for increases in educational provision. This group of relationships can be regarded as "contingency" generalizations.

Using our third independent variable, rate of change, we can suggest that in the short-run high rates of educational development may accentuate competition for educational access between different groups, resulting in greater inequality in access to schooling. This we may view as a "duplication" effect in the context of our present discussion.

Finally, regardless of contrasts in their actual rate of educational development, there is very limited variation in most new nations in the definition of what constitutes a "good" education. Individuals perceive schooling not only in occupational-instrumental terms but also as the key to participation in a more universal cultural community. In this sense it is not only the historical impact of the metropole that is significant but the cultural influence that it continues to exert on the contemporary scene. Perhaps this is one of the most universal legacies of colonization.

# CONTRIBUTORS

ELLIOT J. BERG is professor of economics and director of the Center for Research on Economic Development at the University of Michigan. He has published extensively on problems of economic development in sub-Saharan Africa.

REMI CLIGNET is professor in the Department of Sociology and on the faculty of the African Studies Program at Northwestern University. He is the author of articles concerned with social change in contemporary Africa, and his most recent major work is *Many Wives, Many Powers* (1970), a study of polygyny.

PHILIP FOSTER is professor of education and sociology at the University of Chicago and assistant director of the Comparative Education Center at that university. He is the author of *Education and Social Change in Ghana* (1965) and coauthor (with Remi Clignet) of *The Fortunate Few: A Study of Secondary Schools and Students in the Ivory Coast* (1966).

REGINALD H. GREEN is economic advisor to the Treasury, United Republic of Tanzania and honorary professor of economics at the University of Dar es Salam. He is coauthor of *Unity or Poverty: The Economics of Pan-Africanism* (1968) and has contributed numerous articles on problems of economic development in middle Africa.

MARTIN KILSON is associate professor of government at Harvard University. He has made several extended visits to West Africa and has contributed many articles on politics in that area. Apart from his major work *Political Change in a West African State* (1966), he has coedited several volumes on African and Afro-American affairs.

JON KRAUS is assistant professor in the Department of Political Science at the State University College of New York, Fredonia. He is the author of articles in the *Journal of Modern African Studies, Africa Report, Problems of Communism,* and *World Affairs* and has contributed papers to recent volumes on the Ghanaian coup d'etat and the military in Africa.

ALAIN A. LEVASSEUR received most of his early training in France and spent 1966–67 as professeur, Ecole nationale d'administration, Abidjan, Ivory Coast. He is currently assistant professor at Tulane University Law School and has published several manuals and articles on civil law.

BEVERLEY POOLEY is currently professor of law at the University of Michigan. He was formerly lecturer at the University of Ghana and has written extensively on problems of the modernization of legal systems in sub-Saharan Africa.

RICHARD E. STRYKER is on the faculty of the Department of Political Science, Indiana University. He conducted field research in the Ivory Coast from 1965 to 1967 and received his doctorate from UCLA in 1970.

DOROTHY DEE VELLENGA is on the faculty at Ripon College, Wisconsin, and spent 1968–69 conducting fieldwork in Ghana on changes in the marriage laws. She is a former student of the Department of Sociology, Columbia University.

IMMANUEL WALLERSTEIN is professor of sociology at Columbia University and was a fellow of the Center for Advanced Study in the Behavioral Sciences in 1970–71. He is the author of *The Road to Independence: Ghana and the Ivory Coast* (1964); *Africa: The Politics of Unity* (1969), and numerous other books and articles on social change in modern Africa.

ARISTIDE R. ZOLBERG is professor and chairman, Department of Political Science, University of Chicago. His principal works to date are *One Party Government in the Ivory Coast* (1964 and 1969) and *Creating Political Order: The Party States of West Africa* (1966).

# INDEX